OXFORD PHILOSOPHICAL TEXTS

Series Editor: John Cottingham

The Oxford Philosophical Texts series consists of authoritative teaching editions of canonical texts in the history of philosophy from the ancient world down to modern times. Each volume provides a clear, well laid out text together with a comprehensive introduction by a leading specialist, giving the student detailed critical guidance on the intellectual context of the work and the structure and philosophical importance of the main arguments. Endnotes are supplied which provide further commentary on the arguments and explain unfamiliar references and terminology, and a full bibliography and index are also included.

The series aims to build up a definitive corpus of key texts in the Western philosophical tradition, which will form a reliable and enduring resource for students and teachers alike.

PUBLISHED IN THIS SERIES:

Berkeley *A Treatise Concerning the Principles of Human Knowledge* (edited by Jonathan Dancy)
Berkeley *Three Dialogues between Hylas and Philonous* (edited by Jonathan Dancy)
Hume *An Enquiry concerning the Principles of Morals* (edited by Tom L. Beauchamp)
Leibniz *Philosophical Texts* (edited by R. S. Woolhouse and Richard Francks)
Mill *Utilitarianism* (edited by Roger Crisp)

FORTHCOMING TITLES INCLUDE:

Frege *Philosophical Writings* (edited by Anthony Kenny)
Hume *A Treatise of Human Nature* (edited by David Fate Norton and Mary J. Norton)
Kant *Groundwork for the Metaphysics of Morals* (edited by Thomas E. Hill and Arnulf Zweig)
Kant *Prolegomena to Any Future Metaphysics* (edited by Günter Zöller)
Spinoza *Ethics* (edited by G. H. R. Parkinson)

OXFORD PHILOSOPHICAL TEXTS

David Hume

An Enquiry concerning the
Principles of Morals

DAVID HUME

An Enquiry concerning the Principles of Morals

EDITED BY
TOM L. BEAUCHAMP

Oxford · New York
OXFORD UNIVERSITY PRESS

OXFORD
UNIVERSITY PRESS

Great Clarendon Street, Oxford OX2 6DP

Oxford University Press is a department of the University of Oxford.
It furthers the University's objective of excellence in research, scholarship,
and education by publishing worldwide in

Oxford New York

Auckland Cape Town Dar es Salaam Hong Kong Karachi
Kuala Lumpur Madrid Melbourne Mexico City Nairobi
New Delhi Shanghai Taipei Toronto

With offices in

Argentina Austria Brazil Chile Czech Republic France Greece
Guatemala Hungary Italy Japan Poland Portugal Singapore
South Korea Switzerland Thailand Turkey Ukraine Vietnam

Oxford is a registered trade mark of Oxford University Press
in the UK and in certain other countries

Published in the United States
by Oxford University Press Inc., New York

British Library Cataloguing in Publication Data

Data available

Library of Congress Cataloging in Publication Data

Hume, David, 1711-1776
An enquiry concerning the principles of morals / David Hume;
editied by Tom L. Beauchamp.
(Oxford Philosophical texts)
Includes Bibliographical references and index.
1. Ethics. I. Beauchamp, Tom L. II. Title. III. Series.
B1466.B43 1997 171'.2–dc21 97-39960

Data available

Typeset by Cepha Imaging
Printed in Great Britain
on acid-free paper by
Ashord Colour Press Ltd, Gosport, Hants

ISBN 978-0-19-875184-7

10 11 12 13 14 15 16 17 18 19

Contents

PART 1
Introductory Material

How to Use this Book

In this edition the text of *An Enquiry concerning the Principles of Morals* is surrounded by a body of editorial material. The purpose of this material is to help students understand the context in which the work was written and to interpret difficult passages.

Prior to the text, an Editor's Introduction explains Hume's history and intellectual context, his general philosophy, and his moral philosophy. The bulk of this introduction is devoted to a treatment of topical issues in his moral philosophy. A short note following the introduction explains the editorial basis of this particular text. Additional Supplementary Readings are recommended to students in the next section. Included is information about Hume's philosophical works, early modern writings in moral philosophy, and a selection of books and recent articles about Hume's moral philosophy.

After the text, several editorial aids are provided. The first is the Annotations to the *Enquiry*, a section that explains particular passages in the text. Small daggers that have been entered in the text indicate each point at which there is a corresponding annotation. At the head of the annotations for each section is a summary–analysis of the argument in the section. Also included in the annotations are translations of all French, Latin, and Greek quotations and information on the context or content of a work that Hume identifies or to which he alludes.

Terms that had somewhat different meanings when Hume wrote are defined or explained in the Glossary. Often, but not always, these words are now rarely used. Words that occur only once and that are defined in the annotations do not reappear in the Glossary.

The reader will also find a reference list. The authors and works in this list are either cited by Hume or by the editor in the annotations or the introduction. This list thus captures all references to published works in the volume.

Finally, it deserves mention that numbers appear in the margin at the head of each paragraph in Hume's text. These numbers are provided by the editor to establish a universal reference system that allows precise citation without the need for page numbers. This reference system is used throughout the present volume.

Students may wish to use this editorial material in a variety of ways. Perhaps the most suitable strategy is to begin by ignoring editorial material and reading Hume's text uninstructed, except for reference to the definitions in the Glossary. However, this approach is not always the most efficient. Many students want to understand Hume's history and goals before they begin reading, and many students will want to follow the annotations as they encounter puzzling passages. The advantage of a wide variety of editorial aids is that one can venture and select as one sees fit.

List of Abbreviations

Editor's Introduction

Just before his death, David Hume declared *An Enquiry concerning the Principles of Morals* (hereafter *EPM*) the best of his many writings. This small book developed from his youthful struggles to gain an audience for a system of novel and controversial philosophical doctrines. Two and a half centuries later, Hume is almost universally ranked among the world's foremost moral philosophers.

EPM is primarily a book about what Hume calls 'personal merit' and 'virtue'. From the outset, Hume says he will 'analyze that complication of mental qualities, which form what, in common life, we call PERSONAL MERIT' (1.10). He means that he will examine qualities such as bravery and kindness that receive our approval or disapproval. We all know 'in common life', as Hume puts it, that a difference exists between a much admired person and a hateful person. Hume's problem is to figure out why we make such distinctions. Why, he asks, is one set of qualities praised and admired, another set condemned and disdained? Why not the other way around, as happens when groups of robbers and pirates admire villainy and teach vice?

Hume provides many intriguing examples of questions he poses in *EPM*. Here is one, adapted to the twentieth century: When we go to theatres and see modern films about the ancient Greeks and Romans, why does everyone in the theatre regard some figures as cruel and depraved, and others as worthy and admirable? What causes in a mature and impartial person feelings of approbation for some figures and disapprobation for others? When we have these feelings, what *moral* significance do they have? Are persons admirable or despicable, honest or dishonest, fair or unfair merely because we *feel* they are? Is there no universality in our moral judgements that transcends the subjective feelings we have about people? Does reason correct our feelings and tell us that we sometimes reach unreliable conclusions when we allow our judgements to be affected by our feelings?

Hume's explorations of these questions about merit reach beyond what we ordinarily think of as the moral qualities and virtues of persons. He sees that we often associate a person's merit with social rank, power, wealth, beauty, good judgement, athletic skill, worldly success, and the like. *EPM* investigates these forms of personal merit almost as thoroughly as moral virtue.

1. Life and Early Publishing History

How did Hume become interested in these subjects, and how did he differ in his interests and beliefs from other moral philosophers in the eighteenth century?

Hume was born in 1711 in Edinburgh. An unusually gifted young student, he entered the university in Edinburgh during the 1722–3 session.[1] There he received a liberal arts education in the classics, literature, political theory, philosophy, natural science, mathematics, and history. In 1725 he ended his course of studies and briefly considered a career in law, but soon relinquished this ambition in order to become a scholar and literary figure. He reported that 'My studious Disposition, my Sobriety, and my Industry gave my Family a Notion that the Law was a proper Profession for me: But I found an unsurmountable Aversion to every thing but the pursuits of Philosophy and general Learning.'[2]

The Treatise *and its Recasting*

When he was 23, Hume wrote a self-reflective report about a special period in his youth:

[W]hen I was about 18 Years of Age [1729], there seem'd to be open'd up to me a new Scene of Thought, which transported me beyond Measure, & made me, with an Ardor natural to young men, throw up every other Pleasure or Business to apply entirely to it. The Law . . . appear'd nauseous to me, & I cou'd think of no other way of pushing my Fortune in the World, but that of a Scholar & Philosopher.[3]

Hume is referring to his earliest ideas for the formulation of a comprehensive philosophical system about human nature, a system he later claimed to have drafted before he was 25 years old. He published this work anonymously in 1739 and 1740 as *A Treatise of Human Nature* (hereafter *Treatise*).

---

[1] See Barfoot, 'Hume and the Culture of Science', 151 n. 2. All materials cited in footnotes are referenced in the References.
[2] 'My Own Life' 3 (cited by paragraph numbers), in *Letters of David Hume*, 1: 1–7 (hereafter *Letters*).
[3] Mar. or Apr. 1734, to a doctor, *Letters*, 1: 13.

Hume grappled in this book with the great philosophers and the classical Greek and Roman writers who were then staples of Scottish higher education. However, the *Treatise* was not a success in Hume's lifetime. He said it 'fell *dead-born from the Press*'.[4] Few readers grasped the book's significance and originality. As a result, Hume judged himself harshly and regretted his decision to publish the *Treatise* so early in life. 'I was', he said, 'carry'd away by the Heat of Youth & Invention to publish too precipitately'.[5]

During the early 1740s Hume decided to set the *Treatise* aside rather than attempt a second edition. He concluded that he should substantially correct its *style* while retaining many of its principal *doctrines*. The retained doctrines were then reformulated and issued in several new works, one being *EPM*. In these reformulations, Hume laboured to make his prose more graceful and readable. He admired the elegant style of popular essayists such as Joseph Addison, and he attempted to achieve a similarly cultivated form of communication with the broader literate community. This objective helps account for the many literary and historical references in *EPM* that are not found in the *Treatise*.

As Hume distanced himself from the *Treatise*, he began to 'cast anew'[6] its three books as separate publications, in each case using a popular essay style. Book 3 was heavily revised in both style and substance and published in 1751 as *EPM*, now widely known as Hume's Second Enquiry. The First Enquiry was his recasting of Book 1 of the *Treatise*.

The Second Enquiry

Shorter and more graceful than Book 3 of the *Treatise*, *EPM* both compressed and revised the complex views presented in the earlier work. In 'My Own Life' Hume recalls the writing and publishing of the Second Enquiry:

I went down in 1749 and lived two Years with my Brother at his Country house: For my Mother was now dead. I there composed . . . my Enquiry concerning the Principles of Morals, which is another part of my Treatise, that I cast anew. . . . [M]y Enquiry concerning the Principles of Morals . . . in my own opinion (who ought not to judge on that subject) is of all my writings, historical, philosophical, or literary, incomparably the best.[7]

---

[4] 'My Own Life' 6, in *Letters*, 1: 2.
[5] Mar. or Apr. 1751, to Gilbert Elliot of Minto, *Letters*, 1: 158.
[6] 'My Own Life' 8–9, in *Letters*, 1: 3.
[7] Ibid. pars. 9–10, in *Letters*, 1: 3–4.

Hume apparently had been rethinking the revision of Book 3 for several years, but he wrote the bulk of *EPM* between early summer 1749 and late 1750. He then published it in 1751 together with the short work entitled 'A Dialogue', which has always been published as if it were a final appendix to *EPM*.

No later than March 1753, Hume revised *EPM* for a second edition.[8] A year later he declared it his 'favourite Performance' as a writer.[9] For many years thereafter he continued to revise and perfect it. In its second edition, *EPM* began to be published together with several other works in a collection entitled *Essays and Treatises on Several Subjects*.[10] From 1758 until the final of the several revised editions that he prepared, this 1,000-page edition contained all of Hume's philosophical, political, and literary works that remained continuously in print.

Throughout his remarkable publishing career Hume wrote on a vast array of topics in history, literature, politics, economics, and philosophy. Although a scholar and literary figure of great renown, he was not a professor or, in the usual sense, an academic. Nor was he a reclusive philosopher, as René Descartes (1596–1650), Baruch de Spinoza (1632–77), and many others had been. Like G. W. Leibniz (1646–1716) and John Locke (1632–1704), Hume was frequently involved in public affairs. He was, at different times, secretary to a British general, keeper of the Advocates' Library in Edinburgh, embassy secretary and later chargé d'affaires of the embassy in Paris, and under-secretary of state in the Northern Department of the British government. These practical interests often inspired the examples and references in *EPM*.

2. Hume's General Philosophy

A few philosophical methods and tenets are common to virtually all of Hume's philosophical writings. These ingredients—notably, his empiricism, opposition to rationalism, and scepticism—play a major role in the assumptions and arguments of *EPM*.

---

[8] See 3 May 1753, to Sir David Dalrymple, *Letters*, 1: 174.

[9] 5 Nov. 1755, to the Abbé le Blanc, *Letters*, 1: 227.

[10] *EPM*, 2nd edn., is vol. 3 in *Essays and Treatises on Several Subjects*, 4 vols. (London: Strahan for A. Millar, 1753).

Empiricism and the Role of Experience

Hume is often referred to as an empiricist, that is, one who believes that experience rather than pure reason is the source of our information about matters of fact. Although the word 'empiricist' should be used with caution, some central features of Hume's philosophy have understandably been so labelled.

Like his predecessor Locke, Hume held that no ideas and no awareness of matters of fact are discoverable by pure reason. Locke referred to the mind's contents as *ideas*; Hume's parallel term is *perception*, a category under which he distinguishes *impressions* and *ideas*. Impressions are the items that come directly before the mind, such as colours, sounds, shapes, and feelings. Hume defines impressions as *original* perceptions (original sensations, passions, and emotions) and ideas as *copies* or 'faint images' of impressions. His point is this: Impressions are the materials first presented to the mind. Ideas are derived from these impressions and then become instruments for remembering, imagining, thinking, reflecting, and symbolizing. Jointly they comprise the constituents of the human mental world. Like many philosophers of his time, Hume believed that objects, events, other people, and the like are known to us only by perceptions.[11] All conceptions and beliefs derive from these perceptions.

However, Hume did not think that every belief is acquired directly from experience. For example, beliefs often arise from dreams, from inaccurate memories of events, and from an active imagination. Through the imagination we combine ideas into more complex ideas, which may have no corresponding impressions—for example, 'A virtuous horse we can conceive; because, from our own feeling, we can conceive virtue; and this we may unite to the figure and shape of a horse, which is an animal familiar to us.'[12]

We are not *acquainted* with virtuous horses, even if we conceive and believe in them. We thus lack a sound basis in experience for belief in virtuous horses. To have a solid basis, each idea must have come originally from one or more impressions and must adequately represent the original source or sources. This thesis is a cardinal point in Hume's thinking, one so integral that it becomes for him a foundational methodological principle.

---

[11] Unlike Locke, Hume did not have a causal theory of perception. Hume maintained that we do not know the causes of our perceptions because we have no access to them.

[12] Hume, *An Enquiry concerning Human Understanding* 2.5 (hereafter *EHU*; cited by section and paragraph numbers).

He 'promises to draw no conclusions but where . . . authorized by experience' and says he will speak 'with contempt of hypotheses' unless they can be confirmed in experience.[13] Hume's empiricism, then, requires good evidence from experience and avoidance of speculative hypotheses that cannot be empirically confirmed.

The Science of Human Nature and the Experimental Method

Hume's empiricism is operative in his examination of the human mind, an approach that he hoped would provide laws of psychology that are as well confirmed as the laws of physics. He described his philosophy as an attempt to develop a 'science of human nature', which means a systematic explanation of the human mind, including its moral sentiments. It seems odd today to say that the goal of a philosophy is to generate a science, but this ambition is fundamental in Hume's philosophy.

Hume also claimed to follow an 'experimental method' in his pursuit of a science. What he means by a *science* and an *experimental method* are not entirely clear, but we know he was influenced by principles of method published by the scientist Isaac Newton (1642–1727). Newton rejected speculative explanations, demanded scientific observations, and attempted to formulate testable scientific laws.[14] For example, when Newton wrote about the planets moving around the sun, he explained their motions in terms of laws of gravitational attraction. He knew that the idea of gravitation was obscure, and he did not pretend to have discovered esoteric forces or forms of 'attraction' that explain gravity. He used the term 'gravity' to refer to the complex set of effects and relationships that he had observed, which he formulated as the laws of observable movements.

Hume hoped to develop an analogous science of human nature by examining the inner world of perception, desire, feeling, belief, reasoning, and inference. This science would also examine publicly observable human behaviour. The workings of the inner mind and human behaviour are natural events, and therefore a science ideally should be able to explain them using methods like those it uses to explain other events in nature:

[T]he only solid foundation we can give to this science [of human nature] must be laid on experience and observation. . . . [T]he essence of the mind being equally

---

[13] Hume, *Abstract* (of *Treatise*), pars. 2–3.

[14] Newton, *Mathematical Principles*, 400; see also 1, 13–14, 398–400 for Definition 2, Laws 1 and 3, and Rules 1–3.

unknown to us with that of external bodies, it must be equally impossible to form any notion of its powers and qualities otherwise than from careful and exact experiments, and the observation of those particular effects, which result from its different circumstances and situations. . . . We must therefore glean up our experiments in this science from a cautious observation of human life, and take them as they appear in the common course of the world, by men's behaviour in company, in affairs, and in their pleasures.[15]

Hume's philosophy begins with the 'phenomena'—that is, with the appearances and events that we experience directly. In moral philosophy, he began with moral phenomena, such as the ways in which we approve and disapprove of various forms of human conduct. After closely inspecting both his own mental faculties and observing the behaviour of other people, he searched for the explanatory principles and causes that would elevate his observations to the status of a science.

In an attempt to discover the general principles that associate or connect ideas, Hume observed and described how ideas regularly enter and exit his mind. He argued that ideas are related to other ideas by 'principles of connexion'. That is, certain types of ideas introduce other types of ideas in regular and predictable patterns.[16] He also tried to find patterns in the ways people behave in the company of other persons, in how they conduct their affairs, and the like. In *EPM* Hume uses these observations to formulate the principles and laws of psychology that underlie moral reasoning and judgement:

The only object of reasoning is to discover the circumstances on both sides, which are common . . . and thence to reach the foundation of ethics, and find those universal principles, from which all censure or approbation is ultimately derived. As this is a question of fact . . . we can only expect success, by following the experimental method, and deducing general maxims from a comparison of particular instances. (1.10)

A major goal of *EPM* is to discover the conditions under which persons approve and disapprove of human motives and actions, thereby accounting for personal merit or virtue. Hume tries to show that impartial persons approve of only those motives and actions that are either useful or agreeable to oneself or others and disapprove of only those that are harmful or disagreeable. The success of his inquiry depends heavily on how well he has defended this thesis. In its defence, he gives a prominent place to what he calls the *passions*.

---

[15] *Treatise*, Introduction 7–8, 10 (Introduction cited by paragraph numbers).
[16] See *EHU* 3.1–3.

The Place of the Passions

Hume's account of the human passions, which he often calls *sentiments*, is one of his distinctive contributions to philosophy. For him, all passions are perceptions and can be studied like other perceptions. Passions are impressions caused in the mind by previous impressions or ideas. For example, we currently fear, hope, and desire based on some prior experience, such as witnessing an event or meeting another person.

Many philosophers before Hume had disapproved of behaviour driven by passion. Plato (5th–4th c. BC), the Stoics, St Augustine (4th–5th c. AD), Spinoza, and others viewed the passions as irrational and sometimes overpowering influences needing the disciplined control of reason. These philosophers regarded the passions as alien forces, not parts of one's real self or one's intended actions; a person is acted upon by passions, rather than acting as an agent. Spinoza, for example, said that a 'passion of the mind is a confused idea' and that persons are often in bondage to their passions, from which reason alone can 'free' them.[17]

Hume, by contrast, thought that passions need not be confused, misleading, or censurable. They are vital and worthy dimensions of human nature, and Hume regarded it as incorrect to say that reason should always control the passions. Such advice will only distract persons from proper moral behaviour and make them miserable. We should accept our nature rather than fight it. Reason cannot move us to action and cannot liberate us from the passions. Reason can only be the faithful servant of the passions. For example, the desire to promote a friend's happiness motivates us to acts of friendship, and reason helps us figure out the best means to achieve those goals. Passions such as love, hope, and fellow-feeling all have constructive roles in Hume's ethics, eclipsing the role attributed to reason in other philosophers' systems.

The Limits of Reason

Because Hume elevated the importance of the passions and lowered expectations of reason, he is sometimes regarded as an irrationalist who reduces human actions to natural instinct. However, this interpretation distorts his position. Hume wanted to show that reason has sharp limits in philosophy and ordinary life, not that it has no significant powers.

Hume is particularly concerned to show that human rational capacities

---

[17] Spinoza, *Ethics* 3, Conclusion. See also the language of 'bondage', 'service', and 'affect' at many points in Spinoza's *Ethics*.

are more limited than some of his predecessors (called *rationalists* below) had maintained. They held that reason is capable of grasping fundamental truths about the natural, mental, and moral worlds in a manner analogous to the way in which reason grasps mathematical truths. Hume thinks that this belief cannot be sustained by an examination of reason and experience. He denies that reason has the capacity to deliver knowledge and truth in areas that many persons have supposed it could, including the realm of morality. One of Hume's goals is to situate moral judgement outside the domain of reasoned proof, a view that has prompted some to label Hume a 'moral sceptic'.

The Attractions of Scepticism

Hume was widely regarded as a sceptic by his contemporaries, a reputation that persists today. In the eighteenth century, sceptics were regarded as philosophers who maintained that no absolute certainty exists and that a person should suspend judgement rather than cling to dogmatic beliefs. Sceptics of this description thought that methods of reasoning often leave us unable to choose between competing truth claims. Hume accepts the proposition that we do not know anything with absolute certainty about matters of fact and that truth is not achievable in many areas of inquiry. However, he also maintains that science gives good reasons for belief in matters of fact. The general label 'sceptic', then, is not a perfect fit for his views.

None the less, there are at least two reasons why Hume has been regarded as a sceptic about *morals*. First, by grounding morals in taste and passion, while denying all grounding in reason, Hume places morals beyond demonstration, knowledge, and truth. Moral judgements cannot be supported exclusively by appeal to facts and cannot, therefore, be demonstrated to be correct or incorrect. Second, Hume denies that moral values of goodness, obligation, and virtue exist independently of the human mind. That is, moral values require human nature and human responses for their existence. They do not exist in the form of objects in the world or in the form of divine commands. These philosophical theses seem plausible in many matters of morals. Compassion, for example, requires a compassionate person; moral compassion does not exist unless compassionate persons exist. However, Hume's theses are less obvious in other areas of moral conduct. For example, is justice like compassion? Are there not objective moral standards of justice that are independent of human responses?

Hume maintains that all moral values, from love and generosity to justice and human dignity, require either some form of human sensitivity *or* some form of agreement among human agents. Many moral standards, including justice, are conventions that humans accept with the intent of facilitating communal living. In this respect, standards of justice do not exist in a realm beyond human nature any more than compassion does. Hume is therefore a sceptic about claims to know moral properties that are independent of human nature and about the powers of reason to deliver moral truths.

These claims seem to his critics so sceptical and dangerous that they threaten the existence of morality. However, this representation needs careful examination, because Hume did not think of his views either as sceptical of conventional moral standards or as a threat to those standards. His goal was to explain the nature and origin of those standards. In *EPM* Hume defends the universality of moral values and the importance of impartiality in forming moral beliefs.

Hume often seems more of a sceptic about certain moral philosophies and moral theologies than a sceptic about morality. His criticisms are aimed especially at philosophical theories about morality that promote objectivity and rationality. Rarely is he critical or sceptical about morality as a social institution or about the possibility of a science of moral psychology. He adopts sceptical attitudes primarily when he suspects that good evidence for claims is not possible and when the wrong sort of claim is being made (for example, when moral judgements are taken to be like mathematical judgements).

He also rejects what he calls *excessive* scepticism, while accepting *mitigated* scepticism. Hume admired a group of moderate ancient philosophers known as academic sceptics and regarded their views as preventing uncritical and dogmatic assumptions, undue enthusiasm, and speculative hypotheses that exceed scientific or experiential evidence.[18] He respected their forms of doubt and withholding of judgement as appropriate ways to prevent arrogance and dogmatism. Excessive or radical scepticism, by contrast, doubts everything, including the trustworthiness of the very human faculties we use to form beliefs. This scepticism promotes universal doubt, and Hume judged it to be futile and self-defeating.[19] He did not think that good evidence for beliefs can be achieved

---

[18] Modern scholars have pointed out that Hume's information about academic scepticism may have been in some respects incorrect. However, his views were generally in the mainstream of 17th- and 18th-century interpretations.

[19] *EHU* 12.

in any domain if all human faculties are distrusted, because all conclusions reached by use of those faculties would have to be distrusted.

The merits of mitigated scepticism are its capacity to show the true limits of human reason and its challenge to dogmatic assumptions. To be appropriately sceptical, Hume maintained, is to attend carefully to the weight of the evidence, to work at eliminating prejudice, to remain open to new discoveries and insights, and to appreciate the limits of our mental capacities. Hume regarded such scepticism as useful, not futile like excessive scepticism. It affects our beliefs as well as our conduct, and it undermines religious fanatics, philosophical ideologues, and moral zealots.

3. Background Controversies in Moral Philosophy

Hume's moral philosophy grew out of his science of human nature and his assignment of appropriate roles to reason and passion, but his subject-matter came from philosophical, psychological, and theological controversies of his period. The first word in *EPM* is 'disputes'. After discussing philosophical disputes for two paragraphs, Hume introduces a central controversy that he will confront in *EPM*:

There has been a controversy started of late . . . concerning the general foundation of MORALS; whether they be derived from REASON, or from SENTIMENT; whether we attain the knowledge of them by a chain of argument and induction, or by an immediate feeling and finer internal sense; whether, like all sound judgment of truth and falsehood, they should be the same to every rational intelligent being; or whether, like the perception of beauty and deformity, they be founded entirely on the particular fabric and constitution of the human species. (1.3)

The rationalists, or partisans of reason, held that moral judgement is founded on a rational apprehension of eternal standards of right and wrong. The sentimentalists, or those who appeal to a moral sense and human feelings, held that moral judgement is founded on an internal sense or set of sentiments distinct from reason.

Hume is constantly engaged with this dispute and related controversies. As the seventeenth and early eighteenth centuries unfolded, four leading types of moral philosophy emerged: (1) *natural law theory*, (2) *rationalism*, (3) *egoism*, and (4) *moral sense theory* (sentimentalism). Hume supported a revised and qualified version of (4) and found at least some merit in (1), while opposing the main strands of (2) and (3). None the less, Hume took seriously the leading writers representing all four of these types of theory. He often writes as a conciliator attempting to avoid extremes by retaining the best elements in each type of theory, while ignoring or arguing against the extreme and unacceptable ingredients.

Three Rivals of Moral Sense Theory

NATURAL LAW THEORIES

Hume refers to writers on the laws of nature twice in *EPM* (3.29, 3.48). He might be referring to classical Aristotelian or Stoic writers, or to modern followers of St Thomas Aquinas (1225?–74).[20] More likely, however, Hume is referring to figures in the natural law tradition who were influential at the time he wrote—chiefly the Dutch jurist and political figure Hugo Grotius (1583–1645) and the German jurist and historian Samuel Pufendorf (1632–94), both of whom Hume cited, at least perfunctorily, in one or more editions of *EPM*.

In the older natural law tradition deriving from Aquinas, moral guidelines were interpreted as part of nature. Their existence was held to account for the objectivity of morals and the justifiability of moral judgements. This view was popular in the Anglican Church, the Roman Catholic Church, Tory political thought, and divine right monarchism during the early modern period. However, the premise of a moral objectivity in nature was abandoned by natural law philosophers such as Grotius and Pufendorf (and by Hume). These thinkers regarded moral obligations and rights as created in human communities. Because they viewed non-human nature as containing no ethics, they thought that we must learn about ethics through the study of human nature. From this study, they sought to develop dependable guide-lines in morals and politics that transcend local customs and traditions. They referred to these guidelines as the laws of nature. As Hume notes, rules of property and rules of international law and justice were among the more important rules they discussed.

The goal of these theories was to achieve consensus, universality, and practical moral guidance in societies that, without appropriate laws to govern them, would remain deeply divided. Universality is necessary to

---

[20] E.g. the Jesuit Francisco Suarez (1548–1617) and the Anglican Richard Hooker (1553/4–1600). Some commentators regard Hume's own moral philosophy as an extension, or perhaps type, of natural law theory.

arbitrate the many conflicting interests present in society and in international relations. Some writers emphasized the *rights* that all persons possess, irrespective of the laws and customs of particular communities; other writers emphasized fundamental *obligations*. Like these natural law theorists, Hume started from a belief in a universal human nature and emphasized universal moral norms. However, Hume offered a primarily descriptive account of morality, whereas natural law theorists produced a primarily prescriptive account. In this respect, his theory differs markedly from theirs, though both take human nature as the proper starting-point in moral theory.[21]

RATIONALISM

The rationalists,[22] as noted previously, regarded sentiment as a dangerously inadequate and even subversive basis for morality. They held that actions are in themselves either right or wrong, and they argued that both sentiment and self-interest can and should be overcome by adequate ideas of what is eternally good and evil. The source of these ideas is reason, which has the power to apprehend fundamental truths about goodness, virtue, benevolence, justice, honesty, and the like, just as reason has the power to grasp axioms in mathematics.

Rationalists such as John Balguy had been writing in opposition to moral sense theories near the time that Hume was drafting *EPM*, generating an ongoing exchange in the reason–sentiment controversy. Despite their differences, rationalists and moral sense theorists agreed on matters such as the presence of benevolence in human nature and the importance of impartiality, and both opposed egoism. This agreement opened the way for Hume to reject rationalist views about objectivity and truth in morals, while concurring with rationalists on the nature and acceptability of everyday morality.

EGOISM

Primarily a psychological theory of human motivation, egoism is the theory that persons do *only* what pleases them or what is in their perceived self-interest. The subtle egoism of Thomas Hobbes (1588–1679) and the provocative egoism of Bernard Mandeville (*c.*1670–1733) put this theory at

---

[21] For Hume, universal laws (laws of human nature) are structural features of human nature; they are not normative premises or systems.
[22] E.g. Ralph Cudworth (1617–88), Samuel Clarke (1675–1729), William Wollaston (1659–1724), and John Balguy (1686–1748). In *EPM* Hume also mentions Nicolas Malebranche in this connection. See n. 12.

the forefront of moral controversy in the eighteenth century. In *EPM*, Hume refers explicitly to Hobbes and Locke (and implicitly to Mandeville) as espousing a 'selfish system of morals', because they accept the principle that 'no passion is, or can be disinterested; that the most generous friendship, however sincere, is a modification of self-love' (Appx. 2.1–3). Hume and his contemporaries categorized this theory as sceptical because it denied the reality of what they thought essential to morality: a moral motive.[23] That is, acting from selfishness is not a *moral* motive even if the resulting action is morally right. A moral motive has the interests of others in view and entails acting from a desire to be generous, friendly, helpful, and the like.

Mandeville argued that the motive underlying human action is private interest and that humans are naturally neither sociable nor benevolent. He thought that self-interested motivation has good results, because the public benefits from the economic activity undertaken by those who attempt to improve their circumstances. Mandeville offered a shocking thesis: Vice rather than virtue maximally benefits society by creating a higher standard of living. The so-called vices of eating, drinking, and buying luxury goods employ many people and thus create better lives for everyone. A 'vice', in Mandeville's terminology, is a self-interested desire for luxury and happiness. Character traits such as competitiveness, envy, a passion for luxury, and ambition for personal success are all vices. In short, each person acts 'viciously' for personal betterment, and thereby inadvertently promotes the welfare of all.

Hume argues that egoism rests on a faulty moral psychology. However, he also regarded egoism as containing an insight into human nature by pointing to the limited scope of both benevolence and reason.

Moral Sense Theories

An alternative to these three types of moral philosophy emerged in the early eighteenth century in the writings of a group of philosophers who held that the moral life does not depend on knowledge of natural laws, eternal truths, or self-interest. They described an innate, non-rational capacity to make moral judgements.

---

[23] See *EPM* 5.6. Hume discusses this 'fallacy' in his essay 'Of the Dignity or Meanness of Human Nature' 10–11 (all essays cited by paragraph numbers). Mandeville is associated with the theory that Hume attacks (as Hume notes in his essay 'Of Refinement in the Arts' 21 n. 2). See Mandeville, *The Fable of the Bees*, 1: 18–24, 39–41, 324.

SHAFTESBURY'S RESPONSE TO HOBBES AND LOCKE

The originator of this theory was the third earl of Shaftesbury (Anthony Ashley Cooper, 1671–1713), who depicted Hobbes as eliminating moral motivation and the moral virtues by reducing them to self-love. Shaftesbury argued that self-interest and fear of either human or divine authority are improper motives in the moral life.[24] He did not hold that all persons are by nature virtuous, only that ordinary persons have natural capacities both to act virtuously and to distinguish right from wrong.[25]

To explain the moral sense as a form of moral judgement, Shaftesbury depicted how we react internally to objects and events that we experience. Beauty, he noted, requires a spontaneous reaction by perceivers to perceived objects, and the moral sense is like the sense of beauty in that it detects the 'moral beauty' that is present in the ways that persons respond to other persons.[26] This natural capacity to react explains how the common person can judge the moral correctness or incorrectness of the motives and actions of others.[27] Hume was attracted to this account and praised Shaftesbury. Although he abandoned the language of 'moral sense' in *EPM* and substituted 'internal sense', he retained some of the ingredients of moral sense theory as Shaftesbury had delineated it.

HUTCHESON'S RESPONSE TO MANDEVILLE

Criticisms quickly mounted against various features of Shaftesbury's moral psychology—Mandeville's barbs cutting particularly deeply. In response, philosopher and Presbyterian preacher Francis Hutcheson (1694–1746) developed Shaftesbury's rudimentary ideas about a moral sense in the form of a direct reply to the egoism of Mandeville. Hutcheson argued that in addition to the senses of sight, hearing, touch, smell, and taste, we have an internal (he thought God-given) sense that generates moral judgements, moral distinctions, and moral knowledge.[28] We

[24] Shaftesbury, 'Sensus Communis: Essay on the Freedom of Wit and Humour', in *Characteristics*, 1: 65–9, 81–5.

[25] See 'An Inquiry concerning Virtue, or Merit', in *Characteristics*, 1: 251–4, 258–66.

[26] Shaftesbury condemned inferences to the conclusion that the capacity for moral judgement is not natural; see Letter to Michael Ainsworth, 3 June 1709, in *The Life, Unpublished Letters, and Philosophical Regimen of Anthony, Earl of Shaftesbury*, 403–5.

[27] See 'An Inquiry concerning Virtue, or Merit', in *Characteristics*, 1: 251–5.

[28] Hutcheson, *System* 1.1.5; *Inquiry*, Treatise 1, sect. 1.

perceive moral qualities of persons and evaluate human actions and motives through this moral sense, just as through the external senses we perceive sensible qualities of objects.

For Hutcheson, actions are virtuous because the motives that produce the actions please those who observe the actions, and do so irrespective of self-advantage. He maintained that we sometimes rightly regard an action as virtuous even when it displeases us and undercuts our interests. I might, for example, recognize genuine honourableness in an enemy leader, although this leader is thwarting my interests and my country's interests. We also sometimes approve of a vicious and illegal act of another person—for instance, when we react favourably to someone's violent retaliation in response to unjust acts.

Hutcheson encountered a problem that many have claimed to be a problem for Hume's ethics. If actions or motives are virtuous *because* we approve them, then any action or motive that receives our approval is virtuous. Hutcheson compounded the problem by saying that we aim at virtue because virtuous acts please us and that we avoid vicious acts because they displease us. This theory suggests that a person who is not pleased by virtuous acts will not have a motive to act virtuously, and that a person who is pleased by vice will have a motive to vice. In advancing this theory, Hutcheson seems more to embrace than rebuff Hobbes and Mandeville.

Hutcheson attempted to overcome this problem by appealing to God's providential design of persons: God made us benevolent agents who favourably judge benevolent responses in others. Here Hutcheson and Hume differ profoundly. In *EPM*, Hume embraces or comes close to embracing many themes in Hutcheson's ethics, but he detaches his philosophy entirely from theological moorings. Only the 'design' inherent in human nature, not the way a deity designed that nature, accounts in Hume's philosophy for our moral capacities and sensitivity.

The Influence of these Moral Theories on Hume

Many scholars of Hume have aspired to discover which philosopher or set of philosophers most deeply influenced him. Three prevalent strategies are (1) to link him to Locke and George Berkeley (1685–1753) in the evolution of British empiricism, (2) to link him to the moral sense tradition of Shaftesbury and Hutcheson, and (3) to trace the influence of the ancient (and perhaps modern) sceptics on Hume. The most abiding and influential of these interpretations for Hume's moral theory has been a combination of (1) and (2). The influential Hume scholar Norman Kemp Smith offered the following interpretation:

[I]t was under the *direct influence* of Francis Hutcheson that [Hume] was led to recognise that . . . judgments of value of whatever type are based . . . *solely* on feeling; and that what then 'open'd up to [him] a new Scene of Thought' . . . was the discovery that this point of view could be carried over into the theoretical domain, and could there be employed in the solution of several of the chief problems to which Locke and Berkeley had drawn attention.[29]

The thesis that Hume modelled his moral philosophy on Hutcheson's is perhaps still the ruling interpretation, but it is an over-reaction to Hume's actual indebtedness. Hume's formal education, his large correspondence, and the references in his works indicate that he drew from many philosophers and non-philosophers, not merely from one individual philosopher or type of philosophy. Attempts in Hume scholarship to reduce his system of philosophy to other philosophers' schemes, including moral sense theorists, are more misleading than illuminating. Hume's moral philosophy is difficult to interpret without an appreciation of the intellectual climate in which it evolved; none the less, it is a distinctive and original moral philosophy.

4. Hume's Moral Philosophy

Many interpretations of Hume's moral philosophy in *EPM* have been published since the eighteenth century. As we shift to textual interpretation, the reader should appreciate that commentators do not always agree on the meaning of his text.

Principles of Morals

Hume chose a title for *EPM* that included 'the principles of morals' because he was looking for 'the general principles of human nature, as discovered in common life and practice' (5.43). These principles are formulated with as much precision as possible in the science of human nature. In a footnote, Hume indicates why and how his moral philosophy refers to principles (n. 19):

[29] Norman Kemp Smith, *The Philosophy of David Hume*, 12–13 (italics added).

It is needless to push our researches so far as to ask, why we have humanity or a fellow-feeling with others. It is sufficient, that this is experienced to be a principle in human nature. We must stop somewhere in our examination of causes; and there are, in every science, some general principles, beyond which we cannot hope to find any principle more general. . . . [W]e may here safely consider these principles as original.

Hume maintains that these general and universal principles are 'original' features of human nature, just as the principles of nature studied in physics are laws of physical nature. All persons, however they differ in belief and conduct, have these principles in their nature. In *EPM* Hume is concerned with principles such as humanity and benevolence (two terms that generally carry identical or near-identical meanings[30]), because these principles are essential to the portion of the science of human nature that investigates morality and human moral responsiveness.

Today, principles are usually treated in moral philosophy as normative guide-lines, that is, as rules that state conditions of the permissibility, obligatoriness, rightness, or wrongness of actions. 'Do not kill' and 'Respect the rights of others' are examples. Hume generally does not use the term 'principle' in this normative sense. His principles are conditions in human nature that can be studied empirically and formulated in his science of human nature. Benevolence appears to be his most important principle, but 'benevolence' is also a general term for a class of *virtues* rooted in goodwill, generosity, and love directed at others. Hume depicts benevolence in its many manifestations (friendship, charity, compassion, etc.) as an ingredient of human nature, unlike rules of justice, which require human conventions (see below, pp. 35–7). Although he speaks of both benevolence and justice as social virtues (1.11), only benevolence is a *principle* of human *nature*.

Hume is also interested in principles of human nature that are not *moral* principles. For example, he depicts self-love as a principle of human nature that competes with moral principles such as benevolence. He recognizes that some principles of our nature can override other principles in particular circumstances. Sometimes a moral principle prevails; at other times a non-moral principle such as self-love dominates.

---

[30] 'Humanity', which appears fifty-eight times in *EPM*, does not have a single, easily expressed meaning. However, in general, humanity is the moral character or quality of being human through goodwill, kindness, gentleness, courtesy, civility, benevolence, affability, and the like. See esp. 2.5; n. 19; 5.18; 5.46; Dial. 7.

Benevolence and Self-Love

Hume accepts the egoists' claim that self-love is a principle of human nature, but maintains that egoism generalized to all human conduct rests on a faulty psychology. Egoism is too simple because its account of human nature is too streamlined. Normally we assume, in any field, that one theory is preferable to another theory if the first theory has fewer explanatory principles than the second, with no loss of content. Egoists seemed to him to find, quite dogmatically, what they set out to find in human nature—namely, a single principle of self-love that motivates all human actions, even those we call 'moral'.

Hume thinks that any observer will see that in addition to this principle there are 'such dispositions as benevolence and generosity; such affections as love, friendship, compassion, gratitude' (Appx. 2.6). A devoted mother is among his favourite examples:

Tenderness to their offspring, in all sensible beings, is commonly able alone to counterbalance the strongest motives of self-love, and has no manner of dependence on that affection. What interest can a fond mother have in view, who loses her health by assiduous attendance on her sick child, and afterwards languishes and dies of grief, when freed, by its death, from the slavery of that attendance? . . . These and a thousand other instances are marks of a general benevolence in human nature, where no *real* interest binds us to the object. (Appx. 2.9, 11)

Hume thinks that natural benevolence 'accounts, in great part, for the origin of morality' (5.17). He suggests that benevolence, sympathy, fellow-feeling, concern for others, and the like are key ingredients in human nature. It is but a short step to his conclusion in Section 9 that our common humanity accounts for why moral responses are 'universal and comprehensive' (9.5).

None the less, the presence of a principle of self-love led Hume to accept some aspects of the egoists' claims about human motivation. He acknowledges many motives in human nature and uses metaphors of the dove, wolf, and serpent to illustrate a mixture of elements in our nature (9.4): 'There is some benevolence . . . some spark of friendship for human kind; some particle of the dove, kneaded into our frame, along with the elements of the wolf and serpent.' This thesis that generous elements and self-interested elements are fused in human nature is an attempt to advance a balanced moral psychology.

Whereas the egoist views human nature as limited to motives such as fear and self-love, Hume regards persons as motivated by a variety of passions, both generous and ungenerous. He also believes that these elements vary by degree from person to person. Lacking distinctive information about a particular individual, we cannot know whether in that person benevolence typically dominates and controls self-love, or the converse.

Universal Sensibility and Universality in Morals

One of Hume's chief explanatory mechanisms is an 'internal sense or feeling, which nature has made universal' (1.9).[31] Following Hutcheson, though at some distance, Hume treats this internal sense as a capacity of *judgement*, but not a capacity of *reason*.

The terms 'moral sentiment' and 'internal sense' were sometimes used loosely and without careful definition in eighteenth-century philosophy. For example, 'sentiment' referred both to ideas or feelings caused by operations of the mind and to the mental operations themselves.[32] The term also referred to feelings, opinions, and judgements. Hume uses the term broadly in *EPM* to refer to refined feeling, internal sensing, attitude, and opinion, including approvals, disapprovals, and evaluations. When he says that 'morality is determined by sentiment' (Appx. 1.10), he seems to mean little more than that moral perceptions require mental capacities without which moral darkness would prevail, just as awareness of colours and a feeling of warmth require that specific sensory capacities exist in persons.

Hume's theory has been criticized for making the subjective self the sole source of moral approval and disapproval, virtue and vice, and right and wrong. The basis of this interpretation is rooted in statements such as the following from the *Treatise*: 'vice entirely escapes you, as long as you consider the object. You never can find it, till you turn your reflection into your own breast, and find a sentiment of disapprobation, which arises in you'.[33] Such statements have led some commentators to maintain that Hume makes morality relative to each individual's particular feelings and tastes.

Whatever the merits of this interpretation (see pp. 33–4, 44–5 below), it cannot be the whole story, because Hume argues that moral sentiment has

---

[31] Although Hume does not use 'moral sense' in *EPM*, see *Treatise* 3.1.2, entitled 'Moral distinctions deriv'd from a moral sense'. Hume's language in *EPM* suggests a development in his views.

[32] See Ephraim Chambers, *Cyclopaedia*, 'Thought'.   [33] *Treatise* 3.1.1.26.

a *universal* dimension. 'The notion of morals implies some sentiment common to all mankind, which recommends the same object to general approbation, and makes every man, or most men, agree in the same opinion or decision concerning it. It also implies some sentiment, so universal and comprehensive as to extend to all mankind' (9.5). Non-moral beliefs and sentiments are often relative to the particular responses of individuals, but Hume thinks that persons universally have the same moral sentiments and universally reach the same moral judgements when unbiassed and placed in relevantly similar circumstances (9.7). For example, when we have the same information about and an impartial view of another person, we all make the same judgements about that person's virtues and vices. By definition, virtue is *'a quality of the mind agreeable to or approved of by every one'* (n. 50). Hume presents his views about universality in morals as follows:

When a man denominates another his *enemy*, his *rival*, his *antagonist*, his *adversary*, he is understood . . . to express sentiments, peculiar to himself, and arising from his particular circumstances and situation. But when he bestows on any man the epithets of *vicious* or *odious* or *depraved*, he then speaks another language, and expresses sentiments, in which, he expects, all his audience are to concur with him. He must here, therefore, depart from his private and particular situation, and must choose a point of view, common to him with others: He must move some universal principle of the human frame, and touch a string, to which all mankind have an accord and symphony. . . . The humanity of one man is the humanity of every one; and the same object touches this passion in all human creatures. (9.6)

Connections between Hume's theory of the passions, his universalism, and his science of human nature emerge in this passage. The common point of view is the perspective of an agent who retreats from his or her 'private and particular situation' to achieve an impartial perspective. By abstracting from particular situations and personal sentiments, the agent is affected only by sentiments of humanity. In the light of this theory, it is inaccurate to say that Hume renders morality entirely dependent on the particular feelings of individual observers. Moral responses rest on features that are uniform in human nature. When differences in moral viewpoint occur, as they do, Hume regards them either as based on different underlying information, a lack of impartiality or specific traditions and practices in particular communities.

To ascertain whether we have appropriate moral responses in particular cases, Hume says we must place our sentiments—our approvals, preferences, recommendations, and the like—into the public arena to see if impartial persons concur. Only then can we reliably discover whether we 'touch a string, to which all mankind have an accord'. If our views are morally appropriate, then any 'impartial enquirer'—as Hume in *EPM* calls an unbiassed investigator—with the relevant background experience would have the requisite sentiment of approbation. This standard of impartiality and public endorsement is reflected in the following passage from Hume's essay 'Of the Original Contract': 'Though an appeal to general opinion may justly, in the speculative sciences of metaphysics, natural philosophy, or astronomy, be deemed unfair and inconclusive, yet in all questions with regard to morals, as well as criticism, there is really no other standard, by which any controversy can ever be decided.'[34]

Virtue and Vice

Hume does not seem to mean that we must actually *experience* feelings of approbation or disapprobation whenever we make a moral judgement about a person's virtue. He apparently means that the actions and character traits that we call *virtuous* would not qualify as virtuous unless they had already been widely approved, creating a 'general opinion' in society. To designate someone as having a virtue requires a social history through which the character traits we denominate virtues have been distinguished from other character traits, such as ingenuity and endurance.

THE DEFINITION OF VIRTUE

Hume defines 'virtue' as follows: 'It is the nature, and, indeed, the definition of virtue, that it is *a quality of the mind agreeable to or approved of by every one, who considers or contemplates it*' (n. 50). This definition, and the surrounding analysis in the text, indicate that a virtue is a fusion of two analytically distinct components: (1) a mental quality in the person contemplated, and (2) a perception by those who contemplate the person. The latter perception is not merely a single individual's perception; many individuals must have the requisite perception. Virtues exist only if the component parts are fused: neither (1) nor (2) is sufficient by itself to qualify as a virtue—although many interpreters of Hume have read him as saying either that (1) is sufficient for virtue or that (2) is sufficient for virtue. The reason is that Hume himself often abridges his meaning: he calls something a virtue while mentioning only (1) or (2).

---

[34] 'Original Contract' 46; cf. *Treatise* 3.2.8.8.

His unabridged thesis is that virtues are mental qualities that produce pleasure in impartial observers; the pleasure then produces esteem for those mental qualities. Conversely, vices are mental qualities that provoke displeasure in impartial observers, producing contempt for those qualities. Every quality of mind that is useful or agreeable—either to individuals who possess the quality or to other persons—'communicates a pleasure to the [unprejudiced] spectator', leading to the classification of that quality as a virtue (9.12; n. 50).

The postulate that virtues are approved of by all impartial inquirers leads Hume to say that qualities such as 'friendship, sympathy, mutual attachment, and fidelity' are 'esteemed in all nations and all ages' (Dial. 28). This thesis of universality appears to be Hume's way of making morality a matter of sentiment without rendering it a matter of 'sentiments, peculiar to [oneself] . . . arising from [one's] particular circumstances and situation' (9.6). A mental quality is a virtue if and only if it evokes universal commendation; a mental quality is a vice if and only if the quality evokes universal condemnation. To this account it must be appended that we *make* mental qualities virtues and vices through the processes of universal approval and condemnation. (This theory is treated in the section below on objectivity and subjectivity.)

The possession of virtue in this sense is the basis of a person's merit. Hume often uses the terms 'virtue' and 'personal merit' synonymously.[35] He indicates that philosophical analysis of personal merit is at the very heart of his work in *EPM*:

We shall analyze that complication of mental qualities, which form what, in common life, we call PERSONAL MERIT: We shall consider every attribute of the mind, which renders a man an object either of esteem and affection, or of hatred and contempt; every habit or sentiment or faculty, which, if ascribed to any person, implies either praise or blame. . . . The . . . universal [capacity for moral judgements found] among mankind, gives a philosopher sufficient assurance, that he can never be considerably mistaken in framing the catalogue [of the virtues] . . . (1.10)

THE CATALOGUE OF THE VIRTUES

To construct the catalogue of the virtues, Hume says that he must discover by experimental reasoning the common features of the many personal qualities that we praise and blame. Ultimately this experimental reasoning will yield a correct catalogue and also conclusions about that in

---

[35] However, 'personal merit' sometimes encompasses both virtue and vice.

which personal merit consists, which is 'the usefulness or agreeableness of qualities' (9.13).

Hume presents a fourfold categorization of the mental qualities that form personal merit or virtue:[36]

1. Qualities useful to others.
2. Qualities useful to ourselves.
3. Qualities immediately agreeable to ourselves.
4. Qualities immediately agreeable to others.

Using these categories, Hume develops his catalogue of the virtues and a corresponding catalogue of the vices. A catalogue is not for him merely a comprehensive roll or list; it is a structured, systematic list that follows from this fourfold classification. The virtues listed under each category share a specific function, such as furthering the interests of society, though some virtues fit under more than one category.

These categories and the qualities Hume treats as virtues occupy more space than any topic in *EPM*. Hume's table of contents in *EPM* indicates the importance of the last three categories (2–4) by the titles he placed on Sections 6–8. The first category (1) does not appear in the table of contents, but only because several early sections include content that falls into this category. The specific mental qualities include the following:

1. *Qualities useful to others* (Sections 2–5):
   benevolence (and the related notions of sociability, being good-natured, humanity, mercifulness, generosity), gratitude, friendliness, truthfulness, justice, fidelity, honour, allegiance, chastity, charity, affability, lenity, mercy, and moderation.

2. *Qualities useful to ourselves* (Section 6):
   discretion, industry, frugality, caution, strength of mind, wisdom, memory, enterprise, assiduity, frugality, economy, good sense, prudence, discernment, temperance, sobriety, patience, constancy, perseverance, judgement, forethought, considerateness, secrecy, order, insinuation, address, presence of mind, quickness of conception, and facility of expression.

3. *Qualities immediately agreeable to ourselves* (Section 7):
   cheerfulness, greatness of mind, courage, restrained pride, dignity, tranquillity, poetic talent, serenity, and delicacy of taste.

---

[36] See his summary titles in nn. 53–6 of *EPM* and the corresponding text.

4. *Qualities immediately agreeable to others* (Section 8):
   good manners, wit, ingenuity, eloquence, affability, genius, modesty, decency, politeness, genteelness, and cleanliness.

By definition, as we have seen, Hume's catalogue is comprised entirely of mental qualities. Although many bodily qualities such as muscular strength and agility in running are useful or agreeable, they cannot qualify as virtues.

Hume's catalogue of the virtues in *EPM* is comprised, roughly speaking, of the virtues listed under the above four major categories. An abbreviated summary statement of his list is found in the Conclusion to *EPM*, where he says that the 'whole class of virtues and accomplishments' in the catalogue could not be listed even in several pages (9.12).[37] Hume says that he uses the experimental method to arrive at his typology by locating the circumstances in which we approve or disapprove and praise or blame these mental qualities. By comparing many particular instances, he isolates the common features of the items that are approved, praised, disapproved, and blamed.

In the case of the qualities in category (1), Hume thinks that we approve of them because these qualities 'promote the interests of our species, and bestow happiness on human society' (2.22). The social utility of these mental qualities explains our approval. Part of the argument in Sections 1–5 of *EPM* is a defence of this thesis. In Sections 6–8 Hume shifts from these 'social virtues' to the remaining categories of personal merit. In Section 6 he considers qualities that are useful to their possessors and are for this reason approved of by others, though they are of no benefit to others (6.21). In Section 7, Hume analyses qualities immediately agreeable to those who possess them, and in Section 8 he considers qualities immediately agreeable to those who observe the qualities in others. He says that we approve of the person who has these qualities without consideration of the social utility of the qualities and without regard for our personal interest. By the time he reaches his conclusion in Section 9, Hume is positioned to argue that 'PERSONAL MERIT consists altogether in the possession of mental qualities, *useful* or *agreeable* to the *person himself* or to *others*' (9.1).

Moral Motives

An account of moral motives is closely connected to this account of personal merit and moral virtue. Building on a key premise in ancient ethics

---

[37] See *Treatise* 3.3 (also 3.2) for virtues and vices that help fill out Hume's catalogue.

and in Hutcheson's ethics, Hume argues that actors receive moral approval not of the *action* they perform, but of their *motive*—or, Hume sometimes says, their *intention*. Proper motive alone makes actions morally worthy. These motives are often important because they are signs of a person's character. Hume believes that what generally matters most to us about persons is their character—their morally relevant internalized principles and dispositions—not their actions, however important these actions may be.

When we evaluate others, Hume argues, the only way for us to gain access to their motives, and thereby to their virtues and character, is to infer the motive from their external behaviour. For example, if we judge someone's action to be friendly, we assume from the person's behaviour that the action is motivated by a desire to be friendly. If we later discover that an act we thought friendly was actually performed to manipulate us, we no longer regard the act as friendly or praiseworthy. Hume's statement of this position is clearest in the *Treatise*:

'Tis evident, that when we praise any actions, we regard only the motives that produc'd them, and consider the actions as signs or indications of certain principles in the mind and temper. The external performance has no merit. We must look within to find the moral quality. This we cannot do directly; and therefore fix our attention on actions, as on external signs. But these actions are still consider'd as signs; and the ultimate object of our praise and approbation is the motive, that produc'd them.[38]

Although *EPM* contains no comparably explicit discussion of the relationship between action, motive, and virtue, the same basic doctrine emerges. Judgements of an agent's virtue or vice and personal merit or demerit, Hume maintains, are inherently tied to the agent's motives. For example, a person's act of benefiting someone merits moral praise only if the person's motive is to benefit the other person; it cannot be a moral motive if the action springs primarily from a desire to receive a reward for supplying the benefit. Right motive is essential for virtue, and a virtuous character is constituted by having an appropriate and enduring motivational structure.

Consider the following case as an example of Hume's point. A person discharges an obligation because it is an obligation, but intensely dislikes being placed in a position in which the interests of others must be placed

---

[38] *Treatise* 3.2.1.2. Hume once wrote to Hutcheson explaining his point: 'Actions are not virtuous nor vicious; but only so far as they are proofs of certain Qualitys or durable Principles in the Mind' (17 Sept. 1739, *Letters*, 1: 34). Cf. *Treatise* 3.3.1.4.

first. This person does not love, feel friendly towards, or cherish others and respects their wishes only because obligation requires it. This person none the less performs the morally right action and even has a well-formed disposition to perform such actions. A disposition to follow moral rules and perform moral obligations exists in this person, but the motive is not morally approvable. In Hume's theory, if a person characteristically lacks approvable motives, a necessary condition of virtuous character is missing.

Objectivity and Subjectivity

This account of virtue in persons and the earlier account of universal response and judgement contrast sharply with a type of objectivism that Hume rejected. The fact that some moral beliefs are held universally does not, he thinks, indicate either that these beliefs rest on moral values that are objective parts of the universe (as some rationalists and natural law thinkers proposed) or that the beliefs are true or false. Hume believed that statements of empirical fact (for example, 'My car is parked on First Avenue') and statements of the relations of ideas (for example, 'Cars are motorized vehicles') are either true or false, whereas moral assertions are neither true nor false. In the first appendix in *EPM*, he summarizes his conclusions (Appx. 1.21):

The distinct boundaries and offices of *reason* and of *taste* are easily ascertained. The former conveys the knowledge of truth and falsehood: The latter gives the sentiment of beauty and deformity, vice and virtue. The one discovers objects, as they really stand in nature, without addition or diminution: The other has a productive faculty, and gilding or staining all natural objects with the colours, borrowed from internal sentiment, raises, in a manner, a new creation.

In asserting that the faculty of taste 'gilds' objects (that is, metaphorically, coats or gold-plates objects), Hume does not deny that we discover and rely in the gilding process on qualities that the objects gilded actually possessed. For example, a truthful person objectively has the quality or trait of truthfulness. Hume's point is that this property of persons counts as a *virtue* of truthfulness (a gilded rather than a bare truthfulness) only because we make it a virtue through our powers of approval. We gild the truthful person with the virtue of truthfulness by adding something (one essential component of virtue) that was not there previously. Whereas virtue requires a history of public approbation, the mere property of being truthful does not. Many properties, qualities, or traits of persons are *not* gilded in this way and therefore are not virtues. For example, fear of flying in aeroplanes and love of classical music are not virtues, though in principle they could be virtues if human nature led us to respond with approbation to these mental qualities as we do to truthful persons.

We correctly attribute virtue to a person only if the person objectively possesses the properties that are essential to the subjective response of approbation that gilds the properties with virtue. In this respect, virtue does exist independently of the approval of *any particular* human observer, and a person can be virtuous irrespective of others noticing that the person is virtuous, just as a person can be inebriated without anyone noticing the inebriation. This fact has suggested to some commentators that Hume believes in objective qualities of virtue that are independent of the subjective responses of persons.

There is a point to this interpretation, but it is easy to push Hume's universalism and theory of mental qualities too far in this direction. As noted previously, virtue *requires* some process of universal subjective response and gilding by impartial persons. Consistent with this position, Hume maintains that honest persons are honest and virtuous irrespective of whether others *believe* they are honest or *regard* them as virtuous. As Hume maintained in the *Treatise*, a virtuous person cast into a dungeon remains virtuous even when the virtue is lost to the rest of the world: 'Virtue in rags is still virtue'.[39] His thesis is that character traits such as honesty cannot qualify as virtues unless there has been a history of approbation by impartial observers; but once that history is in place, it is irrelevant whether observers actually notice that a person is virtuous.

To say that '*X* is morally virtuous' therefore entails that the relevant type of mental quality—a motive of honesty, for example—consistently stimulates approbation in all impartial persons. However paradoxical, Hume's theory is based on the premiss that moral attributions of virtue in persons both refer to objective properties independent of observers' minds (factual properties) and append something to those objective properties (moral characteristics) through the process of gilding. This interpretation seems warranted in light of Hume's text, but the reader should appreciate that Hume's philosophy is being *interpreted*. Hume never uses the language of 'objective' or 'objectivity' in *EPM*, and his typical language to express impartiality—another term he never uses in *EPM* (though he twice uses 'impartial')—is 'a point of view, common . . . with others',

---

[39] *Treatise* 3.3.1.19.

'unprejudiced notions', 'proper discernment', 'proper sentiment', and the like. Some readers may prefer to stick closer to this language than to use terms such as *objectivity* or *impartiality*.

Justice and Utility

In the *Treatise* Hume held that we have both *natural* virtues—those qualities native to or embedded in human nature, such as benevolence, generosity, moderation, and meekness—and *artificial* virtues, such as justice, which are acquired only through a public agreement. Hume abandons the language of natural and artificial virtues in *EPM*, but part of his reason for making this distinction remains, as we shall now see.

Unlike benevolence, justice requires a system of socially constructed rules. Rules of justice spring up, grow, and develop over time. 'Justice' is, in effect, Hume's term for the virtue of following the rules and institutions that society creates to thwart the elements of the wolf and serpent in our nature, whereas 'benevolence' is his term for the element of the dove. Despite these differences, benevolence and justice both have to do with promoting utility. Benevolent acts are directed at promoting the good of our intimates and close associates. The more diversified a social arrangement becomes and the greater the extent to which persons are strangers rather than intimates, the more useful Hume considers the rules of justice and the less useful natural benevolence.

Justice has often been depicted in contemporary moral philosophy as starkly different from social utility, on grounds that obligations of justice are independent of what is socially useful. However, Hume attempts to bring justice and utility into amicable association. At the outset of Section 3, he announces his intention to prove that 'public utility is the *sole* origin of justice' (3.1). Some interpret Hume as meaning that rules of justice are justified by a more foundational principle of utility, but this problem of justification is not Hume's problem. His concern is to explain the *origin* and *nature* of rules of justice, not to *justify* particular frameworks of rules. He neither proposes nor defends particular norms of justice; instead, he explains the nature, function, and source of all such norms.

THE CIRCUMSTANCES OF JUSTICE AND THE UTILITY OF JUSTICE

Hume begins by examining the circumstances in which rules of justice arise and the way in which rules function in those circumstances. He maintains that rules of justice emerge and become accepted in a society because they promote social utility. To persuade us that rules of social justice arise for this reason, Hume reflects on situations in which rules of justice would be useless, unnecessary, or impossible—that is, without social utility. The circumstances that he considers are (1) an unlimited availability of the goods a person desires, (2) an unlimited benevolence in the members of society, (3) an extreme lack of necessary resources (because of famine or war), and (4) a situation in which we must interact with persons or creatures who are ignorant of the rules of justice.

In Hume's framework, justice requires both personal conflict and social co-operation. Conflict is simply part of the human condition. We are by nature partial to ourselves and those close to us, but our beneficence is usually confined to this small group of intimates. Strangers are not the benefactors of our benevolence, except on rare occasions. Justice arises because almost all persons have this natural partiality and limited benevolence. They want as many goods as possible in life, and they seek stability in the possession of their goods. Rules of justice are the means to these ends. These rules are developed in order to ameliorate problems that arise from the competition for scarce resources, the limited benevolence in persons, and the vulnerability of personal property to damage or theft.

Hume maintains that justice 'would never once have been dreamed of' (3.3) if we lived in a society in which goods were freely available and every desire satisfied. However, many goods are scarce and competition for them is keen. To avoid destructive forms of competition, we institute conventions of justice that establish rights for individuals and that protect the common interest. These rules are not devised for completely rational, completely sympathetic, or completely benevolent persons, but for typical members of society who are limited in rationality, sympathy, and benevolence.

THE CONVENTIONS OF JUSTICE

This account of justice is 'conventionalist'. That is, moral rules, institutions, and practices arise and gain acceptability through social arrangements. 'Convention' in Hume's sense need not involve an explicit consent, promise, or social contract (Appx. 3.7). Conventions are rules that almost all members of society follow in almost all circumstances. For example, Hume regards basic rules of language, etiquette, promise-keeping, and contracting as conventions. His claim about justice, in particular, is that justice requires a background framework of publicly accepted rules that are inlaid in the social mosaic of expected behaviours. Each person who follows the rules understands that the interests of everyone in society are advanced by conformity to these rules.

Hume concisely expressed the main line of his views about justice and convention in the *Treatise*:

After . . . [a] convention, concerning abstinence from the possessions of others, is enter'd into, and every one has acquir'd a stability in his possessions, there immediately arise the ideas of justice and injustice; as also those of *property*, *right*, and *obligation*. The latter are altogether unintelligible without first understanding the former. . . . Those rules, by which property, right, and obligation are determin'd, . . . have all of them a direct and evident tendency to public good, and the support of society. . . . [E]very individual person must find himself a gainer, on ballancing the account; since, without justice, society must immediately dissolve.[40]

People signal to others that they are willing to behave in certain ways when they realize that everyone will benefit from those forms of conduct. As stability, reciprocity, and trust grow, the conventions are strengthened and their social utility increases. Formal contracts and informal promises and agreements conform to the conventions, but they are not the *basis* of the original social conventions. Similarly, the members of a community accept governments, laws, and various social institutions when these institutions promote social utility. If the utility of these institutions erodes or vanishes, causing a slippage in the trust and social co-operation that originally allowed the institutions to flourish, the mutual respect that supports the institutions will be impaired or lost. The institutions can then be expected to disintegrate.

THE MOTIVATION TO JUSTICE

Hume believed that every prudent person will see that it is in his or her interest to abide by the rules of justice, as long as others do so. He argues that our recognition that rules of justice protect personal interest motivates us to accept and abide by these rules. This thesis about why we are motivated to act justly seems egoistic (more like than unlike Hobbes), because self-interest alone summons us to accept rules of justice. Yet if Hume's analysis were a thoroughgoing egoism, he could not consistently depict justice as a moral virtue or its rules as moral obligations.

Hume resolves this problem as follows. Self-interest initially motivates us to accept co-operative rules of justice. Once the rules are in place, it is

---

[40] *Treatise* 3.2.2.11; 3.2.6.6; 3.2.2.22.

public-spiritedness—a motive to act in the common interest—that motivates us to abide by the rules. This motive is more like benevolence than self-interest. Persons develop this secondary motive because their natural humanity or fellow-feeling leads them to promote the good of others, and they see that abiding by the rules of justice does promote the good of others. Hume calls this personal identification with the rules of justice a 'sense of common interest' and the 'sentiment of justice' (Appx. 3.7, 9). This sense of justice is reinforced by parents, teachers, peers, and politicians.[41]

JUSTICE AS A VIRTUE

Hume also presents justice as a virtue of persons. Justice is a virtue when the motivation to act justly is a stable trait of a person's character. The person must respect the rules of justice and internalize the regulation of conduct by these rules in order to be just. Merely acting in accordance with rules of justice is not enough for a person to possess the virtue of justice. Moral approval and disapproval have motive and character as their objects, not mere conformity to rules. Again we see the supremacy of *virtue* as a moral category in Hume's ethics, even when he is writing primarily about the utility of social rules and institutions.

The Sensible Knave Problem

Hume recognizes that circumstances sometimes arise in which persons will apparently not further their own interests by acting justly. None the less, obligations of justice suggest that we should sacrifice self-interest, obey moral rules, and promote the interests of others even when our own interests might not, in particular circumstances, be advanced. In a famous passage, Hume considers the acts of a 'sensible knave' who occasionally acts unjustly while concealing his immoral acts through deception (9.22). Hume indicates that this knave's true interests are subject to competing interpretations. On the one hand, the knave is constantly in danger of exposing his deception and cunning, with the ruinous consequence of a 'total loss of reputation, and the forfeiture of all future trust and confidence' (9.24). On the other hand, the knave might be willing to take this risk and sacrifice his peace of mind and sense of integrity for worldly bene-

---

[41] See Hume's rich account of the 'original motive' to justice in his *Treatise* 3.2.1.13–16; 3.2.2.19, 23–4.

fits. The knave will have his own perspective on how to balance the benefits, risks, and losses of his activities, and his balance may differ from another person's evaluation.

In general, Hume believes that acting morally returns benefits to the actor, because it produces favourable responses in other persons. From this perspective, Hume can appeal to the knave's instinctive self-interest as a reason for acting in accordance with moral rules of justice. The problem, however, is that acting unjustly often seems personally beneficial in *particular* cases. Some philosophers have therefore thought that Hume's knave presents a sober challenge to the rationality and justifiability of internalizing the moral point of view. Hume himself acknowledges that we may not be able to supply a convincing answer to the knave's question about why he should act morally, especially if we must assume exactly what the knave assumes about his interests (9.23).

None the less, Hume offers some answers to the knave that follow from previous arguments in *EPM*. One answer reiterates his psychological thesis that self-interest does not always triumph over moral sentiment in persons with an uncorrupted moral nature. The needs of others frequently motivate us to act in their behalf, irrespective of foreseen outcomes for self-interest. Hume also thinks that the knave has been duped because he will sacrifice the enjoyments that flow from the esteem of others and from personal self-regard for 'worthless toys' (9.25). The knave simply fails to appreciate the value of a sense of integrity and self-respect, which themselves profoundly contribute to a person's happiness and sense of well-being.

Hume seems to recognize however, that his line of argument is not decisive. A truly clever knave can selectively reject those aspects of morality that do not serve self-interest. The knave can agree that Hume correctly presents the advantages of rules of justice for all members of society and still go on to ask why these rules should be followed on every occasion. Hume's purpose in presenting and then briskly dismissing his knave in two pages of *EPM* may not be to respond to this question as much as to reassure readers who already possess a sense of justice and a well-formed character that these possessions are worthy and ultimately rewarding.

Hume may think that this answer to the knave's question is all that can be or need be provided, but, as he seems to recognize, the problem of the sensible knave represents a severe test of his theory, just as it does for any theory of morality.

A Utilitarian Moral Philosophy?

Because utility is the sole origin of justice for Hume, he is often interpreted as a utilitarian, that is, as one who accepts the moral theory that we are obligated to act to maximize human welfare and minimize harmful outcomes in all circumstances. Do his theses about utility constitute utilitarianism?

Hume supports a utility-centred account of personal merit that features the useful and agreeable qualities of persons. This theory, like his account of justice, gives *EPM* a utilitarian appearance. However, unlike classical utilitarians, Hume does not develop a normative theory in which the principle of utility reigns as the supreme foundational principle. His theory is a descriptive explaining of moral approval in terms of character traits and social practices that have utility. Hume uses the term 'utility' to refer to whatever promotes the happiness of members of society or advances the public good. He does not develop a theory about maximizing aggregate welfare or about whether one system of rules is, on balance, better than another system of rules in producing utilitarian outcomes. His reflections are centred on the comparative value of having a system of conventional rules rather than no rules at all.

In Section 5, entitled 'Why Utility Pleases', Hume argues that the utility of actions is the *chief* reason we welcome and praise them and also 'the chief circumstance' whereby *virtues* 'derive their merit' (5.4). This thesis too derives from his account of human nature and social morality, not from a conviction that we are obligated to maximize the welfare of all affected parties.

The Nature of Obligations

In several passages in *EPM* Hume uses the language of 'duty' and 'obligation', yet he never supplies a developed account of obligation or of how persons come to be obligated. It often seems unclear whether Hume has a normative theory of obligation or merely an account of human nature that explains how we come to feel obligated. A related question is whether Hume takes *obligation* seriously as a moral category or is so concerned with *virtue* that obligation is a side issue.

At various points in *EPM* Hume attempts to explain the relationships among feelings, motives, obligations, and virtues, including how we acquire and learn to recognize obligations when no natural motive or inclination such as self-interest or benevolence motivates us. His comments are difficult to interpret, but he seems to employ at least two senses of 'obligation' (using also the synonym 'duty'). These two senses can be called *psychological* obligation and *social* obligation.

First, in *psychological obligation* a person is morally obligated whenever the person experiences a moral sentiment that prompts action. This sense of obligation is motivational and causal: Moral sentiments motivate action, causing us to feel that we must perform the action. Rather than implying that one *ought* to act in accordance with the sentiment felt as obliging, this account is based on motivation by a moral sentiment: The universality of moral sentiment implies that all similarly situated persons who take an impartial perspective feel the same moral sentiments (a psychological thesis). These universally felt sentiments generate universally embraced moral rules, which are normative. When Hume speaks of a 'rule of right' being established through this process (9.5; Appx. 1.9), he presumably thinks that any rule of this description obligates persons. However, he is not entirely clear on the point, and this interpretation may capture the spirit more than the letter of his moral philosophy. Many commentators would find this normative interpretation speculative, even if they view the psychological interpretation as well supported in his writings.

Second, consider *social obligation*. Obligations of justice and all obligations based on social rules are normative. A rule of property, for example, demands that persons refrain from taking the possessions of other persons. In society we first learn the advantages of moral conventions and positive laws that secure rights of liberty and property. We then abide by these conventions because they establish mutually beneficial arrangements. These arrangements establish our expectations of others, and failure to conform to these expectations provides grounds for disapprobation, condemnation, and blame. Obligations are established by the rules of expected behaviour. In both *EPM* and the *Treatise*, Hume offers an analogy to multiple oarsmen who are motivated by a commonly accepted convention to pull a boat efficiently without the existence of any formal contract or promise, because doing so is in their mutual interest (Appx. 3.8). Once conventions are in place, obligations (to row, to act justly, etc.) exist and must be discharged even if we find them inconvenient, arduous, or displeasing.

An example of Hume's theory of social obligation is found in his account in *Treatise* 3.2.5 of the obligation of promise-keeping. He argues that the source of this obligation is conventional (both 'customary' and 'artificial'), rather than natural. That is, the obligation is based on a social practice established to promote human goals and interests, such as peace and stability, that would be seriously threatened without it. All persons are advantaged by abiding by rules of promise-keeping, which promote reciprocation and trust. Once the convention is in place, a person cannot escape the obligation to keep a promise merely by appealing to personal desires, plans, interests, or beliefs. Such personal pursuits do not validly override a promise. An obligation to keep the promise exists whenever the person says 'I promise' and means it, because in this act of speech the person wills and assumes the obligation.[42]

We can generalize this account of social obligation as follows. Obligation ultimately derives from social expectations and conventions. Blame and disapproval follow from disappointments of social expectations and violations of conventions. This is the origin of obligation and accounts for its normative force. From this perspective, when Hume speaks of duties of humanity, obligations of justice, duties of honesty, and the like, we can interpret him as accepting the normative thesis that all members of society have these duties or obligations, not merely the psychological thesis that persons view themselves as obligated by social rules.

Hume provides only a few sentences about obligation in *EPM*, including a discussion of obligations of loyalty to governments and international laws (4.1–3). The reason for his relative neglect of *obligation* is that his centre-piece category is *virtue*. His focus on persons rather than their actions led him to make 'virtue' and 'vice' the preferred language over 'obligation' and 'duty'. At the same time, Hume sometimes indicates that we have obligations to avoid vices, and he never abandons the category of obligation altogether.

In one of his essays he wrote that 'If a man have a lively sense of honour and virtue, with moderate passions, his conduct will always be conformable to the rules of morality; or if he depart from them [the rules], his return will be easy and expeditious.'[43] This passage suggests that persons

---

[42] However, part of understanding this convention is understanding that it is not always morally required that a person keep a stated promise. One might be making a promise to a thief or might encounter a conflicting obligation that justifies not keeping the promise. Obligations can be validly overridden. This vision of obligations is introduced in *EPM* (4.3) during a brief discussion of the justification of moral actions and the balancing of conflicting moral and political obligations: 'All politicians will allow, and most philosophers, that REASONS of STATE may, in particular emergencies, dispense with the rules of justice. . . . But nothing less than the most extreme necessity, it is confessed, can justify individuals in a breach of promise, or an invasion of the properties of others.'

[43] Hume, 'The Sceptic' 29.

of virtue can be relied upon to recognize their obligations and meet them. This comment may help explain why in *EPM* Hume places the premium on virtues rather than obligations.

Customary Practices and Specific Rules

In discussing rules of justice and obligation, Hume points out that the rules are specified in different ways in different societies. Particular duties and rights vary from one society to the next, each of which gives a different specific content to the general rules found in all societies. Hume compares different ways of building houses to different ways of developing rules of property: People in many different times and places construct houses, but construct them differently; similarly, persons in many different times and places fashion rules of property, but design them differently in accordance with the necessities of the particular society. In the case of traditions of house construction and laws of property, 'their chief outlines pretty regularly concur; because the purposes, to which they tend, are every where exactly similar' (3.44–5).

Conventions of property hold a special fascination for Hume. These conventions are specified in societies by systems of social rules of justice, typically enforceable laws. The rules specify legitimate forms of the possession and transfer of property and state the obligations, rights, and responsibilities of the various parties. These rules vary in accordance with historical circumstance and culture. For example, different countries establish different holdings in land and water, different lengths of time that property can be held, different rules about permissible gifts and inheritances, and different laws governing the transfer of rights. For this reason, substantive rules of justice regarding property and rights cannot be provided by abstract philosophical theories of distributive justice; answers can only come from within the framework of conventional social systems.

Hume's interest in the specification of duties and rights in different cultures led him to consider the nature and role of social practices. He provides an account of 'common life and practice' (5.43) in which, despite the existence of many of 'the same rules' (3.47) in all cultures, the different practices in different cultures can be explained by the different utilities the practices have in those communities. He argues that many forms of human conduct in these cultures make no sense unless we grasp the underlying practices. For example, conventions surrounding the exchange of private property make sense only to someone who already understands the 'institution of property' and its accompanying practices (3.44). If two parties sign a contract to sell a house and the buyer hands over a deposit, this transaction is understandable only if practices of owning, selling, contracting, depositing, and the like are understood. There could, of course, be a society in which no private property exists and no transfer of property occurs. Actions of buying and selling property would seem bizarre or inexplicable to persons in this culture.

Custom, Relativity, and Disagreement

Some critics maintain that rules and practices are legitimate forms of social morality in Hume's philosophy merely because they are customary. They object to Hume's ethics on grounds that it is overly conventionalist, landing us in a moral relativism. That is, they think Hume must hold that all moral beliefs and principles are relative to the rules and responses of individual cultures or persons, so that notions of moral rightness and wrongness vary from place to place or person to person.

Hume's theory has more resources than this interpretation suggests. Moral rules and practices are always *utility-promoting* and *universally approved* by impartial persons. Hume condemns customary rules and laws that fail to meet these conditions: 'Where a civil law is so perverse as to cross all the interests of society, it loses all its authority, and men judge by the ideas of natural justice, which are conformable to those interests. . . . Thus, the interests of society require, that contracts be fulfilled; and there is not a more material article either of natural or civil justice' (n. 12). Customs, traditions, or standards that fail to be utility-promoting or to be approvable by impartial persons have no authority. These systems need revision to promote the interests of society and to gain the approval of those governed by them. However, beyond these general conditions for acceptable rules, Hume is reluctant to judge the acceptability or unacceptability of a community's particular moral rules. He indicates that any set of conventional rules that has been adopted in a particular moral or legal system is satisfactory if it satisfies these general conditions.

In 'A Dialogue' Hume considers these problems and cautiously supports the universalism for which he argues throughout *EPM*. He suggests that many apparent moral disagreements and forms of diversity stem from an undue narrowness of perspective on the part of moral agents or cultural groups. They lack either a proper understanding of the relevant facts or a proficiency in making the judgements that need to be made.

Hume also insists that 'All the circumstances of the case are supposed to be laid before us, ere we can fix any sentence of blame or approbation. . . . In moral decisions, all the circumstances and relations must be previously known' (Appx. 1.11). This theme reappears in 'A Dialogue': Social disagreement arises when persons have an inadequate grasp of the circumstances, have divergent views about the utility of an action, rely on narrow rather than impartial viewpoints, or fail to surmount their own self-interest.

Hume appreciated the diversity of customs and practices in the morals of groups, but as a philosopher his inclination was to peer through this heterogeneity and probe for common and uniform principles, especially principles in human nature. As he puts it in the mouth of a figure in 'A Dialogue', 'the *principles* upon which men reason in morals are always the same; though the *conclusions* which they draw are often very different' (Dial. 36; italics added).

This statement suggests that Hume accepts a relativity of particular social rules, practices, and judgements, but not a relativity of the general principles of human nature that underlie those rules, practices, and judgements. For example, all morally serious persons and societies react to kidnappings in their community with moral sentiments that lead to cultural prohibitions of such theft; however, the particular forms of condemnation, how children are understood as property, and the types of punishment for kidnapping vary considerably. Hume's conventionalism and historicism allow for this moral diversity, but do not translate into either a pure conventionalism or an unqualified cultural or historical relativism of standards.

The Role of Reason

Because Hume relies heavily on taste, passion, sentiment, and the like in his account of morals, some commentators believe that he has acknowledged no role for reason in moral thinking and is altogether a sceptic about reason in morals. However, this interpretation is one-sided. Hume assigns reason (or understanding) a vital role in moral thinking, just as he assigns it a central role in the scientific investigation of moral behaviour that forms part of his science of human nature.

In the *Treatise* (2.3.3.4), Hume made a famous statement in an attempt to describe reason's proper role: *Reason is, and ought only to be the slave of the passions*. He called this view an extraordinary opinion, and it has provoked criticism down to the present day. No such statement is found in *EPM*, but the doctrine is similar, because reason is again depicted as playing a subsidiary role to passion. Hume argues that sentiments present our goals in life and that reason then assists us in achieving those goals. Being incapable by itself of providing goals, reason discovers the means to achieve them. Hume insists that reason and passion, so understood, can never be in opposition or compete for the role of determining the will.

Many philosophers have faulted this thesis, on grounds that Hume is at odds with common opinion, which holds that in the domain of morality reason must control desire, rather than desire controlling reason. When, for example, we desire to promote our personal interest above the interests of others, reason informs us of what is inappropriate and unreasonable in our conduct. These critics of Hume believe that desire and reason often conflict and that desire can be contrary to reason. They maintain that reason has the power to determine how we should act, and they see moral actions as undertaken for ends that reason approves.[44]

Although Hume does deny that conflicts can exist between reason and desire, he acknowledges that reason can control our actions by giving us information that will redirect our desires and attitudes. He also argues that moral conflict can occur between motives of self-interest and moral motives. In opposing the 'selfish system of morals' (Appx. 2.3), Hume points to conflicts such as the following: 'The most obvious objection to the selfish hypothesis, is, that . . . [self-love] is contrary to common feeling and our most unprejudiced notions . . . [such] as benevolence and generosity' (Appx. 2.6); and, Hume adds, 'by such universal principles are the particular sentiments of self-love frequently controuled and limited' (9.8).

Hume thus acknowledges that there are cases in which personal desire conflicts with a moral faculty, and he holds that this claim shows some similarity to common views of reason. He recognizes that *calm desire*, for example, is similar in function to what other philosophers call reason. When Hume uses the language of 'cool preference' (5.39; 9.4) and 'cool approbation' (5.43) in *EPM*, he is reflecting this view. In cool moments of inner conflict, Hume maintains that a calm desire has mitigated or overridden a more intense or violent desire. He thinks that rationalists mistake the clash between calm and agitated desires for a clash between reason and

---

[44] See e.g. Terence Penelhum, 'Hume's Moral Psychology', in Norton (ed.), *The Cambridge Companion to Hume*, 139–40; Baier, *The Moral Point of View*, 258–60.

desire. For example, if a desire to contact the police about a crime takes precedence over an intensely violent urge to take personal revenge for the crime, Hume would say that a calm desire, not reason, has gained ascendancy over a violent desire.

Hume thinks that the rationalists misunderstand human nature when they argue that reason controls the desire for revenge. To fathom Hume's opposition to such philosophical claims about reason, we need to distinguish the rationalistic conception of reason that he rejected from the service role for reason that he accepted.

THE ROLE FOR REASON THAT HUME REJECTS

Hume is often interpreted as arguing that no value judgement—however extreme, obscene, or cruel—is reasonable or unreasonable, just as no value judgement is factual. This interpretation needs careful assessment. A passion is 'unreasonable' for Hume not because the passion is *inappropriate*, as we suggest today when we say, 'It was unreasonable of him to be angry', but because the passion is based on an *erroneous judgement*, as when we say, 'It is unreasonable to have a desire to do what is impossible'. For example, if I desire to see my dead grandfather at a restaurant tonight and this desire together with my peculiar belief that he will be there lead me to go to the restaurant, my desire is unreasonable because the judgement that he is alive and will be at the restaurant is unreasonable. Hume thinks that the judgement, not the passion, is unreasonable.

Some philosophers have argued that Hume is mistaken, on grounds that the term 'reasonable' can be properly applied to an emotion or desire that is inappropriate. Obviously Hume is not prepared to accept this sense of 'reasonable' if it literally means 'based on reason'. None the less, Hume does not maintain that grossly immoral beliefs about torture, genocide, and slavery that are accompanied by correct judgements of fact are 'reasonable' in the broad sense that we now often use the term 'reasonable'. He himself uses 'reasonable' in this broader sense. For example, he speaks in *EPM* of 'the conduct of any reasonable man' (3.20) and 'a reasonable frugality' (6.11). Moral convictions are unreasonable in this sense when passion-driven judgements are inappropriate, immoderate, or excessive.

This problem of what is reasonable obviously depends on how broadly or narrowly one uses the terms 'reason' and 'passion'. Hume generally uses them in stark opposition: Reason is non-passionate; passion is nonrational. Hume believes that human motivation comes fundamentally from desires, aversions, and the like, not from reason.[45] If reason could inform us which desires and aversions are rational or otherwise acceptable, then reason alone could lead us to act. But reason is impotent in this regard. Hume's dismissal of reason as a motivating force is blunt and uncompromising from the earliest passages in *EPM* (1.7): 'What is honourable, what is fair, what is becoming, what is noble, what is generous, takes possession of the heart, and animates us to embrace and maintain it. What is intelligible, what is evident, what is probable, what is true, procures only the cool assent of the understanding' (that is, reason).

THE ROLE FOR REASON THAT HUME ACCEPTS

Hume summarizes the role he assigns to reason in morals as follows:

One principal foundation of moral praise being supposed to lie in the usefulness of any quality or action; it is evident, that *reason* must enter for a considerable share in all decisions of this kind; since nothing but that faculty can instruct us in the tendency of qualities and actions, and point out their beneficial consequences to society and to their possessor. (Appx. 1.2)

Information about the consequences of acting on what we desire can make a decisive difference to the actions we select or reject. If a person discovers through reason that an outcome will be more costly than beneficial, desire may turn to aversion. For example, if a calorie-conscious person discovers that a particularly tasty delicacy is very fattening, the passion for it may disappear. Similarly, a person who wants to be healthy and discovers through reason that aerobic exercise is very healthy can come to have a desire for aerobic exercise that did not previously exist. Reason, in this manner, can modify desire and redirect action by turning aspiration into aversion and lack of desire into desire: 'Reason, being cool and disengaged, is no motive to action, and directs only the impulse received from appetite or inclination, by showing us the means of attaining happiness or avoiding misery' (Appx. 1.21).

Another passage about the proper role for reason clarifies Hume's theory: '[I]n order to pave the way for . . . a sentiment, and give a proper discernment of its object, it is often necessary, we find, that much reasoning should precede, that nice distinctions be made, just conclusions drawn, distant comparisons formed, complicated relations examined, and general

---

[45] For details, see *Treatise* 2.3.3, 'Of the influencing motives of the will'. Hume there considers the inadequacies of theories that reason and passion conflict and that passion must be brought under the control of reason. He argues that reason in no respect directly influences the will or causes action.

facts fixed and ascertained' (1.9). The person who reasons as here depicted appeals to these procedures prior to forming a sentiment or judgement. Today we might say that reason itself requires that we use the methods mentioned in this passage, but Hume's narrow use of the term 'reason' leads him to say only that there is a prior role for reason.

Religious Scepticism and the Autonomy of Morals

In contrast to many writers of his period, Hume was sceptical about claims that a religious foundation is needed for morals. He drops hints in *EPM* indicating his disdain for a religiously motivated morality. For example, he caustically dismisses the 'monkish virtues' celebrated by persons under religious vows of poverty, chastity, humility, and obedience to religious authority (9.3). In his catalogue of virtues, he surprised his contemporaries by substituting restrained pride, affability, delicacy of taste, and the like in the place of certain virtues sanctioned by religious traditions. This catalogue and his distaste for parts of the religious catalogue show a clear rejection of Christian ethics (most obviously in its Roman Catholic and puritan forms).

Although raised in a strong Calvinistic environment, Hume overthrew his religious beginnings and dedicated himself to showing that the moral life can be lived and fully explained without the resources of religion. He sought to cut the moral sense tradition free of reliance on divine authority by relying entirely on categories such as *natural virtues* and the *rules of civilized society*. Hume laboured in writing *EPM* to show that moral beliefs and practices can be accounted for exclusively through our native resources (for example, benevolence) and social conventions (for example, rules of justice). Hume's scepticism about religious foundations for morals is therefore not a scepticism about all foundations for morals. He located those foundations in human nature.

Hume's ethics is among the first thoroughly secular theories in British philosophy. This divorce from religion may be one reason why he aligns himself with 'the ancient moralists'. Cicero (1st c. BC), Aristotle (4th c. BC), and other ancient moralists were right, in his view, to stress the virtues and their connections to inner motivation. Hume's appeal to these ancient authorities was a vital means of communicating with his audience. If he could convince his readers that widely admired figures such as Cicero held a secular view of morals, he stood a better chance of having his own views accepted.

5. The Structure of the Text

Hume's major topics, arguments, and conclusions in moral philosophy are sometimes hidden from view because so much of his effort goes into his observations about human nature. The present section is devoted exclusively to the structure of *EPM* and the main topics in his moral philosophy.

The title of *EPM* indicates Hume's abiding interest in 'the principles of morals'. The first three sections and the first three appendices discuss principles and virtues, especially benevolence and justice. These six major parts of *EPM* are grouped together in the outline below under the heading 'Basic Moral Categories and Distinctions'. Sections 4 and 5 extend the analysis of benevolence and justice to political society and to the variety of social circumstances in which promoting utility is of social importance. These topics are grouped in the outline under the heading 'The Role of Utility'. Sections 6, 7, and 8 provide an account of additional qualities of persons (those not already handled in previous sections) that qualify as moral virtues or as some other form of personal merit. Appendix 4 deepens this analysis by delineating the origins and boundaries of virtues and talents. These topics are arranged in the outline below under the heading 'Personal Merit and Moral Virtue'. Section 9 is Hume's 'Conclusion' to his arguments on all of the above topics, and this heading is retained in the outline below. Finally, the short essay entitled 'A Dialogue' is appended at the end as more or less a fifth appendix to *EPM*. Its topics are placed in the outline below under the heading 'Relativity and Universality in Morals'.

Basic Moral Categories and Distinctions
A Controversy over the Foundation of Morals (Section 1 and Appendix 1)
Benevolence: A Principle and a Social Virtue (Section 2 and Appendix 2)
Justice: Social Rules and Social Virtues (Section 3 and Appendix 3)

The Role of Utility
The Role of Utility in Political Society and Political Obligation (Section 4)
Why Utility Pleases (Section 5)

Personal Merit and Moral Virtue
Qualities Useful to Ourselves (Section 6)
Qualities Immediately Agreeable to Ourselves (Section 7)
Qualities Immediately Agreeable to Others (Section 8)
Origins and Boundaries of Different Types of Qualities (Appendix 4)

Conclusions (Section 9)

Relativity and Universality in Morals ('A Dialogue')

Analytical summaries of each of these sections and appendices are found in the Annotations to the *Enquiry*. Readers who seek more information about the *argument* that runs through these sections should consult these summaries.

One qualification is in order: The groupings in the above outline place an organization on Hume's text that a reader should use cautiously. The concerns of Hume's Section 1 are different in many respects from those of Sections 2 and 3, and Sections 2 and 3 are in some respects closely related to Section 4. Similar comments could be made about relationships among the other sections. One could group Hume's concerns in different ways, and thoughtful readers will wish to do so. The outline in this section should be interpreted as an aid to orient the reader to Hume's structure, not as his recommended conception or as the only defensible conception.

6. Conclusion: Hume's Influence

Hume has influenced many great philosophers and has attracted many critics and adherents in the last 250 years. Among those he influenced were the greatest moral philosophers of his and later periods. In his own time, Hume profoundly affected the most eminent British moralists of the late eighteenth century, including Adam Smith (1723–90), Richard Price (1723–91), and Thomas Reid (1710–96). Hume and Smith were reasonably close, personally and philosophically, and Smith praised Hume 'as approaching as nearly to the idea of a perfectly wise and virtuous man, as perhaps the nature of human frailty will admit'.[46] Price and Reid each offered a negative appraised on Hume's philosophy, and their views became highly influential. None the less, they admired Hume for his achievements, appreciated the power of his arguments, and treated him with the utmost respect as a philosopher. Reid, for example, wrote to Hume that 'I have learned more from your writings [about human nature] . . . than from all others put together'.[47]

---

[46] 9 Nov. 1776, Adam Smith to William Strahan, *Letters*, 2: 452.
[47] 18 Mar. 1763, Reid to Hume, in Burton (ed.), *Letters of Eminent Persons Addressed to David*

By many accounts today, the greatest philosopher of the eighteenth century in any nation was the German philosopher Immanuel Kant (1724–1804). Kant admired and profited from the writings of Hutcheson, Hume, and Smith in moral philosophy and was deeply influenced by other parts of Hume's philosophy, which he said had awakened him from his 'dogmatic slumbers'. However, rarely were philosophers, at least on the surface, more opposed than Hume and Kant in their moral theories. Hume was the informed sentimentalist sceptical of the powers of pure reason, Kant the defender of pure reason against the corrupting powers of sentiment. Hume produced no normative theory of obligation, whereas Kant placed such inquiry at the forefront of his moral philosophy. Hume made utility central in moral theory; Kant downgraded it.

The great utilitarian thinkers dominated moral philosophy in Britain in the nineteenth century, and they too acknowledged an indebtedness to Hume's writings in moral, political, and economic theory. Jeremy Bentham (1748–1832), the philosopher generally regarded as the founder or at least the architect of this movement, credited Hume with a profound influence on his thinking and said that 'the name of the principle of utility . . . was the name adopted from David Hume'.[48] John Stuart Mill (1806–73), the most prominent utilitarian, said that Hume had an unparalleled ability to challenge cultural preconceptions and to criticize arguments. He added that 'If Bentham had merely continued the work of Hume, he would scarcely have been heard of in philosophy; for he was far inferior to Hume in Hume's qualities.'[49] This appraisal is no depreciation of Bentham, who was Mill's godfather and philosophical inspiration. Mill simply recognized in Hume a genius rarely found in any culture at any time.

In the first half of the twentieth century, Hume was overshadowed in writings on moral philosophy by some of the very figures he had influenced so deeply, especially Kant and Mill. Shortly after mid-century, however, philosophers began to return to Hume's writings. Scholarship on Hume and Humean theories of ethics began to flourish. This trend continues at present, and respect for Hume among philosophers may

---

Hume, 154–6. In the Dedication to *An Inquiry into the Human Mind*, Reid stated that it was Hume who provoked him to think about how to rescue the principles of the human understanding from the consequences of sceptical assumptions, a major objective of Reid's work as a philosopher. *Works*, 1: 95.

[48] Bentham, *A Fragment on Government*, 'Historical Preface, Intended for the Second Edition' 2, 508.

[49] Mill, 'Bentham', 79–80.

never have been as widespread as it is today. Hume's theories of *taste, sentiment*, and *judgement* have heavily influenced some writers; others have praised Hume's emphasis on *character, virtue*, and *community*, as well as the central role he gives in his theory to intimate relationships, which have too long been neglected in moral theory. The power of his synoptic vision as a moral philosopher can often be seen in these writings.

In the quarter-century when Hume was able to witness the attention that his peers paid to *An Enquiry concerning the Principles of Morals*, he saw his views more rejected than received. None the less, he probably took comfort in preparing each of his nine revised editions of *EPM*. He would today be gratified to learn that this book is read by a larger audience than at any time in its history, and continues, together with his *Treatise*, to exert an influence in moral philosophy unmatched by that of any other writer in the English language, excepting, perhaps, Thomas Hobbes and John Stuart Mill.

The Text Printed in this Edition

An Enquiry concerning the Principles of Morals was first published in 1751. The last edition seen through the press with Hume's supervision, published in 1772, is the basis of the text (the copytext) in the present edition. The posthumous edition of 1777 has been consulted for evidence of late changes by the author and has almost always been followed for substantive changes of wording. The order of sections, parts, and appendices also follows the 1777 edition. The methods used in converting the copytext into the definitive or 'critical' text of the present edition and a history of Hume's revisions are provided in the Clarendon critical edition, which also explains editorial policy with regard to the choice of copytext, emendation, correction of errors, and the recording of substantive variants.

The sources cited by Hume in his notes have been checked against appropriate early modern editions and corrected whenever Hume or his compositor introduced errors in the citation of units such as page, book, and chapter numbers. Footnotes have been supplemented by the editor to provide more complete information, including precise titles, volumes, books, chapters, sections, and lines. This editorial amplification appears within square brackets to distinguish it from Hume's text. No editorial intrusions have been allowed in the text itself except for daggers to indicate where an annotation appears in the back matter and numbers introduced by the editor in the margin at the head of each paragraph, which are provided to establish a universal reference system that allows precise citation without reference to page numbers.

Supplementary Reading

This bibliography provides information about Hume's philosophical works, early modern writings in moral philosophy that may have influenced Hume, and a selection of books and recent articles about Hume's moral philosophy. Those seeking a more extensive list of materials should consult the bibliographical materials cited at the end of this list, in Section 8. The literature on Hume is extensive, and the list below is largely confined, in its references to secondary literature, to works that treat Hume's *moral* philosophy. Even for this category the listing is highly selective. Several substantial works in Hume scholarship are not listed because they are too remote from moral philosophy.

1. WRITINGS BY HUME

A list of Hume's writings, in chronological order, appears immediately below, with the year of first publication (but with the final title, if a change of title occurred). These works have been published in innumerable editions, many still in print. Several electronic editions are also available.

EARLY
A Treatise of Human Nature (1739–40).
An Abstract of . . . A Treatise of Human Nature (1740).
Essays: Moral and Political (1741–2).
A Letter from a Gentleman to his Friend in Edinburgh (1745).

MID-LIFE
An Enquiry concerning Human Understanding (1748).
An Enquiry concerning the Principles of Morals (1751).
Essays: Political Discourses (1752).
A Dissertation on the Passions (1757).
The Natural History of Religion (1757).
The History of England (1754–62).

POSTHUMOUS
My Own Life (1777).
Dialogues concerning Natural Religion (1779).
Essays on Suicide and the Immortality of the Soul (1783).

Oxford University Press is currently in the process of publishing a critical edition of Hume's philosophical, political, and literary works under the editorship of Tom L. Beauchamp, David Fate Norton, and M. A. Stewart. At present there is no critical or standard edition of Hume's philosophical or historical publications. The closest approximation is the following outdated collection: *The Philosophical Works of David Hume*, ed. T. H. Green and T. H. Grose, 4 vols. (London, 1882–86; fac. Darmstadt: Scientia, 1964).

In the absence of scholarly editions, various editions have been relied upon in the study of Hume's texts. The following list presents (1) original edition titles (in chronological order) and, as appropriate, (2) modern editions that have deservedly earned a reputation as superior in some features to other editions.

'Hume's Early Memoranda, 1729–1740', ed. E. C. Mossner, *Journal of the History of Ideas*, 9 (1948), 492–518.

A Treatise of Human Nature: Being an Attempt to Introduce the Experimental Method of Reasoning into Moral Subjects, 3 vols. (London, 1739–40). See *A Treatise of Human Nature*, ed. David Fate Norton and Mary Norton (Oxford: Clarendon Press, forthcoming).

An Abstract of a Book lately Published; Entituled, A Treatise of Human Nature, &c. wherein the Chief Argument of that Book is farther Illustrated and Explained (London, 1740). See in *A Treatise of Human Nature*, ed. Norton and Norton, above.

Essays Moral and Political, 2 vols. (Edinburgh, 1741–2); *Political Discourses* (Edinburgh, 1752); and part of *Four Dissertations* (London, 1757). See *Essays*, ed. Eugene Miller, 2nd edn. (Indianapolis: LibertyClassics, 1987); *Political Essays*, ed. Knud Haakonssen (Cambridge: Cambridge University Press, 1994); and *David Hume: Selected Essays*, ed. Stephen Copley and Andrew Edgar (Oxford: Oxford University Press, 1993).

A Letter from a Gentleman to his Friend in Edinburgh: Containing Some Observations on A Specimen of the Principles concerning Religion and Morality, said to be maintain'd in a Book lately publish'd, Entituled, A Treatise of Human Nature, &c. (Edinburgh, 1745). See *A Letter from a Gentleman to his Friend in Edinburgh*, ed. Ernest C. Mossner and John V. Price (Edinburgh, 1745; fac. Edinburgh: University Press, 1967).

An Enquiry concerning Human Understanding, first published as *Philosophical Essays concerning Human Understanding* (London, 1748). See *An Enquiry concerning Human Understanding*, ed. Tom L. Beauchamp (Oxford: Clarendon Press, forthcoming).

An Enquiry concerning the Principles of Morals (London, 1751).

Four Dissertations (London, 1757). The items in this work were eventually included in *Essays and Treatises on Several Subjects*. See *The Natural History of Religion*, ed. A. Wayne Colver (Oxford: Clarendon Press, 1976); and *A Dissertation on the Passions*, in *Philosophical Works*, ed. Green and Grose, above. For the other two dissertations, see *Essays*, ed. Miller, above.

Supplementary Reading

The History of England from the Invasion of Julius Caesar to The Revolution in 1688 (London, 1754–62). See *The History of England*, 6 vols., foreword by William B. Todd (Indianapolis: LibertyClassics, 1983).

Dialogues concerning Natural Religion (London, 1779). See *Hume's Dialogues concerning Natural Religion*, ed. Norman Kemp Smith (Oxford: Clarendon Press, 1935), 2nd edn. with supplement (Edinburgh: Nelson, 1947; repr. Indianapolis: Bobbs-Merrill, 1962).

Currently, three computer-readable electronic collections of Hume's texts are available. The most comprehensive is available in both disk and CD-ROM form in the Past Masters Series of the Intelex Corporation. Hume's *Treatise* and two *Enquiries* are available from Oxford University Press, which uses the outdated, but classic Selby-Bigge editions. Finally, HUMETEXT 1.0, prepared by Tom L. Beauchamp, David Fate Norton, and M. A. Stewart, is available from the Department of Philosophy, Georgetown University. This collection includes Hume's philosophical, political, and literary works, prepared in pure form from eighteenth-century editions, without modern editing, and corrected for errors.

2. HUME'S LIFE AND CORRESPONDENCE

The following books provide ample data and scholarship regarding Hume's life, publishing history, and personal relationships. Except for Mossner, these works are primarily for advanced scholarship. Although Mossner's biography should be used with caution because of occasional historical inaccuracies, it contains a store of useful information about Hume's life not readily available elsewhere and is, on the whole, the best biography. Greig as well as Klibansky and Mossner are important (though incomplete) collections of Hume's many letters. Burton is outdated in some respects, but remains the only collection of letters to Hume. Numerous additional letters written by Hume have been published since these volumes, sprinkled in several journals and books. A comprehensive edition of the correspondence of Hume is currently under preparation for the Oxford University Press by David Raynor.

BURTON, JOHN HILL, *Letters of Eminent Persons Addressed to David Hume* (Edinburgh, 1849; repr. Bristol: Thoemmes Antiquarian Books, 1989).

GREIG, J. Y. T., *The Letters of David Hume*, 2 vols. (Oxford: Clarendon Press, 1932).

KLIBANSKY, RAYMOND, and MOSSNER, ERNEST C. (eds.), *New Letters of David Hume* (Oxford: Clarendon Press, 1954).

MOSSNER, ERNEST C., *The Life of David Hume*, 2nd edn. (Oxford: Clarendon Press, 1980).

3. SOURCES IN EARLY MODERN PHILOSOPHY
PRIOR TO 1751

The following books were available for Hume to read prior to the publication of
EPM in 1751. All played important roles in the moral philosophy of the period in
which Hume formed his ideas. It has been documented that Hume knew several of
these works. Books of importance in eighteenth-century moral philosophy after
EPM (such as Lord Kames's *Essays on the Principles of Morality and Natural Religion*
and Adam Smith's *Theory of the Moral Sentiments*) are not included; however, some
of these works are mentioned in the Editor's Introduction to the present volume.

BALGUY, JOHN, *The Foundation of Moral Goodness* (1727–8), 2 vols. in 1 (London:
    1728–9; fac. New York: Garland, 1976).

BAYLE, PIERRE, *The Dictionary Historical and Critical of Mʳ Peter Bayle* (1697), ed. and
    trans. Pierre Desmaizeaux, 2nd edn., 5 vols. (London, 1734–8; fac. New York:
    Garland, 1984).

BUTLER, JOSEPH, *Fifteen Sermons Preached at the Rolls Chapel* (1726), in vol. 2 of *The
    Works of Joseph Butler*, ed. W. E. Gladstone, 2 vols. (Oxford: Clarendon Press,
    1896).

CLARKE, SAMUEL, *A Discourse concerning the Unchangeable Obligations of Natural
    Religion, and the Truth and Certainty of the Christian Revelation* (1705), in vol. 2 of
    The Works of Samuel Clarke, D. D., 4 vols. (London, 1738; fac. New York:
    Garland, 1978).

CUDWORTH, RALPH, *A Treatise concerning Eternal and Immutable Morality* (London,
    1731; fac. New York: Garland, 1976).

GROTIUS, HUGO, *De jure belli ac pacis [On the Law of War and Peace]* (1625), in James
    Brown Scott (ed.), Classics of International Law, 2 vols. (Oxford: Clarendon
    Press, 1925), vol. 1, fac. Amsterdam, 1646; vol. 2, Eng. trans. Francis W. Kelsey
    et al.

HOBBES, THOMAS, *Leviathan* (1651), ed. Edwin Curley (Indianapolis: Hackett,
    1994).

HUTCHESON, FRANCIS, *An Essay on the Nature and Conduct of the Passions and
    Affections. With Illustrations on the Moral Sense* (London, 1728), in vol. 2 of
    Collected Works of Francis Hutcheson.

——*An Inquiry into the Original of our Ideas of Beauty and Virtue; In Two Treatises*
    (London, 1725), in vol. 1 of *Collected Works of Francis Hutcheson*.

——*A Short Introduction to Moral Philosophy* (London, 1747), in vol. 4 of *Collected
    Works of Francis Hutcheson*.

——*Collected Works of Francis Hutcheson*, 7 vols., fac. edn. by Bernhard Fabian
    (Hildesheim: Olms, 1969–71).

LOCKE, JOHN, *An Essay concerning Human Understanding* (1690), 4th edn., ed. Peter
    H. Nidditch (Oxford: Clarendon Press, 1975).

——*Two Treatises of Government* (1690), ed. Peter Laslett, student edn.
    (Cambridge: Cambridge University Press, 1988).

MALEBRANCHE, NICOLAS, *The Search after Truth* (1674–5), trans. Thomas M. Lennon and Paul J. Olscamp (Columbus: Ohio State University Press, 1980).

MANDEVILLE, BERNARD DE, *The Fable of the Bees; or, Private Vices, Publick Benefits* (1714), ed. F. B. Kaye, vol. 1 (Oxford: Clarendon Press, 1924; repr. Indianapolis: LibertyClassics, 1988).

MONTESQUIEU, CHARLES LOUIS DE SECONDAT, BARON DE, *The Persian Letters* (1721), 'Cashan edition, done into English' (London: Athenaeum, 1901).

——*The Spirit of Laws* (1748), ed. and trans. Anne Cohler, Basia Miller, and Harold Stone (Cambridge: Cambridge University Press, 1989).

PUFENDORF, SAMUEL, *De jure naturae et gentium* [*On the Law of Nature and Nations*] (1672), trans. C. H. Oldfather and W. A. Oldfather, 2 vols. (Oxford: Clarendon Press, 1934), vol. 1, fac. 1688; vol. 2, translation.

SHAFTESBURY, ANTHONY ASHLEY COOPER, THIRD EARL OF, *Characteristics of Men, Manners, Opinions, Times* (1711), ed. John M. Robertson, 2 vols. in 1 (London, 1900; repr. Indianapolis: Bobbs-Merrill, 1964).

SPINOZA, BARUCH DE, *Ethics* (1677, posthum.), in vol. 1 of *The Collected Works of Spinoza*, ed. and trans. Edwin Curley (Princeton: Princeton University Press, 1985).

WOLLASTON, WILLIAM, *The Religion of Nature Delineated* (1722) (London, 1724; fac. New York: Garland, 1978).

4. ANTHOLOGIES IN EARLY MODERN MORAL PHILOSOPHY

The following materials include selections from several of the authors listed above and many others as well. Selby-Bigge and Raphael contain extensive material from British sources; Schneewind is particularly valuable for continental European sources.

RAPHAEL, D. D. (ed.), *British Moralists 1650–1800*, 2 vols. (Oxford: Clarendon Press, 1969; repr. Indianapolis: Hackett, 1991).

SCHNEEWIND, JEROME B. (ed.), *Moral Philosophy from Montaigne to Kant*, 2 vols. (Cambridge: Cambridge University Press, 1990).

SELBY-BIGGE, L. A. (ed.), *British Moralists: Being Selections from Writers Principally of the Eighteenth Century*, 2 vols. (Oxford: Clarendon Press, 1897; repr. New York: Dover, 1965).

5. GENERAL STUDIES OF HUME

5.1. Introductory Surveys

The following clearly written works sometimes range beyond Hume's moral theory, but all contain sections that introduce Hume's moral philosophy. Both

Norton (an anthology) and Penelhum (which contains material from Hume's writings) are outstanding guides to Hume scholarship and to the Hume literature. Baier is the best available brief overview of Hume's ethics. MacNabb is exceptionally clear, but in some respects dated.

BAIER, ANNETTE, 'Hume, David', *Encyclopedia of Ethics*, ed. Lawrence Becker and Charlotte Becker (New York: Garland, 1992), vol. 1.

MACNABB, D. G. C., *David Hume: His Theory of Knowledge and Morality*, 2nd edn. (London: Hutchinson, 1951; repr. Hamden, Conn.: Archon Books, 1966).

NORTON, DAVID FATE (ed.), *The Cambridge Companion to Hume* (Cambridge: Cambridge University Press, 1993).

PENELHUM, TERENCE, *David Hume: An Introduction to his Philosophical System* (West Lafayette, Ind.: Purdue University Press, 1992).

5.2. Advanced Surveys and General Interpretations

These wide-ranging works consider both historical and philosophical problems. They are primarily for the advanced student. Smith's book has been more influential on Hume scholars than any work in the twentieth century; it is primarily historical and textual, and its interpretation of Hume and his history remain controversial. Students often find it easier to read Smith's article before his book. Stroud provides a philosophical work that follows more or less in the path of Smith's 'naturalistic' interpretation. Norton is critical of both Stroud and Smith and provides an erudite account of Hume's intellectual background. Penelhum's book covers the broadest territory and, like Stroud and Norton, is very clearly written. Mackie's book has been widely discussed for its interpretation and criticism, as Broad's had been in previous decades.

BRICKE, JOHN, *Mind and Morality: An Examination of Hume's Moral Psychology* (Oxford: Oxford University Press, 1996).

BROAD, C. D., *Five Types of Ethical Theory* (London: Routledge & Kegan Paul, 1930), ch. 4.

MACKIE, JOHN, *Hume's Moral Theory* (London: Routledge & Kegan Paul, 1980).

NORTON, DAVID FATE, *David Hume: Common Sense Moralist, Sceptical Metaphysician* (Princeton: Princeton University Press, 1982).

PENELHUM, TERENCE, *Hume* (New York: St Martin's Press, 1975).

SMITH, NORMAN KEMP, 'The Naturalism of Hume', *Mind*, 14 (1905), 149–73, 335–47.

——*The Philosophy of David Hume* (London: Macmillan, 1941; fac. New York: St Martin's Press, 1966).

STROUD, BARRY, *Hume* (London: Routledge & Kegan Paul, 1977).

5.3. Anthologies and Collected Essays

Several anthologies and collected essays on Hume have been published, none dealing exclusively with his moral philosophy. The collections below are all recommended, though some are thin on Hume's moral philosophy. The journal *Hume Studies* is a particularly vital source of Hume scholarship. It is the only journal exclusively devoted to Hume and is an official journal of the Hume Society, which meets at conventions several times each year.

CHAPPELL, V. C. (ed.), *Hume: A Collection of Critical Essays* (New York: Doubleday, 1966; repr. Notre Dame, Ind.: University of Notre Dame Press, 1966).

Hume Studies, pub. Apr. and Nov. Available through and published by the Hume Society, University of Utah. Available in printed and electronic forms. Pub. in revised format as of vol. 19, no. 1 (Nov. 1993).

LIVINGSTON, DONALD, and KING, JAMES (eds.), *Hume: A Re-evaluation* (New York: Fordham University Press, 1976).

NORTON, DAVID FATE, *et al.* (eds.), *McGill Hume Studies* (San Diego: Austin Hill Press, 1979).

STEWART, M. A., and WRIGHT, JOHN (eds.), *Hume and Hume's Connexions* (Edinburgh: Edinburgh University Press; University Park: Pennsylvania State University Press, 1995).

6. STUDIES OF HUME BY TOPIC

6.1. *Passions, Sentiments, and Moral Psychology*

The works below rely more heavily on Hume's *Treatise* than on his subsequent work, but they are the best materials on these subjects. Árdal's book was influential in the 1970s and 1980s; and Baier's book may be headed for a similar reception a quarter-century later. Hearn and Immerwahr present stimulating interpretations that are very different from those of Árdal and Mercer, below.

ÁRDAL, PÁLL S., *Passion and Value in Hume's* Treatise (Edinburgh: Edinburgh University Press, 1966).

BAIER, ANNETTE, *A Progress of Sentiments* (Cambridge, Mass.: Harvard University Press, 1991).

HEARN, THOMAS K., 'General Rules and the Moral Sentiments in Hume's *Treatise*', *Review of Metaphysics*, 30 (1976), 57–72.

IMMERWAHR, JOHN, 'Hume on Tranquillizing the Passions', *Hume Studies*, 18 (1992), 293–314.

6.2. *Reason and its Limitations*

The works below treat several different questions about Hume's account of reason and the reasonable, often contrasting the roles of reason with those of sentiment or taste. Falk's interpretation is a speculative and creative interpretation, but not closely grounded in the text. Harrison treats the meaning of reason, practical reason, rationality, and rational demonstration. Kydd's book is considered by some scholars to be a pioneering work in twentieth-century scholarship on Hume, but it is now infrequently cited. Nuyen maintains that Hume's concern with reason is to defeat rationalist views. Winters cautions against the dangers of a univocal interpretation of the term 'reason' in Hume. Many articles cited above and below also deal with themes of reason and reasonableness.

FALK, W. D., 'Hume on Practical Reason', *Philosophical Studies*, 27 (1975), 1–18.
HARRISON, JONATHAN, *Hume's Moral Epistemology* (Oxford: Clarendon Press, 1976).
KYDD, R. M., *Reason and Conduct in Hume's* Treatise (London: Oxford University Press, 1946).
NUYEN, A. T., 'David Hume on Reason, Passions and Morals', *Hume Studies*, 10 (1984), 26–45.
WINTERS, BARBARA, 'Hume on Reason', *Hume Studies*, 5 (1979), 20–35.

6.3. Benevolence, Humanity, and Sympathy

These themes have received less attention in the scholarly literature than might be expected. The following approaches and conclusions are primarily centred on the *Treatise*. See also Shaver, 'Hume and the Duties of Humanity' (section 6.9 below).

JENKINS, JOHN J., 'Hume's Account of Sympathy—Some Difficulties', in V. Hope (ed.), *Philosophers of the Scottish Enlightenment* (Edinburgh: Edinburgh University Press, 1984), 91–104.
McCRACKEN, D. J., 'David Hume and the Sentiment of Humanity', *Actes du XIᵉ Congress International de Philosophie*, 8 (1953), 100–3.
MERCER, PHILIP, *Sympathy and Ethics: A Study of the Relationship between Sympathy and Morality, with Special Reference to Hume's* Treatise (Oxford: Clarendon Press, 1972).
VANTERPOOL, RUDOLPH V., 'Hume on the "Duty" of Benevolence', *Hume Studies*, 14 (Apr. 1988), 93–110.

6.4. Justice, Convention, and Natural Law Theory

Justice has been one of the most thoroughly treated topics in the Hume literature. The following are recommended for their treatments of specific subjects: Buckle and Harrison provide exceptionally thorough and comprehensive coverage of the topics mentioned in their titles. Haakonssen's work is more a treatment of Smith than Hume, but is illuminating on both. Westerman challenges Haakonssen and Buckle on natural law theory. Gauthier interprets Hume as a contractarian without a formal contract and as a non-utilitarian. Some important books and articles on themes of justice in Hume cited elsewhere in this bibliography are Árdal, *Passion and Value in Hume's* Treatise (section 6.1 above), Macleod, 'Rule-Utilitarianism and Hume's Theory of Justice' (section 6.5 below), and

Norton, *David Hume* (section 5.2 above). On the topic of conventionalism, in addition to Gauthier (and others), see Snare, *Morals, Motivation, and Convention* (section 6.8 below). On natural law, see also Forbes, *Hume's Philosophical Politics* (section 6.10 below).

BUCKLE, STEPHEN, *Natural Law and the Theory of Property: Grotius to Hume* (Oxford: Clarendon Press, 1991).

GAUTHIER, DAVID, 'David Hume, Contractarian', *Philosophical Review*, 88 (1979), 3–38.

HAAKONSSEN, KNUD, *The Science of the Legislator: The Natural Jurisprudence of David Hume and Adam Smith* (Cambridge: Cambridge University Press, 1981).

HARRISON, JONATHAN, *Hume's Theory of Justice* (Oxford: Clarendon Press, 1981).

WESTERMAN, PAULINE C., 'Hume and the Natural Lawyers: A Change of Landscape', in Stewart and Wright (eds.), *Hume and Hume's Connexions* (section 5.3 above), 83–104.

6.5. *Utility and Utilitarianism*

These articles raise historical and philosophical questions about the utilitarian and non-utilitarian character of Hume's moral philosophy. However, they do not adequately treat broader questions about the role of utility in Hume's theory. See the topics of *Benevolence* and *Justice*, sections 6.3 and 6.4 above, especially Gauthier, 'David Hume, Contractarian', which contains an important anti-utilitarian interpretation of Hume.

DARWALL, STEPHEN, 'Hume and the Invention of Utilitarianism', in Stewart and Wright (eds.), *Hume and Hume's Connexions* (section 5.3 above), 58–82.

GLOSSOP, RONALD J., 'Is Hume a "Classical Utilitarian"?', *Hume Studies*, 2 (1976), 1–16.

MACLEOD, ALISTAIR, 'Rule-Utilitarianism and Hume's Theory of Justice', *Hume Studies*, 7 (1981), 74–84.

MARTIN, MARIE A., 'Utility and Morality: Adam Smith's Critique of Hume', *Hume Studies*, 16 (1990), 107–20.

6.6. *Virtues, Moral Sense, and Moral Objectivity*

A. MacIntyre contains an influential critique of Hume on these subjects. J. McIntyre deals with largely non-ethical considerations of the analysis of character needed for the account of the virtues. Raphael deals extensively with Hume's intellectual context, as does Hope, who compares the moral philosophies of Hutcheson, Hume, and Smith. Norton and Pitson discuss whether Hume is a realist or a projectionist; both deny that he is a projectionist. Baxter and Blackburn probe the comparison often made between moral qualities and secondary qualities. Martin focuses on the classical foundations of Hume's thought, especially his account of the virtues. Mackie, *Hume's Moral Theory* (section 5.2), Norton, *David Hume* (section 5.2), Árdal, *Passion and Value in Hume's* Treatise (section 6.1), Harrison, *Hume's Theory of Justice* (section 6.4), and Baier, *A Progress of Sentiments* (section 6.1), are all important studies of Hume on some aspects of the topics in this section.

BAXTER, DONALD L. M., 'Hume on Virtue, Beauty, Composites, and Secondary Qualities', *Pacific Philosophical Quarterly*, 71 (1990), 103–18.

BLACKBURN, SIMON, 'Hume on the Mezzanine Level', *Hume Studies*, 19 (1993), 273–88.

HOPE, VINCENT M., *Virtue by Consensus* (Oxford: Clarendon Press, 1989).

MACINTYRE, ALASDAIR, *Whose Justice? Which Rationality?* (Notre Dame, Ind.: University of Notre Dame Press, 1988).

MCINTYRE, JANE L., 'Character: A Humean Account', *History of Philosophy Quarterly*, 7 (1990), 193–206.

MARTIN, MARIE A., 'Hume on Human Excellence', *Hume Studies*, 18 (1992), 383–99.

NORTON, DAVID FATE, 'Hume's Moral Ontology', *Hume Studies*, 10th Anniversary edn. (1985), 189–214.

PITSON, A. E., 'Projectionism, Realism, and Hume's Moral Sense Theory', *Hume Studies*, 15 (1989), 61–92.

RAPHAEL, D. D., *The Moral Sense* (London: Oxford University Press, 1947).

6.7. The Sensible Knave Problem

The following are all useful treatments of this topic. Gauthier treats the sensible knave problem in the context of self-interested motives for accepting the rules of justice. He is criticized by Baier in the same journal issue for an undue narrowness of interpretation. Postema concentrates on the subtle replies open to the knave and assesses the adequacy of Hume's answer to the challenge. Costa reaches beyond the sensible knave problem to Hume's reasons for treating the problem and to the problem of why we should be just. See also Darwall, 'Motive and Obligation in Hume's Ethics' (section 6.9 below).

BAIER, ANNETTE, 'Artificial Virtues and the Equally Sensible Non-Knaves: A Response to Gauthier', *Hume Studies*, 18 (1992), 429–39.

COSTA, MICHAEL J., 'Why Be Just? Hume's Response in the Inquiry', *Southern Journal of Philosophy*, 22 (1984), 469–80.

GAUTHIER, DAVID, 'Artificial Virtues and the Sensible Knave', *Hume Studies*, 18 (1992), 401–27.

—— 'Three against Justice: The Foole, the Sensible Knave, and the Lydian Shepherd', *Midwest Studies in Philosophy VII* (Minneapolis: University of Minnesota Press, 1982), 11–29.

POSTEMA, GERALD, 'Hume's Reply to the Sensible Knave', *History of Philosophy Quarterly*, 5 (1988), 23–40.

Supplementary Reading

6.8. Moral Motivation and the Causes of Action

Bricke's work is set in the context of an analysis of Hume's moral psychology. The discussions in Snare, Coleman, and Shaw are rooted in distinctly twentieth-century discussions of motivation, explanation, and justification. Snare's book is rich, but complex and difficult. See also Harrison, *Hume's Moral Epistemology* (section 6.2 above), and Darwall, 'Motive and Obligation in Hume's Ethics' (section 6.9 below).

BRICKE, JOHN, 'Hume, Motivation and Morality', *Hume Studies*, 14 (Apr. 1988), 1–24.

COLEMAN, DOROTHY, 'Hume's Internalism', *Hume Studies*, 18 (1992), 331–47.

SHAW, DANIEL, 'Hume's Theory of Motivation', pts. 1 and 2, *Hume Studies*, 15 (1989), 163–83 and 18 (1992), 19–39.

SNARE, FRANCIS, *Morals, Motivation, and Convention: Hume's Influential Doctrines* (Cambridge: Cambridge University Press, 1991).

6.9. Obligation

The nature of obligation (or duty) is a relatively underexplored theme in Hume's writings. The essay by Darwall is especially recommended for its depth and range. He treats the subject of the power of morality to obligate in Hume and his predecessors, especially the obligation to be just. Cohen argues that Hume presents a normative ethics and subscribes to the thesis that moral judgements are universalizable, so that everyone in relevantly similar circumstances is similarly obligated. Shaver attempts to piece together Hume's account of obligation and apply it to the natural virtue of humanity. Haakonssen presents the conditions of obligation in Hume and the connection between obligation and usefulness. Pitson and Vitek debate the nature of the obligation involved in promising.

COHEN, MENDEL F., 'Obligation and Human Nature in Hume's Philosophy', *Philosophical Quarterly*, 40 (1990), 316–41.

DARWALL, STEPHEN, 'Motive and Obligation in Hume's Ethics', *Nous*, 27 (1993), 415–48.

HAAKONSSEN, KNUD, 'Hume's Obligations', *Hume Studies*, 4 (1978), 7–17.

PITSON, A. E., 'Hume on Promises and their Obligation', *Hume Studies*, 14 (1988), 176–90.

SHAVER, ROBERT, 'Hume and the Duties of Humanity', *Journal of the History of Philosophy*, 30 (1992), 545–56.

VITEK, WILLIAM, 'The Humean Promise: Whence Comes its Obligation?', *Hume Studies*, 12 (1986), 160–76.

6.10. The Intersection of Moral, Political, and Legal Philosophy

The following are well written books on this subject, which has recently increased in importance in Hume scholarship. This topic is often combined with justice (section 6.4 above), and publications sometimes bring Hume's essays and *History of England* into the interpretation of his moral thought. Forbes's historical and natural law interpretation of Hume is both influential and controversial. Miller presents Hume's account of judgement and how Hume combined it with the establishment ideology and aristocratic values. Stewart provides a controversial interpretation of Hume as a liberal moral and political philosopher and proponent of moral reform. Whelan's analysis is a treatment of Hume's principal moral and political problems that is influenced by political theory. See also Harrison, *Hume's Theory of Justice* (section 6.4 above).

FORBES, DUNCAN, *Hume's Philosophical Politics* (Cambridge: Cambridge University Press, 1975).

MILLER, DAVID, *Philosophy and Ideology in Hume's Political Thought* (Oxford: Clarendon Press, 1981).

STEWART, JOHN B., *The Moral and Political Philosophy of David Hume* (New York: Columbia University Press, 1963).

——*Opinion and Reform in Hume's Political Philosophy* (Princeton: Princeton University Press, 1992).

WHELAN, FREDERICK G., *Order and Artifice in Hume's Political Philosophy* (Princeton: Princeton University Press, 1985).

7. GENERAL BIBLIOGRAPHICAL MATERIALS

The work of Jessop, Hall, and the follow-up articles in *Hume Studies* (by Hall and Morris) are indispensable bibliographical materials for serious research in the Hume literature. The *Philosopher's Index* is pivotal for research in the current literature and for electronic searching on the literature post-1985.

HALL, ROLAND, *50 Years of Hume Scholarship* (Edinburgh: Edinburgh University Press, 1978).

——and [later] MORRIS, WILLIAM E., 'The Hume Literature [for *Years*]', *Hume Studies*, vol. 4 and many later volumes. Updated frequently (after vol. 4); pub. as a supplement to *50 Years of Hume Scholarship*.

JESSOP, T. E., *A Bibliography of David Hume and of Scottish Philosophy, from Francis Hutcheson to Lord Balfour* (London: Brown, 1938; repr. New York: Garland, 1983).

LINEBACK, RICHARD H. (ed.), *Philosopher's Index* (Bowling Green: Philosophy Documentation Center, Bowling Green State University, Ohio). Issued quarterly in printed edition. Also available in CD-ROM and On-Line versions. Includes bibliographic citations and abstracts from approximately 270 journals.

8. ADVANCED AND SPECIALIZED BIBLIOGRAPHICAL MATERIALS

The extensive literature surveys by Capaldi *et al.* and Yalden-Thomson are useful for all levels of research on major topics. Details of the earliest editions of Hume's works are presented in Todd, and a large collection of Hume's surviving correspondence, manuscripts, and other materials once held by the Royal Society of Edinburgh—now at the National Library of Scotland—are presented in Greig and Beynon as well as Cunningham. These materials are specialized and of value only for scholars and advanced students. The Chuo University publications contain a bibliography of both Hume's lifetime editions and eighteenth-century British publications by other authors. The Nortons present a study and reference list of the remnants of Hume's Library, as it was merged with the library of Hume's nephew David Hume the Younger; it is invaluable for research on the editions Hume may have used and titles he may have read.

CAPALDI, NICHOLAS, KING, JAMES, and LIVINGSTON, DONALD, 'The Hume Literature of the 1970s', *Philosophical Topics*, 12 (1981), 167–92.

——'The Hume Literature of the 1980s', *American Philosophical Quarterly*, 28 (1991), 255–72.

CHUO UNIVERSITY, *David Hume and the Eighteenth Century British Thought: An Annotated Catalogue*, ed. Sadao Ikeda, 2 vols. (Tokyo: Chuo University Library, 1986, 1988).

CUNNINGHAM, IAN C., 'The Arrangement of the Royal Society of Edinburgh's David Hume Collection', *The Bibliotheck*, 15 (1988), 8–22.

GREIG, J. Y. T., and BEYNON, HAROLD, *Calendar of Hume MSS. in the Possession of the Royal Society of Edinburgh* (Edinburgh: Royal Society of Edinburgh, 1932; repr. New York: Garland, 1990).

NORTON, DAVID FATE, and NORTON, MARY J., *The David Hume Library* (Edinburgh: Edinburgh Bibliographical Society, 1996).

TODD, W. B., 'David Hume: A Preliminary Bibliography', in W. B. Todd (ed.), *Hume and the Enlightenment: Essays Presented to Ernest Campbell Mossner* (Edinburgh: Edinburgh University Press, 1974).

YALDEN-THOMSON, D. C., 'Recent Work on Hume', *American Philosophical Quarterly*, 20 (1983), 1–22.

PART 2
The Text

AN ENQUIRY CONCERNING THE
PRINCIPLES OF MORALS

SECTION 1

OF THE GENERAL PRINCIPLES
OF MORALS

1   DISPUTES with men, pertinaciously obstinate in their principles, are, of all others, the most irksome; except, perhaps, those with persons, entirely disingenuous, who really do not believe the opinions they defend, but engage in the controversy, from affectation, from a spirit of opposition, or from a desire of showing wit[†] and ingenuity, superior to the rest of mankind. The same blind adherence to their own arguments is to be expected in both; the same contempt of their antagonists; and the same passionate vehemence, in enforcing sophistry and falsehood. And as reasoning is not the source, whence either disputant derives his tenets; it is in vain to expect, that any logic, which speaks not to the affections, will ever engage him to embrace sounder principles.

2   Those who have denied the reality of moral distinctions,[†] may be ranked among the disingenuous disputants; nor is it conceivable, that any human creature could ever seriously believe, that all characters and actions were alike entitled to the affection and regard of every one. The difference, which nature has placed between one man and another, is so wide, and this difference is still so much farther widened, by education, example, and habit, that, where the opposite extremes come at once under our apprehension, there is no scepticism so scrupulous, and scarce any assurance so determined, as absolutely to deny all distinction between them. Let a man's insensibility be ever so great, he must often be touched with the images of RIGHT and WRONG; and let his prejudices be ever so obstinate, he must observe, that others are susceptible of like impressions. The only way, therefore, of converting an antagonist[†] of this kind, is to leave him to himself. For, finding that no body keeps up the controversy with him, it is probable he will, at last, of himself, from mere weariness, come over to the side of common sense and reason.

3   There has been a controversy started of late, much better worth examination, concerning the general foundation of MORALS;[†] whether they be

see p.93 *Enquiry concerning the Principles of Morals*

derived from REASON, or from SENTIMENT; whether we attain the knowledge of them by a chain of argument and induction, or by an immediate feeling and finer internal sense;[†] whether, like all sound judgment of truth and falsehood, they should be the same to every rational intelligent being; or whether, like the perception of beauty and deformity, they be founded entirely on the particular fabric and constitution of the human species.

4   The ancient philosophers, though they often affirm, that virtue is nothing but conformity to reason, yet, in general, seem to consider morals as deriving their existence from taste[†] and sentiment. On the other hand, our modern enquirers,[†] though they also talk much of the beauty of virtue, and deformity of vice, yet have commonly endeavoured to account for these distinctions by metaphysical reasonings, and by deductions from the most abstract principles of the understanding. Such confusion reigned in these subjects, that an opposition[†] of the greatest consequence could   SBN 171 prevail between one system and another, and even in the parts of almost each individual system; and yet no body, till very lately, was ever sensible of it. The elegant Lord SHAFTESBURY,[†] who first gave occasion to remark this distinction, and who, in general, adhered to the principles of the ancients, is not, himself, entirely free from the same confusion.

5   It must be acknowledged, that both sides of the question are susceptible of specious arguments.[†] Moral distinctions, it may be said, are discernible by pure *reason*: Else, whence the many disputes that reign in common life, as well as in philosophy, with regard to this subject: The long chain of proofs often produced on both sides; the examples cited, the authorities appealed to, the analogies employed, the fallacies detected, the inferences drawn, and the several conclusions adjusted to their proper principles. Truth is disputable; not taste:[†] What exists in the nature of things is the standard of our judgment; what each man feels within himself is the standard of sentiment. Propositions in geometry may be proved, systems in physics[†] may be controverted; but the harmony of verse, the tenderness of passion, the brilliancy of wit, must give immediate pleasure. No man reasons concerning another's beauty; but frequently concerning the justice or injustice of his actions. In every criminal trial the first object of the prisoner is to disprove the facts alleged, and deny the actions imputed to him: The second to prove, that, even if these actions were real, they might be justified, as innocent and lawful. It is confessedly by deductions of the understanding, that the first point is ascertained: How can we suppose that a different faculty of the mind is employed in fixing the other?[†]

1. Of the General Principles of Morals

6   On the other hand, those who would resolve all moral determinations into *sentiment*, may endeavour to show, that it is impossible for reason[†] ever to draw conclusions of this nature. To virtue, say they, it belongs to be *amiable*, and vice *odious*. This forms their very nature or essence. But can   SBN 172
reason or argumentation distribute these different epithets to any subjects, and pronounce before-hand, that this must produce love, and that hatred? Or what other reason can we ever assign for these affections, but the original fabric and formation of the human mind, which is naturally adapted to receive them?

7   The end of all moral speculations is to teach us our duty; and, by proper representations of the deformity of vice and beauty of virtue, beget correspondent habits,[†] and engage us to avoid the one, and embrace the other.   Vr - habit
But is this ever to be expected from inferences and conclusions of the   R cannot
understanding, which of themselves have no hold of the affections, nor set   produce
in motion the active powers of men? They discover truths: But where the   H
truths which they discover are indifferent, and beget no desire or aversion, they can have no influence on conduct and behaviour. What is honourable, what is fair, what is becoming, what is noble, what is generous, takes possession of the heart, and animates us to embrace and maintain it. What is intelligible, what is evident, what is probable, what is true, procures only the cool assent of the understanding; and gratifying a speculative curiosity, puts an end to our researches.

8   Extinguish all the warm feelings and prepossessions in favour of virtue, and all disgust or aversion to vice: Render men totally indifferent towards these distinctions; and morality is no longer a practical study,[†] nor has any tendency to regulate our lives and actions.

9   These arguments on each side (and many more might be produced) are   AM :
so plausible, that I am apt to suspect, they may, the one as well as the other,   R + S
be solid and satisfactory, and that *reason* and *sentiment* concur[†] in almost all moral determinations and conclusions. The final sentence,[†] it is probable, which pronounces characters and actions amiable or odious, praiseworthy or blameable; that which stamps on them the mark of honour or   SBN 173
infamy, approbation or censure; that which renders morality an active   we affective
principle, and constitutes virtue our happiness, and vice our misery: It is   attitudes to
probable, I say, that this final sentence depends on some internal sense or   Vc / Vr
feeling, which nature has made universal in the whole species. For what   Vr.
else can have an influence of this nature? But in order to pave the way for   moral
such a sentiment, and give a proper discernment of its object, it is often   sense
necessary, we find, that much reasoning should precede, that nice distinctions be made, just conclusions drawn, distant comparisons formed,

but King nec (as in taste)

method: examine personal merit 152
(estimable/
blameable Qines)

complicated relations examined, and general facts fixed and ascertained. Some species of beauty, especially the natural kinds, on their first appearance, command our affection and approbation; and where they fail of this effect, it is impossible for any reasoning to redress their influence, or adapt them better to our taste and sentiment. But in many orders of beauty, particularly those of the finer arts, it is requisite to employ much reasoning, in order to feel the proper sentiment; and a false relish† may frequently be corrected by argument and reflection. There are just grounds to conclude, that moral beauty partakes much of this latter species, and demands the assistance of our intellectual faculties, in order to give it a suitable influence on the human mind.

10   But though this question, concerning the general principles of morals, be curious and important, it is needless for us, at present, to employ farther care in our researches concerning it. For if we can be so happy, in the course of this enquiry, as to discover the true origin of morals, it will then easily appear how far either sentiment or reason enters into all determinations of this nature.[1] In order to attain this purpose, we shall endeavour to follow a very simple method: We shall analyze that complication of mental qualities,† which form what, in common life, we call PERSONAL MERIT: We shall consider every attribute of the mind, which renders a man   SBN 174 an object either of esteem and affection, or of hatred and contempt; every habit or sentiment or faculty, which, if ascribed to any person, implies either praise or blame,† and may enter into any panegyric or satire† of his character and manners. The quick sensibility, which, on this head, is so universal† among mankind, gives a philosopher sufficient assurance, that he can never be considerably mistaken in framing the catalogue,† or incur any danger of misplacing the objects of his contemplation: He needs only enter into his own breast for a moment, and consider whether or not he should desire to have this or that quality ascribed to him, and whether such or such an imputation would proceed from a friend or an enemy. The very nature of language guides us almost infallibly in forming a judgment of this nature; and as every tongue possesses one set of words which are taken in a good sense, and another in the opposite,† the least acquaintance with the idiom suffices,† without any reasoning, to direct us in collecting and arranging the estimable or blameable qualities of men. The only object of reasoning is to discover the circumstances on both sides, which are common to these qualities; to observe that particular in which the estimable qualities agree on the one hand, and the blameable on the other;

---

[1] See Appendix 1.

76

and thence to reach the foundation of ethics, and find those universal prin-   *empiricism*
ciples,[†] from which all censure or approbation is ultimately derived. As this
is a question of fact, not of abstract science,[†] we can only expect success,
by following the experimental method,[†] and deducing general maxims
from a comparison of particular instances. The other scientifical method,[†]
where a general abstract principle is first established, and is afterwards
branched out into a variety of inferences and conclusions, may be more
perfect in itself, but suits less the imperfection of human nature, and is a
common source of illusion and mistake in this as well as in other subjects.
Men are now cured of their passion for hypotheses and systems in natural   SBN 175
philosophy, and will hearken to no arguments but those which are derived
from experience. It is full time they should attempt a like reformation in all
moral disquisitions; and reject every system of ethics, however subtile or
ingenious, which is not founded on fact and observation.

11   We shall begin our enquiry on this head by the consideration of the
social virtues,[†] benevolence and justice. The explication of them will probably give us an opening by which the others may be accounted for.

benevolence most {estimable?} Qy
{amiable}

SECTION 2

OF BENEVOLENCE

PART 1

1   IT may be esteemed, perhaps, a superfluous task to prove, that the benevolent or softer affections† are ESTIMABLE; and wherever they appear, engage the approbation, and good-will of mankind. The epithets *sociable, good-natured, humane, merciful, grateful, friendly, generous, beneficent*, or their equivalents, are known in all languages, and universally express the highest merit, which *human nature* is capable of attaining. Where these amiable qualities are attended with birth and power and eminent abilities, and display themselves in the good government or useful instruction of mankind, they seem even to raise the possessors of them above the rank of *human nature*, and make them approach in some measure to the divine. Exalted capacity, undaunted courage, prosperous success;† these may only expose a hero or politician to the envy and ill-will of the public: But as soon as the praises are added of humane and beneficent; when instances are displayed of lenity, tenderness, or friendship; envy itself is silent, or joins the general voice of approbation and applause.

2   When PERICLES,† the great ATHENIAN statesman and general, was on his death-bed, his surrounding friends, deeming him now insensible, began to indulge their sorrow for their expiring patron, by enumerating his great qualities and successes, his conquests and victories, the unusual length of his administration, and his nine trophies† erected over the enemies of the republic. "You forget," cries the dying hero, who had heard all, "you forget the most eminent of my praises, while you dwell so much on those vulgar advantages, in which fortune had a principal share. You have not observed, that no citizen has ever yet worne mourning on my account."[2]

3   In men of more ordinary talents and capacity, the social virtues become, if possible, still more essentially requisite; there being nothing

---

[2] PLUTARCH. in PERICLE. [Plutarch, *Lives*, 'Pericles', ch. 38, §4, 173 C.]

eminent, in that case, to compensate for the want of them, or preserve the person from our severest hatred, as well as contempt. A high ambition, an elevated courage, is apt, says Cicero,[†] in less perfect characters, to degenerate into a turbulent ferocity. The more social and softer virtues are there chiefly to be regarded. These are always good and amiable.[3]

4   The principal advantage, which Juvenal[†] discovers in the extensive capacity of the human species is, that it renders our benevolence also more extensive, and gives us larger opportunities of spreading our kindly influence than what are indulged to the inferior creation.[4] It must, indeed, be confessed, that by doing good only, can a man truly enjoy the advantages of being eminent. His exalted station, of itself, but the more exposes him to danger and tempest. His sole prerogative[†] is to afford shelter to inferiors, who repose themselves under his cover and protection.

5   But I forget, that it is not my present business to recommend generosity and benevolence, or to paint, in their true colours, all the genuine charms of the social virtues. These, indeed, sufficiently engage every heart, on the first apprehension of them; and it is difficult to abstain from some sally of panegyric,[†] as often as they occur in discourse or reasoning. But our object here being more the speculative,[†] than the practical part of morals, it will   SBN 178 suffice to remark, (what will readily, I believe, be allowed) that no qualities are more entitled to the general good-will and approbation of mankind, than beneficence and humanity,[†] friendship and gratitude, natural affection and public spirit, or whatever proceeds from a tender sympathy with others, and a generous concern for our kind and species. These, wherever they appear, seem to transfuse[†] themselves, in a manner, into each beholder, and to call forth, in their own behalf, the same favourable and affectionate sentiments, which they exert on all around.

PART 2

6 We may observe, that, in displaying the praises of any humane, beneficent man, there is one circumstance which never fails to be amply insisted on, namely, the happiness and satisfaction, derived to society from his intercourse and good offices.[†] To his parents, we are apt to say, he endears himself by his pious attachment and duteous care, still more than by the

---

[3] Cic. de officiis, lib. 1. [Cicero, *De officiis*, bk. 1, ch. 19, §§ 62–3, ch. 44, § 157.]
[4] Sat. 15. 139. & seq. [Juvenal, *Satires* 15, lines 139–47.]

connexions of nature. His children never feel his authority, but when employed for their advantage. With him, the ties of love are consolidated by beneficence and friendship. The ties of friendship approach, in a fond observance of each obliging office, to those of love and inclination. His domestics and dependents have in him a sure resource; and no longer dread the power of fortune, but so far as she exercises it over him. From him the hungry receive food, the naked cloathing, the ignorant and slothful skill and industry. Like the sun, an inferior minister[†] of providence, he cheers, invigorates, and sustains the surrounding world.

7   If confined to private life, the sphere of his activity is narrower; but his influence is all benign and gentle. If exalted into a higher station,[†] mankind and posterity reap the fruit of his labours.

8   As these topics of praise[†] never fail to be employed, and with success,   SBN 1 where we would inspire esteem for any one; may it not thence be concluded, that the UTILITY, resulting from the social virtues, forms, at least, a *part* of their merit,[†] and is one source of that approbation and regard so universally paid to them?

9   When we recommend even an animal or a plant as *useful* and *beneficial*, we give it an applause and recommendation suited to its nature. As, on the other hand, reflection on the baneful influence of any of these inferior beings always inspires us with the sentiment of aversion. The eye is pleased with the prospect of corn-fields and loaded vineyards; horses grazing, and flocks pasturing: But flies the view of briars and brambles, affording shelter to wolves and serpents.

10   A machine, a piece of furniture, a vestment, a house well contrived for use and conveniency, is so far beautiful, and is contemplated with pleasure and approbation. An experienced eye is here sensible to many excellencies, which escape persons ignorant and uninstructed.

11   Can any thing stronger be said in praise of a profession, such as merchandize or manufacture, than to observe the advantages which it procures to society? And is not a monk and inquisitor[†] enraged when we treat his order as useless or pernicious to mankind?

12   The historian exults in displaying the benefit arising from his labours. The writer of romance alleviates or denies the bad consequences ascribed to his manner of composition.

13   In general, what praise is implied in the simple epithet *useful*! What reproach in the contrary!

14   Your gods, says CICERO,[5†] in opposition to the EPICUREANS, cannot justly

---

[5] De nat. Deor. lib. 1. [Cicero, *De natura deorum*, bk. 1, ch. 36, §§ 100–1.]

claim any worship or adoration, with whatever imaginary perfections you may suppose them endowed. They are totally useless and unactive. Even the EGYPTIANS, whom you so much ridicule, never consecrated any animal but on account of its utility. SBN 180

15   The sceptics assert,[6†] though absurdly, that the origin of all religious worship was derived from the utility of inanimate objects, as the sun and moon, to the support and well-being of mankind. This is also the common reason assigned by historians, for the deification[†] of eminent heroes and legislators.[7]

16   To plant a tree, to cultivate a field, to beget children; meritorious acts, according to the religion of ZOROASTER.[†]

17   In all determinations of morality, this circumstance of public utility is ever principally in view; and wherever disputes arise, either in philosophy or common life, concerning the bounds of duty, the question cannot, by any means, be decided with greater certainty, than by ascertaining, on any side, the true interests of mankind. If any false opinion, embraced from appearances, has been found to prevail; as soon as farther experience and sounder reasoning have given us juster notions of human affairs; we retract our first sentiment, and adjust anew the boundaries of moral good and evil.

18   Giving alms to common beggars is naturally praised; because it seems to carry relief to the distressed and indigent: But when we observe the encouragement thence arising to idleness and debauchery, we regard that species of charity rather as a weakness than a virtue.

19   *Tyrannicide,*[†] or the assassination of usurpers and oppressive princes, was highly extolled in ancient times; because it both freed mankind from many of these monsters, and seemed to keep the others in awe, whom the sword or poinard could not reach. But history and experience having since convinced us, that this practice encreases the jealousy and cruelty of princes, a TIMOLEON and a BRUTUS, though treated with indulgence on account of the prejudices of their times, are now considered as very improper models for imitation. SBN 181

20   Liberality in princes[†] is regarded as a mark of beneficence: But when it occurs, that the homely bread of the honest and industrious is often thereby converted into delicious cates for the idle and the prodigal, we soon retract our heedless praises. The regrets of a prince, for having lost a day, were noble and generous: But had he intended to have spent it in acts

---

⁶ SEXT. EMP. adversus mathem. lib. 9. [Sextus Empiricus, *Against the Physicists*, bk. 1, §18 (*Adversus mathematicos*, bk. 9, §18).]

⁷ DIOD. SIC. passim. [Diodorus Siculus, *Historical Library*, bk. 4, ch. 1, §§4–7, ch. 2, §§1 ff.]

of generosity to his greedy courtiers, it was better lost than misemployed
after that manner.

21   Luxury,[†] or a refinement on the pleasures and conveniencies of life, had
long been supposed the source of every corruption in government, and
the immediate cause of faction, sedition, civil wars, and the total loss of
liberty. It was, therefore, universally regarded as a vice, and was an object
of declamation to all satirists, and severe moralists. Those, who prove, or
attempt to prove, that such refinements rather tend to the encrease of
industry, civility, and arts, regulate anew[†] our *moral* as well as *political* sentiments, and represent, as laudable and innocent, what had formerly been
regarded as pernicious or blameable.

22   Upon the whole, then, it seems undeniable, *that* nothing can bestow
more merit on any human creature than the sentiment of benevolence in
an eminent degree; and *that* a *part*, at least, of its merit arises from its tendency to promote the interests of our species, and bestow happiness on
human society. We carry our view into the salutary consequences of such
a character and disposition; and whatever has so benign an influence, and
forwards so desirable an end,[†] is beheld with complacency and pleasure.
The social virtues are never regarded without their beneficial tendencies,
nor viewed as barren and unfruitful. The happiness of mankind, the order
of society, the harmony of families, the mutual support of friends, are   SBN 18
always considered as the result of their gentle dominion over the breasts[†]
of men.

23   How considerable a *part* of their merit we ought to ascribe to their
utility, will better appear from future disquisitions;[8†] as well as the reason,
why this circumstance has such a command over our esteem and
approbation.[9]

---

[8] Section 3d and 4th.   [9] Section 5th.

SECTION 3

OF JUSTICE

PART 1

1   THAT justice is useful to society, and consequently that *part* of its merit, at least, must arise from that consideration, it would be a superfluous undertaking to prove. That public utility is the *sole* origin of justice,† and that reflections on the beneficial consequences of this virtue are the *sole* foundation of its merit; this proposition, being more curious and important, will better deserve our examination and enquiry.

2   Let us suppose, that nature has bestowed on the human race such profuse *abundance* of all *external* conveniencies, that, without any uncertainty in the event, without any care or industry on our part, every individual finds himself fully provided with whatever his most voracious appetites can want, or luxurious imagination wish or desire. His natural beauty, we shall suppose, surpasses all acquired ornaments: The perpetual clemency of the seasons renders useless all cloaths or covering: The raw herbage affords him the most delicious fare; the clear fountain, the richest beverage. No laborious occupation required: No tillage: No navigation. Music, poetry, and contemplation form his sole business: Conversation, mirth, and friendship his sole amusement.

3   It seems evident, that, in such a happy state, every other social virtue would flourish, and receive tenfold encrease; but the cautious, jealous virtue of justice would never once have been dreamed of. For what purpose make a partition of goods, where every one has already more than enough? Why give rise to property, where there cannot possibly be any injury? Why call this object *mine*, when, upon the seizing of it by another, I need but stretch out my hand to possess myself of what is equally valuable? Justice, in that case, being totally USELESS, would be an idle ceremonial, and could never possibly have place in the catalogue of virtues.

4   We see, even in the present necessitous condition of mankind, that,

wherever any benefit is bestowed by nature in an unlimited abundance, we leave it always in common among the whole human race, and make no subdivisions of right and property. Water and air, though the most necessary of all objects, are not challenged as the property of individuals; nor can any man commit injustice by the most lavish use and enjoyment of these blessings. In fertile extensive countries, with few inhabitants, land is regarded on the same footing. And no topic is so much insisted on by those, who defend the liberty of the seas, as the unexhausted use of them in navigation. Were the advantages, procured by navigation, as inexhaustible, these reasoners had never had any adversaries to refute; nor had any claims ever been advanced of a separate, exclusive dominion over the ocean.

5   It may happen, in some countries, at some periods, that there be established a property in water, none in land;[10†] if the latter be in greater abundance than can be used by the inhabitants, and the former be found, with difficulty, and in very small quantities.

6   Again; suppose, that, though the necessities of human race continue the same as at present, yet the mind is so enlarged, and so replete with friendship and generosity, that every man has the utmost tenderness for   SBN 1 every man, and feels no more concern for his own interest than for that of his fellows: It seems evident, that the USE of justice would, in this case, be suspended[†] by such an extensive benevolence, nor would the divisions and barriers of property and obligation have ever been thought of. Why should I bind another, by a deed or promise, to do me any good office, when I know that he is already prompted, by the strongest inclination, to seek my happiness, and would, of himself, perform the desired service; except the hurt, he thereby receives, be greater than the benefit accruing to me? In which case, he knows, that, from my innate humanity and friendship, I should be the first to oppose myself to his imprudent generosity. Why raise land-marks between my neighbour's field and mine, when my heart has made no division between our interests; but shares all his joys and sorrows with the same force and vivacity[†] as if originally my own? Every man, upon this supposition, being a second self[†] to another, would trust all his interests to the discretion of every man; without jealousy, without partition, without distinction. And the whole human race would form only one family; where all would lie in common,[†] and be used freely, without regard to property; but cautiously too, with as entire regard to the

---

[10] Genesis, chap. 13. and 21. [Gen. 13: 7–12; 21: 25–30.]

3. Of Justice

necessities of each individual, as if our own interests were most intimately concerned.

7   In the present disposition of the human heart,[†] it would, perhaps, be difficult to find compleat instances of such enlarged affections; but still we may observe, that the case of families approaches towards it; and the stronger the mutual benevolence is among the individuals, the nearer it approaches; till all distinction of property be, in a great measure, lost and confounded among them. Between married persons, the cement of friendship is by the laws supposed so strong as to abolish all division of possessions; and has often, in reality, the force ascribed to it. And it is observable, that, during the ardour of new enthusiasms, when every principle is enflamed into extravagance, the community of goods has frequently been attempted; and nothing but experience of its inconveniencies, from the returning or disguised selfishness of men, could make the imprudent fanatics[†] adopt anew the ideas of justice and of separate property. So true is it, that this virtue derives its existence entirely from its necessary *use* to the intercourse and social state of mankind.

8   To make this truth more evident, let us reverse the foregoing suppositions;[†] and carrying every thing to the opposite extreme, consider what would be the effect of these new situations. Suppose a society to fall into such want of all common necessaries,[†] that the utmost frugality and industry cannot preserve the greater number from perishing, and the whole from extreme misery: It will readily, I believe, be admitted, that the strict laws of justice are suspended, in such a pressing emergence, and give place to the stronger motives of necessity and self-preservation. Is it any crime, after a shipwreck, to seize whatever means or instrument of safety one can lay hold of, without regard to former limitations of property? Or if a city besieged were perishing with hunger; can we imagine, that men will see any means of preservation before them, and lose their lives, from a scrupulous regard to what, in other situations, would be the rules of equity and justice? The USE and TENDENCY of that virtue is to procure happiness and security, by preserving order in society: But where the society is ready to perish from extreme necessity, no greater evil can be dreaded from violence and injustice; and every man may now provide for himself by all the means, which prudence can dictate, or humanity permit. The public, even in less urgent necessities, opens granaries,[†] without the consent of proprietors; as justly supposing, that the authority of magistracy[†] may, consistent with equity, extend so far: But were any number of men to assemble, without the tye of laws or civil jurisdiction; would an equal partition of

bread in a famine, though effected by power and even violence, be regarded as criminal or injurious?

9   Suppose likewise, that it should be a virtuous man's fate to fall into the society of ruffians, remote from the protection of laws and government; what conduct must he embrace in that melancholy situation? He sees such a desperate rapaciousness prevail; such a disregard to equity, such contempt of order, such stupid blindness to future consequences, as must immediately have the most tragical conclusion, and must terminate in destruction to the greater number, and in a total dissolution of society to the rest. He, mean while, can have no other expedient than to arm himself, to whomever the sword he seizes, or the buckler, may belong: To make provision of all means of defence and security: And his particular regard to justice being no longer of USE to his own safety or that of others, he must consult the dictates of self-preservation alone, without concern for those who no longer merit his care and attention.

10   When any man, even in political society, renders himself, by his crimes, obnoxious to the public, he is punished by the laws in his goods and person; that is, the ordinary rules of justice are, with regard to him, suspended[†] for a moment, and it becomes equitable to inflict on him, for the *benefit* of society, what, otherwise, he could not suffer without wrong or injury.

11   The rage and violence of public war; what is it but a suspension of justice among the warring parties, who perceive, that this virtue is now no longer of any *use* or advantage to them? The laws of war,[†] which then succeed to those of equity and justice, are rules calculated for the *advantage* and *utility* of that particular state, in which men are now placed. And were a civilized nation engaged with barbarians, who observed no rules even of war; the former must also suspend their observance of them, where they no longer serve to any purpose; and must render every action or rencounter as bloody and pernicious as possible to the first aggressors.   SBN 18

12   Thus, the rules of equity or justice depend entirely on the particular state and condition, in which men are placed, and owe their origin[†] and existence to that UTILITY, which results to the public from their strict and regular observance. Reverse, in any considerable circumstance, the condition of men: Produce extreme abundance or extreme necessity: Implant in the human breast perfect moderation and humanity, or perfect rapaciousness and malice: By rendering justice totally *useless*, you thereby totally destroy its essence, and suspend its obligation upon mankind.

13   The common situation of society is a medium amidst all these extremes. We are naturally partial to ourselves, and to our friends; but are

capable of learning the advantage resulting from a more equitable conduct. Few enjoyments are given us from the open and liberal hand of nature; but by art, labour, and industry, we can extract them in great abundance. Hence the ideas of property become necessary in all civil society: Hence justice derives its usefulness to the public: And hence alone arises its merit and moral obligation.

4   These conclusions are so natural and obvious, that they have not escaped even the poets, in their descriptions of the felicity, attending the golden age or the reign of SATURN.[†] The seasons, in that first period of nature, were so temperate, if we credit these agreeable fictions, that there was no necessity for men to provide themselves with cloaths and houses, as a security against the violence of heat and cold: The rivers flowed with wine and milk: The oaks yielded honey; and nature spontaneously produced her greatest delicacies. Nor were these the chief advantages of that happy age. Tempests were not alone removed from nature; but those more furious tempests were unknown to human breasts, which now cause such uproar, and engender such confusion. Avarice, ambition, cruelty, selfishness, were never heard of: Cordial affection, compassion, sympathy, were the only movements with which the mind was yet acquainted. Even the punctilious distinction of *mine* and *thine* was banished from among that happy race of mortals, and carried with it the very notion of property and obligation, justice and injustice.

SBN 189

5   This *poetical* fiction of the *golden age* is, in some respects, of a piece[†] with the *philosophical* fiction of the *state of nature*;[†] only that the former is represented as the most charming and most peaceable condition, which can possibly be imagined; whereas the latter is painted out as a state of mutual war and violence, attended with the most extreme necessity. On the first origin of mankind, we are told, their ignorance and savage nature[†] were so prevalent, that they could give no mutual trust, but must each depend upon himself, and his own force or cunning for protection and security. No law was heard of: No rule of justice known: No distinction of property regarded: Power was the only measure of right; and a perpetual war of all against all was the result of men's untamed selfishness and barbarity.[11]

---

[11] This fiction of a state of nature, as a state of war, was not first started by Mr. HOBBES, as is commonly imagined. PLATO endeavours to refute an hypothesis very like it in the 2d, 3d, and 4th books de republica. CICERO, on the contrary, supposes it certain and universally acknowledged in the following passage. "Quis enim vestrum, judices, ignorat, ita naturam rerum tulisse, ut quodam tempore homines, nondum neque naturali, neque civili jure descripto, fusi per agros, ac dispersi vagarentur tantumque haberent quantum manu ac viribus, per cædem ac

animals have no rights

16   Whether such a condition of human nature could ever exist, or if it did,
could continue so long as to merit the appellation of a *state*, may justly be
doubted. Men are necessarily born in a family-society, at least; and are
trained up by their parents to some rule of conduct and behaviour. But this
must be admitted, that, if such a state of mutual war and violence was ever
real, the suspension of all laws of justice, from their absolute inutility, is a
necessary and infallible consequence.

17   The more we vary our views of human life, and the newer and more
unusual the lights are, in which we survey it, the more shall we be convinced, that the origin here assigned for the virtue of justice is real and
satisfactory.[†]

18   Were there a species of creatures,[†] intermingled with men, which,
though rational, were possessed of such inferior strength, both of body
and mind, that they were incapable of all resistance, and could never, upon
the highest provocation, make us feel the effects of their resentment; the
necessary consequence, I think, is, that we should be bound, by the laws of
humanity, to give gentle usage to these creatures, but should not, properly
speaking, lie under any restraint of justice with regard to them, nor could
they possess any right or property, exclusive of such arbitrary lords. Our
intercourse with them could not be called society, which supposes a
degree of equality; but absolute command on the one side, and servile
obedience on the other. Whatever we covet, they must instantly resign:
Our permission is the only tenure, by which they hold their possessions:
Our compassion and kindness the only check, by which they curb our
lawless will: And as no inconvenience ever results from the exercise of
a power, so firmly established in nature, the restraints of justice and
property, being totally *useless*, would never have place in so unequal a
confederacy.

19   This is plainly the situation of men, with regard to animals; and how far
these may be said to possess reason,[†] I leave it to others to determine. The

vulnera, aut eripere, aut retinere potuissent? Qui igitur primi virtute & consilio præstanti
exiterunt, ii perspecto genere humanæ docilitatis ac ingenii, dissipatos, unum in locum con-
gregarunt, eosque ex feritate illa ad justitiam ac mansuetudinem transduxerunt. Tum res ad
communem utilitatem, quas publicas appellamus, tum conventicula hominum, quæ postea
civitates nominatæ sunt, tum domicilia conjuncta, quas urbes dicamus, invento & divino &
humano jure, mœnibus sepserunt. Atque inter hanc vitam, perpolitam humanitate, & illam
immanem, nihil tam interest quam jus atque vis. Horum utro uti nolimus, altero est utendum.
Vim volumus extingui? Jus valeat necesse est, id est, judicia, quibus omne jus continetur. Judicia
displicent, aut nulla sunt? Vis dominetur necesse est. Hæc vident omnes." Pro Sext. lib. 42.
[Thomas Hobbes, *Leviathan*, pt. 1, chs. 13–14; pt. 2, chs. 17, 21. Plato, *Republic*, bk. 2, 358 E ff.
Cicero, *Pro Sestio*, ch. 42, §§ 91–2.]

great superiority of civilized Europeans above barbarous Indians,[†] tempted us to imagine ourselves on the same footing with regard to them, and made us throw off all restraints of justice, and even of humanity, in our treatment of them. In many nations, the female sex are reduced to like slavery,[†] and are rendered incapable of all property, in opposition to their lordly masters. But though the males, when united, have, in all countries, bodily force sufficient to maintain this severe tyranny; yet such are the insinuation, address, and charms of their fair companions, that women are commonly able to break the confederacy, and share with the other sex in all the rights and privileges of society.

20   Were the human species so framed by nature as that each individual possessed within himself every faculty, requisite both for his own preservation and for the propagation of his kind: Were all society and intercourse cut off between man and man, by the primary intention of the Supreme Creator: It seems evident, that so solitary a being would be as much incapable of justice, as of social discourse and conversation. Where mutual regards and forbearance serve to no manner of purpose, they would never direct the conduct of any reasonable man. The headlong course of the passions would be checked by no reflection on future consequences. And as each man is here supposed to love himself alone, and to depend only on himself and his own activity for safety and happiness, he would, on every occasion, to the utmost of his power, challenge the preference above every other being, to none of which he is bound by any ties,   SBN 192 either of nature or of interest.

21   But suppose the conjunction of the sexes to be established in nature, a family immediately arises; and particular rules being found requisite for its subsistence, these are immediately embraced; though without comprehending the rest of mankind within their prescriptions. Suppose, that several families unite together into one society, which is totally disjoined from all others, the rules, which preserve peace and order, enlarge themselves to the utmost extent of that society; but becoming then entirely useless, lose their force when carried one step farther. But again suppose, that several distinct societies maintain a kind of intercourse for mutual convenience and advantage, the boundaries of justice still grow larger,[†] in proportion to the largeness of men's views, and the force of their mutual connexions. History, experience, reason sufficiently instruct us in this natural progress of human sentiments, and in the gradual enlargement of our regards to justice, in proportion as we become acquainted with the extensive utility of that virtue.

PART 2

22 If we examine the *particular* laws, by which justice is directed, and property determined; we shall still be presented with the same conclusion. The good of mankind is the only object of all these laws and regulations. Not only it is requisite, for the peace and interest of society, that men's possessions should be separated; but the rules, which we follow, in making the separation, are such as can best be contrived to serve farther the interests of society.

23 We shall suppose, that a creature, possessed of reason, but unacquainted with human nature, deliberates with himself what RULES of justice or property would best promote public interest, and establish peace and security among mankind: His most obvious thought would be, to assign the largest possessions to the most extensive virtue, and give every one the power of doing good, proportioned to his inclination. In a perfect theocracy,[†] where a being, infinitely intelligent, governs by particular volitions, this rule would certainly have place, and might serve to the wisest purposes: But were mankind to execute such a law; so great is the uncertainty of merit, both from its natural obscurity, and from the self-conceit of each individual, that no determinate rule of conduct would ever result from it; and the total dissolution of society must be the immediate consequence. Fanatics may suppose, *that dominion is founded on grace,*[†] and *that saints alone inherit the earth;*[†] but the civil magistrate very justly puts these sublime theorists[†] on the same footing with common robbers, and teaches them by the severest discipline, that a rule, which, in speculation, may seem the most advantageous to society, may yet be found, in practice, totally pernicious and destructive.

24 That there were *religious* fanatics[†] of this kind in ENGLAND, during the civil wars, we learn from history; though it is probable, that the obvious *tendency* of these principles excited such horror in mankind, as soon obliged the dangerous enthusiasts to renounce, or at least conceal their tenets. Perhaps, the *levellers,*[†] who claimed an equal distribution of property, were a kind of *political* fanatics, which arose from the religious species, and more openly avowed their pretensions;[†] as carrying a more plausible appearance, of being practicable in themselves, as well as useful to human society.

25 It must, indeed, be confessed, that nature is so liberal[†] to mankind, that, were all her presents equally divided among the species, and improved by art and industry, every individual would enjoy all the necessaries, and even most of the comforts of life; nor would ever be liable to any ills, but such as

3. Of Justice

might accidentally arise from the sickly frame and constitution of his body.   SBN 194
It must also be confessed, that, wherever we depart from this equality, we
rob the poor[†] of more satisfaction than we add to the rich, and that the
slight gratification of a frivolous vanity,[†] in one individual, frequently costs
more than bread to many families, and even provinces. It may appear
withal, that the rule of equality, as it would be highly *useful*, is not altogether *impracticable*; but has taken place, at least in an imperfect degree, in
some republics; particularly that of SPARTA;[†] where it was attended, it is
said, with the most beneficial consequences. Not to mention, that the
AGRARIAN laws,[†] so frequently claimed in ROME, and carried into execution
in many GREEK cities, proceeded, all of them, from a general idea of the
utility of this principle.

26   But historians, and even common sense, may inform us, that, however
specious these ideas of *perfect* equality may seem, they are really, at
bottom, *impracticable*; and were they not so, would be extremely *pernicious*
to human society. Render possessions ever so equal, men's different
degrees of art, care, and industry will immediately break that equality.[†] Or
if you check these virtues,[†] you reduce society to the most extreme indi-
gence; and instead of preventing want and beggary in a few, render it
unavoidable to the whole community. The most rigorous inquisition too is
requisite to watch every inequality on its first appearance; and the most
severe jurisdiction, to punish and redress it. But besides, that so much
authority must soon degenerate into tyranny, and be exerted with great
partialities; who can possibly be possessed of it, in such a situation as is
here supposed? Perfect equality of possessions, destroying all subordina-
tion, weakens extremely the authority of magistracy, and must reduce all
power nearly to a level, as well as property.

27   We may conclude, therefore, that, in order to establish laws for the regulation of property, we must be acquainted with the nature and situation of
man; must reject appearances, which may be false, though specious;[†] and   SBN 195
must search for those rules, which are, on the whole, most *useful* and *beneficial*. Vulgar sense and slight experience are sufficient for this purpose;
where men give not way to too selfish avidity, or too extensive
enthusiasm.[†]

28   Who sees not, for instance, that whatever is produced or improved by a
man's art or industry ought, for ever, to be secured to him, in order to give
encouragement to such *useful* habits and accomplishments? That the property ought also to descend to children and relations, for the same *useful*
purpose? That it may be alienated by consent,[†] in order to beget that commerce and intercourse, which is so *beneficial* to human society? And that all

inheritance just

contracts and promises ought carefully to be fulfilled, in order to secure mutual trust and confidence, by which the general *interest* of mankind is so much promoted?

29   Examine the writers on the laws of nature;[†] and you will always find, that, whatever principles they set out with, they are sure to terminate here at last, and to assign, as the ultimate reason for every rule which they establish, the convenience and necessities of mankind. A concession thus extorted, in opposition to systems, has more authority, than if it had been made in prosecution of them.[†]

30   What other reason, indeed, could writers ever give, why this must be *mine* and that *yours*; since uninstructed nature,[†] surely, never made any such distinction? The objects, which receive those appellations, are, of themselves, foreign to us; they are totally disjoined and separated from us; and nothing but the general interests of society can form the connexion.

31   Sometimes, the interests of society may require a rule of justice in a particular case; but may not determine any particular rule, among several, which are all equally beneficial. In that case, the slightest *analogies*[†] are laid hold of, in order to prevent that indifference and ambiguity, which would be the source of perpetual dissention. Thus possession alone, and first possession, is supposed to convey property, where no body else has any preceding claim and pretension. Many of the reasonings of lawyers are of this analogical nature, and depend on very slight connexions of the imagination.   SBN 19

32   Does any one scruple, in extraordinary cases, to violate all regard to the private property of individuals, and sacrifice to public interest a distinction, which had been established for the sake of that interest? The safety of the people is the supreme law:[†] All other particular laws are subordinate to it, and dependent on it: And if, in the *common* course of things, they be followed and regarded; it is only because the public safety and interest *commonly* demand so equal and impartial an administration.

33   Sometimes both *utility* and *analogy* fail, and leave the laws of justice in total uncertainty. Thus, it is highly requisite, that prescription or long possession should convey property; but what number of days or months or years should be sufficient for that purpose, it is impossible for reason alone to determine. *Civil laws* here supply the place of the natural *code*,[†] and assign different terms for prescription, according to the different *utilities*,[†] proposed by the legislator. Bills of exchange and promissory notes, by the laws of most countries, prescribe sooner than bonds, and mortgages, and contracts of a more formal nature.

3. Of Justice

34   In general, we may observe, that all questions of property are subordinate to the authority of civil laws, which extend, restrain, modify, and alter the rules of natural justice, according to the particular *convenience* of each community.† The laws have, or ought to have, a constant reference to the constitution of government, the manners, the climate, the religion, the commerce, the situation of each society. A late author† of genius, as well as learning, has prosecuted this subject at large, and has established, from these principles, a system of political knowledge, which abounds in ingenious and brilliant thoughts, and is not wanting in solidity.[12]   SBN 197

35   *What is a man's property?* Any thing, which it is lawful for him, and for him alone, to use. *But what rule have we, by which we can distinguish these objects?* Here we must have recourse to statutes, customs, precedents, analogies, and a hundred other circumstances; some of which are constant and inflexible, some variable and arbitrary. But the ultimate point, in which they all professedly terminate, is, the interest and happiness of human society. Where this enters not into consideration, nothing can appear more whimsical, unnatural, and even superstitious, than all or most of the laws of justice and of property.   SBN 198

36   Those, who ridicule vulgar superstitions, and expose the folly of

---

[12] The author of *L'Esprit des Loix.* [Charles Louis de Secondat Montesquieu, *De l'esprit des loix* [*The Spirit of Laws*].] This illustrious writer, however, sets out with a different theory, and supposes all right to be founded on certain *rapports* or relations; which is a system, that, in my opinion, never will be reconciled with true philosophy. Father MALEBRANCHE, as far as I can learn, was the first that started this abstract theory of morals, which was afterwards adopted by CUDWORTH, CLARKE, and others; and as it excludes all sentiment, and pretends to found every thing on reason, it has not wanted followers in this philosophic age. See Section 1. and Appendix 1. With regard to justice, the virtue here treated of, the inference against this theory seems short and conclusive. Property is allowed to be dependent on civil laws; civil laws are allowed to have no other object, but the interest of society: This therefore must be allowed to be the sole foundation of property and justice. Not to mention, that our obligation itself to obey the magistrate and his laws is founded on nothing but the interests of society.   SBN 197

If the ideas of justice, sometimes, do not follow the dispositions of civil law; we shall find, that these cases, instead of objections, are confirmations of the theory delivered above. Where a civil law is so perverse as to cross all the interests of society, it loses all its authority, and men judge by the ideas of natural justice, which are conformable to those interests. Sometimes also civil laws, for useful purposes, require a ceremony or form to any deed; and where that is wanting, their decrees run contrary to the usual tenor of justice; but one who takes advantage of such chicanes, is not commonly regarded as an honest man. Thus, the interests of society require, that contracts be fulfilled; and there is not a more material article either of natural or civil justice: But the omission of a trifling circumstance will often, by law, invalidate a contract, *in foro humano*, but not *in foro conscientiæ*,† as divines express themselves. In these cases, the magistrate is supposed only to withdraw his power of enforcing the right, not to have altered the right. Where his intention extends to the right, and is conformable to the interests of society; it never fails to alter the right; a clear proof of the origin of justice and of property, as assigned above.

particular regards[†] to meats, days, places, postures, apparel, have an easy task; while they consider all the qualities and relations of the objects, and discover no adequate cause for that affection or antipathy, veneration or horror, which have so mighty an influence over a considerable part of mankind. A Syrian would have starved rather than taste pigeon; an Egyptian[†] would not have approached bacon: But if these species of food be examined by the senses of sight, smell, or taste, or scrutinized by the sciences of chymistry, medicine, or physics; no difference is ever found between them and any other species, nor can that precise circumstance be pitched on,[†] which may afford a just foundation for the religious passion. A fowl on Thursday is lawful food; on Friday abominable: Eggs, in this house, and in this diocese, are permitted during Lent; a hundred paces farther, to eat them is a damnable sin. This earth or building, yesterday was profane; to-day, by the muttering of certain words, it has become holy and sacred. Such reflections as these, in the mouth of a philosopher, one may safely say, are too obvious to have any influence; because they must always, to every man, occur at first sight; and where they prevail not, of themselves, they are surely obstructed by education, prejudice, and passion, not by ignorance or mistake.

37   It may appear to a careless view, or rather, a too abstracted reflection, that there enters a like superstition into all the sentiments of justice; and that, if a man expose its object, or what we call property, to the same scrutiny of sense and science, he will not, by the most accurate enquiry, find any foundation for the difference made by moral sentiment. I may SBN 19 lawfully nourish myself from this tree; but the fruit of another of the same species, ten paces off, it is criminal for me to touch. Had I worne this apparel an hour ago, I had merited the severest punishment; but a man, by pronouncing a few magical syllables, has now rendered it fit for my use and service. Were this house placed in the neighbouring territory, it had been immoral for me to dwell in it; but being built on this side the river, it is subject to a different municipal law, and, by its becoming mine, I incur no blame or censure. The same species of reasoning, it may be thought, which so successfully exposes superstition, is also applicable to justice; nor is it possible, in the one case more than in the other, to point out, in the object, that precise quality or circumstance, which is the foundation of the sentiment.

38   But there is this material difference between *superstition* and *justice*, that the former is frivolous, useless, and burdensome; the latter is absolutely requisite to the well-being of mankind and existence of society. When we abstract from this circumstance (for it is too apparent ever to be over-

3. Of Justice

looked) it must be confessed, that all regards to right and property, seem entirely without foundation, as much as the grossest and most vulgar superstition. Were the interests of society nowise concerned, it is as unintelligible, why another's articulating certain sounds,[†] implying consent, should change the nature of my actions with regard to a particular object, as why the reciting of a liturgy by a priest, in a certain habit and posture, should dedicate a heap of brick and timber, and render it, thenceforth and for ever, sacred.[13]

[13] It is evident, that the will or consent alone never transfers property, nor causes the obligation of a promise, (for the same reasoning extends to both) but the will must be expressed by words or signs, in order to impose a tye upon any man. The expression being once brought in as subservient to the will, soon becomes the principal part of the promise; nor will a man be less bound by his word, though he secretly give a different direction to his intention, and with-hold the assent of his mind. But though the expression makes, on most occasions, the whole of the promise, yet it does not always so; and one who should make use of any expression, of which he knows not the meaning, and which he use without any sense of the consequences, would not certainly be bound by it. Nay, though he know its meaning, yet if he use it in jest only, and with such signs as evidently show, that he has no serious intention of binding himself, he would not lie under any obligation of performance; but it is necessary, that the words be a perfect expression of the will, without any contrary signs. Nay, even this we must not carry so far as to imagine, that one, whom, by our quickness of understanding, we conjecture, from certain signs, to have an intention of deceiving us, is not bound by his expression or verbal promise, if we accept of it; but must limit this conclusion to those cases where the signs are of a different nature from those of deceit. All these contradictions are easily accounted for, if justice arise entirely from its usefulness to society; but will never be explained on any other hypothesis.

It is remarkable, that the moral decisions of the JESUITS and other relaxed casuists, were commonly formed in prosecution of some such subtilties of reasoning as are here pointed out, and proceeded as much from the habit of scholastic refinement as from any corruption of the heart, if we may follow the authority of Mons. BAYLE. See his *Dictionary*, article LOYOLA.[†] [Pierre Bayle, *Dictionnaire historique et critique*, 'Loyola', n. (T).] And why has the indignation of mankind risen so high against these casuists; but because every one perceived, that human society could not subsist were such practices authorized, and that morals must always be handled with a view to public interest, more than philosophical regularity? If the secret direction of the intention, said every man of sense, could invalidate a contract; where is our security? And yet a metaphysical schoolman might think, that, where an intention was supposed to be requisite, if that intention really had not place, no consequence ought to follow, and no obligation be imposed. The casuistical subtilties may not be greater than the subtilties of lawyers, hinted at above; but as the former are *pernicious*, and the latter *innocent* and even *necessary*, this is the reason of the very different reception they meet with from the world.

It is a doctrine of the church of ROME, that the priest, by a secret direction of his intention, can invalidate any sacrament.[†] This position is derived from a strict and regular prosecution of the obvious truth, that empty words alone, without any meaning or intention in the speaker, can never be attended with any effect. If the same conclusion be not admitted in reasonings concerning civil contracts, where the affair is allowed to be of so much less consequence than the eternal salvation of thousands, it proceeds entirely from men's sense of the danger and inconvenience of the doctrine in the former case: And we may thence observe, that however positive, arrogant, and dogmatical any superstition may appear, it never can convey any thorough persuasion of the reality of its objects, or put them, in any degree, on a balance[†]

[people not as convinced of relig. as of prac. life]

39   These reflections are far from weakening the obligations of justice, or SBN 20
diminishing any thing from the most sacred attention to property. On the SBN 20
contrary, such sentiments must acquire new force from the present reasoning. For what stronger foundation can be desired or conceived for any
duty, than to observe, that human society, or even human nature could not
subsist, without the establishment of it; and will still arrive at greater
degrees of happiness and perfection, the more inviolable the regard is,
which is paid to that duty?

40   The dilemma seems obvious: As justice evidently tends to promote
public utility and to support civil society, the sentiment of justice is either
derived from our reflecting on that tendency, or like hunger, thirst, and
other appetites, resentment, love of life, attachment to offspring, and
other passions, arises from a simple original instinct† in the human breast,
which nature has implanted for like salutary purposes. If the latter be the
case, it follows, that property, which is the object of justice, is also distinguished by a simple, original instinct, and is not ascertained by any argument or reflection. But who is there that ever heard of such an instinct? Or
is this a subject, in which new discoveries can be made? We may as well
expect to discover, in the body, new senses, which had before escaped the
observation of all mankind.

41   But farther, though it seems a very simple proposition to say, that
nature, by an instinctive sentiment, distinguishes property, yet in reality
we shall find, that there are required for that purpose ten thousand different instincts, and these employed about objects of the greatest intricacy
and nicest discernment. For when a definition of *property* is required, that SBN 20
relation is found to resolve itself into any possession acquired by occupation, by industry, by prescription, by inheritance, by contract, &c. Can we
think, that nature, by an original instinct, instructs us in all these methods
of acquisition?

42   These words too, *inheritance* and *contract*, stand for ideas infinitely complicated; and to define them exactly, a hundred volumes of laws, and a
thousand volumes of commentators, have not been found sufficient. Does
nature, whose instincts in men are all simple, embrace such complicated
and artificial objects, and create a rational creature, without trusting any
thing to the operation of his reason?

43   But even though all this were admitted, it would not be satisfactory.
Positive laws can certainly transfer property. Is it by another original

with the common incidents of life, which we learn from daily observation and experimental
reasoning.

instinct, that we recognize the authority of kings and senates, and mark all the boundaries of their jurisdiction? Judges too, even though their sentence be erroneous and illegal, must be allowed, for the sake of peace and order, to have decisive authority, and ultimately to determine property. Have we original, innate ideas† of prætors and chancellors and juries? Who sees not, that all these institutions arise merely from the necessities of human society?

44 All birds of the same species, in every age and country, build their nests alike: In this we see the force of instinct. Men, in different times and places, frame their houses differently: Here we perceive the influence of reason and custom. A like inference may be drawn from comparing the instinct of generation and the institution of property.

45 How great soever the variety of municipal laws, it must be confessed, that their chief outlines pretty regularly concur; because the purposes, to which they tend, are every where exactly similar. In like manner, all houses have a roof and walls, windows and chimneys; though diversified in their shape, figure, and materials. The purposes of the latter, directed to the   SBN 203
conveniencies of human life, discover not more plainly their origin from reason and reflection, than do those of the former, which point all to a like end.

46 I need not mention the variations, which all the rules of property receive from the finer turns and connexions of the imagination, and from the subtilties and abstractions of law-topics and reasonings. There is no possibility of reconciling this observation to the notion of original instincts.

47 What alone will beget a doubt concerning the theory, on which I insist, is the influence of education and acquired habits, by which we are so accustomed to blame injustice, that we are not, in every instance, conscious of any immediate reflection on the pernicious consequences of it. The views the most familiar to us are apt, for that very reason, to escape us; and what we have very frequently performed from certain motives, we are apt likewise to continue mechanically, without recalling, on every occasion, the reflections, which first determined us. The convenience, or rather necessity, which leads to justice, is so universal, and every where points so much to the same rules, that the habit takes place in all societies; and it is not without some scrutiny, that we are able to ascertain its true origin. The matter, however, is not so obscure, but that, even in common life, we have, every moment, recourse to the principle of public utility, and ask, *What must become of the world, if such practices prevail? How could society subsist under such disorders?* Were the distinction or separation of

Jice based only on its Ut) to socy

possessions entirely useless, can any one conceive, that it ever should have obtained in society?

48   Thus we seem, upon the whole, to have attained a knowledge of the force of that principle here insisted on, and can determine what degree of esteem or moral approbation may result from reflections on public interest and utility. The necessity of justice to the support of society is the SOLE foundation of that virtue; and since no moral excellence[†] is more highly esteemed, we may conclude, that this circumstance of usefulness has, in general, the strongest energy,[†] and most entire command over our sentiments. It must, therefore, be the source of a considerable part of the merit ascribed to humanity, benevolence, friendship, public spirit, and other social virtues of that stamp; as it is the SOLE source of the moral approbation paid to fidelity, justice, veracity, integrity, and those other estimable and useful qualities and principles. It is entirely agreeable to the rules of philosophy,[†] and even of common reason; where any principle has been found to have a great force and energy in one instance, to ascribe to it a like energy in all similar instances. This indeed is NEWTON's chief rule of philosophizing.[14]

SBN 204

[14] Principia, lib. 3. [Isaac Newton, *Philosophiae naturalis principia mathematica*, bk. 3.]

our attitudes governed most by Ut)

value of soc¹ Vrs ᴬ mostly ← Ut)   *117 136*
*   "   "   other Vrs ᴮ wholly   "   "*
[ᴸsocietal']

SECTION 4[†]

OF POLITICAL SOCIETY

1 HAD every man sufficient *sagacity* to perceive, at all times, the strong interest, which binds him to the observance of justice and equity, and *strength of mind* sufficient to persevere in a steady adherence to a general and a distant interest, in opposition to the allurements of present pleasure and advantage; there had never, in that case, been any such thing as government or political society, but each man, following his natural liberty, had lived in entire peace and harmony with all others. What need of positive law, where natural justice† is, of itself, a sufficient restraint? Why create magistrates, where there never arises any disorder or iniquity? Why abridge our native freedom, when, in every instance, the utmost exertion of it is found innocent and beneficial? It is evident, that, if government were totally useless, it never could have place, and that the SOLE foundation of the duty of ALLEGIANCE is the *advantage*, which it procures to society, by preserving peace and order among mankind.

2 When a number of political societies are erected, and maintain a great intercourse together, a new set of rules are immediately discovered to be *useful* in that particular situation; and accordingly take place under the title of LAWS OF NATIONS.† Of this kind are, the sacredness of the person of ambassadors, abstaining from poisoned arms, quarter in war,† with others of that kind, which are plainly calculated for the *advantage* of states and kingdoms, in their intercourse with each other.

3 The rules of justice, such as prevail among individuals, are not entirely suspended among political societies. All princes pretend a regard to the rights of other princes; and some, no doubt, without hypocrisy. Alliances and treaties are every day made between independent states, which would only be so much waste of parchment, if they were not found, by experience, to have *some* influence and authority. But here is the difference between kingdoms and individuals. Human nature cannot, by any means, subsist, without the association of individuals; and that association never could have place, were no regard paid to the laws of equity and justice.

Disorder, confusion, the war of all against all,[†] are the necessary consequences of such a licentious conduct. But nations can subsist without intercourse. They may even subsist, in some degree, under a general war. The observance of justice, though useful among them, is not guarded by so strong a necessity as among individuals; and the *moral obligation* holds proportion with the *usefulness*.[†] All politicians will allow, and most philosophers, that REASONS of STATE[†] may, in particular emergencies, dispense with the rules of justice, and invalidate any treaty or alliance, where the strict observance of it would be prejudicial, in a considerable degree, to either of the contracting parties. But nothing less than the most extreme necessity, it is confessed, can justify individuals in a breach of promise, or an invasion of the properties of others.

4   In a confederated commonwealth, such as the ACHÆAN republic of old, or the SWISS Cantons and United Provinces[†] in modern times; as the league has here a peculiar *utility*, the conditions of union have a peculiar sacredness and authority, and a violation of them would be regarded as no less, or even as more criminal, than any private injury or injustice.

5   The long and helpless infancy of man requires the combination of parents for the subsistence of their young; and that combination requires the virtue of CHASTITY[†] or fidelity to the marriage bed. Without such a *utility*, it will readily be owned, that such a virtue would never have been thought of.[15]   SBN 20

6   An infidelity of this nature is much more *pernicious* in *women* than in *men*. Hence the laws of chastity are much stricter over the one sex than over the other.

7   These rules have all a reference to generation; and yet women past child-bearing are no more supposed to be exempted from them than those in the flower of their youth and beauty. *General rules* are often extended

---

[15] The only solution, which PLATO[†] gives to all the objections that might be raised against the community of women, established in his imaginary commonwealth, is, Κάλλιστα γὰρ δὴ τοῦτο καὶ λέγεται καὶ λελέξεται, ὅτι τὸ μὲν ὠφέλιμον καλόν, τὸ δὲ βλαβερὸν αἰσχρόν. "Scite enim istud & dicitur & dicetur, Id quod utile sit, honestum esse: quod autem inutile sit, turpe esse." De rep. lib. 5. p. 457. ex edit. Serr. And this maxim will admit of no doubt, where public utility is concerned; which is PLATO's meaning. And indeed to what other purpose do all the ideas of chastity and modesty serve? "Nisi utile est quod facimus, stulta est gloria," says PHÆDRUS.[†] Καλὸν τῶν βλαβερῶν οὐδέν, says PLUTARCH,[†] de vitioso pudore. "Nihil eorum quæ damnosa sunt, pulchrum est." The same was the opinion of the STOICS. Φασὶν οὖν οἱ Στωικοὶ ἀγαθὸν εἶναι ὠφέλειαν ἢ οὐχ ἕτερον ὠφελείας, ὠφελεῖν μὲν λέγοντες τὴν ἀρετὴν καὶ τὴν σπουδαίαν πρᾶξιν. SEXT. EMP.[†] lib. 3. cap. 20. [Plato, *Republic*, bk. 5, 457 B, in *Opera*, trans. Ioanne Serranus (1578 edn.), 457. Phaedrus, *Aesopic Fables*, bk. 3, fable 17, line 12. Plutarch, *Moralia*, 'On False Shame', ch. 3, 529 E. Sextus Empiricus, *Outlines of Pyrrhonism*, bk. 3, ch. 22 (20 in older editions), § 169.]

beyond the principle, whence they first arise; and this in all matters of taste and sentiment. It is a vulgar story at PARIS, that, during the rage of the MISSISSIPPI, a hump-backed fellow went every day into the RUE DE QUINCEMPOIX, where the stock-jobbers[†] met in great crowds, and was well paid for allowing them to make use of his hump as a desk, in order to sign their contracts upon it. Would the fortune, which he raised by this expedient, make him a handsome fellow; though it be confessed, that personal beauty arises very much from ideas of utility?[†] The imagination is influenced by associations of ideas; which, though they arise at first from the judgment, are not easily altered by every particular exception that occurs to us. To which we may add, in the present case of chastity, that the example of the old would be pernicious to the young; and that women,   SBN 208 continually foreseeing that a certain time would bring them the liberty of indulgence,[†] would naturally advance that period, and think more lightly of this whole duty, so requisite to society.

8   Those who live in the same family have such frequent opportunities of licence of this kind, that nothing could preserve purity of manners, were marriage allowed among the nearest relations, or any intercourse of love between them ratified by law and custom. INCEST, therefore, being *pernicious* in a superior degree, has also a superior turpitude and moral deformity annexed to it.

9   What is the reason, why, by the ATHENIAN laws, one might marry a half-sister by the father, but not by the mother? Plainly this: The manners of the ATHENIANS were so reserved, that a man was never permitted to approach the women's apartment, even in the same family, unless where he visited his own mother. His step-mother and her children were as much shut up from him as the women of any other family, and there was as little danger of any criminal correspondence between them. Uncles and nieces, for a like reason, might marry at ATHENS; but neither these, nor half-brothers and sisters, could contract that alliance at ROME, where the intercourse[†] was more open between the sexes. Public utility is the cause of all these variations.

10   To repeat, to a man's prejudice, any thing that escaped[†] him in private conversation, or to make any such use of his private letters, is highly blamed. The free and social intercourse of minds must be extremely checked, where no such rules of fidelity are established.

11   Even in repeating stories, whence we can foresee no ill consequences to result, the giving of one's author[†] is regarded as a piece of indiscretion, if not of immorality. These stories, in passing from hand to hand, and receiving all the usual variations, frequently come about to the persons

concerned, and produce animosities and quarrels among people, whose   SBN 209
intentions are the most innocent and inoffensive.

12   To pry into secrets, to open or even read the letters of others, to play the
spy upon their words and looks and actions; what habits more inconvenient in society? What habits, of consequence, more blameable?

13   This principle is also the foundation of most of the laws of good
manners; a kind of lesser morality,[†] calculated for the ease of company and
conversation. Too much or too little ceremony are both blamed, and every
thing, which promotes ease, without an indecent familiarity, is useful and
laudable.

14   Constancy in friendships, attachments, and familiarities, is commendable, and is requisite to support trust and good correspondence in society.
But in places of general, though casual concourse, where the pursuit of
health and pleasure brings people promiscuously together,[†] public conveniency has dispensed with this maxim; and custom there promotes an
unreserved conversation for the time, by indulging the privilege of drop-
ping afterwards every indifferent acquaintance,[†] without breach of civility
or good manners.

15   Even in societies, which are established on principles the most immoral,
and the most destructive to the interests of the general society, there are
required certain rules, which a species of false honour, as well as private
interest, engages the members to observe. Robbers and pirates,[†] it has
often been remarked, could not maintain their pernicious confederacy,
did they not establish a new distributive justice among themselves, and
recall those laws of equity, which they have violated with the rest of
mankind.

16   *I hate a drinking companion*, says the GREEK proverb, *who never forgets.*[†]
The follies of the last debauch should be buried in eternal oblivion, in
order to give full scope to the follies of the next.

17   Among nations, where an immoral gallantry, if covered with a thin veil   SBN 210
of mystery, is, in some degree, authorized by custom, there immediately
arise a set of rules, calculated for the conveniency of that attachment. The
famous court or parliament of love in PROVENCE[†] formerly decided all difficult cases of this nature.

18   In societies for play,[†] there are laws required for the conduct of the
game; and these laws are different in each game. The foundation, I own, of
such societies is frivolous; and the laws are, in a great measure, though not
altogether, capricious and arbitrary. So far is there a material difference
between them and the rules of justice, fidelity, and loyalty. The general
societies of men are absolutely requisite for the subsistence of the species;

and the public conveniency,[†] which regulates morals, is inviolably established in the nature of man, and of the world, in which he lives. The comparison, therefore, in these respects, is very imperfect. We may only learn from it the necessity of rules, wherever men have any intercourse with each other.

19   They cannot even pass each other on the road without rules. Waggoners, coachmen, and postilions have principles, by which they give the way;[†] and these are chiefly founded on mutual ease and convenience. Sometimes also they are arbitrary, at least dependent on a kind of capricious analogy, like many of the reasonings of lawyers.[16]

20   To carry the matter farther, we may observe, that it is impossible for men so much as to murder each other without statutes, and maxims, and an idea of justice and honour. War has its laws as well as peace; and even   SBN 211
that sportive kind of war, carried on among wrestlers, boxers, cudgel-players, gladiators, is regulated by fixed principles. Common interest and utility beget infallibly a standard of right and wrong among the parties concerned.

---

[16] That the lighter machine yield to the heavier, and, in machines of the same kind, that the   SBN 210
empty yield to the loaded; this rule is founded on convenience. That those who are going to the
capital take place of those who are coming from it; this seems to be founded on some idea of
the dignity of the great city, and of the preference of the future to the past. From like reasons,
among foot-walkers, the right-hand entitles a man to the wall, and prevents jostling, which
peaceable people find very disagreeable and inconvenient.

SECTION 5

WHY UTILITY PLEASES

PART 1

1 It seems so natural a thought to ascribe to their utility the praise, which we bestow on the social virtues, that one would expect to meet with this principle every where in moral writers, as the chief foundation of their reasoning and enquiry. In common life, we may observe, that the circumstance of utility is always appealed to; nor is it supposed, that a greater eulogy can be given to any man, than to display his usefulness to the public, and enumerate the services, which he has performed to mankind and society. What praise, even of an inanimate form, if the regularity and elegance of its parts destroy not its fitness for any useful purpose! And how satisfactory an apology for any disproportion or seeming deformity, if we can show the necessity of that particular construction for the use intended! A ship appears more beautiful to an artist, or one moderately skilled in navigation, where its prow is wide and swelling beyond its poop, than if it were framed with a precise geometrical regularity, in contradiction to all the laws of mechanics. A building, whose doors and windows were exact squares, would hurt the eye by that very proportion; as ill adapted to the figure of a human creature, for whose service the fabric was intended.† What wonder then, that a man, whose habits and conduct are hurtful to society, and dangerous or pernicious to every one who has an intercourse with him, should, on that account, be an object of disapprobation, and communicate to every spectator the strongest sentiments of disgust and hatred?[17]

---

[17] We ought not to imagine, because an inanimate object may be useful as well as a man, that therefore it ought also, according to this system, to merit the appellation of *virtuous*. The sentiments, excited by utility, are, in the two cases, very different; and the one is mixed with affection, esteem, approbation, &c. and not the other. In like manner, an inanimate object may have good colour and proportions as well as a human figure. But can we ever be in love with the former? There are a numerous set of passions and sentiments, of which thinking rational beings are, by the original constitution of nature, the only proper objects: And though the very same qualities be transferred to an insensible, inanimate being, they will not excite the same

5. Why Utility Pleases

2   But perhaps the difficulty of accounting for these effects of usefulness,[†] or its contrary, has kept philosophers from admitting them into their systems of ethics, and has induced them rather to employ any other principle, in explaining the origin of moral good and evil. But it is no just reason for rejecting any principle, confirmed by experience, that we cannot give a satisfactory account of its origin, nor are able to resolve it into other more general principles. And if we would employ a little thought on the present subject, we need be at no loss to account for the influence of utility, and to deduce it from principles, the most known and avowed in human nature.

3   From the apparent usefulness of the social virtues, it has readily been SBN 214 inferred by sceptics, both ancient and modern, that all moral distinctions arise from education,[†] and were, at first, invented, and afterwards encouraged, by the art of politicians, in order to render men tractable, and subdue their natural ferocity and selfishness, which incapacitated them for society. This principle, indeed, of precept and education, must so far be owned to have a powerful influence, that it may frequently encrease or diminish, beyond their natural standard, the sentiments of approbation or dislike; and may even, in particular instances, create, without any natural principle,[†] a new sentiment of this kind; as is evident in all superstitious practices and observances: But that *all* moral affection or dislike arises from this origin, will never surely be allowed by any judicious enquirer. Had nature made no such distinction, founded on the original constitution[†] of the mind, the words, *honourable* and *shameful*, *lovely* and *odious*, *noble* and *despicable*, had never had place in any language;[†] nor could politicians, had they invented these terms, ever have been able to render them intelligible, or make them convey any idea to the audience. So that nothing can be more superficial than this paradox of the sceptics;[†] and it were well, if, in the abstruser studies of logic and metaphysics, we could as easily obviate the cavils of that sect, as in the practical and more intelligible sciences of politics and morals.

4   The social virtues must, therefore, be allowed to have a natural beauty

sentiments. The beneficial qualities of herbs and minerals are, indeed, sometimes called their SBN 213 *virtues*; but this is an effect of the caprice of language, which ought not be regarded in reasoning. For though there be a species of approbation attending even inanimate objects, when beneficial, yet this sentiment is so weak, and so different from that which is directed to beneficent magistrates or statesmen, that they ought not to be ranked under the same class or appellation.

    A very small variation of the object, even where the same qualities are preserved, will destroy a sentiment. Thus, the same beauty, transferred to a different sex, excites no amorous passion, where nature is not extremely perverted.

and amiableness, which, at first, antecedent to all precept or education, recommends them to the esteem of uninstructed mankind, and engages their affections. And as the public utility of these virtues is the chief circumstance, whence they derive their merit, it follows, that the end, which they have a tendency to promote, must be some way agreeable to us, and take hold of some natural affection. It must please, either from considerations of self-interest, or from more generous motives and regards.

5   It has often been asserted, that, as every man has a strong connexion with society, and perceives the impossibility of his solitary subsistence, he becomes, on that account, favourable to all those habits or principles, which promote order in society, and ensure to him the quiet possession of so inestimable a blessing. As much as we value our own happiness and welfare, as much must we applaud the practice of justice and humanity, by which alone the social confederacy[†] can be maintained, and every man reap the fruits of mutual protection and assistance.

6   This deduction of morals from self-love, or a regard to private interest, is an obvious thought, and has not arisen wholly from the wanton sallies and sportive assaults of the sceptics.[†] To mention no others, POLYBIUS,[†] one of the gravest and most judicious, as well as most moral writers of antiquity, has assigned this selfish origin to all our sentiments of virtue.[18] But though the solid, practical sense of that author, and his aversion to all vain subtilties, render his authority on the present subject very considerable; yet is not this an affair to be decided by authority, and the voice of nature and experience seems plainly to oppose the selfish theory.[†]

7   We frequently bestow praise on virtuous actions, performed in very distant ages and remote countries; where the utmost subtilty of imagination would not discover any appearance of self-interest,[†] or find any connexion of our present happiness and security with events so widely separated from us.

8   A generous, a brave, a noble deed, performed by an adversary, commands our approbation; while in its consequences it may be acknowledged prejudicial to our particular interest.

9   Where private advantage concurs with general affection for virtue, we

---

[18] Undutifulness to parents is disapproved of by mankind, προορωμένους τὸ μέλλον, καὶ συλλογιζομένους ὅτι τὸ παραπλήσιον ἑκάστοις αὐτῶν συγκυρήσει. Ingratitude for a like reason (though he seems there to mix a more generous regard) συναγανακτοῦντας μὲν τῷ πέλας, ἀναφέροντας δ' ἐπ' αὐτοὺς τὸ παραπλήσιον ἐξ ὧν ὑπογίγνεταί τις ἔννοια παρ' ἑκάστῳ τῆς τοῦ καθήκοντος δυνάμεως καὶ θεωρίας. Lib. vi. cap. 4. [Polybius, *Histories*, bk. 6, ch. 6, §§ 2–7.] Perhaps the historian only meant, that our sympathy and humanity was more enlivened, by our considering the similarity of our case with that of the person suffering; which is a just sentiment.

readily perceive and avow the mixture of these distinct sentiments, which have a very different feeling and influence on the mind. We praise, perhaps, with more alacrity, where the generous, humane action contributes to our particular interest: But the topics of praise, which we insist on, are very wide of[†] this circumstance. And we may attempt to bring over others to our sentiments, without endeavouring to convince them, that they reap any advantage from the actions which we recommend to their approbation and applause.

10   Frame the model of a praise-worthy character, consisting of all the most amiable moral virtues: Give instances, in which these display themselves after an eminent and extraordinary manner: You readily engage the esteem and approbation of all your audience, who never so much as enquire in what age and country the person lived, who possessed these noble qualities: A circumstance, however, of all others, the most material to self-love, or a concern for our own individual happiness.

11   Once on a time, a statesman, in the shock and contest of parties, prevailed so far as to procure, by his eloquence, the banishment of an able adversary; whom he secretly followed, offering him money for his support during his exile, and soothing him with topics of consolation in his misfortunes. "Alas!" cries the banished statesman, "with what regret must I leave my friends in this city, where even enemies are so generous!" Virtue, SBN 217 though in an enemy, here pleased him: And we also give it the just tribute of praise and approbation; nor do we retract these sentiments, when we hear, that the action passed at ATHENS, about two thousand years ago, and that the persons' names were ÆSCHINES and DEMOSTHENES.[†]

12   *What is that to me?* There are few occasions, when this question is not pertinent: And had it that universal, infallible influence supposed, it would turn into ridicule every composition, and almost every conversation, which contain any praise or censure of men and manners.

13   It is but a weak subterfuge, when pressed by these facts and arguments, to say, that we transport ourselves, by the force of imagination, into distant ages[†] and countries, and consider the advantage, which we should have reaped from these characters, had we been contemporaries, and had any commerce with the persons. It is not conceivable, how a *real* sentiment or passion can ever arise from a known *imaginary* interest; especially when our *real* interest is still kept in view,[†] and is often acknowledged to be entirely distinct from the imaginary, and even sometimes opposite to it.

14   A man, brought to the brink of a precipice,[†] cannot look down without trembling; and the sentiment of *imaginary* danger actuates him, in

Enquiry concerning the Principles of Morals

opposition to the opinion and belief of *real* safety. But the imagination is here assisted by the presence of a striking object; and yet prevails not, except it be also aided by novelty, and the unusual appearance of the object. Custom soon reconciles us to heights and precipices, and wears off these false and delusive terrors. The reverse is observable in the estimates, which we form of characters and manners; and the more we habituate ourselves to an accurate scrutiny of morals, the more delicate feeling do we acquire of the most minute distinctions between vice and virtue. Such frequent occasion, indeed, have we, in common life, to pronounce all kinds of moral determinations, that no object of this kind can be new or unusual to us; nor could any *false* views or prepossessions maintain their ground against an experience, so common and familiar. Experience being chiefly what forms the associations of ideas,[†] it is impossible, that any association could establish and support itself, in direct opposition to that principle.[†]

SBN 218

15   Usefulness is agreeable, and engages our approbation. This is a matter of fact, confirmed by daily observation. But, *useful?* For what? For some body's interest, surely. Whose interest then? Not our own only: For our approbation frequently extends farther. It must, therefore, be the interest of those, who are served by the character or action approved of; and these we may conclude, however remote, are not totally indifferent to us. By opening up this principle, we shall discover one great source of moral distinctions.

PART 2

16   Self-love is a principle in human nature of such extensive energy, and the interest of each individual is, in general, so closely connected with that of the community, that those philosophers were excusable, who fancied, that all our concern for the public might be resolved into a concern for our own happiness and preservation. They saw, every moment, instances of approbation or blame, satisfaction or displeasure towards characters and actions; they denominated the objects of these sentiments, *virtues* or *vices*; they observed, that the former had a tendency to encrease the happiness, and the latter the misery of mankind; they asked, whether it were possible that we could have any general concern for society, or any disinterested resentment of the welfare or injury of others; they found it simpler[†] to consider all these sentiments as modifications of self-love; and

SBN 219

they discovered a pretence, at least, for this unity of principle,[†] in that close union of interest, which is so observable between the public and each individual.

17 But notwithstanding this frequent confusion of interests, it is easy to attain what natural philosophers, after Lord BACON, have affected to call the *experimentum crucis*,[†] or that experiment, which points out the right way in any doubt or ambiguity. We have found instances, in which private interest was separate from public; in which it was even contrary: And yet we observed the moral sentiment to continue, notwithstanding this disjunction of interests.[†] And wherever these distinct interests sensibly concurred, we always found a sensible encrease of the sentiment, and a more warm affection to virtue, and detestation of vice, or what we properly call, *gratitude* and *revenge*. Compelled by these instances, we must renounce the theory, which accounts for every moral sentiment by the principle of self-love. We must adopt a more public affection, and allow, that the interests of society are not, even on their own account, entirely indifferent to us. Usefulness is only a tendency to a certain end; and it is a contradiction in terms,[†] that any thing pleases as means to an end, where the end itself nowise affects us. If usefulness, therefore, be a source of moral sentiment, and if this usefulness be not always considered with a reference to self; it follows, that every thing, which contributes to the happiness of society, recommends itself directly to our approbation and good-will. Here is a principle, which accounts, in great part, for the origin of morality: And what need we seek for abstruse and remote systems, when there occurs one so obvious and natural?[19]

18 Have we any difficulty to comprehend the force of humanity and benevolence?[†] Or to conceive, that the very aspect of happiness, joy, prosperity, gives pleasure; that of pain, suffering, sorrow, communicates uneasiness? The human countenance, says HORACE,[20†] borrows smiles or tears from the human countenance. Reduce a person to solitude, and he

SBN 220

---

[19] It is needless to push our researches so far as to ask, why we have humanity or a fellow-feeling with others. It is sufficient, that this is experienced to be a principle in human nature. We must stop somewhere in our examination of causes; and there are, in every science, some general principles, beyond which we cannot hope to find any principle more general. No man is absolutely indifferent to the happiness and misery of others. The first has a natural tendency to give pleasure; the second, pain. This every one may find in himself. It is not probable, that these principles can be resolved into principles more simple and universal, whatever attempts may have been made to that purpose. But if it were possible, it belongs not to the present subject; and we may here safely consider these principles as original: Happy, if we can render all the consequences sufficiently plain and perspicuous!

[20] "Uti ridentibus arrident, ita flentibus adflent
Humani vultus." HOR. [Horace, *Art of Poetry*, lines 101–2.]

SBN 219

SBN 220

loses all enjoyment, except either of the sensual or speculative kind; and that because the movements of his heart are not forwarded by correspondent movements in his fellow-creatures. The signs of sorrow and mourning, though arbitrary, affect us with melancholy; but the natural symptoms, tears and cries and groans, never fail to infuse compassion and uneasiness. And if the effects of misery touch us in so lively a manner; can we be supposed altogether insensible or indifferent towards its causes; when a malicious or treacherous character and behaviour are presented to us?

19   We enter, I shall suppose, into a convenient, warm, well-contrived apartment: We necessarily receive a pleasure from its very survey; because it presents us with the pleasing ideas of ease, satisfaction, and enjoyment. The hospitable, good-humoured, humane landlord appears. This circumstance surely must embellish the whole; nor can we easily forbear reflecting, with pleasure, on the satisfaction which results to every one from his intercourse and good offices. SBN 22

20   His whole family, by the freedom, ease, confidence, and calm enjoyment, diffused over their countenances, sufficiently express their happiness. I have a pleasing sympathy[†] in the prospect of so much joy, and can never consider the source of it, without the most agreeable emotions.

21   He tells me, that an oppressive and powerful neighbour had attempted to dispossess him of his inheritance, and had long disturbed all his innocent and social pleasures. I feel an immediate indignation arise in me against such violence and injury.

22   But it is no wonder, he adds, that a private wrong should proceed from a man, who had enslaved provinces, depopulated cities, and made the field and scaffold stream with human blood. I am struck with horror at the prospect of so much misery, and am actuated by the strongest antipathy against its author.

23   In general, it is certain, that, wherever we go, whatever we reflect on or converse about, every thing still presents us with the view of human happiness or misery, and excites in our breast a sympathetic movement of pleasure or uneasiness. In our serious occupations, in our careless amusements, this principle still exerts its active energy.

24   A man, who enters the theatre, is immediately struck with the view of so great a multitude, participating of one common amusement; and experiences, from their very aspect, a superior sensibility[†] or disposition of being affected with every sentiment, which he shares with his fellow-creatures.

25   He observes the actors to be animated by the appearance of a full audi-

110

5. Why Utility Pleases

ence, and raised to a degree of enthusiasm, which they cannot command in any solitary or calm moment.

26   Every movement of the theatre, by a skilful poet, is communicated, as it were by magic, to the spectators; who weep, tremble, resent, rejoice, and are enflamed with all the variety of passions, which actuate the several personages of the drama.   SBN 222

27   Where any event crosses our wishes,[†] and interrupts the happiness of the favourite characters, we feel a sensible anxiety and concern. But where their sufferings proceed from the treachery, cruelty, or tyranny of an enemy, our breasts are affected with the liveliest resentment against the author of these calamities.

28   It is here esteemed contrary to the rules of art to represent any thing cool and indifferent. A distant friend, or a confident, who has no immediate interest in the catastrophe, ought, if possible, to be avoided by the poet; as communicating a like indifference to the audience, and checking the progress of the passions.

29   Few species of poetry are more entertaining than *pastoral*; and every one is sensible, that the chief source of its pleasure arises from those images of a gentle and tender tranquillity, which it represents in its personages, and of which it communicates a like sentiment to the reader. SANNAZARIUS,[†] who transferred the scene to the sea-shore, though he presented the most magnificent object in nature, is confessed to have erred in his choice. The idea of toil, labour, and danger, suffered by the fishermen, is painful; by an unavoidable sympathy, which attends every conception of human happiness or misery.

30   When I was twenty, says a FRENCH poet,[†] OVID was my favourite: Now I am forty, I declare for HORACE. We enter, to be sure, more readily into sentiments, which resemble those we feel every day: But no passion, when well represented, can be entirely indifferent to us; because there is none, of which every man has not, within him, at least the seeds and first principles. It is the business of poetry to bring every affection near to us by lively imagery and representation, and make it look like truth and reality: A certain proof, that, wherever that reality is found, our minds are disposed to be strongly affected by it.   SBN 223

31   Any recent event or piece of news, by which the fate of states, provinces, or many individuals is affected, is extremely interesting even to those whose welfare is not immediately engaged. Such intelligence is propagated with celerity, heard with avidity, and enquired into with attention and concern. The interest of society appears, on this occasion, to be, in some degree, the interest of each individual. The imagination is sure to

111

be affected; though the passions excited may not always be so strong and steady as to have great influence on the conduct and behaviour.

32   The perusal of a history seems a calm entertainment; but would be no entertainment at all, did not our hearts beat with correspondent movements to those which are described by the historian.

33   THUCYDIDES and GUICCIARDIN[†] support with difficulty our attention; while the former describes the trivial rencounters of the small cities of GREECE, and the latter the harmless wars of PISA. The few persons interested, and the small interest fill not the imagination, and engage not the affections. The deep distress of the numerous ATHENIAN army before SYRACUSE; the danger, which so nearly threatens VENICE; these excite compassion; these move terror and anxiety.

34   The indifferent, uninteresting style of SUETONIUS, equally with the masterly pencil of TACITUS,[†] may convince us of the cruel depravity of NERO or TIBERIUS: But what a difference of sentiment! While the former coldly relates the facts; and the latter sets before our eyes the venerable figures of a SORANUS and a THRASEA, intrepid in their fate, and only moved by the melting sorrows of their friends and kindred. What sympathy then touches every human heart! What indignation against the tyrant, whose causeless fear or unprovoked malice gave rise to such detestable barbarity!   SBN 2

35   If we bring these subjects nearer: If we remove all suspicion of fiction and deceit: What powerful concern is excited, and how much superior, in many instances, to the narrow attachments of self-love and private interest! Popular sedition, party zeal, a devoted obedience to factious leaders; these are some of the most visible, though less laudable effects of this social sympathy in human nature.

36   The frivolousness[†] of the subject too, we may observe, is not able to detach us entirely from what carries an image of human sentiment and affection.

37   When a person stutters, and pronounces with difficulty, we even sympathize with this trivial uneasiness, and suffer for him. And it is a rule in criticism,[†] that every combination of syllables or letters, which gives pain to the organs of speech in the recital, appears also, from a species of sympathy, harsh and disagreeable to the ear. Nay, when we run over a book with our eye, we are sensible of such unharmonious composition; because we still imagine, that a person recites it to us, and suffers from the pronunciation of these jarring sounds. So delicate is our sympathy!

38   Easy and unconstrained postures and motions are always beautiful: An

5. Why Utility Pleases

air of health and vigour is agreeable: Cloaths which warm, without burdening the body; which cover, without imprisoning the limbs, are well-fashioned. In every judgment of beauty, the feelings of the person affected enter into consideration, and communicate to the spectator similar touches of pain or pleasure.[21] What wonder, then, if we can pronounce no judgment concerning the character and conduct of men, without considering the tendencies of their actions, and the happiness or misery which thence arises to society? What association of ideas would ever operate, were that principle here totally unactive?[22] $\quad$ SBN 225

If any man, from a cold insensibility, or narrow selfishness of temper, is unaffected with the images of human happiness or misery, he must be equally indifferent to the images of vice and virtue: As, on the other hand, it is always found, that a warm concern for the interests of our species is attended with a delicate feeling of all moral distinctions; a strong resentment of injury done to men; a lively approbation of their welfare. In this particular, though great superiority is observable of one man above another; yet none are so entirely indifferent to the interest of their fellow-creatures, as to perceive no distinctions of moral good and evil, in consequence of the different tendencies of actions and principles. How, indeed, can we suppose it possible in any one, who wears a human heart, that, if there be subjected to his censure,† one character or system of conduct, which is beneficial, and another, which is pernicious, to his species or community, he will not so much as give a cool preference to the former, or $\quad$ SBN 226 ascribe to it the smallest merit or regard? Let us suppose such a person ever so selfish; let private interest have ingrossed ever so much his attention; yet

[21] "Decentior equus cujus astricta sunt ilia; sed idem velocior. Pulcher aspectu sit athleta, $\quad$ SBN 224 cujus lacertos exercitatio expressit; idem certamini paratior. Nunquam enim *species* ab *utilitate* dividitur. Sed hoc quidem discernere modici judicii est." QUINTILIAN,† Inst. lib. 8. cap. 3. [Quintilian, *Institutes*, bk. 8, ch. 3, §§10–11.]

[22] In proportion to the station which a man possesses, according to the relations in which he $\quad$ SBN 225 is placed; we always expect from him a greater or less degree of good, and when disappointed, blame his inutility; and much more do we blame him, if any ill or prejudice arise from his conduct and behaviour. When the interests of one country interfere with those of another, we estimate the merits of a statesman by the good or ill, which results to his own country from his measures and councils, without regard to the prejudice which he brings on its enemies and rivals. His fellow-citizens are the objects, which lie nearest the eye, while we determine his character. And as nature has implanted in every one a superior affection to his own country, we never expect any regard to distant nations, where a competition arises. Not to mention, that, while every man consults the good of his own community, we are sensible, that the general interest of mankind is better promoted, than by any loose indeterminate views to the good of a species, whence no beneficial action could ever result, for want of a duly limited object, on which they could exert themselves.

Enquiry concerning the Principles of Morals

in instances, where that is not concerned, he must unavoidably feel *some* propensity to the good of mankind, and make it an object of choice, if every thing else be equal. Would any man, who is walking along, tread as willingly on another's gouty toes, whom he has no quarrel with, as on the hard flint and pavement? There is here surely a difference in the case. We surely take into consideration the happiness and misery of others, in weighing the several motives of action, and incline to the former, where no private regards draw us to seek our own promotion or advantage by the injury of our fellow-creatures. And if the principles of humanity[†] are capable, in many instances, of influencing our actions, they must, at all times, have *some* authority over our sentiments, and give us a general approbation of what is useful to society, and blame of what is dangerous or pernicious. The degrees of these sentiments may be the subject of controversy; but the reality of their existence, one should think, must be admitted, in every theory or system.

40   A creature, absolutely malicious and spiteful, were there any such in nature, must be worse than indifferent to the images of vice and virtue. All his sentiments must be inverted, and directly opposite to those, which prevail in the human species. Whatever contributes to the good of mankind, as it crosses the constant bent of his wishes and desires, must produce uneasiness and disapprobation; and on the contrary, whatever is the source of disorder and misery in society, must, for the same reason, be regarded with pleasure and complacency. TIMON, who, probably from his affected spleen, more than any inveterate malice, was denominated the man-hater, embraced ALCIBIADES,[†] with great fondness. "Go on, my boy!" cried he, "acquire the confidence of the people: You will one day, I foresee, be the cause of great calamities to them:"[23] Could we admit the two principles of the MANICHEANS,[†] it is an infallible consequence, that their sentiments of human actions, as well as of every thing else, must be totally opposite, and that every instance of justice and humanity, from its necessary tendency, must please the one deity and displease the other. All mankind so far resemble the good principle, that, where interest or revenge or envy perverts not our disposition, we are always inclined, from our natural philanthropy,[†] to give the preference to the happiness of society, and consequently to virtue, above its opposite. Absolute, unprovoked, disinterested malice has never, perhaps, place in any human breast; or if it had, must there pervert all the sentiments of morals, as well as the feelings of humanity. If the cruelty of NERO be allowed entirely voluntary,

    SBN 22

[23] PLUTARCH. in vita ALC. [Plutarch, *Lives*, 'Alcibiades', ch. 16, §6, 199 C–D.]

no disint[d] malice

and not rather the effect of constant fear and resentment; it is evident, that TIGELLINUS, preferably to SENECA or BURRHUS,[†] must have possessed his steady and uniform approbation.

41   A statesman or patriot, who serves our own country, in our own time, has always a more passionate regard paid to him, than one whose beneficial influence operated on distant ages or remote nations; where the good, resulting from his generous humanity, being less connected with us, seems more obscure, and affects us with a less lively sympathy. We may own the merit to be equally great, though our sentiments are not raised to an equal height, in both cases. The judgment here corrects the inequalities[†] of our internal emotions and perceptions; in like manner, as it preserves us from error, in the several variations of images, presented to our external senses. The same object, at a double distance, really throws on the eye a picture of but half the bulk; yet we imagine that it appears of the same size in both situations; because we know, that, on our approach to it, its image would expand on the eye, and that the difference consists not in the object itself, but in our position with regard to it. And, indeed, without such a correction of appearances, both in internal and external sentiment, men could never think or talk steadily on any subject; while their fluctuating situations produce a continual variation on objects, and throw them into such different and contrary lights and positions.[24]

2   The more we converse with mankind, and the greater social intercourse we maintain, the more shall we be familiarized to these general preferences and distinctions, without which our conversation and discourse could scarcely be rendered intelligible to each other. Every man's interest is peculiar to himself, and the aversions and desires, which result from it, cannot be supposed to affect others in a like degree. General language, therefore, being formed for general use, must be moulded on some more general views, and must affix the epithets of praise or blame, in

---

[24] For a like reason, the tendencies of actions and characters, not their real accidental consequences,[†] are alone regarded in our moral determinations or general judgments; though in our real feeling or sentiment, we cannot help paying greater regard to one whose station, joined to virtue, renders him really useful to society, than to one, who exerts the social virtues only in good intentions and benevolent affections. Separating the character from the fortune, by an easy and necessary effort of thought, we pronounce these persons alike, and give them the same general praise. The judgment corrects or endeavours to correct the appearance: But is not able entirely to prevail over sentiment.

Why is this peach-tree said to be better than that other; but because it produces more or better fruit? And would not the same praise be given it, though snails or vermin had destroyed the peaches, before they came to full maturity? In morals too, is not *the tree known by the fruit?* And cannot we easily distinguish between nature and accident, in the one case as well as in the other?

Moral law enshrines gen' soc' stds
wh transcend selfish evaln 147   selfish θ
                                              108 119

Enquiry concerning the Principles of Morals

conformity to sentiments, which arise from the general interests of the
community. And if these sentiments, in most men, be not so strong as   SBN 2
those, which have a reference to private good; yet still they must make
some distinction, even in persons the most depraved and selfish; and must
attach the notion of good to a beneficent conduct, and of evil to the contrary. Sympathy, we shall allow, is much fainter than our concern for ourselves, and sympathy with persons remote from us, much fainter than that
with persons near and contiguous; but for this very reason, it is necessary
for us, in our calm judgments and discourse concerning the characters of
men, to neglect all these differences, and render our sentiments more
public and social. Besides, that we ourselves often change our situation in
this particular, we every day meet with persons, who are in a situation different from us, and who could never converse with us, were we to remain
constantly in that position and point of view, which is peculiar to ourselves. The intercourse of sentiments,[†] therefore, in society and conversation, makes us form some general unalterable standard, by which we may
approve or disapprove of characters and manners. And though the heart
takes not part entirely with[†] those general notions, nor regulates all its love
and hatred, by the universal, abstract differences of vice and virtue,
without regard to self, or the persons with whom we are more intimately
connected; yet have these moral differences a considerable influence, and
being sufficient, at least, for discourse, serve all our purposes in company,
in the pulpit, on the theatre, and in the schools.[25]

43   Thus, in whatever light we take this subject, the merit, ascribed to the   SBN
social virtues, appears still uniform, and arises chiefly from that regard,
which the natural sentiment of benevolence engages us to pay to the interests of mankind and society. If we consider the principles of the human
make, such as they appear to daily experience and observation; we must, *a
priori*, conclude it impossible for such a creature as man to be totally indifferent to the well or ill-being of his fellow-creatures, and not readily, of
himself, to pronounce, where nothing gives him any particular biass, that
what promotes their happiness is good, what tends to their misery is evil,
without any farther regard or consideration. Here then are the faint rudi-
ments, at least, or outlines, of a *general* distinction between actions; and in

[25] It is wisely ordained by nature, that private connexions should commonly prevail over uni-   SBN
versal views and considerations; otherwise our affections and actions would be dissipated and
lost, for want of a proper limited object. Thus a small benefit done to ourselves, or our near
friends, excites more lively sentiments of love and approbation than a great benefit done to a
distant commonwealth: But still we know here, as in all the senses, to correct these inequalities
by reflection, and retain a general standard of vice and virtue, founded chiefly on general
usefulness.

5. Why Utility Pleases

proportion as the humanity of the person is supposed to encrease, his connexion with those who are injured or benefited, and his lively conception of their misery or happiness; his consequent censure or approbation acquires proportionable vigour.[†] There is no necessity, that a generous action, barely mentioned in an old history or remote gazette,[†] should communicate any strong feelings of applause and admiration. Virtue, placed at such a distance, is like a fixed star,[†] which, though to the eye of reason, it may appear as luminous as the sun in his meridian,[†] is so infinitely removed, as to affect the senses, neither with light nor heat. Bring this virtue nearer, by our acquaintance or connexion with the persons, or even by an eloquent recital of the case; our hearts are immediately caught, our sympathy enlivened, and our cool approbation converted into the warmest sentiments of friendship and regard. These seem necessary and infallible consequences of the general principles of human nature, as discovered in common life and practice.

Again; reverse these views and reasonings: Consider the matter *a posteriori*; and weighing the consequences, enquire if the merit of social virtue be not, in a great measure, derived from the feelings of humanity, with which it affects the spectators. It appears to be matter of fact, that the circumstance of *utility*, in all subjects, is a source of praise and approbation: That it is constantly appealed to in all moral decisions concerning the merit and demerit of actions: That it is the *sole* source of that high regard paid to justice, fidelity, honour, allegiance, and chastity: That it is inseparable from[†] all the other social virtues, humanity, generosity, charity, affability, lenity, mercy, and moderation: And, in a word, that it is a foundation of the chief part of morals, which has a reference to mankind and our fellow-creatures.

It appears also, that, in our general approbation of characters and manners, the useful tendency of the social virtues moves us not by any regards to self-interest, but has an influence much more universal and extensive. It appears, that a tendency to public good, and to the promoting of peace, harmony, and order in society, does always, by affecting the benevolent principles of our frame, engage us on the side of the social virtues. And it appears, as an additional confirmation, that these principles of humanity and sympathy enter so deeply into all our sentiments, and have so powerful an influence, as may enable them to excite the strongest censure and applause. The present theory is the simple result of all these inferences, each of which seems founded on uniform experience and observation.

Were it doubtful, whether there were any such principle in our nature as

SBN 231

117

humanity or a concern for others, yet when we see, in numberless instances, that whatever has a tendency to promote the interests of society, is so highly approved of, we ought thence to learn the force of the benevolent principle; since it is impossible for any thing to please as means to an end, where the end is totally indifferent.[†] On the other hand, were it doubtful, whether there were, implanted in our nature, any general principle of moral blame and approbation, yet when we see, in numberless instances, the influence of humanity, we ought thence to conclude, that it is impossible, but that every thing, which promotes the interest of society, must communicate pleasure, and what is pernicious give uneasiness. But when these different reflections and observations concur in establishing the same conclusion,[†] must they not bestow an undisputed evidence upon it?

47   It is however hoped, that the progress of this argument will bring a farther confirmation of the present theory, by showing the rise of other sentiments of esteem and regard from the same or like principles.

SBN 2

SECTION 6

OF QUALITIES USEFUL TO OURSELVES

PART 1

1 IT seems evident, that where a quality or habit is subjected to our examination, if it appear, in any respect, prejudicial to the person possessed of it,
or such as incapacitates him for business and action, it is instantly blamed,
and ranked among his faults and imperfections. Indolence, negligence,
want of order and method, obstinacy, fickleness, rashness, credulity; these
qualities were never esteemed by any one indifferent to a character; much
less, extolled as accomplishments or virtues. The prejudice, resulting from
them, immediately strikes our eye, and gives us the sentiment of pain and
disapprobation.

2 No quality, it is allowed, is absolutely either blameable or praise-worthy.
It is all according to its degree. A due medium, say the PERIPATETICS,[†] is the
characteristic of virtue. But this medium is chiefly determined by utility. A
proper celerity, for instance, and dispatch[†] in business, is commendable.
When defective, no progress is ever made in the execution of any purpose:
When excessive, it engages us in precipitate and ill-concerted measures
and enterprizes: By such reasonings, we fix the proper and commendable
mediocrity in all moral and prudential disquisitions; and never lose view of
the advantages, which result from any character or habit.

3 Now as these advantages are enjoyed by the person possessed of the
character, it can never be *self-love* which renders the prospect of them
agreeable to us, the spectators, and prompts our esteem and approbation.
No force of imagination can convert us into another person, and make us
fancy, that we, being that person, reap benefit from those valuable qualities, which belong to him. Or if it did, no celerity of imagination could
immediately transport us back, into ourselves, and make us love and
esteem the person, as different from us. Views and sentiments, so opposite
to known truth, and to each other, could never have place, at the same

time, in the same person. All suspicion, therefore, of selfish regards, is here totally excluded. It is a quite different principle, which actuates our bosom, and interests us in the felicity of the person whom we contemplate. Where his natural talents and acquired abilities give us the prospect of elevation, advancement, a figure in life, prosperous success, a steady command over fortune, and the execution of great or advantageous undertakings; we are struck with such agreeable images, and feel a complacency and regard immediately arise towards him. The ideas of happiness, joy, triumph, prosperity, are connected with every circumstance of his character, and diffuse over our minds a pleasing sentiment of sympathy and humanity.[26]

4   Let us suppose a person originally framed† so as to have no manner of   SBN 2
concern for his fellow-creatures, but to regard the happiness and misery of all sensible beings with greater indifference than even two contiguous shades of the same colour. Let us suppose, if the prosperity of nations were laid on the one hand, and their ruin on the other, and he were desired to choose; that he would stand, like the schoolman's ass,† irresolute and undetermined, between equal motives; or rather, like the same ass between two pieces of wood or marble, without any inclination or propensity to either side. The consequence, I believe, must be allowed just, that such a person, being absolutely unconcerned, either for the public good of a community or the private utility of others, would look on every quality, however pernicious, or however beneficial, to society, or to its possessor, with the same indifference as on the most common and uninteresting object.

5   But if, instead of this fancied monster, we suppose a *man* to form a judgment or determination in the case, there is to him a plain foundation of preference, where every thing else is equal; and however cool his choice may be, if his heart be selfish, or if the persons interested be remote from him; there must still be a choice or distinction between what is useful, and

---

[26] One may venture to affirm, that there is no human creature, to whom the appearance of   SBN 2
happiness (where envy or revenge has no place) does not give pleasure, that of misery, uneasiness. This seems inseparable from our make and constitution. But they are only the more generous minds, that are thence prompted to seek zealously the good of others, and to have a real passion for their welfare. With men of narrow and ungenerous spirits, this sympathy goes not beyond a slight feeling of the imagination, which serves only to excite sentiments of complacency or censure, and makes them apply to the object either honourable or dishonourable appellations. A griping miser, for instance, praises extremely *industry* and *frugality* even in others, and sets them, in his estimation, above all the other virtues. He knows the good that results from them, and feels that species of happiness with a more lively sympathy, than any   SBN 2
other you could represent to him; though perhaps he would not part with a shilling to make the fortune of the industrious man, whom he praises so highly.

6. Of Qualities Useful to Ourselves

what is pernicious. Now this distinction is the same in all its parts, with the *moral distinction*, whose foundation has been so often, and so much in vain, enquired after. The same endowments of the mind, in every circumstance, are agreeable to the sentiment of morals and to that of humanity; the same temper is susceptible of high degrees of the one sentiment and of the other; and the same alteration in the objects, by their nearer approach or by connexions, enlivens the one and the other. By all the rules of philosophy,[†] therefore, we must conclude, that these sentiments are originally the same; since, in each particular, even the most minute, they are governed by the same laws, and are moved by the same objects.

6   Why do philosophers infer, with the greatest certainty, that the moon is kept in its orbit by the same force of gravity, that makes bodies fall near the surface of the earth, but because these effects are, upon computation, found similar and equal? And must not this argument bring as strong conviction, in moral as in natural disquisitions?[†]

7   To prove, by any long detail, that all the qualities, useful to the possessor, are approved of, and the contrary censured, would be superfluous. The least reflection on what is every day experienced in life, will be sufficient. We shall only mention a few instances, in order to remove, if possible, all doubt and hesitation.

8   The quality, the most necessary for the execution of any useful enterprize, is DISCRETION; by which we carry on a safe intercourse with others, give due attention to our own and to their character, weigh each circumstance of the business which we undertake, and employ the surest and safest means for the attainment of any end or purpose. To a CROMWELL,[†] perhaps, or a DE RETZ,[†] discretion may appear an alderman-like virtue, as Dr. SWIFT[†] calls it; and being incompatible with those vast designs, to which their courage and ambition prompted them, it might really, in them, be a fault or imperfection. But in the conduct of ordinary life, no virtue is more requisite, not only to obtain success, but to avoid the most fatal miscarriages and disappointments. The greatest parts without it, as observed by an elegant writer, may be fatal to their owner; as POLYPHEMUS,[†] deprived of his eye, was only the more exposed, on account of his enormous strength and stature.

9   The best character, indeed, were it not rather too perfect for human nature, is that which is not swayed by temper of any kind; but alternately employs enterprize and caution, as each is *useful* to the particular purpose intended. Such is the excellence which St. EVREMOND ascribes to mareschal TURENNE,[†] who displayed every campaign, as he grew older, more temerity in his military enterprizes; and being now, from long experience,

SBN 236

SBN 237

perfectly acquainted with every incident in war, he advanced with greater firmness and security, in a road so well known to him. FABIUS, says MACHIAVEL, was cautious; SCIPIO[†] enterprizing: And both succeeded, because the situation of the ROMAN affairs, during the command of each, was peculiarly adapted to his genius; but both would have failed, had these situations been reversed. He is happy, whose circumstances suit his temper; but he is more excellent, who can suit his temper to any circumstances.

10   What need is there to display the praises of INDUSTRY, and to extol its advantages, in the acquisition of power and riches, or in raising what we call a *fortune* in the world? The tortoise, according to the fable, by his perseverance, gained the race[†] of the hare, though possessed of much superior swiftness. A man's time, when well husbanded, is like a cultivated field, of which a few acres produce more of what is useful to life, than extensive provinces, even of the richest soil, when over-run with weeds and brambles.

11   But all prospect of success in life, or even of tolerable subsistence, must fail, where a reasonable FRUGALITY is wanting. The heap, instead of encreasing, diminishes daily, and leaves its possessor so much more unhappy, as, not having been able to confine his expences to a large revenue, he will still less be able to live contentedly on a small one. The SBN 2 souls of men, according to PLATO,[27†] enflamed with impure appetites, and losing the body, which alone afforded means of satisfaction, hover about the earth, and haunt the places, where their bodies are deposited; possessed with a longing desire to recover the lost organs of sensation.[†] So may we see worthless prodigals,[†] having consumed their fortune in wild debauches, thrusting themselves into every plentiful table, and every party of pleasure, hated even by the vicious, and despised even by fools.

12   The one extreme of frugality is *avarice*,[†] which, as it both deprives a man of all use of his riches, and checks hospitality and every social enjoyment, is justly censured on a double account. *Prodigality*, the other extreme, is commonly more hurtful to a man himself; and each of these extremes is blamed above the other, according to the temper of the person who censures, and according to his greater or less sensibility to pleasure, either social or sensual.

13   QUALITIES often derive their merit from complicated sources. *Honesty*,

---

[27] Phædo. [Plato, *Phaedo*, 80 c–81 E.]

6. *Of Qualities Useful to Ourselves*

fidelity, truth, are praised for their immediate tendency to promote the interests of society; but after those virtues are once established upon this foundation, they are also considered as advantageous to the person himself, and as the source of that trust and confidence, which can alone give a man any consideration in life. One becomes contemptible, no less than odious, when he forgets the duty, which, in this particular, he owes to himself as well as to society.

14   Perhaps, this consideration is one *chief* source of the high blame, which is thrown on any instance of failure among women in point of *chastity.*[†] The greatest regard, which can be acquired by that sex, is derived from their fidelity; and a woman becomes cheap and vulgar, loses her rank, and is exposed to every insult, who is deficient in this particular. The smallest failure is here sufficient to blast her character. A female has so many opportunities of secretly indulging these appetites, that nothing can give us security but her absolute modesty and reserve; and where a breach is once made, it can scarcely ever be fully repaired. If a man behave with cowardice on one occasion, a contrary conduct reinstates him in his character. But by what action can a woman, whose behaviour has once been dissolute, be able to assure us, that she has formed better resolutions, and has self-command enough to carry them into execution?

SBN 239

15   All men, it is allowed, are equally desirous of happiness; but few are successful in the pursuit: One considerable cause is the want of STRENGTH of MIND, which might enable them to resist the temptation of present ease or pleasure, and carry them forward in the search of more distant profit[†] and enjoyment. Our affections, on a general prospect of their objects, form certain rules of conduct, and certain measures of preference of one above another: And these decisions, though really the result of our calm passions[†] and propensities, (for what else can pronounce any object eligible or the contrary?) are yet said, by a natural abuse of terms, to be the determinations of pure *reason*[†] and reflection. But when some of these objects approach nearer[†] to us, or acquire the advantages of favourable lights and positions, which catch the heart or imagination; our general resolutions are frequently confounded, a small enjoyment preferred, and lasting shame and sorrow entailed[†] upon us. And however poets may employ their wit and eloquence, in celebrating present pleasure, and rejecting all distant views to fame, health, or fortune; it is obvious, that this practice is the source of all dissoluteness and disorder, repentance and misery. A man of a strong and determined temper adheres tenaciously to his general resolutions, and is neither seduced by the allurements of pleasure, nor

terrified by the menaces of pain; but keeps still in view those distant pursuits, by which he, at once, ensures his happiness and his honour.

16   Self-satisfaction, at least in some degree, is an advantage, which equally
attends the FOOL and the WISE MAN: But it is the only one; nor is there any
other circumstance in the conduct of life, where they are upon an equal
footing. Business, books, conversation; for all of these, a fool is totally incapacitated, and except condemned by his station to the coarsest drudgery,
remains a *useless* burden upon the earth. Accordingly, it is found, that men
are extremely jealous of their character in this particular; and many
instances are seen of profligacy and treachery, the most avowed and unreserved; none of bearing patiently the imputation of ignorance and stupidity. DICÆARCHUS, the MACEDONIAN general, who, as POLYBIUS[†] tells us,[28]
openly erected one altar to impiety, another to injustice, in order to bid
defiance to mankind; even he, I am well assured, would have started[†] at the
epithet of *fool*, and have meditated revenge for so injurious an appellation.
Except the affection of parents, the strongest and most indissoluble bond
in nature, no connexion has strength sufficient to support the disgust
arising from this character. Love itself, which can subsist under treachery,
ingratitude, malice, and infidelity, is immediately extinguished by it, when
perceived and acknowledged; nor are deformity and old age more fatal to
the dominion of that passion. So dreadful are the ideas of an utter inca-
pacity for any purpose or undertaking, and of continued error and mis-
conduct in life!

17   When it is asked, *Whether a quick or a slow apprehension be most valuable?*
Whether one, that, at first view, penetrates far into a subject, but can perform
nothing upon study;[†] *or a contrary character, which must work out every thing by*
dint of application?[†] *Whether a clear head or a copious invention? Whether a pro-*
found genius or a sure judgment? In short, what character, or peculiar turn of
understanding is more excellent than another? It is evident, that we can
answer none of these questions, without considering which of those qualities capacitates a man best for the world, and carries him farthest in any
undertaking.

18   If refined sense and exalted sense[†] be not so *useful* as common sense,
their rarity, their novelty, and the nobleness of their objects make some
compensation, and render them the admiration of mankind: As gold,
though less serviceable than iron, acquires, from its scarcity, a value, which
is much superior.

---

[28] Lib. 17. cap. 35. [Polybius, *Histories*, bk. 18 (17 in older editions), ch. 54 (35 in older
editions), §§ 6–10.]

6. Of Qualities Useful to Ourselves

19   The defects of judgment can be supplied by no art or invention; but those of MEMORY frequently may, both in business and in study, by method and industry, and by diligence in committing every thing to writing; and we scarcely ever hear a short memory given as a reason for a man's failure in any undertaking. But in ancient times, when no man could make a figure[†] without the talent of speaking, and when the audience were too delicate to bear such crude, undigested harangues as our extemporary orators offer to public assemblies; the faculty of memory was then of the utmost consequence, and was accordingly much more valued than at present. Scarce any great genius is mentioned in antiquity, who is not celebrated for this talent; and CICERO enumerates it among the other sublime qualities of CÆSAR[†] himself.[29]

20   Particular customs and manners alter the usefulness of qualities: They also alter their merit. Particular situations and accidents have, in some degree, the same influence. He will always be more esteemed, who possesses those talents and accomplishments, which suit his station and profession, than he whom fortune has misplaced in the part which she has assigned him. The private or selfish virtues[†] are, in this respect, more arbitrary than the public and social. In other respects, they are, perhaps, less liable to doubt and controversy.

SBN 242

21   In this kingdom, such continued ostentation, of late years, has prevailed among men in *active* life with regard to *public spirit*, and among those in *speculative* with regard to *benevolence*;[†] and so many false pretensions to each have been, no doubt, detected, that men of the world are apt, without any bad intention, to discover a sullen incredulity on the head of[†] those moral endowments, and even sometimes absolutely to deny their existence and reality. In like manner, I find, that, of old, the perpetual cant[†] of the STOICS and CYNICS concerning *virtue*, their magnificent professions and slender performances, bred a disgust in mankind; and LUCIAN,[†] who, though licentious with regard to pleasure, is yet, in other respects, a very moral writer, cannot, sometimes, talk of virtue, so much boasted, without betraying symptoms of spleen and irony.[30] But surely this peevish delicacy, whence-ever it arises, can never be carried so far as to make us deny the

---

[29] "Fuit in illo ingenium, ratio, memoria, literæ, cura, cogitatio, diligentia," &c. PHILIP. 2. [Cicero, *Philippics* 2, ch. 45, § 116.]

[30] Ἀρετήν τινα καὶ ἀσώματα καὶ λήρους μεγάλῃ τῇ φωνῇ ξυνειρόντων. LUCIAN. TIMON. Again, Καὶ συνάγοντες (οἱ φιλόσοφοι) εὐεξαπάτητα μειράκια τήν τε πολυθρύλλητον ἀρετὴν τραγῳδοῦσι. IСURO-MEN. In another place, Ἡ ποῦ γάρ ἐστιν ἡ πολυθρύλλητος ἀρετή, καὶ φύσις, καὶ εἱμαρμένη, καὶ τύχη, ἀνυπόστατα καὶ κενὰ πραγμάτων ὀνόματα. Deor. concil. [Lucian, *Timon; or, The Misanthrope*, § 9; *Icaromenippus; or, The Sky Man*, § 30; *The Parliament of the Gods*, § 13.]

Enquiry concerning the Principles of Morals

existence of every species of merit, and all distinction of manners and behaviour. Besides *discretion, caution, enterprize, industry, assiduity, frugality, œconomy, good sense, prudence, discernment*; besides these endowments, I say, whose very names force an avowal of their merit, there are many others, to which the most determined scepticism cannot, for a moment, refuse the tribute of praise and approbation. *Temperance, sobriety, patience, constancy, perseverance, forethought, considerateness, secrecy, order, insinuation, address, presence of mind, quickness of conception, facility of expression;* these, and a thousand more of the same kind, no man will ever deny to be excellencies and perfections. As their merit consists in their tendency to serve the person, possessed of them, without any magnificent claim to public and social desert, we are the less jealous of their pretensions, and readily admit them into the catalogue of laudable qualities. We are not sensible, that, by this concession, we have paved the way for all the other moral excellencies, and cannot consistently hesitate any longer, with regard to disinterested benevolence, patriotism, and humanity.

SBN 24

22   It seems, indeed, certain, that first appearances are here, as usual, extremely deceitful, and that it is more difficult, in a speculative way, to resolve into self-love the merit, which we ascribe to the selfish virtues[†] above-mentioned, than that even of the social virtues, justice and beneficence. For this latter purpose, we need but say, that whatever conduct promotes the good of the community is loved, praised, and esteemed by the community, on account of that utility and interest, of which every one partakes: And though this affection and regard be, in reality, gratitude, not self-love, yet a distinction, even of this obvious nature, may not readily be made by superficial reasoners; and there is room, at least, to support the cavil and dispute for a moment. But as qualities, which tend only to the utility of their possessor, without any reference to us, or to the community, are yet esteemed and valued; by what theory or system can we account for this sentiment from self-love, or deduce it from that favourite origin? There seems here a necessity for confessing that the happiness and misery of others are not spectacles entirely indifferent to us; but that the view of the former, whether in its causes or effects, like sun-shine or the prospect of well-cultivated plains, (to carry our pretensions no higher) communicates a secret joy and satisfaction; the appearance of the latter, like a lowering cloud or barren landscape, throws a melancholy damp over the imagination. And this concession being once made, the difficulty is over; and a natural, unforced interpretation of the phænomena of human life[†] will afterwards, we may hope, prevail among all speculative enquirers.

SBN 24

PART 2

23   It may not be improper, in this place, to examine the influence of bodily endowments, and of the goods of fortune,[†] over our sentiments of regard and esteem, and to consider whether these phænomena fortify or weaken the present theory. It will naturally be expected, that the beauty of the body, as is supposed by all ancient moralists, will be similar, in some respects, to that of the mind; and that every kind of esteem, which is paid to a man, will have something similar in its origin, whether it arise from his mental endowments, or from the situation of his exterior circumstances.

24   It is evident, that one considerable source of *beauty* in all animals is the advantage, which they reap from the particular structure of their limbs and members, suitably to the particular manner of life, to which they are by nature destined. The just proportions of a horse,[†] described by Xenophon and Virgil, are the same, that are received at this day by our modern jockeys;[†] because the foundation of them is the same, namely, experience of what is detrimental or useful in the animal.

25   Broad shoulders, a lank belly, firm joints, taper legs; all these are beautiful in our species, because signs of force and vigour. Ideas of utility and its contrary, though they do not entirely determine what is handsome or deformed, are evidently the source of a considerable part of approbation or dislike.   SBN 245

26   In ancient times, bodily strength and dexterity, being of greater *use* and importance in war, was also much more esteemed and valued, than at present. Not to insist on Homer and the poets, we may observe, that historians scruple not to mention *force of body* among the other accomplishments even of Epaminondas, whom they acknowledge to be the greatest hero, statesman, and general of all the Greeks.[31] A like praise is given to Pompey,[†] one of the greatest of the Romans.[32] This instance is similar to what we observed above, with regard to memory.

27   What derision and contempt, with both sexes, attend *impotence*; while

---

[31] Diodorus Siculus, lib. 15. [Diodorus Siculus, *Historical Library*, bk. 15, ch. 88, §§ 3–4.] It may not be improper to give the character of Epaminondas, as drawn by the historian, in order to show the ideas of perfect merit, which prevailed in those ages. In other illustrious men, says he, you will observe, that each possessed some one shining quality, which was the foundation of his fame: In Epaminondas all the *virtues* are found united; force of body, eloquence of expression, vigour of mind, contempt of riches, gentleness of disposition, and *what is chiefly to be regarded*, courage and conduct in war.

[32] "Cum alacribus, saltu; cum velocibus, cursu; cum validis recte certabat." Sallust. apud Veget.[†] [Vegetius, *De re militari*, bk. 1, ch. 9, lines 14–15 (quoting Sallust).]

nat'l respect for , rich & powrful
(∴ Ns)

the unhappy object is regarded as one deprived of so capital a pleasure in life, and at the same time, as disabled from communicating it to others. *Barrenness* in women, being also a species of *inutility*, is a reproach, but not in the same degree: Of which the reason is very obvious, according to the present theory.

28 There is no rule in painting or statuary more indispensible than that of balancing the figures, and placing them with the greatest exactness on their proper center of gravity. A figure, which is not justly balanced, is ugly; because it conveys the disagreeable ideas of fall, harm, and pain.[33]

29 A disposition or turn of mind, which qualifies a man to rise in the world, and advance his fortune, is entitled to esteem and regard, as has already been explained. It may, therefore, naturally be supposed, that the actual possession of riches and authority will have a considerable influence over these sentiments.

30 Let us examine any hypothesis, by which we can account for the regard paid to the rich and powerful: We shall find none satisfactory, but that which derives it from the enjoyment communicated to the spectator by the images of prosperity, happiness, ease, plenty, authority, and the gratification of every appetite. Self-love, for instance, which some affect so much to consider as the source of every sentiment, is plainly insufficient for this purpose. Where no good-will or friendship appears, it is difficult to conceive on what we can found our hope of advantage from the riches of others; though we naturally respect the rich, even before they discover any such favourable disposition towards us.

31 We are affected with the same sentiments, when we lie so much out of the sphere of their activity, that they cannot even be supposed to possess the power of serving us. A prisoner of war, in all civilized nations, is treated with a regard suited to his condition; and riches, it is evident, go far towards fixing the condition of any person. If birth and quality enter for a share, this still affords us an argument to our present purpose. For what is it we call a man of birth, but one who is descended from a long succession

[33] All men are equally liable to pain and disease and sickness; and may again recover health and ease. These circumstances, as they make no distinction between one man and another, are no source of pride or humility, regard or contempt. But comparing our own species to superior ones, it is a very mortifying consideration, that we should all be so liable to diseases and infirmities; and divines accordingly employ this topic, in order to depress self-conceit and vanity. They would have more success, if the common bent of our thoughts were not perpetually turned to compare ourselves with others. The infirmities of old age are mortifying; because a comparison with the young may take place. The king's evil[†] is industriously concealed, because it affects others, and is often transmitted to posterity. The case is nearly the same with such diseases as convey any nauseous or frightful images; the epilepsy, for instance, ulcers, sores, scabs, &c.

of rich and powerful ancestors, and who acquires our esteem by his connexion with persons whom we esteem? His ancestors, therefore, though dead, are respected, in some measure, on account of their riches; and consequently, without any kind of expectation.

32   But not to go so far as prisoners of war or the dead, to find instances of this disinterested regard for riches; we may only observe, with a little attention, those phænomena, which occur in common life and conversation. A man, who is himself, we shall suppose, of a competent fortune, and of no profession, being introduced to a company of strangers, naturally treats them with different degrees of respect, as he is informed of their different fortunes and conditions; though it is impossible that he can so suddenly propose, and perhaps he would not accept of,[†] any pecuniary advantage from them. A traveller is always admitted into company, and meets with civility, in proportion as his train and equipage speak him a man of great or moderate fortune. In short, the different ranks of men are, in a great measure, regulated by riches; and that with regard to superiors as well as inferiors, strangers as well as acquaintance.

33   What remains, therefore, but to conclude, that, as riches are desired for ourselves only as the means of gratifying our appetites, either at present or in some imaginary future period; they beget esteem in others merely from their having that influence? This indeed is their very nature or essence: They have a direct reference to the commodities, conveniencies, and pleasures of life: The bill of a banker, who is broke, or gold in a desert island, would otherwise be full as valuable. When we approach a man, who is, as we say, at his ease, we are presented with the pleasing ideas of plenty, satisfaction, cleanliness, warmth; a cheerful house, elegant furniture, ready service, and whatever is desirable in meat, drink, or apparel. On the contrary, when a poor man appears, the disagreeable images of want, penury, hard labour, dirty furniture, coarse or ragged cloaths, nauseous meat and distasteful liquor, immediately strike our fancy. What else do we mean by saying that one is rich, the other poor? And as regard or contempt is the natural consequence of those different situations in life; it is easily seen what additional light and evidence this throws on our preceding theory, with regard to all moral distinctions.[34]

SBN 248

---

[34] There is something extraordinary, and seemingly unaccountable in the operation of our passions, when we consider the fortune and situation of others. Very often another's advancement and prosperity produces envy, which has a strong mixture of hatred, and arises chiefly from the comparison of ourselves with the person. At the very same time, or at least, in very short intervals, we may feel the passion of respect, which is a species of affection or good-will, with a mixture of humility. On the other hand, the misfortunes of our fellows often cause pity, which has in it a strong mixture of good-will. This sentiment of pity is nearly allied to

34   A man, who has cured himself of all ridiculous prepossessions, and is fully, sincerely, and steadily convinced, from experience as well as philosophy, that the difference of fortune makes less difference in happiness than is vulgarly imagined; such a one does not measure out degrees of esteem according to the rent-rolls of his acquaintance. He may, indeed, externally pay a superior deference to the great lord above the vassal; because riches are the most convenient, being the most fixed and determinate, source of distinction: But his internal sentiments are more regulated by the personal characters of men, than by the accidental and capricious favours of fortune.[†]

35   In most countries of EUROPE, family, that is, hereditary riches, marked with titles and symbols from the sovereign, is the chief source of distinction. In ENGLAND, more regard is paid to present opulence and plenty. Each SBN 249 practice has its advantages and disadvantages. Where birth is respected, unactive, spiritless minds remain in haughty indolence, and dream of nothing but pedigrees and genealogies: The generous and ambitious seek honour and authority and reputation and favour. Where riches are the chief idol, corruption, venality, rapine prevail: Arts, manufactures, commerce, agriculture flourish. The former prejudice, being favourable to military virtue, is more suited to monarchies. The latter, being the chief spur to industry, agrees better with a republican government.[†] And we accordingly find, that each of these forms of government, by varying the *utility* of those customs, has commonly a proportionable effect on the sentiments of mankind.

---

contempt, which is a species of dislike, with a mixture of pride. I only point out these phænom- SBN 246 ena, as a subject of speculation to such as are curious with regard to moral enquiries. It is sufficient for the present purpose to observe in general, that power and riches commonly cause respect, poverty and meanness contempt, though particular views and incidents may sometimes raise the passions of envy and of pity.[†]

SECTION 7

OF QUALITIES IMMEDIATELY AGREEABLE TO OURSELVES

1 WHOEVER has passed an evening with serious melancholy people, and has observed how suddenly the conversation was animated, and what sprightliness diffused itself over the countenance, discourse, and behaviour of every one, on the accession of a good-humoured, lively companion; such a one will easily allow, that CHEERFULNESS carries great merit with it, and naturally conciliates the good-will of mankind. No quality, indeed, more readily communicates itself to all around; because no one has a greater propensity to display itself, in jovial talk and pleasant entertainment. The flame spreads through the whole circle; and the most sullen and morose are often caught by it. That the melancholy hate the merry, even though HORACE[†] says it, I have some difficulty to allow; because I have always observed, that, where the jollity is moderate and decent,[†] serious people are so much the more delighted, as it dissipates the gloom, with which they are commonly oppressed; and gives them an unusual enjoyment.

2 From this influence of cheerfulness, both to communicate itself, and to engage approbation, we may perceive, that there is another set of mental qualities, which, without any utility or any tendency to farther good, either of the community or of the possessor, diffuse a satisfaction on the beholders, and procure friendship and regard. Their immediate sensation, SBN 251 to the person possessed of them, is agreeable: Others enter into the same humour, and catch the sentiment, by a contagion or natural sympathy: And as we cannot forbear loving whatever pleases, a kindly emotion arises towards the person, who communicates so much satisfaction. He is a more animating spectacle: His presence diffuses over us more serene complacency and enjoyment: Our imagination, entering into his feelings and disposition, is affected in a more agreeable manner, than if a melancholy, dejected, sullen, anxious temper were presented to us. Hence the affection

Enquiry concerning the Principles of Morals

and approbation, which attend the former: The aversion and disgust, with which we regard the latter.[35]

3   Few men would envy the character, which CÆSAR gives of CASSIUS.[†]

> He loves no play,
> As thou do'st, ANTHONY: He hears no music:
> Seldom he smiles; and smiles in such a sort,
> As if he mock'd himself, and scorn'd his spirit
> That could be mov'd to smile at any thing.

Not only such men, as CÆSAR adds, are commonly *dangerous*, but also, having little enjoyment within themselves, they can never become agreeable to others, or contribute to social entertainment. In all polite nations and ages,[†] a relish for pleasure, if accompanied with temperance and decency, is esteemed a considerable merit, even in the greatest men; and becomes still more requisite in those of inferior rank and character. It is an agreeable representation, which a FRENCH writer[†] gives of the situation of his own mind in this particular, "Virtue I love," says he, "without austerity: Pleasure, without effeminacy: And life, without fearing its end."[36]   SBN 25

4   Who is not struck with any signal instance of GREATNESS of MIND[†] or Dignity of Character; with elevation of sentiment, disdain of slavery, and with that noble pride and spirit, which arises from conscious virtue? The sublime, says LONGINUS,[†] is often nothing but the echo or image of magnanimity; and where this quality appears in any one, even though a syllable be not uttered, it excites our applause and admiration; as may be observed of the famous silence of AJAX[†] in the ODYSSEY, which expresses more noble disdain and resolute indignation, than any language can convey.[37]

5   "Were I ALEXANDER," said PARMENIO, "I would accept of these offers made by DARIUS." "So would I too," replied ALEXANDER, "were I PARMENIO."[†] This saying is admirable, says LONGINUS, from a like principle.[38†]

---

[35] There is no man, who, on particular occasions, is not affected with all the disagreeable passions, fear, anger, dejection, grief, melancholy, anxiety, &c. But these, so far as they are natural, and universal, make no difference between one man and another, and can never be the object of blame. It is only when the disposition gives a *propensity* to any of these disagreeable passions, that they disfigure the character, and by giving uneasiness, convey the sentiment of disapprobation to the spectator.   SBN 25

[36] "J'aime la vertu, sans rudesse;   SBN 25
J'aime le plaisir, sans molesse;
J'aime la vie, & n'en crains point la fin." ST. EVREMOND.

[Seigneur de Saint-Évremond, 'Lettre à M. le Comte Magalotti'.]
[37] Cap. 9. [Anon., *On the Sublime*, ch. 9, §§2–3.]   [38] Idem. [Ibid., § 4.]

7. Of Qualities Agreeable to Ourselves

6   "Go!" cries the same hero to his soldiers, when they refused to follow[†] him to the INDIES, "go tell your countrymen, that you left ALEXANDER compleating the conquest of the world." "ALEXANDER," said the Prince of CONDE,[†] who always admired this passage, "abandoned by his soldiers, among Barbarians, not yet fully subdued, felt in himself such a dignity and right of empire, that he could not believe it possible, that any one would refuse to obey him. Whether in EUROPE or in ASIA, among GREEKS or PERSIANS, all was indifferent to him: Wherever he found men, he fancied he should find subjects."

7   The confident of MEDEA in the tragedy recommends caution and submission; and enumerating all the distresses of that unfortunate heroine, asks her, what she has to support her against her numerous and implacable enemies. "Myself," replies she; "Myself, I say, and it is enough." BOILEAU   SBN 253 justly recommends this passage as an instance of true sublime.[39†]

8   When PHOCION, the modest, the gentle PHOCION, was led to execution, he turned to one of his fellow-sufferers, who was lamenting his own hard fate. "Is it not glory enough for you," says he, "that you die with PHOCION?"[40†]

9   Place in opposition the picture, which TACITUS draws of VITELLIUS,[†] fallen from empire, prolonging his ignominy from a wretched love of life, delivered over to the merciless rabble; tossed, buffeted, and kicked about; constrained, by their holding a poinard under his chin, to raise his head, and expose himself to every contumely. What abject infamy! What low humiliation! Yet even here, says the historian, he discovered some symptoms of a mind not wholly degenerate. To a tribune, who insulted him, he replied, "I am still your emperor."[41]

10   We never excuse the absolute want of spirit and dignity of character, or a proper sense of what is due to one's self, in society and the common intercourse of life. This vice constitutes what we properly call *meanness*; when a man can submit to the basest slavery, in order to gain his ends; fawn upon those who abuse him; and degrade himself by intimacies and familiarities with undeserving inferiors. A certain degree of generous pride[†] or

[39] Réflexion 10 sur LONGIN. [Nicolas Boileau-Despréaux, *Réflexions critiques sur quelques passages de Longin*, Réflexion 10.]

[40] PLUTARCH. in PHOC. [Plutarch, *Lives*, 'Phocion', ch. 36, §§ 2–3, 758 D.]

[41] TACIT. hist. lib. 3. [Tacitus, *Histories*, bk. 3, chs. 84–5.] The author entering upon the narration, says, "*Laniata veste, fœdum spectaculum ducebatur, multis increpantibus, nullo inlacrimante: deformitas exitus misericordiam abstulerat.*" To enter thoroughly into this method of thinking, we must make allowance for the ancient maxims, that no one ought to prolong his life after it became dishonourable; but, as he had always a right to dispose of it, it then became a duty to part with it.

self-value is so requisite, that the absence of it in the mind displeases, after the same manner as the want of a nose, eye, or any of the most material features of the face or members of the body.[42]

11   The utility of COURAGE, both to the public and to the person possessed of it, is an obvious foundation of merit: But to any one who duly considers of the matter, it will appear, that this quality has a peculiar lustre, which it derives wholly from itself, and from that noble elevation inseparable from it. Its figure, drawn by painters and by poets, displays, in each feature, a sublimity and daring confidence; which catches the eye, engages the affections, and diffuses, by sympathy, a like sublimity of sentiment[†] over every spectator.

SBN 254

12   Under what shining colours does DEMOSTHENES[43] represent PHILIP;[†] where the orator apologizes for his own administration, and justifies that pertinacious love of liberty, with which he had inspired the ATHENIANS. "I beheld PHILIP," says he, "he with whom was your contest, resolutely, while in pursuit of empire and dominion, exposing himself to every wound; his eye goared, his neck wrested, his arm, his thigh pierced, whatever part of his body fortune should seize on, that cheerfully relinquishing; provided that, with what remained, he might live in honour and renown. And shall it be said, that he, born in PELLA,[†] a place heretofore mean and ignoble, should be inspired with so high an ambition and thirst of fame: While you, ATHENIANS, &c." These praises excite the most lively admiration; but the views presented by the orator, carry us not, we see, beyond the hero himself, nor ever regard the future advantageous consequences of his valour.

13   The martial temper of the ROMANS, enflamed by continual wars, had raised their esteem of courage so high, that, in their language, it was called *virtue*, by way of excellence and of distinction from all other moral qualities. "The SUEVI",[†] in the opinion of TACITUS,[44] "dressed their hair with a laudable intent: Not for the purpose of loving or being loved: They adorned themselves only for their enemies, and in order to appear more

SBN 255

---

[42] The absence of a virtue may often be a vice; and that of the highest kind; as in the instance of ingratitude, as well as meanness. Where we expect a beauty, the disappointment gives an uneasy sensation, and produces a real deformity. An abjectness of character, likewise, is disgustful and contemptible in another view. Where a man has no sense of value in himself, we are not likely to have any higher esteem of him. And if the same person, who crouches to his superiors, is insolent to his inferiors (as often happens), this contrariety of behaviour, instead of correcting the former vice, aggravates it extremely by the addition of a vice, still more odious. See Section 8.

SBN 253
SBN 254

[43] Pro corona. [Demosthenes, *On the Crown*, §§ 67–8.]

[44] De moribus GERM. [Tacitus, *Germania*, ch. 38.]

7. Of Qualities Agreeable to Ourselves

terrible." A sentiment of the historian, which would sound a little oddly in other nations and other ages.

14   The SCYTHIANS, according to HERODOTUS,[45†] after scalping their enemies, dressed the skin like leather, and used it as a towel; and whoever had the most of those towels was most esteemed among them. So much had martial bravery, in that nation, as well as in many others, destroyed the sentiments of humanity; a virtue surely much more useful and engaging.

15   It is indeed observable, that, among all uncultivated nations, who have not, as yet, had full experience of the advantages attending beneficence, justice, and the social virtues, courage[†] is the predominant excellence; what is most celebrated by poets, recommended by parents and instructors, and admired by the public in general. The ethics of HOMER[†] are, in this particular, very different from those of FENELON,[†] his elegant imitator; and such as were well suited to an age, when one hero, as remarked by THUCYDIDES,[46†] could ask another, without offence, whether he were a robber or not. Such also, very lately, was the system of ethics, which prevailed in many barbarous parts of IRELAND; if we may credit SPENCER,[†] in his judicious account of the state of that kingdom.[47]

if . .

16   Of the same class of virtues with courage is that undisturbed philosophical TRANQUILLITY, superior to pain, sorrow, anxiety, and each assault of adverse fortune. Conscious of his own virtue, say the philosophers, the sage elevates himself[†] above every accident of life; and securely placed in the temple of wisdom, looks down on inferior mortals, engaged in pursuit of honours, riches, reputation, and every frivolous enjoyment. These pretensions, no doubt, when stretched to the utmost, are, by far, too magnificent[†] for human nature. They carry, however, a grandeur with them, which seizes the spectator, and strikes him with admiration. And the nearer we can approach in practice, to this sublime tranquillity and indifference (for we must distinguish it from a stupid insensibility) the more secure enjoyment shall we attain within ourselves, and the more greatness of mind shall we discover to the world. The philosophical tranquillity may, indeed, be considered only as a branch of magnanimity.[†]

SBN 256

[45] Lib. 4. [Herodotus, *History*, bk. 4, ch. 46.]

SBN 255

[46] Lib. 1. [Thucydides, *History*, bk. 1, ch. 5, §§ 2–3.]

[47] "It is a common use", says he, "amongst their gentlemen's sons, that, as soon as they are able to use their weapons, they straight gather to themselves three or four stragglers or kern, with whom wandering a while up and down idly the country, taking only meat, he at last falleth into some bad occasion, that shall be offered; which being once made known, he is thenceforth counted a man of worth, in whom there is courage." [Edmund Spenser, *A View of the (Present) State of Ireland.*]

17 Who admires not SOCRATES; his perpetual serenity and contentment, amidst the greatest poverty and domestic vexations; his resolute contempt of riches, and his magnanimous care of preserving liberty, while he refused all assistance from his friends and disciples, and avoided even the dependence of an obligation? EPICTETUS[†] had not so much as a door to his little house or hovel; and therefore, soon lost his iron lamp, the only furniture which he had worth taking. But resolving to disappoint all robbers for the future, he supplied its place with an earthen lamp, of which he very peaceably kept possession ever after.

18 Among the ancients, the heroes in philosophy, as well as those in war and patriotism, have a grandeur and force of sentiment, which astonishes our narrow souls,[†] and is rashly rejected as extravagant and supernatural. They, in their turn, I allow, would have had equal reason to consider as romantic and incredible, the degree of humanity, clemency, order, tranquillity, and other social virtues, to which, in the administration of government, we have attained in modern times, had any one been then able to have made a fair representation of them. Such is the compensation, which nature, or rather education, has made in the distribution of excellencies and virtues, in these different ages.

SBN 25

19 The merit of BENEVOLENCE, arising from its utility, and its tendency to promote the good of mankind, has been already explained, and is, no doubt, the source of a *considerable* part of that esteem, which is so universally paid to it. But it will also be allowed, that the very softness and tenderness of the sentiment, its engaging endearments, its fond expressions, its delicate attentions, and all that flow of mutual confidence and regard, which enters into a warm attachment of love and friendship: It will be allowed, I say, that these feelings, being delightful in themselves,[†] are necessarily communicated to the spectators, and melt them into the same fondness and delicacy. The tear naturally starts in our eye on the apprehension of a warm sentiment of this nature: Our breast heaves, our heart is agitated, and every humane tender principle of our frame is set in motion, and gives us the purest and most satisfactory enjoyment.

20 When poets form descriptions of ELYSIAN fields,[†] where the blessed inhabitants stand in no need of each other's assistance, they yet represent them as maintaining a constant intercourse of love and friendship, and sooth our fancy with the pleasing image of these soft and gentle passions. The idea of tender tranquillity in a pastoral ARCADIA[†] is agreeable from a like principle, as has been observed above.[48]

[48] Section 5. Part 2.

7. Of Qualities Agreeable to Ourselves

21   Who would live amidst perpetual wrangling, and scolding, and mutual reproaches? The roughness and harshness of these emotions disturb and displease us: We suffer by contagion and sympathy; nor can we remain SBN 258 indifferent spectators, even though certain, that no pernicious consequences would ever follow from such angry passions.

22   As a certain proof, that the whole merit of benevolence is not derived from its usefulness, we may observe, that, in a kind way of blame, we say, a person is *too good*; when he exceeds his part in society, and carries his attention for others beyond the proper bounds. In like manner, we say a man is *too high-spirited, too intrepid, too indifferent about fortune*: Reproaches, which really, at bottom, imply more esteem than many panegyrics.[†] Being accustomed to rate the merit and demerit of characters chiefly by their useful or pernicious tendencies, we cannot forbear applying the epithet of blame,[†] when we discover a sentiment, which rises to a degree that is hurtful: But it may happen, at the same time, that its noble elevation, or its engaging tenderness so seizes the heart, as rather to encrease our friendship and concern for the person.[49]

23   The amours and attachments of HARRY the IVth of FRANCE, during the civil wars of the league,[†] frequently hurt his interest and his cause; but all the young, at least, and amorous, who can sympathize with the tender passions, will allow, that this very weakness (for they will readily call it such) chiefly endears that hero, and interests them in his fortunes.

24   The excessive bravery and resolute inflexibility of CHARLES the XIIth[†] ruined his own country, and infested all his neighbours; but have such splendour and greatness in their appearance, as strikes us with admiration; and they might, in some degree, be even approved of, if they betrayed not sometimes too evident symptoms of madness and disorder.

25   The ATHENIANS pretended to the first invention of agriculture and of SBN 259 laws; and always valued themselves extremely on the benefit thereby procured to the whole race of mankind. They also boasted, and with reason, of their warlike enterprizes; particularly against those innumerable fleets and armies of PERSIANS, which invaded GREECE during the reigns of DARIUS and XERXES.[†] But though there be no comparison, in point of utility, between these peaceful and military honours; yet we find, that the orators, who have writ such elaborate panegyrics on that famous city, have chiefly triumphed in displaying the warlike atchievements. LYSIAS, THUCYDIDES, PLATO, and ISOCRATES[†] discover, all of them, the same

---

[49] Cheerfulness could scarce admit of blame from its excess, were it not that dissolute mirth, without a proper cause or subject, is a sure symptom and characteristic of folly, and on that account disgustful.   SBN 258

partiality; which, though condemned by calm reason and reflection, appears so natural in the mind of man.

26   It is observable, that the great charm of poetry consists in lively pictures of the sublime passions, magnanimity, courage, disdain of fortune; or those of the tender affections, love and friendship; which warm the heart, and diffuse over it similar sentiments and emotions. And though all kinds of passion, even the most disagreeable, such as grief and anger, are observed, when excited by poetry, to convey a satisfaction,[†] from a mechanism of nature, not easy to be explained: Yet those more elevated or softer affections have a peculiar influence, and please from more than one cause or principle. Not to mention, that they alone interest us in the fortune of the persons represented, or communicate any esteem and affection for their character.

27   And can it possibly be doubted, that this talent itself of poets, to move the passions, this PATHETIC and SUBLIME[†] of sentiment, is a very considerable merit; and being enhanced by its extreme rarity, may exalt the person possessed of it, above every character of the age in which he lives? The prudence, address, steadiness, and benign government of AUGUSTUS, adorned with all the splendour of his noble birth and imperial crown, render him but an unequal competitor for fame with VIRGIL,[†] who lays nothing into the opposite scale but the divine beauties of his poetical genius.   SBN 260

28   The very sensibility to these beauties, or a DELICACY of taste,[†] is itself a beauty in any character; as conveying the purest, the most durable, and most innocent of all enjoyments.

29   These are some instances of the several species of merit, that are valued for the immediate pleasure, which they communicate to the person possessed of them. No views of utility or of future beneficial consequences enter into this sentiment of approbation; yet is it of a kind similar to that other sentiment, which arises from views of a public or private utility. The same social sympathy, we may observe, or fellow-feeling[†] with human happiness or misery, gives rise to both; and this analogy, in all the parts of the present theory, may justly be regarded as a confirmation of it.

SECTION 8

OF QUALITIES IMMEDIATELY AGREEABLE TO OTHERS[50]

1   As the mutual shocks, in *society*, and the oppositions of interest and self-love have constrained mankind to establish the laws of *justice*; in order to preserve the advantages of mutual assistance and protection: In like manner, the eternal contrarieties,[†] in *company*, of men's pride and self-conceit, have introduced the rules of GOOD MANNERS or POLITENESS;[†] in order to facilitate the intercourse of minds, and an undisturbed commerce and conversation. Among well-bred people, a mutual deference is affected: Contempt of others disguised: Authority concealed: Attention given to each in his turn: And an easy stream of conversation maintained, without vehemence, without interruption, without eagerness for victory, and without any airs of superiority. These attentions and regards are immediately *agreeable* to others, abstracted from any consideration of utility or beneficial tendencies: They conciliate affection, promote esteem, and extremely enhance the merit of the person, who regulates his behaviour by them.

2   Many of the forms of breeding are arbitrary and casual: But the thing expressed by them is still the same. A SPANIARD goes out of his own house before his guest, to signify that he leaves him master of all. In other countries, the landlord walks out last, as a common mark of deference and regard.

3   But, in order to render a man perfect *good company*, he must have WIT and INGENUITY as well as good manners. What wit is, it may not be easy to define;[†] but it is easy surely to determine, that it is a quality immediately *agreeable* to others, and communicating, on its first appearance, a lively

---

[50] It is the nature, and, indeed, the definition of virtue, that it is *a quality of the mind agreeable* *to or approved of by every one, who considers or contemplates it*. But some qualities produce pleasure, because they are useful to society, or useful or agreeable to the person himself; others produce it more immediately: Which is the case with the class of virtues here considered.

joy and satisfaction to every one who has any comprehension of it. The most profound metaphysics, indeed, might be employed, in explaining the various kinds and species of wit; and many classes of it, which are now received on the sole testimony of taste and sentiment, might, perhaps, be resolved into more general principles. But this is sufficient for our present purpose, that it does affect taste and sentiment, and bestowing an immediate enjoyment, is a sure source of approbation and affection.

4   In countries, where men pass most of their time in conversation, and visits, and assemblies, these *companionable* qualities, so to speak, are of high estimation, and form a chief part of personal merit. In countries, where men live a more domestic life, and either are employed in business, or amuse themselves in a narrower circle of acquaintance, the more solid qualities† are chiefly regarded. Thus, I have often observed, that, among the FRENCH, the first questions, with regard to a stranger, are, *Is he polite? Has he wit?* In our own country, the chief praise bestowed, is always that of a *good-natured, sensible fellow.*

5   In conversation, the lively spirit of dialogue is *agreeable*, even to those who desire not to have any share in the discourse: Hence the teller of long stories, or the pompous declaimer, is very little approved of. But most men desire likewise their turn in the conversation, and regard, with a very evil eye,† that *loquacity*, which deprives them of a right they are naturally so jealous of.   SBN 26:

6   There is a sort of harmless *liars*, frequently to be met with in company, who deal much in the marvellous. Their usual intention is to please and entertain; but as men are most delighted with what they conceive to be truth, these people mistake extremely the means of pleasing, and incur universal blame. Some indulgence, however, to lying or fiction is given in *humorous* stories; because it is there really agreeable and entertaining; and truth is not of any importance.

7   Eloquence, genius of all kinds, even good sense, and sound reasoning, when it rises to an eminent degree, and is employed upon subjects of any considerable dignity and nice discernment;† all these endowments seem immediately agreeable, and have a merit distinct from their usefulness. Rarity, likewise, which so much enhances the price of every thing, must set an additional value on these noble talents of the human mind.

8   Modesty may be understood in different senses, even abstracted from chastity,† which has been already treated of. It sometimes means that tenderness and nicety of honour, that apprehension of blame, that dread of

intrusion or injury towards others, that PUDOR,[†] which is the proper guardian of every kind of virtue, and a sure preservative against vice and corruption. But its most usual meaning is when it is opposed to *impudence* and *arrogance*, and expresses a diffidence of our own judgment, and a due attention and regard for others. In young men chiefly, this quality is a sure sign of good sense; and is also the certain means of augmenting that endowment, by preserving their ears open to instruction, and making them still grasp after new attainments. But it has a farther charm to every spectator; by flattering every man's vanity, and presenting the appearance of a docile pupil, who receives, with proper attention and respect, every word they utter.

SBN 264

9   Men have, in general, a much greater propensity to over-value than under-value themselves; notwithstanding the opinion of ARISTOTLE.[51†] This makes us more jealous of the excess on the former side, and causes us to regard, with a peculiar indulgence, all tendency to modesty and self-diffidence; as esteeming the danger less of falling into any vicious extreme of that nature. It is thus, in countries, where men's bodies are apt to exceed in corpulency, personal beauty is placed in a much greater degree of slenderness, than in countries, where that is the most usual defect. Being so often struck with instances of one species of deformity, men think they can never keep at too great a distance from it, and wish always to have a leaning to the opposite side. In like manner, were the door opened to self-praise, and were MONTAIGNE's maxim[†] observed, that one should say as frankly, *I have sense, I have learning, I have courage, beauty, or wit*; as it is sure we often think so; were this the case, I say, every one is sensible, that such a flood of impertinence would break in upon us, as would render society wholly intolerable. For this reason custom has established it as a rule, in common societies,[†] that men should not indulge themselves in self-praise, or even speak much of themselves; and it is only among intimate friends or people of very manly behaviour, that one is allowed to do himself justice. No body finds fault with MAURICE, Prince of ORANGE, for his reply to one, who asked him, whom he esteemed the first general of the age, "The marquis of SPINOLA",[†] said he, "is the second." Though it is observable, that the self-praise implied is here better implied, than if it had been directly expressed, without any cover or disguise.

10   He must be a very superficial thinker, who imagines, that all instances of mutual deference are to be understood in earnest, and that a man would

SBN 265

---

[51] Ethic. ad Nicomachum. [Aristotle, *Nicomachean Ethics*, bk. 4, ch. 3, esp. 1125ᵃ19–34.]   SBN 264

Enquiry concerning the Principles of Morals

be more esteemable for being ignorant of his own merits and accomplish-ments. A small biass towards modesty, even in the internal sentiment,[†] is favourably regarded, especially in young people; and a strong biass is required in the outward behaviour: But this excludes not a noble pride[†] and spirit, which may openly display itself in its full extent, when one lies under calumny or oppression of any kind. The generous contumacy of SOCRATES,[†] as CICERO calls it, has been highly celebrated in all ages; and when joined to the usual modesty of his behaviour, forms a shining char-acter. IPHICRATES,[†] the ATHENIAN, being accused of betraying the interests of his country, asked his accuser, "Would you," says he, "have, on a like occasion, been guilty of that crime?" "By no means," replied the other. "And can you then imagine," cried the hero, "that IPHICRATES would be guilty?"[52] In short, a generous spirit and self-value, well founded, decently disguised, and courageously supported under distress and calumny, is a great excellency, and seems to derive its merit from the noble elevation of its sentiment, or its immediate agreeableness to its possessor. In ordinary characters, we approve of a biass towards modesty, which is a quality immediately agreeable to others: The vicious excess of the former virtue, namely, insolence or haughtiness, is immediately disagreeable to others: The excess of the latter is so to the possessor. Thus are the boundaries of these duties adjusted.

11   A desire of fame, reputation, or a character with others, is so far from being blameable, that it seems inseparable from virtue, genius, capacity, and a generous or noble disposition. An attention even to trivial matters, in order to please, is also expected and demanded by society; and no one is surprized, if he find a man in company, to observe a greater elegance of dress and more pleasant flow of conversation, than when he passes his time at home, and with his own family. Wherein, then, consists VANITY, which is so justly regarded as a fault or imperfection? It seems to consist chiefly in such an intemperate display of our advantages, honours, and accomplishments; in such an importunate and open demand of praise and admiration, as is offensive to others, and encroaches too far on *their* secret vanity and ambition. It is besides a sure symptom of the want of true dignity and elevation of mind, which is so great an ornament in any char-acter. For why that impatient desire of applause; as if you were not justly entitled to it, and might not reasonably expect, that it would for ever attend you? Why so anxious to inform us of the great company which you have kept; the obliging things which were said to you; the honours, the dis-

SBN 266

---

[52] QUINTIL. lib. 5. cap. 12. [Quintilian, *Institutes*, bk. 5, ch. 12, §§9–11.]   SBN 26

tinctions which you met with; as if these were not things of course,[†] and what we could readily, of ourselves, have imagined, without being told of them?

12   DECENCY, or a proper regard to age, sex, character, and station in the world, may be ranked among the qualities, which are immediately agreeable to others, and which, by that means, acquire praise and approbation. An effeminate behaviour in a man, a rough manner in a woman; these are ugly, because unsuitable to each character, and different from the qualities which we expect in the sexes. It is as if a tragedy abounded in comic beauties, or a comedy in tragic. The disproportions hurt the eye, and convey a disagreeable sentiment to the spectators, the source of blame and disapprobation. This is that *indecorum*, which is explained so much at large by CICERO[†] in his Offices.

13   Among the other virtues, we may also give CLEANLINESS[†] a place; since it naturally renders us agreeable to others, and is no inconsiderable source of love and affection. No one will deny, that a negligence in this particular is a fault; and as faults are nothing but smaller vices,[†] and this fault can have no   SBN 267
other origin than the uneasy sensation, which it excites in others; we may, in this instance, seemingly so trivial, clearly discover the origin of moral distinctions, about which the learned have involved themselves in such mazes of perplexity and error.

14   But besides all the *agreeable* qualities, the origin of whose beauty, we can, in some degree, explain and account for, there still remains something mysterious and inexplicable, which conveys an immediate satisfaction to the spectator, but how, or why, or for what reason, he cannot pretend to determine. There is a MANNER, a grace, an ease, a genteelness, an I-know-not-what, which some men possess above others, which is very different from external beauty and comeliness, and which, however, catches our affection almost as suddenly and powerfully. And though this *manner* be chiefly talked of in the passion between the sexes, where the concealed magic is easily explained, yet surely much of it prevails in all our estimation of characters, and forms no inconsiderable part of personal merit. This class of accomplishments, therefore, must be trusted entirely to the blind, but sure testimony[†] of taste and sentiment; and must be considered as a part of ethics, left by nature to baffle all the pride of philosophy, and make her sensible of her narrow boundaries and slender acquisitions.

15   We approve of another, because of his wit, politeness, modesty, decency, or any agreeable quality which he possesses; although he be not of our acquaintance, nor has ever given us any entertainment, by means of

these accomplishments. The idea, which we form of their effect on his acquaintance, has an agreeable influence on our imagination, and gives us the sentiment of approbation. This principle enters into all the judgments, which we form concerning manners and characters.

SECTION 9

CONCLUSION

PART 1

1   IT may justly appear surprizing, that any man, in so late an age, should find it requisite to prove, by elaborate reasoning, that PERSONAL MERIT consists altogether in the possession of mental qualities, *useful* or *agreeable* to the *person himself* or to *others*. It might be expected, that this principle would have occurred even to the first rude, unpracticed enquirers concerning morals, and been received from its own evidence, without any argument or disputation. Whatever is valuable in any kind, so naturally classes itself under the division of *useful* or *agreeable*, the *utile* or the *dulce*,† that it is not easy to imagine, why we should ever seek farther, or consider the question as a matter of nice research or enquiry. And as every thing useful or agreeable must possess these qualities with regard either to the *person himself* or to *others*, the compleat delineation or description of merit seems to be performed as naturally as a shadow is cast by the sun, or an image is reflected upon water. If the ground, on which the shadow is cast, be not broken and uneven; nor the surface, from which the image is reflected, disturbed and confused; a just figure is immediately presented, without any art or attention. And it seems a reasonable presumption, that systems and hypotheses have perverted† our natural understanding; when a theory, so simple and obvious, could so long have escaped the most elaborate   examination.

2   But however the case may have fared with philosophy; in common life, these principles are still implicitly maintained, nor is any other topic of praise or blame ever recurred to, when we employ any panegyric or satire, any applause or censure of human action and behaviour. If we observe men, in every intercourse of business or pleasure, in every discourse and conversation; we shall find them no where, except in the schools, at any loss upon this subject. What so natural, for instance, as the following dialogue? You are very happy, we shall suppose one to say, addressing himself

to another, that you have given your daughter to CLEANTHES.† He is a man of honour and humanity. Every one, who has any intercourse with him, is sure of *fair* and *kind* treatment.[53] I congratulate you too, says another, on the promising expectations of this son-in-law; whose assiduous application to the study of the laws, whose quick penetration and early knowledge both of men and business, prognosticate the greatest honours and advancement.[54] You surprize me, replies a third, when you talk of CLEANTHES as a man of business and application. I met him lately in a circle of the gayest company, and he was the very life and soul of our conversation: So much wit with good manners; so much gallantry without affectation; so much ingenious knowledge so genteelly delivered, I have never before observed in any one.[55] You would admire him still more, says a fourth, if you knew him more familiarly. That cheerfulness, which you might remark in him, is not a sudden flash struck out by company: It runs through the whole tenor of his life, and preserves a perpetual serenity on his countenance, and tranquillity in his soul. He has met with severe trials, misfortunes as well as dangers; and by his greatness of mind, was still superior to all of them.[56] The image, gentlemen, which you have here delineated of CLEANTHES, cried I, is that of accomplished merit. Each of you has given a stroke of the pencil† to his figure; and you have unawares exceeded all the pictures drawn by GRATIAN or CASTIGLIONE.† A philosopher might select this character as a model of perfect virtue.   SBN 270

3   And as every quality, which is useful or agreeable to ourselves or others, is, in common life, allowed to be a part of personal merit; so no other will ever be received, where men judge of things by their natural, unprejudiced reason, without the delusive glosses of superstition and false religion. Celibacy, fasting, penance, mortification, self-denial, humility, silence, solitude, and the whole train of monkish virtues;† for what reason are they every where rejected by men of sense, but because they serve to no manner of purpose; neither advance a man's fortune in the world, nor render him a more valuable member of society; neither qualify him for the entertainment of company, nor encrease his power of self-enjoyment? We observe, on the contrary, that they cross all these desirable ends; stupify the understanding and harden the heart, obscure the fancy† and sour the temper. We justly, therefore, transfer them to the opposite column, and place them in the catalogue of vices; nor has any superstition force sufficient, among men of the world, to pervert entirely these natural senti-

---

[53] Qualities useful to others.   [54] Qualities useful to the person himself.
[55] Qualities immediately agreeable to others.
[56] Qualities immediately agreeable to the person himself.   SBN 270

SBN 269

146

9. Conclusion

ments. A gloomy, hair-brained enthusiast,[†] after his death, may have a place in the calendar;[†] but will scarcely ever be admitted, when alive, into intimacy and society, except by those who are as delirious and dismal as himself.

4   It seems a happiness in the present theory, that it enters not into that vulgar dispute[†] concerning the *degrees* of benevolence or self-love, which prevail in human nature; a dispute which is never likely to have any issue,   SBN 271 both because men, who have taken part, are not easily convinced, and because the phænomena, which can be produced on either side, are so dispersed, so uncertain, and subject to so many interpretations, that it is scarcely possible accurately to compare them, or draw from them any determinate inference or conclusion. It is sufficient for our present purpose, if it be allowed, what surely, without the greatest absurdity, cannot be disputed, that there is some benevolence, however small, infused into our bosom; some spark of friendship for human kind; some particle of the dove, kneaded into our frame, along with the elements of the wolf and serpent.[†] Let these generous sentiments be supposed ever so weak; let them be insufficient to move even a hand or finger of our body; they must still direct the determinations of our mind, and where every thing else is equal, produce a cool preference of what is useful and serviceable to mankind, above what is pernicious and dangerous. A *moral distinction*, therefore, immediately arises; a general sentiment of blame and approbation; a tendency, however faint, to the objects of the one, and a proportionable aversion to those of the other. Nor will those reasoners, who so earnestly maintain the predominant selfishness of human kind, be any wise scandalized at hearing of the weak sentiments of virtue, implanted in our nature. On the contrary, they are found as ready to maintain the one tenet as the other; and their spirit of satire (for such it appears, rather than of corruption) naturally gives rise to both opinions; which have, indeed, a great and almost an indissoluble connexion[†] together.

5   Avarice, ambition, vanity, and all passions vulgarly, though improperly, comprized[†] under the denomination of *self-love*, are here excluded from our theory concerning the origin of morals, not because they are too weak, but because they have not a proper direction,[†] for that purpose. The   SBN 272 notion of morals implies some sentiment common to all mankind, which   *'moral'* recommends the same object to general approbation,[†] and makes every   ⇒ man, or most men, agree in the same opinion or decision concerning it. It   U also implies some sentiment, so universal and comprehensive as to extend to all mankind, and render the actions and conduct, even of the persons

.: moral go ← sl 116
selfish & 128 164 sq.

the most remote, an object of applause or censure, according as they agree or disagree with that rule of right which is established. These two requisite circumstances belong alone to the sentiment of humanity here insisted on. The other passions produce, in every breast, many strong sentiments of desire and aversion, affection and hatred; but these neither are felt so much in common, nor are so comprehensive, as to be the foundation of any general system and established theory of blame or approbation.

6   When a man denominates another his *enemy*, his *rival*, his *antagonist*, his *adversary*, he is understood to speak the language of self-love, and to express sentiments, peculiar to himself, and arising from his particular circumstances and situation. But when he bestows on any man the epithets of *vicious* or *odious* or *depraved*, he then speaks another language, and expresses sentiments, in which, he expects, all his audience are to concur with him. He must here, therefore, depart from his private and particular situation, and must choose a point of view, common to him with others: He must move some universal principle of the human frame, and touch a string, to which all mankind have an accord and symphony. If he mean, therefore, to express, that this man possesses qualities, whose tendency is pernicious to society, he has chosen this common point of view, and has touched the principle of humanity, in which every man, in some degree, concurs. While the human heart[†] is compounded of the same elements as at present, it will never be wholly indifferent to public good, nor entirely   SBN 2 unaffected with the tendency of characters and manners. And though this affection of humanity may not generally be esteemed so strong as vanity or ambition, yet, being common to all men, it can alone be the foundation of morals, or of any general system of blame or praise. One man's ambition is not another's ambition; nor will the same event or object satisfy both: But the humanity of one man is the humanity of every one; and the same object touches this passion in all human creatures.

7   But the sentiments, which arise from humanity, are not only the same in all human creatures, and produce the same approbation or censure; but they also comprehend all human creatures; nor is there any one whose conduct or character is not, by their means, an object, to every one, of censure or approbation. On the contrary, those other passions, commonly denominated selfish, both produce different sentiments in each individual, according to his particular situation; and also contemplate the greater part of mankind with the utmost indifference and unconcern. Whoever has a high regard and esteem for me flatters my vanity; whoever expresses contempt mortifies and displeases me: But as my name is known but to a small

part of mankind, there are few, who come within the sphere of this passion, or excite, on its account, either my affection or disgust. But if you represent a tyrannical, insolent, or barbarous behaviour, in any country or in any age of the world; I soon carry my eye to the pernicious tendency of such a conduct, and feel the sentiments of repugnance and displeasure towards it. No character can be so remote as to be, in this light, wholly indifferent to me. What is beneficial to society or to the person himself must still be preferred. And every quality or action, of every human being, must, by this means, be ranked under some class or denomination, expressive of general censure or applause.

8   What more, therefore, can we ask to distinguish the sentiments,   SBN 274 dependent on humanity, from those connected with any other passion, or to satisfy us, why the former are the origin of morals, not the latter? Whatever conduct gains my approbation, by touching my humanity, procures also the applause of all mankind, by affecting the same principle in them: But what serves my avarice or ambition pleases these passions in me alone, and affects not the avarice and ambition of the rest of mankind. There is no circumstance of conduct in any man, provided it have a beneficial tendency, that is not agreeable to my humanity, however remote the person: But every man, so far removed as neither to cross nor serve my avarice and ambition, is regarded as wholly indifferent by those passions. The distinction, therefore, between these species of sentiment being so great and evident, language must soon be moulded upon it, and must invent a peculiar set of terms, in order to express those universal sentiments of censure or approbation, which arise from humanity, or from views of general usefulness and its contrary. Virtue and vice become then known:[†] Morals are recognized: Certain general ideas are framed of human conduct and behaviour: Such measures are expected from men, in such situations: This action is determined to be conformable to our abstract rule; that other, contrary. And by such universal principles are the particular sentiments of self-love frequently controuled and limited.[57]

---

[57] It seems certain, both from reason and experience, that a rude, untaught savage regulates chiefly his love and hatred by the ideas of private utility and injury, and has but faint conceptions of a general rule or system of behaviour. The man who stands opposite to him in battle, he hates heartily, not only for the present moment, which is almost unavoidable, but for ever after; nor is he satisfied without the most extreme punishment and vengeance. But we, accustomed to society, and to more enlarged reflections, consider, that this man is serving his own country and community; that any man, in the same situation, would do the same; that we ourselves, in like circumstances, observe a like conduct; that, in general, human society is best supported on such maxims: And by these suppositions and views, we correct, in some measure, our ruder   SBN 275

9   From instances of popular tumults, seditions, factions, panics, and of all
passions, which are shared with a multitude; we may learn the influence of
society, in exciting and supporting any emotion; while the most ungovern-
able disorders are raised, we find, by that means, from the slightest and
most frivolous occasions. SOLON was no very cruel, though, perhaps, an
unjust legislator, who punished neuters[†] in civil wars; and few, I believe,
would, in such cases, incur the penalty, were their affection and discourse
allowed sufficient to absolve them. No selfishness, and scarce any philosophy, have there force sufficient to support a total coolness and indifference; and he must be more or less than man, who kindles not in the
common blaze.[†] What wonder then, that moral sentiments are found of
such influence in life; though springing from principles, which may
appear, at first sight, somewhat small and delicate? But these principles, we
must remark, are social and universal: They form, in a manner, the *party* of
human kind[†] against vice or disorder, its common enemy: And as the
benevolent concern for others is diffused, in a greater or less degree, over
all men, and is the same in all, it occurs more frequently in discourse, is
cherished by society and conversation, and the blame and approbation,
consequent on it, are thereby rouzed from that lethargy, into which they
are probably lulled, in solitary and uncultivated nature.[†] Other passions,
though perhaps originally stronger, yet being selfish and private, are often
overpowered by its force, and yield the dominion of our breast[†] to those
social and public principles.

10   Another spring of our constitution, that brings a great addition of force
to moral sentiment, is, the love of fame; which rules, with such uncon-
trouled authority, in all generous minds,[†] and is often the grand object of
all their designs and undertakings. By our continual and earnest pursuit of
a character, a name, a reputation in the world, we bring our own deportment and conduct frequently in review, and consider how they appear in
the eyes of those, who approach and regard us. This constant habit of sur-
veying ourselves, as it were, in reflection, keeps alive all the sentiments of
right and wrong, and begets, in noble natures, a certain reverence for
themselves as well as others; which is the surest guardian of every virtue.

and narrower passions. And though much of our friendship and enmity be still regulated by
private considerations of benefit and harm, we pay, at least, this homage to general rules, which
we are accustomed to respect, that we commonly pervert our adversary's conduct, by imputing
malice or injustice to him, in order to give vent to those passions, which arise from self-love
and private interest. When the heart is full of rage, it never wants pretences of this nature;
though sometimes as frivolous, as those from which HORACE, being almost crushed by the fall
of a tree,[†] affects to accuse of parricide the first planter of it. [Horace, *Odes*, bk. 2, ode 13, lines
1–12.]

9. Conclusion

The animal conveniencies and pleasures sink gradually in their value; while every inward beauty and moral grace is studiously acquired, and the mind is accomplished in every perfection,[†] which can adorn or embellish a rational creature.

1   Here is the most perfect morality with which we are acquainted: Here is displayed the force of many sympathies.[†] Our moral sentiment is itself a feeling chiefly of that nature: And our regard to a character with others seems to arise only from a care of preserving a character with ourselves; and in order to attain this end, we find it necessary to prop our tottering judgment on the correspondent approbation of mankind.

2   But, that we may accommodate matters,[†] and remove, if possible, every difficulty, let us allow all these reasonings to be false. Let us allow, that, when we resolve the pleasure, which arises from views of utility, into[†] the sentiments of humanity and sympathy, we have embraced a wrong hypothesis. Let us confess it necessary to find some other explication of that applause, which is paid to objects, whether inanimate, animate, or rational, if they have a tendency to promote the welfare and advantage of mankind. However difficult it be to conceive, that an object is approved of on account of its tendency to a certain end, while the end itself is totally indifferent;[†] let us swallow this absurdity, and consider what are the consequences. The preceding delineation or definition of PERSONAL MERIT must still retain its evidence and authority: It must still be allowed, that every quality of the mind, which is *useful* or *agreeable* to the *person himself* or to *others*, communicates a pleasure to the spectator, engages his esteem, and is admitted under the honourable denomination of virtue or merit. Are not justice, fidelity, honour, veracity, allegiance, chastity, esteemed solely on account of their tendency to promote the good of society? Is not that tendency inseparable from humanity, benevolence, lenity, generosity, gratitude, moderation, tenderness, friendship, and all the other social virtues? Can it possibly be doubted, that industry, discretion, frugality, secrecy, order, perseverance, forethought, judgment, and this whole class of virtues and accomplishments, of which many pages would not contain the catalogue; can it be doubted, I say, that the tendency of these qualities to promote the interest and happiness of their possessor, is the sole foundation of their merit? Who can dispute that a mind, which supports a perpetual serenity and cheerfulness, a noble dignity and undaunted spirit, a tender affection and good-will to all around; as it has more enjoyment within itself, is also a more animating and rejoicing spectacle, than if dejected with melancholy, tormented with anxiety, irritated with rage, or sunk into the most abject baseness and degeneracy? And as to the qualities,

120

SBN 277

Enquiry concerning the Principles of Morals

immediately *agreeable to others*, they speak sufficiently for themselves; and he must be unhappy, indeed, either in his own temper, or in his situation and company, who has never perceived the charms of a facetious wit or flowing affability, of a delicate modesty or decent genteelness of address and manner. SBN 2

13   I am sensible, that nothing can be more unphilosophical than to be positive or dogmatical on any subject; and that, even if *excessive* scepticism[†] could be maintained, it would not be more destructive to all just reasoning and enquiry. I am convinced, that, where men are the most sure and arrogant, they are commonly the most mistaken, and have there given reins to passion, without that proper deliberation and suspence, which can alone secure them from the grossest absurdities.[†] Yet, I must confess, that this enumeration puts the matter in so strong a light, that I cannot, *at present*, be more assured of any truth, which I learn from reasoning and argument, than that personal merit consists entirely in the usefulness or agreeableness of qualities to the person himself possessed of them, or to others, who have any intercourse with him. But when I reflect, that, though the bulk and figure of the earth have been measured and delineated, though the motions of the tides have been accounted for, the order and œconomy of the heavenly bodies[†] subjected to their proper laws, and INFINITE itself[†] reduced to calculation; yet men still dispute concerning the foundation of their moral duties: When I reflect on this, I say, I fall back into diffidence and scepticism, and suspect, that an hypothesis, so obvious, had it been a true one, would, long ere now, have been received by the unanimous suffrage and consent of mankind.

PART 2

14   Having explained the moral *approbation* attending merit or virtue, there remains nothing, but briefly to consider our interested *obligation*[†] to it, and to enquire, whether every man, who has any regard to his own happiness and welfare, will not best find his account[†] in the practice of every moral duty. If this can be clearly ascertained from the foregoing theory,[†] we shall have the satisfaction to reflect, that we have advanced principles, which not only, it is hoped, will stand the test of reasoning and enquiry, but may contribute to the amendment of men's lives,[†] and their improvement in morality and social virtue. And though the philosophical truth of any proposition by no means depends on its tendency to promote the interests SBN 2

9. *Conclusion*

of society; yet a man has but a bad grace, who delivers a theory, however true, which, he must confess, leads to a practice dangerous and pernicious.[†] Why rake into those corners of nature, which spread a nuisance all around? Why dig up the pestilence from the pit, in which it is buried? The ingenuity of your researches may be admired; but your systems will be detested: And mankind will agree, if they cannot refute them, to sink them, at least, in eternal silence and oblivion. Truths, which are *pernicious* to society, if any such there be, will yield to errors, which are salutary and *advantageous*.

15   But what philosophical truths can be more advantageous to society, than those here delivered, which represent virtue in all her genuine and most engaging charms, and make us approach her with ease, familiarity, and affection? The dismal dress falls off, with which many divines,[†] and some philosophers have covered her; and nothing appears but gentleness, humanity, beneficence, affability; nay even, at proper intervals, play, frolic, and gaiety. She talks not of useless austerities and rigours, suffering and self-denial. She declares, that her sole purpose is, to make her votaries and all mankind, during every instant of their existence, if possible, cheerful and happy; nor does she ever willingly part with any pleasure but in hopes of ample compensation in some other period of their lives. The sole trouble, which she demands, is that of just calculation,[†] and a steady preference of the greater happiness. And if any austere pretenders[†] approach her, enemies to joy and pleasure, she either rejects them as hypocrites and deceivers; or if she admit them in her train, they are ranked, however, among the least favoured of her votaries.

anti-religious morality 146

SBN 280

16   And, indeed, to drop all figurative expression, what hopes can we ever have of engaging mankind to a practice, which we confess full of austerity and rigour? Or what theory of morals can ever serve any useful purpose, unless it can show, by a particular detail, that all the duties, which it recommends, are also the true interest of each individual? The peculiar advantage of the foregoing system[†] seems to be, that it furnishes proper mediums for that purpose.

17   That the virtues which are immediately *useful* or *agreeable* to the person possessed of them, are desirable in a view to self-interest, it would surely be superfluous to prove. Moralists, indeed, may spare themselves all the pains, which they often take in recommending these duties. To what purpose collect arguments to evince, that temperance is advantageous, and the excesses of pleasure hurtful? When it appears, that these excesses are only denominated such, because they are hurtful; and that, if the unlimited use of strong liquors, for instance, no more impaired health or

153

the faculties of mind and body than the use of air or water, it would not be a whit more vicious or blameable.

18   It seems equally superfluous to prove, that the *companionable* virtues of good manners and wit, decency and genteelness, are more desirable than the contrary qualities. Vanity alone, without any other consideration, is a sufficient motive to make us wish for the possession of these accomplishments. No man was ever willingly deficient in this particular. All our failures here proceed from bad education, want of capacity, or a perverse and unpliable disposition. Would you have your company coveted, admired, followed; rather than hated, despised, avoided? Can any one seriously deliberate in the case? As no enjoyment is sincere, without some reference to company and society; so no society can be agreeable, or even tolerable, where a man feels his presence unwelcome, and discovers all around him   SBN 2 symptoms of disgust and aversion.

19   But why, in the greater society or confederacy of mankind, should not the case be the same as in particular clubs and companies? Why is it more doubtful, that the enlarged virtues of humanity, generosity, beneficence, are desirable with a view to happiness and self-interest, than the limited endowments of ingenuity and politeness? Are we apprehensive, lest those social affections interfere, in a greater and more immediate degree than any other pursuits, with private utility, and cannot be gratified, without some important sacrifice of honour and advantage? If so, we are but ill instructed in the nature of the human passions, and are more influenced by verbal distinctions than by real differences.

20   Whatever contradiction may vulgarly be supposed between the *selfish* and *social* sentiments[†] or dispositions, they are really no more opposite than selfish and ambitious, selfish and revengeful, selfish and vain. It is requisite, that there be an original propensity of some kind, in order to be a basis to self-love, by giving a relish to the objects of its pursuit; and none more fit for this purpose than benevolence or humanity. The goods of fortune are spent in one gratification or another: The miser, who accumulates his annual income, and lends it out at interest, has really spent it in the gratification of his avarice. And it would be difficult to show, why a man is more a loser by a generous action, than by any other method of expence; since the utmost which he can attain, by the most elaborate selfishness, is the indulgence of some affection.

21   Now if life, without passion, must be altogether insipid and tiresome; let a man suppose that he has full power of modelling his own disposition,[†] and let him deliberate what appetite or desire he would choose for the foundation of his happiness and enjoyment. Every affection, he would

observe, when gratified by success, gives a satisfaction proportioned to its SBN 282 force and violence; but besides this advantage, common to all, the immediate feeling of benevolence and friendship, humanity and kindness, is sweet, smooth, tender, and agreeable, independent of all fortune and accidents. These virtues are besides attended with a pleasing consciousness or remembrance, and keep us in humour with ourselves as well as others; while we retain the agreeable reflection of having done our part towards mankind and society. And though all men show a jealousy of our success in the pursuits of avarice and ambition; yet are we almost sure of their good-will and good-wishes, so long as we persevere in the paths of virtue, and employ ourselves in the execution of generous plans and purposes. What other passion is there where we shall find so many advantages united; an agreeable sentiment, a pleasing consciousness, a good reputation? But of these truths, we may observe, men are, of themselves, pretty much convinced; nor are they deficient in their duty to society, because they would not wish to be generous, friendly, and humane; but because they do not feel themselves such.[†]

22   Treating vice with the greatest candour, and making it all possible concessions, we must acknowledge, that there is not, in any instance, the smallest pretext for giving it the preference above virtue, with a view to self-interest; except, perhaps, in the case of justice, where a man, taking things in a certain light, may often seem to be a loser by his integrity. And though it is allowed, that, without a regard to property, no society could subsist; yet, according to the imperfect way in which human affairs are conducted, a sensible knave,[†] in particular incidents, may think, that an act of iniquity or infidelity will make a considerable addition to his fortune, without causing any considerable breach in the social union and confederacy. That *honesty is the best policy*, may be a good general rule; but is liable to many exceptions: And he, it may, perhaps, be thought, conducts himself SBN 283 with most wisdom, who observes the general rule, and takes advantage of all the exceptions.

23   I must confess, that, if a man think, that this reasoning much requires an answer, it will be a little difficult to find any, which will to him appear satisfactory and convincing. If his heart rebel not against such pernicious maxims, if he feel no reluctance to the thoughts of villany or baseness, he has indeed lost a considerable motive to virtue; and we may expect, that his practice will be answerable to his speculation.[†] But in all ingenuous natures, the antipathy to treachery and roguery is too strong to be counterbalanced by any views of profit or pecuniary advantage. Inward peace of mind, consciousness of integrity, a satisfactory review of our own

Vice does not advance self-int.

conduct; these are circumstances very requisite to happiness, and will be cherished and cultivated by every honest man, who feels the importance of them.

24   Such a one has, besides, the frequent satisfaction of seeing knaves, with all their pretended cunning and abilities, betrayed by their own maxims; and while they purpose to cheat with moderation and secrecy, a tempting incident occurs, nature is frail, and they give into the snare; whence they can never extricate themselves, without a total loss of reputation, and the forfeiture of all future trust and confidence with mankind.

25   But were they ever so secret and successful, the honest man, if he has any tincture of philosophy, or even common observation and reflection, will discover that they themselves are, in the end, the greatest dupes, and have sacrificed the invaluable enjoyment of a character, with themselves at least, for the acquisition of worthless toys and gewgaws. How little is requisite to supply the *necessities* of nature? And in a view to *pleasure*, what comparison between the unbought satisfaction of conversation, society, study, even health and the common beauties of nature, but above all SBN 28 the peaceful reflection on one's own conduct: What comparison, I say, between these, and the feverish, empty amusements of luxury and expence?[†] These natural pleasures, indeed, are really without price; both because they are below all price in their attainment, and above it in their enjoyment.

156

APPENDIX 1

CONCERNING MORAL SENTIMENT

1   I F the foregoing hypothesis be received, it will now be easy for us to determine the question first started,[58][†] concerning the general principles of morals; and though we postponed the decision of that question, lest it should then involve us in intricate speculations, which are unfit for moral discourses, we may resume it at present, and examine how far either *reason* or *sentiment* enters into all decisions of praise or censure.

2   One principal foundation of moral praise being supposed to lie in the usefulness of any quality or action; it is evident, that *reason* must enter for a considerable share in all decisions of this kind; since nothing but that faculty can instruct us in the tendency of qualities and actions, and point out their beneficial consequences to society and to their possessor. In many cases, this is an affair liable to great controversy: Doubts may arise; opposite interests may occur; and a preference must be given to one side, from very nice views, and a small overbalance[†] of utility. This is particularly remarkable in questions with regard to justice; as is, indeed, natural to suppose, from that species of utility, which attends this virtue.[59] Were every single instance of justice, like that of benevolence, useful to society; this would be a more simple state of the case, and seldom liable to great controversy. But as single instances of justice are often pernicious in their first and immediate tendency, and as the advantage to society results only from the observance of the general rule,[†] and from the concurrence and combination of several persons in the same equitable conduct; the case here becomes more intricate and involved. The various circumstances of society; the various consequences of any practice; the various interests, which may be proposed: These, on many occasions, are doubtful, and subject to great discussion and enquiry. The object of municipal laws is to fix all the questions with regard to justice: The debates of civilians; the reflections of politicians; the precedents of history and public records, are all directed to the same purpose. And a very accurate *reason* or *judgment* is

---

[58] Section 1.   [59] See Appendix 3.

*R shows what is pernicious / useful
but does not → blame/approb[n], prefer of useful to
pernicious
∴ St necy*

Enquiry concerning the Principles of Morals

often requisite, to give the true determination, amidst such intricate
doubts arising from obscure or opposite utilities.

3   But though reason, when fully assisted and improved, be sufficient to
instruct us[†] in the pernicious or useful tendency of qualities and actions; it
is not alone sufficient to produce any moral blame or approbation. Utility
is only a tendency to a certain end; and were the end totally indifferent to
us, we should feel the same indifference towards the means. It is requisite a
sentiment should here display itself, in order to give a preference to the
useful above the pernicious tendencies. This sentiment can be no other
than a feeling for the happiness of mankind, and a resentment of their
misery; since these are the different ends, which virtue and vice have a
tendency to promote. Here, therefore, *reason* instructs us in the several
tendencies of actions, and *humanity* makes a distinction in favour of those,
which are useful and beneficial.

4   This partition between the faculties of understanding and sentiment, in
all moral decisions, seems clear from the preceding hypothesis. But I shall
suppose that hypothesis false: It will then be requisite to look out for some   SBN 28
other theory, that may be satisfactory; and I dare venture to affirm, that
none such will ever be found, so long as we suppose reason to be the sole
source of morals. To prove this, it will be proper to weigh the five following considerations.[†]

5   1. It is easy for a false hypothesis to maintain some appearance of truth,
while it keeps wholly in generals, makes use of undefined terms, and
employs comparisons, instead of instances.[†] This is particularly remarkable in that philosophy, which ascribes the discernment of all moral distinctions to reason alone, without the concurrence of sentiment. It is
impossible that, in any particular instance, this hypothesis can so much as
be rendered intelligible; whatever specious figure it may make in general
declamations and discourses. Examine the crime of *ingratitude*, for
instance; which has place,[†] wherever we observe good-will, expressed and
known, together with good offices performed, on the one side, and a
return of ill-will or indifference, with ill-offices or neglect on the other:
Anatomize all these circumstances, and examine, by your reason alone, in
what consists the demerit or blame: You never will come to any issue or
conclusion.

6   Reason judges either of *matter of fact* or of *relations*.[†] Enquire then, *first*,
where is that matter of fact, which we here call *crime*;[†] point it out; determine the time of its existence; describe its essence or nature; explain the
sense or faculty, to which it discovers itself.[†] It resides in the mind of the
person, who is ungrateful. He must, therefore, feel it, and be conscious of

Appx. 1. Concerning Moral Sentiment

it. But nothing is there, except the passion of ill-will or absolute indifference. You cannot say, that these, of themselves, always, and in all circumstances, are crimes. No: They are only crimes, when directed towards persons, who have before expressed and displayed good-will towards us. Consequently, we may infer, that the crime of ingratitude is not any particular individual *fact*; but arises from a complication of circumstances, which, being presented to the spectator, excites the *sentiment* of blame, by the particular structure and fabric of his mind.   SBN 288

7   This representation, you say, is false. Crime, indeed, consists not in a particular *fact*, of whose reality we are assured by *reason*: But it consists in certain *moral relations*, discovered by reason,† in the same manner as we discover, by reason, the truths of geometry or algebra. But what are the relations, I ask, of which you here talk? In the case stated above, I see first good-will and good offices in one person; then ill-will and ill-offices in the other. Between these, there is the relation of *contrariety*. Does the crime consist in that relation? But suppose a person bore me ill-will or did me ill-offices; and I, in return, were indifferent towards him, or did him good offices: Here is the same relation of *contrariety*; and yet my conduct is often highly laudable. Twist and turn this matter as much as you will, you can never rest the morality on relation; but must have recourse to the decisions of sentiment.

8   When it is affirmed, that two and three are equal to the half of ten; this relation of equality, I understand perfectly. I conceive, that if ten be divided into two parts, of which one has as many units as the other; and if any of these parts be compared to two added to three, it will contain as many units as that compound number. But when you draw thence a comparison to moral relations, I own that I am altogether at a loss to understand you. A moral action, a crime, such as ingratitude, is a complicated object. Does the morality consist in the relation of its parts to each other. How? After what manner? Specify the relation: Be more particular and explicit in your propositions; and you will easily see their falsehood.

9   No, say you, the morality consists in the relation of actions to the rule of right; and they are denominated good or ill, according as they agree or disagree with it. What then is this rule of right? In what does it consist? How is it determined? By reason, you say, which examines the moral relations of   SBN 289
actions. So that moral relations are determined by the comparison of actions to a rule. And that rule is determined by considering the moral relations of objects. Is not this fine reasoning?

10   All this is metaphysics, you cry: That is enough: There needs nothing more to give a strong presumption of falsehood. Yes, reply I: Here are

metaphysics surely: But they are all on your side, who advance an abstruse hypothesis, which can never be made intelligible, nor quadrate with any particular instance or illustration. The hypothesis which we embrace is plain. It maintains, that morality is determined by sentiment. It defines virtue[†] to be *whatever mental action or quality gives to a spectator the pleasing sentiment of approbation*; and vice the contrary. We then proceed to examine a plain matter of fact, to wit, what actions have this influence: We consider all the circumstances, in which these actions agree: And thence endeavour to extract some general observations with regard to these sentiments. If you call this metaphysics, and find any thing abstruse here, you need only conclude, that your turn of mind is not suited to the moral sciences.

11   2. When a man, at any time, deliberates concerning his own conduct, (as, whether he had better, in a particular emergence, assist a brother or a benefactor) he must consider these separate relations, with all the circumstances and situations of the persons, in order to determine the superior duty and obligation: And in order to determine the proportion of lines in any triangle, it is necessary to examine the nature of that figure, and the relations which its several parts bear to each other. But notwithstanding this appearing similarity in the two cases, there is, at bottom, an extreme difference between them. A speculative reasoner concerning triangles or circles considers the several known and given relations of the parts of these figures; and thence infers some unknown relation, which is dependent on the former. But in moral deliberations, we must be acquainted, before-hand, with all the objects, and all their relations to each other; and from a comparison of the whole, fix our choice or approbation. No new fact to be ascertained: No new relation to be discovered. All the circumstances of the case are supposed to be laid before us, ere we can fix any sentence of blame or approbation. If any material circumstance be yet unknown or doubtful, we must first employ our enquiry or intellectual faculties to assure us of it; and must suspend for a time all moral decision or sentiment. While we are ignorant, whether a man were aggressor or not, how can we determine whether the person, who killed him, be criminal or innocent? But after every circumstance, every relation is known, the understanding has no farther room to operate, nor any object, on which it could employ itself. The approbation or blame, which then ensues, cannot be the work of the judgment, but of the heart; and is not a speculative proposition or affirmation, but an active feeling or sentiment. In the disquisitions of the understanding,[†] from known circumstances and rela-

tions, we infer some new and unknown. In moral decisions, all the circumstances and relations must be previously known; and the mind, from the contemplation of the whole, feels some new impression of affection or disgust, esteem or contempt, approbation or blame.

12 Hence the great difference between a mistake of *fact* and one of *right*; and hence the reason, why the one is commonly criminal and not the other. When ŒDIPUS killed LAIUS,[†] he was ignorant of the relation, and from circumstances, innocent and involuntary, formed erroneous opinions concerning the action which he committed. But when NERO killed AGRIPPINA,[†] all the relations between himself and the person, and all the circumstances of the fact were previously known to him: But the motive of revenge, or fear, or interest, prevailed in his savage heart over the sentiments of duty and humanity. And when we express that detestation against him, to which he, himself, in a little time, became insensible; it is not, that we see any relations, of which he was ignorant; but that, from the rectitude of our disposition, we feel sentiments, against which he was hardened, from flattery and a long perseverance in the most enormous crimes. In these sentiments, then, not in a discovery of relations of any kind, do all moral determinations consist. Before we can pretend to form any decision of this kind, every thing must be known and ascertained on the side of the object or action. Nothing remains but to feel, on our part, some sentiment of blame or approbation; whence we pronounce the action criminal or virtuous. SBN 291

13 3. This doctrine will become still more evident, if we compare moral beauty with natural, to which, in many particulars, it bears so near a resemblance. It is on the proportion, relation, and position of parts, that all natural beauty depends; but it would be absurd thence to infer, that the perception of beauty, like that of truth in geometrical problems, consists wholly in the perception of relations, and was performed entirely by the understanding or intellectual faculties. In all the sciences, our mind, from the known relations, investigates the unknown: But in all decisions of taste or external beauty, all the relations are before-hand obvious to the eye; and we thence proceed to feel a sentiment of complacency or disgust, according to the nature of the object, and disposition of our organs.

14 EUCLID[†] has fully explained all the qualities of the circle; but has not, in any proposition, said a word of its beauty. The reason is evident. The beauty is not a quality of the circle. It lies not in any part of the line, whose parts are equally distant from a common center. It is only the effect, which that figure produces upon the mind, whose peculiar fabric or structure SBN 292

renders it susceptible of such sentiments. In vain would you look for it in the circle, or seek it, either by your senses or by mathematical reasonings, in all the properties of that figure.

15   Attend to PALLADIO and PERRAULT,[†] while they explain all the parts and proportions of a pillar: They talk of the cornice and frieze and base and entablature and shaft and architrave; and give the description and position of each of these members. But should you ask the description and position of its beauty, they would readily reply, that the beauty is not in any of the parts or members of a pillar, but results from the whole, when that complicated figure is presented to an intelligent mind, susceptible to those finer sensations. Till such a spectator appear, there is nothing but a figure of such particular dimensions and proportions: From his sentiments alone arise its elegance and beauty.

16   Again; attend to CICERO, while he paints the crimes of a VERRES or a CATILINE;[†] you must acknowledge that the moral turpitude results, in the same manner, from the contemplation of the whole, when presented to a being, whose organs have such a particular structure and formation. The orator may paint rage, insolence, barbarity on the one side: Meekness, suffering, sorrow, innocence on the other: But if you feel no indignation or compassion arise in you from this complication of circumstances, you would in vain ask him, in what consists the crime or villany, which he so vehemently exclaims against: At what time, or on what subject it first began to exist: And what has a few months afterwards become of it, when every disposition and thought of all the actors is totally altered, or annihilated. No satisfactory answer can be given to any of these questions, upon the abstract hypothesis of morals; and we must at last acknowledge, that the crime or immorality is no particular fact or relation, which can be the object of the understanding: But arises entirely from the sentiment of disapprobation, which, by the structure of human nature, we unavoidably feel on the apprehension of barbarity or treachery. SBN 29

17   4. Inanimate objects may bear to each other all the same relations, which we observe in moral agents; though the former can never be the object of love or hatred, nor are consequently susceptible of merit or iniquity. A young tree, which over-tops and destroys its parent, stands in all the same relations with NERO, when he murdered AGRIPPINA;[†] and if morality consisted merely in relations, would, no doubt, be equally criminal.

18   5. It appears evident, that the ultimate ends of human actions can never, in any case, be accounted for by *reason*,[†] but recommend themselves entirely to the sentiments and affections of mankind, without any depen-

There is always an ultimate end, wh explains Subordinate ends but can't itself be explained

dence on the intellectual faculties. Ask a man, *why he uses exercise;* he will answer, *because he desires to keep his health.* If you then enquire, *why he desires health,* he will readily reply, *because sickness is painful.* If you push your enquiries farther, and desire a reason, *why he hates pain,* it is impossible he can ever give any. This is an ultimate end, and is never referred to any other object.

19   Perhaps, to your second question, *why he desires health,* he may also reply, that *it is necessary for the exercise of his calling.* If you ask, *why he is anxious on that head,* he will answer, *because he desires to get money.* If you demand *Why? It is the instrument of pleasure,* says he. And beyond this it is an absurdity to ask for a reason. It is impossible there can be a progress *in infinitum;* and that one thing can always be a reason, why another is desired. Something must be desirable on its own account, and because of its immediate accord or agreement with human sentiment and affection.

20   Now as virtue is an end, and is desirable on its own account, without fee or reward, merely for the immediate satisfaction which it conveys; it is requisite that there should be some sentiment, which it touches; some internal taste or feeling, or whatever you please to call it, which distinguishes moral good and evil, and which embraces the one and rejects the other.

Vr an end in itself — desirable for the immed. satisf'n it conveys [to whom?]

SBN 294

21   Thus the distinct boundaries and offices of *reason* and of *taste* are easily ascertained. The former conveys the knowledge of truth and falsehood: The latter gives the sentiment of beauty and deformity, vice and virtue. The one discovers objects, as they really stand in nature, without addition or diminution: The other has a productive faculty, and gilding or staining[†] all natural objects with the colours, borrowed from internal sentiment, raises, in a manner, a new creation. Reason, being cool and disengaged, is no motive to action, and directs only the impulse received from appetite or inclination, by showing us the means of attaining happiness or avoiding misery: Taste, as it gives pleasure or pain, and thereby constitutes happiness or misery, becomes a motive to action, and is the first spring or impulse to desire and volition. From circumstances and relations, known or supposed, the former leads us to the discovery of the concealed and unknown: After all circumstances and relations are laid before us, the latter makes us feel from the whole a new sentiment of blame or approbation. The standard of the one, being founded on the nature of things, is eternal and inflexible,[†] even by the will of the Supreme Being:[†] The standard of the other, arising from the internal frame and constitution of animals, is ultimately derived from that Supreme Will, which bestowed on each being its peculiar nature, and arranged the several classes and orders of existence.

APPENDIX 2[†]

OF SELF-LOVE

2 Φs (i) all "Vr" is delib¹ʸ disguised self-int,
(ii) all concern fr Os' interest really self-int?
concern fw own thos & welfare

1   THERE is a principle,[†] supposed to prevail among many, which is utterly incompatible with all virtue or moral sentiment; and as it can proceed from nothing but the most depraved disposition, so in its turn it tends still further to encourage that depravity. This principle is, that all *benevolence* is mere hypocrisy, friendship a cheat, public spirit a farce, fidelity a snare to procure trust and confidence; and that, while all of us, at bottom, pursue only our private interest, we wear these fair disguises, in order to put others off their guard, and expose them the more to our wiles and machinations.[†] What heart one must be possessed of who professes such principles, and who feels no internal sentiment that belies so pernicious a theory, it is easy to imagine: And also, what degree of affection and benevolence he can bear to a species, whom he represents under such odious colours, and supposes so little susceptible of gratitude or any return of affection. Or if we should not ascribe these principles wholly to a corrupted heart, we must, at least, account for them from the most careless and precipitate examination. Superficial reasoners, indeed, observing many false pretences among mankind, and feeling, perhaps, no very strong restraint in their own disposition, might draw a general and a hasty conclusion, that all is equally corrupted, and that men, different from all   other animals, and indeed from all other species of existence, admit of no degrees of good or bad, but are, in every instance, the same creatures under different disguises and appearances.

2   There is another principle,[†] somewhat resembling the former; which has been much insisted on by philosophers, and has been the foundation of many a system; that, whatever affection one may feel, or imagine he feels for others, no passion is, or can be disinterested; that the most generous friendship, however sincere, is a modification of self-love; and that, even unknown to ourselves, we seek only our own gratification, while we appear the most deeply engaged in schemes for the liberty and happiness of mankind. By a turn of imagination, by a refinement of reflection, by an enthusiasm of passion, we seem to take part in the interests of others, and

imagine ourselves divested of all selfish considerations: But, at bottom, the most generous patriot and most niggardly miser, the bravest hero and most abject coward, have, in every action, an equal regard to their own happiness and welfare.

3   Whoever concludes, from the seeming tendency of this opinion, that those, who make profession of it, cannot possibly feel the true sentiments of benevolence, or have any regard for genuine virtue, will often find himself, in practice, very much mistaken.[†] Probity and honour were no strangers to Epicurus and his sect. Atticus and Horace[†] seem to have enjoyed from nature, and cultivated by reflection, as generous and friendly dispositions as any disciple of the austerer schools.[†] And among the moderns, Hobbes and Locke, who maintained the selfish system[†] of morals, lived irreproachable lives; though the former lay not under any restraint of religion, which might supply the defects of his philosophy.

4   An Epicurean or a Hobbist[†] readily allows, that there is such a thing as   SBN 297 friendship in the world, without hypocrisy or disguise; though he may attempt, by a philosophical chymistry, to resolve the elements of this passion, if I may so speak, into those of another, and explain every affection to be self-love, twisted and moulded, by a particular turn of imagination, into a variety of appearances. But as the same turn of imagination prevails not in every man, nor gives the same direction to the original passion; this is sufficient, even according to the selfish system, to make the widest difference in human characters, and denominate one man virtuous and humane, another vicious and meanly interested.[†] I esteem the man, whose self-love, by whatever means, is so directed as to give him a concern for others, and render him serviceable to society: As I hate or despise him, who has no regard to any thing beyond his own gratifications and enjoyments. In vain would you suggest, that these characters, though seemingly opposite, are, at bottom, the same,[†] and that a very inconsiderable turn of thought forms the whole difference between them. Each character, notwithstanding these inconsiderable differences, appears to me, in practice, pretty durable and untransmutable. And I find not in this, more than in other subjects, that the natural sentiments, arising from the general appearances of things, are easily destroyed by subtile reflections concerning the minute origin of these appearances. Does not the lively, cheerful colour of a countenance inspire me with complacency and pleasure; even though I learn from philosophy,[†] that all difference of complexion arises from the most minute differences of thickness, in the most minute parts of the skin; by means of which a superficies is qualified to reflect one of the original colours of light, and absorb the others?

5   But though the question, concerning the universal or partial selfishness
of man be not so material, as is usually imagined, to morality and practice,
it is certainly of consequence in the speculative science[†] of human nature,
and is a proper object of curiosity and enquiry. It may not, therefore, be   SBN 298
unsuitable, in this place, to bestow a few reflections upon it.[60]

6   The most obvious objection to the selfish hypothesis, is, that, as it is contrary to common feeling and our most unprejudiced notions, there is
required the highest stretch of philosophy to establish so extraordinary a
paradox. To the most careless observer, there appear to be such dispositions as benevolence and generosity; such affections as love, friendship,
compassion, gratitude. These sentiments have their causes, effects,
objects, and operations, marked by common language and observation,
and plainly distinguished from those of the selfish passions. And as this is
the obvious appearance of things, it must be admitted; till some hypothesis be discovered, which, by penetrating deeper into human nature,
may prove the former affections to be nothing but modifications of the
latter. All attempts of this kind have hitherto proved fruitless, and seem to
have proceeded entirely, from that love of *simplicity*,[†] which has been the
source of much false reasoning in philosophy. I shall not here enter into
any detail on the present subject. Many able philosophers have shown the
insufficiency of these systems. And I shall take for granted what, I believe,
the smallest reflection will make evident to every impartial enquirer.

7   But the nature of the subject furnishes the strongest presumption, that
no better system will ever, for the future, be invented, in order to account   SBN 299
for the origin of the benevolent from the selfish affections, and reduce all
the various emotions of the human mind to a perfect simplicity. The case
is not the same in this species of philosophy as in physics. Many an hypothesis in nature, contrary to first appearances, has been found, on more
accurate scrutiny, solid and satisfactory. Instances of this kind are so frequent, that a judicious, as well as witty philosopher,[61†] has ventured to
affirm, if there be more than one way, in which any phænomenon may be

---

[60] Benevolence naturally divides into two kinds, the *general* and the *particular*. The first is,   SBN 298
where we have no friendship or connexion or esteem for the person, but feel only a general
sympathy with him or a compassion for his pains, and a congratulation with his pleasures. The
other species of benevolence is founded on an opinion of virtue, on services done us, or on
some particular connexions. Both these sentiments must be allowed real in human nature; but
whether they will resolve into some nice considerations of self-love, is a question more curious
than important. The former sentiment, to wit, that of general benevolence, or humanity, or
sympathy, we shall have occasion frequently to treat of in the course of this enquiry; and I
assume it as real, from general experience, without any other proof.

[61] Mons. FONTENELLE. [Bernard le Bovier de Fontenelle, *Entretiens sur la pluralité des mondes*.]

Appx. 2. Of Self-Love

produced, that there is a general presumption for its arising from the causes, which are the least obvious and familiar. But the presumption always lies on the other side, in all enquiries concerning the origin of our passions, and of the internal operations of the human mind. The simplest and most obvious cause, which can there be assigned for any phænomenon, is probably the true one. When a philosopher, in the explication of his system, is obliged to have recourse to some very intricate and refined reflections, and to suppose them essential to the production of any passion or emotion, we have reason to be extremely on our guard against so fallacious an hypothesis.[†] The affections are not susceptible of any impression from the refinements of reason or imagination; and it is always found, that a vigorous exertion of the latter faculties, necessarily, from the narrow capacity of the human mind, destroys all activity in the former. Our predominant motive or intention is, indeed, frequently concealed from ourselves, when it is mingled and confounded with other motives,[†] which the mind, from vanity or self-conceit, is desirous of supposing more prevalent: But there is no instance, that a concealment of this nature has ever arisen from the abstruseness and intricacy of the motive. A man, who has lost a friend and patron, may flatter himself, that all his grief arises from generous sentiments, without any mixture of narrow or interested considerations: But a man, that grieves for a valuable friend, who needed his patronage and protection; how can we suppose, that his passionate tenderness arises from some metaphysical regards to a self-interest, which has no foundation or reality? We may as well imagine, that minute wheels and springs, like those of a watch, give motion to a loaded waggon, as account for the origin of passion from such abstruse reflections.

8   Animals are found susceptible of kindness, both to their own species and to ours; nor is there, in this case, the least suspicion of disguise or artifice. Shall we account for all *their* sentiments too, from refined deductions of self-interest? Or if we admit a disinterested benevolence in the inferior species, by what rule of analogy can we refuse it in the superior?

9   Love between the sexes begets a complacency and good-will, very distinct from the gratification of an appetite. Tenderness to their offspring, in all sensible beings, is commonly able alone to counterbalance the strongest motives of self-love, and has no manner of dependence on that affection. What interest can a fond mother[†] have in view, who loses her health by assiduous attendance on her sick child, and afterwards languishes and dies of grief, when freed, by its death, from the slavery of that attendance?

10   Is gratitude no affection of the human breast, or is that a word merely,

not always pres.

animal kindness

love for father children not int'd

gratitude

167

without any meaning or reality? Have we no satisfaction in one man's company above another's, and no desire of the welfare of our friend, even though absence or death should prevent us from all participation in it? Or what is it commonly, that gives us any participation in it, even while alive and present, but our affection and regard to him?

11   These and a thousand other instances are marks of a general benevolence in human nature, where no *real* interest binds us to the object. And how an *imaginary* interest, known and avowed for such, can be the origin of any passion or emotion, seems difficult to explain. No satisfactory hypothesis of this kind has yet been discovered; nor is there the smallest probability, that the future industry of men will ever be attended with more favourable success.

12   But farther, if we consider rightly of the matter, we shall find, that the hypothesis, which allows of a disinterested benevolence, distinct from self-love, has really more *simplicity* in it, and is more conformable to the analogy of nature, than that which pretends to resolve all friendship and humanity into this latter principle. There are bodily wants or appetites, acknowledged by every one, which necessarily precede all sensual enjoyment, and carry us directly to seek possession of the object. Thus, hunger and thirst have eating and drinking for their end; and from the gratification of these primary appetites arises a pleasure, which may become the object of another species of desire or inclination, that is secondary and interested. In the same manner, there are mental passions, by which we are impelled immediately to seek particular objects, such as fame, or power, or vengeance, without any regard to interest; and when these objects are attained, a pleasing enjoyment ensues, as the consequence of our indulged affections. Nature must, by the internal frame and constitution of the mind, give an original propensity to fame, ere we can reap any pleasure from that acquisition,[†] or pursue it from motives of self-love, and a desire of happiness. If I have no vanity, I take no delight in praise: If I be void of ambition, power gives me no enjoyment: If I be not angry, the punishment of an adversary is totally indifferent to me. In all these cases, there is a passion, which points immediately to the object, and constitutes it our good or happiness; as there are other secondary passions, which afterwards arise, and pursue it as a part of our happiness, when once it is constituted such by our original affections. Were there no appetite of any kind antecedent to self-love, that propensity could scarcely ever exert itself; because we should, in that case, have felt few and slender pains or pleasures, and have little misery or happiness to avoid or to pursue.

13   Now where is the difficulty in conceiving, that this may likewise be the

SBN 30

SBN 3(

*the self-gratifying element in bolce, fship &
2ndary, derivative*

Appx. 2. Of Self-Love

case with benevolence and friendship, and that, from the original frame of
our temper, we may feel a desire of another's happiness or good, which,
by means of that affection, becomes our own good, and is afterwards
pursued, from the combined motives of benevolence and self-enjoyment?
Who sees not that vengeance, from the force alone of passion, may be so
eagerly pursued, as to make us knowingly neglect every consideration of
ease, interest, or safety; and, like some vindictive animals, infuse our very
souls into the wounds we give an enemy?[62] And what a malignant philosophy must it be, that will not allow, to humanity and friendship, the same
privileges, which are undisputably granted to the darker passions of
enmity and resentment? Such a philosophy is more like a satire than a true
delineation or description of human nature; and may be a good foundation for paradoxical wit and raillery, but is a very bad one for any serious
argument or reasoning.

[62] "Animasque in vulnere ponunt." VIRG. "Dum alteri noceat, sui negligens", says SENECA[†] of
Anger. De ira, lib. 1. [Virgil, *Georgics*, bk. 4, line 238. Seneca, *Moral Essays*, bk. 3, 'De ira', ch. 1,
§1.]

169

2 kinds social Vr 98
A Hy, benilee &c
B Jice, fidelity &c.
A speed in partic. acts
B only when part of a system

type A soc^l Vrs

APPENDIX 3

SOME FARTHER CONSIDERATIONS
WITH REGARD TO JUSTICE

1   T H E intention of this Appendix is to give some more particular explication of the origin and nature of justice, and to mark some differences between it and the other virtues.

2   The social virtues of humanity and benevolence exert their influence immediately, by a direct tendency or instinct, which chiefly keeps in view the simple object, moving the affections, and comprehends not any scheme or system, nor the consequences resulting from the concurrence, imitation, or example of others. A parent flies to the relief of his child; transported by that natural sympathy, which actuates him, and which affords no leisure to reflect on the sentiments or conduct of the rest of mankind in like circumstances. A generous man cheerfully embraces an opportunity of serving his friend; because he then feels himself under the dominion of the beneficent affections, nor is he concerned whether any other person in the universe were ever before actuated by such noble motives, or will ever afterwards prove their influence. In all these cases, the social passions have in view a single individual object,[†] and pursue the safety or happiness alone of the person loved and esteemed. With this they are satisfied: In this, they acquiesce. And as the good, resulting from their

benign influence, is in itself compleat and entire, it also excites the moral sentiment of approbation, without any reflection on farther conse-quences, and without any more enlarged views of the concurrence or imitation of the other members of society. On the contrary, were the gen-erous friend or disinterested patriot to stand alone in the practice of bene-ficence; this would rather enhance his value in our eyes, and join the praise of rarity and novelty to his other more exalted merits.

3   The case is not the same with the social virtues of justice and fidelity. They are highly useful, or indeed absolutely necessary to the well-being of mankind: But the benefit, resulting from them, is not the consequence of every individual single act; but arises from the whole scheme or system,

concurred in by the whole, or the greater part of the society. General peace and order are the attendants of justice or a general abstinence from the possessions of others: But a particular regard to the particular right of one individual citizen may frequently, considered in itself, be productive of pernicious consequences. The result of the individual acts is here, in many instances, directly opposite to that of the whole system of actions; and the former may be extremely hurtful, while the latter is, to the highest degree, advantageous. Riches, inherited from a parent, are, in a bad man's hand, the instruments of mischief. The right of succession[†] may, in one instance, be hurtful. Its benefit arises only from the observance of the general rule; and it is sufficient, if compensation be thereby made for all the ills and inconveniencies, which flow from particular characters and situations.

4   CYRUS,[†] young and unexperienced, considered only the individual case before him, and reflected on a limited fitness and convenience, when he assigned the long coat to the tall boy, and the short coat to the other of smaller size. His governor instructed him better; while he pointed out   SBN 305 more enlarged views and consequences, and informed his pupil of the general, inflexible rules, necessary to support general peace and order in society.

5   The happiness and prosperity of mankind, arising from the social virtue of benevolence and its subdivisions, may be compared to a wall, built by many hands; which still rises by each stone, that is heaped upon it, and receives encrease proportional to the diligence and care of each workman. The same happiness, raised by the social virtue of justice and its subdivisions, may be compared to the building of a vault,[†] where each individual stone would, of itself, fall to the ground; nor is the whole fabric supported but by the mutual assistance and combination of its corresponding parts.

6   All the laws of nature,[†] which regulate property, as well as all civil laws, are general, and regard alone some essential circumstances of the case, without taking into consideration the characters, situations, and connexions of the person concerned, or any particular consequences which may result from the determination of these laws, in any particular case which offers.[†] They deprive, without scruple, a beneficent man of all his possessions, if acquired by mistake, without a good title; in order to bestow them on a selfish miser, who has already heaped up immense stores of superfluous riches. Public utility requires, that property should be regulated by general inflexible rules; and though such rules are adopted as best serve the same end of public utility, it is impossible for them to prevent all particular hardships, or make beneficial consequences result from every

171

Enquiry concerning the Principles of Morals

individual case. It is sufficient, if the whole plan or scheme be necessary to the support of civil society, and if the balance of good, in the main, does thereby preponderate much above that of evil. Even the general laws of the universe, though planned by infinite wisdom, cannot exclude all evil or inconvenience, in every particular operation. SBN 30(

7   It has been asserted by some, that justice arises from HUMAN CONVENTIONS,[†] and proceeds from the voluntary choice, consent, or combination of mankind. If by convention be here meant a *promise*[†] (which is the most usual sense of the word) nothing can be more absurd than this position. The observance of promises is itself one of the most considerable parts of justice; and we are not surely bound to keep our word, because we have given our word to keep it. But if by convention be meant *a sense of common interest*; which sense each man feels in his own breast, which he remarks in his fellows, and which carries him, in concurrence with others, into a general plan or system of actions, which tends to public utility; it must be owned, that, in this sense, justice arises from human conventions. For if it be allowed (what is, indeed, evident) that the particular consequences of a particular act of justice may be hurtful to the public as well as to individuals; it follows, that every man, in embracing that virtue, must have an eye to the whole plan or system, and must expect the concurrence of his fellows in the same conduct and behaviour. Did all his views terminate in the consequences of each act of his own, his benevolence and humanity, as well as his self-love, might often prescribe to him measures of conduct very different from those, which are agreeable to the strict rules of right and justice.

8   Thus two men pull the oars[†] of a boat by common convention, for common interest, without any promise or contract: Thus gold and silver are made the measures of exchange; thus speech and words and language are fixed, by human convention and agreement. Whatever is advantageous to two or more persons, if all perform their part; but what loses all advantage, if only one perform, can arise from no other principle. There would otherwise be no motive for any one of them to enter into that scheme of conduct.[63] SBN 307

---

[63] This theory concerning the origin of property, and consequently of justice, is, in the main, the same with that hinted at and adopted by GROTIUS.[†] "Hinc discimus, quæ fuerit causa, ob quam a primæva communione rerum primo mobilium, deinde & immobilium discessum est: nimirum quod cum non contenti homines vesci sponte natis, antra habitare, corpore aut nudo agere, aut corticibus arborum ferarumve pellibus vestito, vitæ genus exquisitius delegissent, industria opus fuit, quam singuli rebus singulis adhiberent: Quo minus autem fructus in commune conferrentur, primum obstitit locorum, in quæ homines discesserunt, distantia, deinde justitiæ & amoris defectus, per quem fiebat, ut nec in labore, nec in consumtione fruc-

9   The word, *natural*,[†] is commonly taken in so many senses, and is of so loose a signification, that it seems vain to dispute, whether justice be natural or not. If self-love, if benevolence be natural to man; if reason and forethought be also natural; then may the same epithet be applied to justice, order, fidelity, property, society. Men's inclination, their necessities lead them to combine; their understanding and experience tell them, that this combination is impossible, where each governs himself by no rule, and pays no regard to the possessions of others: And from these passions and reflections conjoined, as soon as we observe like passions and reflections in others, the sentiment of justice, throughout all ages, has infallibly and certainly had place, to some degree or other, in every individual of the human species. In so sagacious an animal, what necessarily arises from the exertion of his intellectual faculties, may justly be esteemed natural.[64]

10   Among all civilized nations, it has been the constant endeavour to   SBN 308
remove every thing arbitrary and partial from the decision of property, and to fix the sentence of judges by such general views and considerations, as may be equal to every member of the society. For besides, that nothing could be more dangerous than to accustom the bench, even in the smallest instance, to regard[†] private friendship or enmity; it is certain, that men, where they imagine, that there was no other reason for the preference of their adversary but personal favour, are apt to entertain the strongest ill-will against the magistrates and judges. When natural reason, therefore, points out no fixed view of public utility, by which a controversy of property can be decided, positive laws[†] are often framed to supply its place, and direct the procedure of all courts of judicature.[†] Where these too fail, as often happens, precedents[†] are called for; and a former decision, though given itself without any sufficient reason, justly becomes a sufficient reason for a new decision. If direct laws and precedents be wanting, imper-

tuum, quæ debebat, æqualitas servaretur. Simul discimus, quomodo res in proprietatem   SBN 307
iverint; non animi actu solo, neque enim scire alii poterant, quid alii suum esse vellent, ut eo abstinerent, & idem velle plures poterant; sed pacto quodam aut expresso, ut per divisionem, aut tacito, ut per occupationem." De jure belli & pacis, lib. 2. cap. 2. §2. art. 4 & 5. [Hugo Grotius, *De jure belli ac pacis*, bk. 2, ch. 2, §2, arts. 4, 5.]

[64] Natural may be opposed, either to what is *unusual*, *miraculous*, or *artificial*. In the two former senses, justice and property are undoubtedly natural. But as they suppose reason, forethought, design, and a social union and confederacy among men, perhaps that epithet cannot strictly, in the last sense, be applied to them. Had men lived without society, property had never   SBN 308
been known, and neither justice nor injustice had ever existed. But society among human creatures, had been impossible, without reason and forethought. Inferior animals, that unite, are guided by instinct, which supplies the place of reason. But all these disputes are merely verbal.[†]

fect and indirect ones are brought in aid; and the controverted case[†] is ranged under them, by analogical reasonings and comparisons, and similitudes, and correspondencies, which are often more fanciful than real. In general, it may safely be affirmed, that jurisprudence is, in this respect, different from all the sciences; and that in many of its nicer questions, there cannot properly be said to be truth or falsehood[†] on either side. If one pleader bring the case under any former law or precedent, by a refined analogy or comparison; the opposite pleader is not at a loss to find an opposite analogy or comparison: And the preference given by the judge is often founded more on taste and imagination than on any solid argument. Public utility is the general object of all courts of judicature;[†] and this utility too requires a stable rule in all controversies: But where several rules, nearly equal and indifferent, present themselves, it is a very slight turn of thought, which fixes the decision in favour of either party.[65]

---

[65] That there be a separation or distinction of possessions, and that this separation be steady and constant; this is absolutely required by the interests of society, and hence the origin of justice and property. What possessions are assigned to particular persons; this is, generally speaking, pretty indifferent; and is often determined by very frivolous views and considerations. We shall mention a few particulars.

Were a society formed among several independent members, the most obvious rule, which could be agreed on, would be to annex property to *present* possession, and leave every one a right to what he at present enjoys. The relation of possession, which takes place between the person and the object, naturally draws on the relation of property.

For a like reason, occupation or first possession becomes the foundation of property.

Where a man bestows labour and industry upon any object, which before belonged to no body; as in cutting down and shaping a tree, in cultivating a field, &c. the alteration, which he produces, causes a relation between him and the object, and naturally engages us to annex it to him by the new relation of property. This cause here concurs with the public utility, which consists in the encouragement given to industry and labour.

Perhaps too, private humanity towards the possessor, concurs, in this instance, with the other motives, and engages us to leave with him what he has acquired by his sweat and labour; and what he has flattered himself in the constant enjoyment of. For though private humanity can, by no means, be the origin of justice; since the latter virtue so often contradicts the former; yet when the rule of separate and constant possession is once formed by the indispensible necessities of society, private humanity, and an aversion to the doing a hardship to another, may, in a particular instance, give rise to a particular rule of property.

I am much inclined to think, that the right of succession or inheritance much depends on those connexions of the imagination, and that the relation to a former proprietor begetting a relation to the object, is the cause why the property is transferred to a man after the death of his kinsman. It is true; industry is more encouraged by the transference of possession to children or near relations: But this consideration will only have place in a cultivated society; whereas the right of succession is regarded even among the greatest Barbarians.

Acquisition of property by *accession* can be explained no way but by having recourse to the relations and connexions of the imagination.

The property of rivers, by the laws of most nations, and by the natural turn of our thought,

11 We may just observe, before we conclude this subject, that, after the   SBN 310
laws of justice are fixed by views of general utility, the injury, the hardship,
the harm, which result to any individual from a violation of them, enter
very much into consideration, and are a great source of that universal
blame, which attends every wrong or iniquity. By the laws of society, this
coat, this horse is mine, and *ought* to remain perpetually in my possession:
I reckon on the secure enjoyment of it: By depriving me of it, you disappoint my expectations, and doubly displease me, and offend every
bystander. It is a public wrong, so far as the rules of equity are violated: It
is a private harm,[†] so far as an individual is injured. And though the second
consideration could have no place, were not the former previously estab-   SBN 311
lished: For otherwise the distinction of *mine* and *thine* would be unknown
in society: Yet there is no question, but the regard to general good is much
enforced by the respect to particular. What injures the community,
without hurting any individual, is often more lightly thought of. But
where the greatest public wrong is also conjoined with a considerable
private one, no wonder the highest disapprobation attends so iniquitous a
behaviour.

is attributed to the proprietors of their banks, excepting such vast rivers as the RHINE or the   SBN 310
DANUBE, which seem too large to follow as an accession to the property of the neighbouring
fields. Yet even these rivers are considered as the property of that nation, through whose
dominions they run; the idea of a nation being of a suitable bulk to correspond with them, and
bear them such a relation in the fancy.

The accessions, which are made to land, bordering upon rivers, follow the land, say the civilians, provided it be made by what they call *alluvion*,[†] that is, insensibly and imperceptibly; which
are circumstances, that assist the imagination in the conjunction.

Where there is any considerable portion torn at once from one bank and added to another, it
becomes not *his* property, whose land it falls on, till it unite with the land, and till the trees and
plants have spread their roots into both. Before that, the thought does not sufficiently join
them.

In short, we must ever distinguish between the necessity of a separation and constancy in
men's possession, and the rules, which assign particular objects to particular persons. The first
necessity is obvious, strong, and invincible: The latter may depend on a public utility more light
and frivolous, on the sentiment of private humanity and aversion to private hardship, on positive laws, on precedents, analogies, and very fine connexions and turns of the imagination.

terminology : excludes 'V.' / 'Vc'

virtue / talent ⎫ no rigid dist" poss.
Vc / defect ⎭

APPENDIX 4

OF SOME VERBAL DISPUTES

1 NOTHING is more usual than for philosophers to encroach upon the
province of grammarians;[†] and to engage in disputes of words, while they
imagine, that they are handling controversies of the deepest importance
and concern. It was in order to avoid altercations, so frivolous and endless,
that I endeavoured to state with the utmost caution the object of our
present enquiry; and proposed simply to collect on the one hand, a list of
those mental qualities which are the object of love or esteem, and form a
part of personal merit, and on the other hand, a catalogue of those qualities, which are the object of censure or reproach, and which detract from
the character of the person, possessed of them; subjoining some reflections concerning the origin of these sentiments of praise or blame. On all
occasions, where there might arise the least hesitation, I avoided the terms
virtue and *vice*; because some of those qualities, which I classed among the
objects of praise, receive, in the ENGLISH language, the appellation of
talents, rather than of virtues;[†] as some of the blameable or censurable
qualities are often called *defects*, rather than vices. It may now, perhaps, be
expected, that, before we conclude this moral enquiry, we should exactly
separate the one from the other; should mark the precise boundaries of
virtues and talents, vices and defects; and should explain the reason and
origin of that distinction. But in order to excuse myself from this under-
taking, which would, at last, prove only a grammatical enquiry,[†] I shall
subjoin the four following reflections, which shall contain all that I intend
to say on the present subject.

2   *First*, I do not find, that in the ENGLISH, or any other modern tongue, the
boundaries are exactly fixed between virtues and talents, vices and defects,
or that a precise definition can be given of the one as contradistinguished
from the other. Were we to say, for instance, that the esteemable qualities
alone, which are voluntary, are entitled to the appellation of virtues; we
should soon recollect the qualities of courage, equanimity, patience, self-
command; with many others, which almost every language classes under

[cf. Note a4 physs courage]

Appx. 4. Of Some Verbal Disputes

this appellation, though they depend little or not at all on our choice. Should we affirm, that the qualities alone, which prompt us to act our part in society, are entitled to that honourable distinction; it must immediately occur, that these are indeed the most valuable qualities, and are commonly denominated the *social* virtues; but that this very epithet supposes, that there are also virtues of another species. Should we lay hold of the distinction between *intellectual* and *moral* endowments,[†] and affirm the last alone to be the real and genuine virtues, because they alone lead to action; we should find, that many of those qualities, usually called intellectual virtues, such as prudence, penetration, discernment, discretion, had also a considerable influence on conduct. The distinction between the *heart* and the *head* may also be adopted: The qualities of the first may be defined such as in their immediate exertion are accompanied with a feeling or sentiment; and these alone may be called the genuine virtues: But industry, frugality, temperance, secrecy, perseverance, and many other laudable powers or habits, generally styled virtues, are exerted without any immediate sentiment in the person possessed of them; and are only known to him by their effects. It is fortunate, amidst all this seeming perplexity, that the question, being merely verbal, cannot possibly be of any importance. A moral, philosophical discourse needs not enter into all these caprices of language, which are so variable in different dialects, and in different ages of the same dialect. But on the whole, it seems to me, that, though it is always allowed, that there are virtues of many different kinds, yet, when a man is called *virtuous*, or is denominated a man of virtue, we chiefly regard his social qualities, which are, indeed, the most valuable. It is, at the same time, certain, that any remarkable defect in courage, temperance, œconomy, industry, understanding, dignity of mind, would bereave even a very good-natured, honest man of this honourable appellation. Who did ever say, except by way of irony, that such a one was a man of great virtue, but an egregious blockhead?

SBN 314

3   But, *secondly*, it is no wonder, that languages should not be very precise in marking the boundaries between virtues and talents, vices and defects; since there is so little distinction made in our internal estimation of them. It seems indeed certain, that the *sentiment* of conscious worth, the self-satisfaction proceeding from a review of a man's own conduct and character; it seems certain, I say, that this sentiment, which, though the most common of all others, has no proper name in our language,[66] arises from

---

[66] The term, *pride*, is commonly taken in a bad sense; but this sentiment seems indifferent, and may be either good or bad, according as it is well or ill founded, and according to the other circumstances which accompany it. The FRENCH express this sentiment by the term, *amour*

177

Enquiry concerning the Principles of Morals

the endowments of courage and capacity, industry and ingenuity, as well as from any other mental excellencies. Who, on the other hand, is not deeply mortified with reflecting on his own folly and dissoluteness, and feels not a secret sting or compunction, whenever his memory presents any past occurrence, where he behaved with stupidity or ill-manners? No time can efface the cruel ideas of a man's own foolish conduct, or of affronts, which cowardice or impudence has brought upon him. They still haunt his solitary hours, damp his most aspiring thoughts, and show him, even to himself, in the most contemptible and most odious colours imaginable.

cf
Wiehsck
[It is
right]

4   What is there too we are more anxious to conceal from others than such blunders, infirmities, and meannesses, or more dread to have exposed by raillery and satire? And is not the chief object of vanity, our bravery or learning, our wit or breeding, our eloquence or address, our taste or abilities? These we display with care, if not with ostentation; and we commonly show more ambition of excelling in them, than even in the social virtues themselves, which are, in reality, of such superior excellence. Good-nature and honesty, especially the latter, are so indispensibly required, that, though the greatest censure attends any violation of these duties, no eminent praise follows such common instances of them, as seem essential to the support of human society. And hence the reason, in my opinion, why, though men often extol so liberally the qualities of their heart, they are shy in commending the endowments of their head: Because the latter virtues, being supposed more rare and extraordinary, are observed to be the more usual objects of pride and self-conceit; and when boasted of, beget a strong suspicion of these sentiments.

5   It is hard to tell, whether you hurt a man's character most by calling him a knave or a coward, and whether a beastly glutton or drunkard be not as odious and contemptible, as a selfish, ungenerous miser. Give me my choice, and I would rather, for my own happiness and self-enjoyment, have a friendly, humane heart, than possess all the other virtues of DEMOSTHENES and PHILIP[†] united: But I would rather pass with the world for[†] one endowed with extensive genius and intrepid courage, and should thence expect stronger instances of general applause and admiration. The figure which a man makes in life, the reception which he meets with in company, the esteem paid him by his acquaintance; all these advantages depend as much upon his good sense and judgment, as upon any other

propre,[†] but as they also express self-love as well as vanity, by the same term, there arises thence a great confusion in ROCHEFOUCAULT, and many of their moral writers. [François de La Rochefoucauld, *Maximes*.]

178

Appx. 4. Of Some Verbal Disputes

part of his character. Had a man the best intentions in the world, and were the farthest removed from all injustice and violence, he would never be able to make himself be much regarded, without a moderate share, at least, of parts and understanding.

6   What is it then we can here dispute about? If sense and courage, temperance and industry, wisdom and knowledge confessedly form a considerable part of *personal merit*: If a man, possessed of these qualities, is both better satisfied with himself, and better entitled to the good-will, esteem, and services of others, than one entirely destitute of them; if, in short, the *sentiments* are similar, which arise from these endowments and from the social virtues; is there any reason for being so extremely scrupulous about a *word*, or disputing whether they be entitled to the denomination of virtues?[†] It may, indeed, be pretended, that the sentiment of approbation, which those accomplishments produce, besides its being *inferior*, is also somewhat *different* from that, which attends the virtues of justice and humanity. But this seems not a sufficient reason for ranking them entirely under different classes and appellations. The character of CÆSAR and that of CATO, as drawn by SALLUST,[†] are both of them virtuous, in the strictest and most limited sense of the word; but in a different way: Nor are the sentiments entirely the same, which arise from them. The one produces love; the other, esteem: The one is amiable; the other awful: We should wish to meet the one character in a friend; the other we should be ambitious of in ourselves. In like manner the approbation, which attends temperance or   SBN 317 industry or frugality, may be somewhat different from that which is paid to the social virtues, without making them entirely of a different species. And, indeed, we may observe, that these endowments, more than the other virtues, produce not, all of them, the same kind of approbation. Good sense and genius beget esteem and regard: Wit and humour excite love and affection.[67]

---

[67] Love and esteem are nearly the same passion, and arise from similar causes. The qualities, which produce both, are such as communicate pleasure. But where this pleasure is severe and serious; or where its object is great, and makes a strong impression; or where it produces any degree of humility and awe: In all these cases, the passion, which arises from the pleasure, is more properly denominated esteem than love. Benevolence attends both: But is connected with love in a more eminent degree. There seems to be still a stronger mixture of pride in contempt than of humility in esteem; and the reason would not be difficult to one, who studied accurately the passions. All these various mixtures and compositions and appearances of sentiment form a very curious subject of speculation, but are wide of our present purpose. Throughout this enquiry, we always consider in general, what qualities are a subject of praise or of censure, without entering into all the minute differences of sentiment, which they excite. It is evident, that whatever is condemned, is also disliked, as well as what is hated; and we here endeavour to take objects, according to their most simple views and appearances. These

7   Most people, I believe, will naturally, without premeditation, assent to the definition of the elegant and judicious poet.[†]

> Virtue (for mere good-nature is a fool)
> Is sense and spirit with humanity.[68]

8   What pretensions has a man to our generous assistance or good offices, who has dissipated his wealth in profuse expences, idle vanities, chimerical projects, dissolute pleasures, or extravagant gaming?[†] These vices (for we scruple not to call them such) bring misery unpitied, and contempt on every one addicted to them.   SBN 3

9   Achæus,[†] a wise and prudent prince, fell into a fatal snare, which cost him his crown and life, after having used every reasonable precaution to guard himself against it. On that account, says the historian, he is a just object of regard and compassion: His betrayers alone of hatred and contempt.[69]

10   The precipitate flight and improvident negligence of Pompey, at the beginning of the civil wars, appeared such notorious blunders to Cicero, as quite palled his friendship towards that great man. "In the same manner," says he, "as want of cleanliness, decency, or discretion in a mistress are found to alienate our affections." For so he expresses himself, where he talks, not in the character of a philosopher, but in that of a statesman and man of the world, to his friend Atticus.[70†]

11   But the same Cicero, in imitation of all the ancient moralists, when he reasons as a philosopher, enlarges very much his ideas of virtue, and comprehends every laudable quality or endowment of the mind, under that honourable appellation. This leads to the *third* reflection, which we proposed to make, to wit, that the ancient moralists, the best models, made no material distinction among the different species of mental endowments and defects, but treated all alike under the appellation of virtues and vices, and made them indiscriminately the object of their moral reasonings. The *prudence* explained in Cicero's *Offices*,[71†] is that sagacity, which leads to the

sciences are but too apt to appear abstract to common readers, even with all the precautions   SBN 3
which we can take to clear them from superfluous speculations, and bring them down to every
capacity.

    [68] *The Art of preserving Health*, Book 4. [John Armstrong, *The Art of Preserving Health*, bk. 4, lines 267–8.]
    [69] Polybius, lib. 8. cap. 2. [Polybius, *Histories*, bk. 8, chs. 20–1.]
    [70] Lib. 9. epist. 10. [Cicero, *Letters to Atticus*, bk. 9, letter 10.]
    [71] Lib. 1. cap. 6. [Cicero, *De officiis*, bk. 1, ch. 6.]

ances do not distinguish wisdom folly & Vr/Vc

discovery of truth, and preserves us from error and mistake. *Magnanimity, temperance, decency,* are there also at large discoursed of. And as that eloquent moralist followed the common received division of the four cardinal virtues,[†] our social duties form but one head, in the general distribution of his subject.[72]   SBN 319

12   We need only peruse the titles of chapters in ARISTOTLE's Ethics[†] to be convinced, that he ranks courage, temperance, magnificence, magnanimity, modesty, prudence, and a manly openness, among the virtues, as well as justice and friendship.

13   To *sustain* and to *abstain*, that is, to be patient and continent, appeared to some of the ancients a summary comprehension of all morals.

14   EPICTETUS has scarcely ever mentioned the sentiment of humanity and compassion, but in order to put his disciples on their guard against it. The virtue of the STOICS seems to consist chiefly in a firm temper and a sound understanding. With them, as with SOLOMON[†] and the eastern moralists, folly and wisdom are equivalent to vice and virtue.   SBN 320

15   Men will praise thee, says DAVID,[73†] when thou dost well unto thyself. I hate a wise man, says the GREEK poet,[†] who is not wise to himself.[74]

16   PLUTARCH[†] is no more cramped by systems in his philosophy than in his history. Where he compares the great men of GREECE and ROME, he fairly sets in opposition all their blemishes and accomplishments of whatever kind, and omits nothing considerable, which can either depress or exalt

---

[72] The following passage of CICERO is worth quoting, as being the most clear and express to our purpose, that any thing can be imagined, and, in a dispute, which is chiefly verbal, must, on account of the author, carry an authority, from which there can be no appeal.   SBN 319

"Virtus autem, quæ est per se ipsa laudabilis, et sine qua nihil laudari potest, tamen habet plures partes, quarum alia est alia ad laudationem aptior. Sunt enim aliæ virtutes, quæ videntur in moribus hominum, et quadam comitate ac beneficentia positæ: aliæ quæ in ingenii aliqua facultate, aut animi magnitudine ac robore. Nam clementia, justitia, benignitas, fides, fortitudo in periculis communibus, jucunda est auditu in laudationibus. Omnes enim hæ virtutes non tam ipsis, qui eas in se habent, quam generi hominum fructuosæ putantur. Sapientia et magnitudo animi, qua omnes res humanæ, tenues et pro nihilo putantur; et in cogitando vis quædam ingenii, et ipsa eloquentia admirationis habet non minus, jucunditatis minus. Ipsos enim magis videtur, quos laudamus, quam illos, apud quos laudamus, ornare ac tueri: sed tamen in laudanda jungenda sunt etiam hæc genera virtutum. Ferunt enim aures hominum, cum illa quæ jucunda et grata, tum etiam illa, quæ mirabilia sunt in virtute, laudari." De orat. lib. 2. cap. 84. [Cicero, *De oratore*, bk. 2, ch. 84, §§ 343–4.]

I suppose, if CICERO were now alive, it would be found difficult to fetter his moral sentiments by narrow systems; or persuade him, that no qualities were to be admitted as *virtues*, or acknowledged to be a part of *personal merit*, but what were recommended by The Whole Duty of Man. [Anon., *The Whole Duty of Man*.]

[73] Psalm 49th. [Ps. 49: 18.]   SBN 320

[74] Μισῶ σοφιστὴν ὅστις οὐχ αὑτῷ σοφός. EURIPIDES. [Euripides, *Fragments*.]

their characters. His moral discourses contain the same free and natural censure of men and manners.

17   The character of HANNIBAL, as drawn by LIVY,[75†] is esteemed partial, but allows him many eminent virtues. Never was there a genius, says the historian, more equally fitted for those opposite offices of commanding and obeying; and it were, therefore, difficult to determine whether he rendered himself *dearer* to the general[†] or to the army. To none would HASDRUBAL entrust more willingly the conduct of any dangerous enterprize; under none, did the soldiers discover more courage and confidence. Great boldness in facing danger; great prudence in the midst of it. No labour could fatigue his body or subdue his mind. Cold and heat were indifferent to him: Meat and drink he sought as supplies to the necessities of nature, not as gratifications of his voluptuous appetites: Waking or rest he used indiscriminately, by night or by day.——These great VIRTUES were balanced by great VICES: Inhuman cruelty; perfidy more than *punic*;[†] no truth, no faith, no regard to oaths, promises, or religion.

18   The character of ALEXANDER the Sixth, to be found in GUICCIARDIN,[76†] is pretty similar, but juster; and is a proof, that even the moderns, where they speak naturally, hold the same language with the ancients. In this pope, says he, there was a singular capacity and judgment: Admirable prudence; a wonderful talent of persuasion; and in all momentous enterprizes, a diligence and dexterity incredible. But these *virtues* were infinitely overbalanced by his *vices*; no faith, no religion, insatiable avarice, exorbitant ambition, and a more than barbarous cruelty.

19   POLYBIUS,[77†] reprehending TIMÆUS for his partiality against AGATHOCLES, whom he himself allows to be the most cruel and impious of all tyrants, says: If he took refuge in SYRACUSE, as asserted by that historian, flying the dirt and smoke and toil of his former profession of a potter; and if proceeding from such slender beginnings, he became master, in a little time, of all SICILY; brought the CARTHAGINIAN state into the utmost danger; and at last died in old age, and in possession of sovereign dignity: Must he not be allowed something prodigious and extraordinary, and to have possessed great talents and capacity for business and action? His historian, therefore, ought not to have alone related what tended to his reproach and infamy; but also what might redound to his PRAISE and HONOUR.

20   In general, we may observe, that the distinction of voluntary or invol-

SBN 32

[75] Lib. 21. cap. 4. [Livy, *History*, bk. 21, ch. 4.]
[76] Lib. 1. [Francesco Guicciardini, *Della historia d'Italia*, bk. 1, ch. 2.]
[77] Lib. 12. [Polybius, *Histories*, bk. 12, ch. 15, esp. §§ 5–12.]

SBN 32
SBN 32

untary was little regarded by the ancients in their moral reasonings; where they frequently treated the question as very doubtful, *whether virtue could be taught*[†] *or not?*[78] They justly considered, that cowardice, meanness, levity, anxiety, impatience, folly, and many other qualities of the mind, might appear ridiculous and deformed, contemptible and odious, though independent of the will.[†] Nor could it be supposed, at all times, in every man's power to attain every kind of mental, more than of exterior beauty.

And here there occurs the *fourth* reflection which I purposed to make, in suggesting the reason, why modern philosophers have often followed a course, in their moral enquiries, so different from that of the ancients. In later times, philosophy of all kinds, especially ethics, have been more closely united with theology than ever they were observed to be among the Heathens; and as this latter science admits of no terms of composition,[†] but bends every branch of knowledge to its own purpose, without much regard to the phænomena of nature, or to the unbiassed sentiments of the mind, hence reasoning, and even language, have been warped from their natural course, and distinctions have been endeavoured to be established, where the difference of the objects was, in a manner, imperceptible. Philosophers, or rather divines under that disguise, treating all morals, as on a like footing with civil laws, guarded by the sanctions of reward and punishment,[†] were necessarily led to render this circumstance, of *voluntary* or *involuntary*, the foundation of their whole theory. Every one may employ *terms* in what sense he pleases: But this, in the mean time, must be allowed, that *sentiments* are every day experienced of blame and praise, which have objects beyond the dominion of the will or choice, and of which it behoves us, if not as moralists, as speculative philosophers at least, to give some satisfactory theory and explication.

A blemish, a fault, a vice, a crime; these expressions seem to denote different degrees of censure and disapprobation; which are, however, all of them, at the bottom, pretty nearly of the same kind or species. The explication of one will easily lead us into a just conception of the others; and it is of greater consequence to attend to things than to verbal appellations. That we owe a duty to ourselves[†] is confessed even in the most vulgar system[†] of morals; and it must be of consequence to examine that duty, in

SBN 322

[78] Vid. PLATO, in MENONE, SENECA, de otio sap. cap. 31. So also HORACE, *Virtutem doctrina paret, naturane donet.* Epist. lib. 1. ep. 18. ÆSCHINES SOCRATICUS, Dial. 1. [Plato, *Meno*, 70 a ff. Seneca, *Moral Essays*, bk. 8, 'De otio', ch. 4 (31 in older editions), esp. § 2. Horace, *Epistles*, bk. 1, ep. 18, line 100. Aeschines Socraticus, *Dialogues* 1.]

SBN 323

SBN 321

order to see, whether it bears any affinity to that which we owe to society. It is probable, that the approbation, attending the observance of both, is of a similar nature, and arises from similar principles; whatever appellation we may give to either of these excellencies.

1   MY friend, PALAMEDES, who is as great a rambler in his principles as in his person, and who has run over, by study and travel, almost every region of the intellectual and material world, surprized me lately with an account of a nation, with whom, he told me, he had passed a considerable part of his life, and whom, he found, in the main, a people extremely civilized and intelligent.

2   There is a country, said he, in the world, called FOURLI,[†] no matter for its longitude or latitude, whose inhabitants have ways of thinking, in many things, particularly in morals, diametrically opposite to ours. When I came among them, I found that I must submit to double pains; first to learn the meaning of the terms in their language, and then to know the import of those terms, and the praise or blame attached to them. After a word had been explained to me, and the character, which it expressed, had been described, I concluded, that such an epithet must necessarily be the greatest reproach in the world; and was extremely surprized to find one in a public company, apply it to a person, with whom he lived in the strictest intimacy and friendship. "You fancy," said I, one day, to an acquaintance, "that CHANGUIS is your mortal enemy: I love to extinguish quarrels; and I must, therefore, tell you, that I heard him talk of you in the most obliging manner."[†] But to my great astonishment, when I repeated CHANGUIS's words, though I had both remembered and understood them perfectly, I found, that they were taken for the most mortal affront, and that I had   SBN 325 very innocently rendered the breach between these persons altogether irreparable.

3   As it was my fortune to come among this people on a very advantageous footing, I was immediately introduced to the best company; and being desired by ALCHEIC to live with him, I readily accepted of his invitation; as I found him universally esteemed for his personal merit,[†] and indeed regarded by every one in FOURLI, as a perfect character.

4   One evening he invited me, as an amusement, to bear him company in a

serenade, which he intended to give to GULKI, with whom, he told me, he was extremely enamoured; and I soon found that his taste was not singular: For we met many of his rivals, who had come on the same errand. I very naturally concluded, that this mistress of his must be one of the finest women in town; and I already felt a secret inclination to see her, and be acquainted with her. But as the moon began to rise, I was much surprized to find, that we were in the midst of the university, where GULKI studied: And I was somewhat ashamed for having attended my friend, on such an errand.

5   I was afterwards told, that ALCHEIC's choice of GULKI was very much approved of by all the good company in town; and that it was expected, while he gratified his own passion, he would perform to that young man the same good office, which he had himself owed to ELCOUF. It seems ALCHEIC had been very handsome in his youth, had been courted by many lovers; but had bestowed his favours chiefly on the sage ELCOUF; to whom he was supposed to owe, in a great measure, the astonishing progress which he had made in philosophy and virtue.

6   It gave me some surprize, that ALCHEIC's wife (who by-the-bye happened also to be his sister) was nowise scandalized at this species of infidelity.

7   Much about the same time I discovered (for it was not attempted to be   SBN 3⌉ kept a secret from me or any body) that ALCHEIC was a murderer and a parricide, and had put to death an innocent person, the most nearly connected with him, and whom he was bound to protect and defend by all the ties of nature and humanity. When I asked, with all the caution and deference imaginable, what was his motive for this action; he replied coolly, that he was not then so much at ease in his circumstances as he is at present, and that he had acted, in that particular, by the advice of all his friends.

8   Having heard ALCHEIC's virtue so extremely celebrated, I pretended to join in the general voice of acclamation, and only asked, by way of curiosity, as a stranger, which of all his noble actions was most highly applauded; and I soon found, that all sentiments were united in giving the preference to the assassination of USBEK.[†] This USBEK had been to the last moment ALCHEIC's intimate friend, had laid many high obligations upon him, had even saved his life on a certain occasion, and had, by his will, which was found after the murder, made him heir to a considerable part of his fortune. ALCHEIC, it seems, conspired with about twenty or thirty more, most of them also USBEK's friends; and falling all together on that unhappy man, when he was not aware, they had torn him with a hundred wounds;

and given him that reward for all his past favours and obligations. Usbek, said the general voice of the people, had many great and good qualities: His very vices were shining, magnificent, and generous: But this action of Alcheic's sets him far above Usbek in the eyes of all judges of merit; and is one of the noblest that ever perhaps the sun shone upon.

9   Another part of Alcheic's conduct, which I also found highly applauded, was his behaviour towards Calish, with whom he was joined in a project or undertaking of some importance. Calish, being a passionate man, gave Alcheic, one day, a sound drubbing; which he took very patiently, waited the return of Calish's good-humour, kept still a fair correspondence with him; and by that means brought the affair, in which they were joined, to a happy issue, and gained to himself immortal honour by his remarkable temper and moderation. SBN 327

10   I have lately received a letter from a correspondent in Fourli, by which I learn, that, since my departure, Alcheic, falling into a bad state of health, has fairly hanged himself; and has died universally regretted and applauded in that country. So virtuous and noble a life, says each Fourlian, could not be better crowned than by so noble an end; and Alcheic has proved by this, as well as by all his other actions, what was his constant principle during his life, and what he boasted of near his last moments, that a wise man is scarcely inferior to the great god, Vitzli.[†] This is the name of the supreme deity among the Fourlians.

11   The notions of this people, continued Palamedes, are as extraordinary with regard to good manners and sociableness, as with regard to morals. My friend Alcheic formed once a party for my entertainment, composed of all the prime wits and philosophers of Fourli; and each of us brought his mess along with him to the place where we assembled. I observed one of them to be worse provided than the rest, and offered him a share of my mess, which happened to be a roasted pullet: And I could not but remark, that he and all the rest of the company smiled at my simplicity. I was told, that Alcheic had once so much interest with his club as to prevail with them to eat in common, and that he had made use of an artifice for that purpose. He persuaded those, whom he observed to be *worst* provided, to offer their mess to the company; after which, the others, who had brought more delicate fare, were ashamed not to make the same offer. This is regarded as so extraordinary an event, that it has since, as I learn, been recorded in the history of Alcheic's life, composed by one of the greatest geniuses of Fourli.

12   Pray, said I, Palamedes, when you were at Fourli, did you also learn the SBN 328 art of turning your friends into ridicule, by telling them strange stories,

and then laughing at them, if they believed you. I assure you, replied he, had I been disposed to learn such a lesson, there was no place in the world more proper. My friend, so often mentioned, did nothing, from morning to night, but sneer, and banter, and rally; and you could scarcely ever distinguish, whether he were in jest or earnest. But you think then, that my story is improbable; and that I have used, or rather abused the privilege of a traveller. To be sure, said I, you were but in jest. Such barbarous and savage manners are not only incompatible with a civilized, intelligent people, such as you said these were; but are scarcely compatible with human nature. They exceed all we ever read of, among the MINGRELIANS, and TOPINAMBOUES.[†]

13   Have a care, cried he, have a care! You are not aware that you are speaking blasphemy, and are abusing your favourites, the GREEKS, especially the ATHENIANS,[†] whom I have couched, all along, under these bizarre names I employed. If you consider aright, there is not one stroke of the foregoing character, which might not be found in the man of highest merit at ATHENS, without diminishing in the least from the brightness of his character. The amours of the GREEKS, their marriages,[79] and the exposing of their children[†] cannot but strike you immediately. The death of USBEK is an exact counterpart to that of CÆSAR.

14   All to a trifle, said I, interrupting him: You did not mention that USBEK was an usurper.

15   I did not, replied he; lest you should discover the parallel I aimed at. But even adding this circumstance, we should make no scruple, according to our sentiments of morals, to denominate BRUTUS, and CASSIUS, ungrateful traitors and assassins:[†] Though you know, that they are, perhaps, the highest characters of all antiquity; and the ATHENIANS erected statues to them; which they placed near those of HARMODIUS and ARISTOGITON, their own deliverers. And if you think this circumstance, which you mention, so material to absolve these patriots, I shall compensate it by another, not mentioned, which will equally aggravate their crime. A few days before the execution of their fatal purpose, they all swore fealty to CÆSAR; and protesting to hold his person ever sacred, they touched the altar with those hands, which they had already armed for his destruction.[80]

16   I need not remind you of the famous and applauded story of THEMISTOCLES, and of his patience towards EURYBIADES,[†] the SPARTAN, his

SBN 321

---

[79] The laws of ATHENS allowed a man to marry his sister by the father. SOLON's law forbid pæderasty to slaves, as being an act of too great dignity for such mean persons.   SBN 321

[80] APPIAN. de bell. civ. lib. 2. SUETONIUS, in vita CÆSARIS. [Appian, *Roman History*, bk. 2, ch. 16, §§ 111–17. Suetonius, *Lives of the Caesars*, bk. 2, 'The Deified Julius', chs. 78–84.]   SBN 321

188

commanding officer, who, heated by debate, lifted his cane to him in a council of war (the same thing as if he had cudgelled him) "Strike!" cries the ATHENIAN, "strike! but hear me."

17 You are too good a scholar not to discover the ironical SOCRATES and his ATHENIAN club in my last story; and you will certainly observe, that it is exactly copied from XENOPHON,[†] with a variation only of the names.[81] And I think I have fairly made it appear, that an ATHENIAN man of merit might be such a one as with us would pass for incestuous, a parricide, an assassin, an ungrateful, perjured traitor, and something else too abominable to be named; not to mention his rusticity and ill-manners. And having lived in this manner, his death might be entirely suitable: He might conclude the scene by a desperate act of self-murder,[†] and die with the most absurd blasphemies in his mouth. And notwithstanding all this, he shall have statues, if not altars, erected to his memory; poems and orations shall be composed in his praise; great sects shall be proud of calling themselves by his name; and the most distant posterity shall blindly continue their admiration: Though were such a one to arise among themselves, they would justly regard him with horror and execration. SBN 330

18 I might have been aware, replied I, of your artifice. You seem to take pleasure in this topic; and are indeed the only man I ever knew, who was well acquainted with the ancients, and did not extremely admire them. But instead of attacking their philosophy, their eloquence, or poetry, the usual subjects of controversy between us, you now seem to impeach their morals,[†] and accuse them of ignorance in a science, which is the only one, in my opinion, in which they are not surpassed by the moderns. Geometry, physics, astronomy, anatomy, botany, geography, navigation; in these we justly claim the superiority: But what have we to oppose to their moralists? Your representation of things is fallacious. You have no indulgence for the manners and customs of different ages. Would you try a GREEK or ROMAN by the common law of ENGLAND? Hear him defend himself by his own maxims; and then pronounce.

19 There are no manners so innocent or reasonable, but may be rendered odious or ridiculous, if measured by a standard, unknown to the persons; especially, if you employ a little art or eloquence, in aggravating some circumstances, and extenuating others, as best suits the purpose of your discourse. All these artifices may easily be retorted on you. Could I inform the ATHENIANS, for instance, that there was a nation, in which adultery,[†] both active and passive, so to speak, was in the highest vogue and esteem:

---

[81] Mem. Soc. lib. 3. sub fine. [Xenophon, *Memorabilia*, bk. 3, ch. 14, §1.] SBN 329

In which every man of education chose for his mistress a married woman, the wife, perhaps, of his friend and companion; and valued himself upon these infamous conquests, as much as if he had been several times a conqueror in boxing or wrestling at the *Olympic* games: In which every man also took a pride in his tameness and facility with regard to his own wife, and was glad to make friends or gain interest by allowing her to prostitute her charms;[†] and even, without any such motive, gave her full liberty and indulgence: I ask, what sentiments the ATHENIANS would entertain of such a people; they who never mentioned the crime of adultery but in conjunction with robbery and poisoning? Which would they admire most, the villany or the meanness of such a conduct? SBN 33

20   Should I add, that the same people were as proud of their slavery[†] and dependence as the ATHENIANS of their liberty; and though a man among them were oppressed, disgraced, impoverished, insulted, or imprisoned by the tyrant, he would still regard it as the highest merit to love, serve, and obey him; and even to die for his smallest glory or satisfaction: These noble GREEKS would probably ask me, whether I spoke of a human society, or of some inferior, servile species.

21   It was then I might inform my ATHENIAN audience, that these people, however, wanted not spirit and bravery. If a man, say I, though their intimate friend, should throw out, in a private company, a raillery against them, nearly approaching any of those, with which your generals and demagogues every day regale each other, in the face of the whole city, they never can forgive him; but in order to revenge themselves, they oblige him immediately to run them through the body, or be himself murdered. And if a man, who is an absolute stranger to them, should desire them, at the peril of their own life, to cut the throat of their bosom-companion, they immediately obey, and think themselves highly obliged and honoured by the commission. These are their maxims of honour: This is their favourite morality.[†]

22   But though so ready to draw their sword against their friends and countrymen; no disgrace, no infamy, no pain, no poverty will ever engage these people to turn the point of it against their own breast.[†] A man of rank would row in the gallies, would beg his bread, would languish in prison, would suffer any tortures; and still preserve his wretched life. Rather than escape his enemies by a generous contempt of death,[†] he would infamously receive the same death from his enemies, aggravated by their triumphant insults, and by the most exquisite sufferings. SBN 33

23   It is very usual too, continue I, among this people to erect jails, where every art of plaguing and tormenting the unhappy prisoners is carefully

studied and practiced: And in these jails it is usual for a parent voluntarily to shut up several of his children; in order, that another child, whom he owns to have no greater or rather less merit than the rest, may enjoy his whole fortune, and wallow in every kind of voluptuousness and pleasure. Nothing so virtuous in their opinion as this barbarous partiality.[†]

24   But what is more singular in this whimsical nation, say I to the ATHENIANS, is, that a frolic of yours during the SATURNALIA,[82†] when the slaves are served by their masters, is seriously continued by them throughout the whole year, and throughout the whole course of their lives; accompanied too with some circumstances, which still farther augment the absurdity and ridicule. Your sport only elevates for a few days those whom fortune has thrown down, and whom she too, in sport, may really elevate for ever above you: But this nation gravely exalts those, whom nature has subjected to them, and whose inferiority and infirmities are absolutely incurable. The women, though without virtue, are their masters and sovereigns: These they reverence, praise, and magnify: To these, they pay the highest deference and respect: And in all places and all times, the superiority of the females is readily acknowledged and submitted to by every one, who has the least pretensions to education and politeness. Scarce any crime would be so universally detested as an infraction of this rule.

25   You need go no further, replied PALAMEDES; I can easily conjecture the   SBN 333
people whom you aim at. The strokes, with which you have painted them, are pretty just; and yet you must acknowledge, that scarce any people are to be found, either in ancient or modern times, whose national character[†] is, upon the whole, less liable to exception.[†] But I give you thanks for helping me out with my argument. I had no intention of exalting the moderns at the expence of the ancients. I only meant to represent the uncertainty of all these judgments concerning characters; and to convince you, that fashion, vogue, custom, and law, were the chief foundation of all moral determinations. The ATHENIANS surely, were a civilized, intelligent people, if ever there were one; and yet their man of merit might, in this age, be held in horror and execration. The FRENCH are also, without doubt, a very civilized, intelligent people; and yet their man of merit might, with the ATHENIANS, be an object of the highest contempt and ridicule, and even hatred. And what renders the matter more extraordinary: These two people are supposed to be the most similar in their national character of

---

[82] The GREEKS kept the feast of SATURN or CHRONUS, as well as the ROMANS. See LUCIAN. epist.   SBN 332
SATURN. [Lucian, *Saturnalia*, §§ 10–39.]

any in ancient and modern times; and while the ENGLISH flatter themselves that they resemble the ROMANS, their neighbours on the continent draw the parallel between themselves and those polite GREEKS. What wide difference, therefore, in the sentiments of morals, must be found between civilized nations and Barbarians, or between nations whose characters have little in common?† How shall we pretend to fix a standard for judgments of this nature?

26   By tracing matters, replied I, a little higher, and examining the first principles, which each nation establishes, of blame or censure. The RHINE flows north, the RHONE south; yet both spring from the *same* mountain, and are also actuated, in their opposite directions, by the *same* principle of gravity. The different inclinations of the ground, on which they run, cause all the difference of their courses.

27   In how many circumstances would an ATHENIAN and a FRENCH man   SBN 334 of merit certainly resemble each other? Good sense, knowledge, wit, eloquence, humanity, fidelity, truth, justice, courage, temperance, constancy, dignity of mind: These you have all omitted; in order to insist only on the points, in which they may, by accident, differ. Very well: I am willing to comply with you; and shall endeavour to account for these differences from the most universal, established principles† of morals.

28   The GREEK loves,† I care not to examine more particularly. I shall only observe, that, however blameable, they arose from a very innocent cause, the frequency of the gymnastic exercises among that people; and were recommended, though absurdly, as the source of friendship, sympathy, mutual attachment, and fidelity;[83] qualities esteemed in all nations and all ages.

29   The marriage of half-brothers and sisters seems no great difficulty. Love between the nearer relations is contrary to reason and public utility; but the precise point, where we are to stop, can scarcely be determined by natural reason; and is therefore a very proper subject for municipal law or custom. If the ATHENIANS went a little too far on the one side, the canon law† has surely pushed matters a great way into the other extreme.[84]

30   Had you asked a parent at ATHENS, why he bereaved his child of that life,† which he had so lately given it. It is because I love it, he would reply; and regard the poverty which it must inherit from me, as a greater evil than death, which it is not capable of dreading, feeling, or resenting.[85]

---

[83] PLAT. symp. p. 182. ex edit. SERR. [Plato, *Symposium*, 182 A–85 C.]

[84] See *Enquiry*, Section 4. [*An Enquiry concerning the Principles of Morals* 4.9.]

[85] PLUTARCH. de amore prolis, sub fine. [Plutarch, *Moralia*, 'On Affection for Offspring', ch. 5, 497 E.]

31 　　How is public liberty, the most valuable of all blessings, to be recovered from the hands of an usurper or tyrant, if his power shields him from public rebellion, and our scruples from private vengeance? That his crime is capital by law, you acknowledge: And must the highest aggravation of his crime, the putting of himself above law, form his full security? You can reply nothing, but by showing the great inconveniencies of assassination; which could any one have proved clearly to the ancients, he had reformed their sentiments in this particular.

SBN 335

32 　　Again, to cast your eye on the picture which I have drawn of modern manners; there is almost as great difficulty, I acknowledge, to justify FRENCH as GREEK gallantry; except only, that the former is much more natural and agreeable than the latter. But our neighbours, it seems, have resolved to sacrifice some of the domestic to the sociable pleasures; and to prefer ease, freedom, and an open commerce to a strict fidelity and constancy. These ends are both good, and are somewhat difficult to reconcile; nor need we be surprized, if the customs of nations incline too much, sometimes to the one side, sometimes to the other.

33 　　The most inviolable attachment to the laws of our country is every where acknowledged a capital virtue; and where the people are not so happy, as to have any legislature but a single person, the strictest loyalty is, in that case, the truest patriotism.

34 　　Nothing surely can be more absurd and barbarous than the practice of duelling; but those, who justify it, say, that it begets civility and good manners. And a duellist, you may observe, always values himself upon his courage, his sense of honour, his fidelity and friendship; qualities, which are here indeed very oddly directed, but which have been esteemed universally, since the foundation of the world.

35 　　Have the gods forbid self-murder?[†] An ATHENIAN allows, that it ought to be forborn. Has the Deity permitted it? A FRENCHMAN allows, that death is preferable to pain and infamy.

36 　　You see then, continued I, that the principles upon which men reason in morals are always the same; though the conclusions which they draw are often very different. That they all reason aright with regard to this subject, more than with regard to any other, it is not incumbent on any moralist to show. It is sufficient, that the original principles of censure or blame are uniform, and that erroneous conclusions can be corrected by sounder reasoning and larger experience. Though many ages have elapsed since the fall of GREECE and ROME; though many changes have arrived in religion, language, laws, and customs; none of these revolutions has ever produced any considerable innovation in the primary sentiments of morals, more

SBN 336

than in those of external beauty. Some minute differences, perhaps, may be observed in both. Horace[86] celebrates a low forehead, and Anacreon[†] joined eye-brows:[87] But the Apollo and the Venus[†] of antiquity are still our models for male and female beauty; in like manner as the character of Scipio continues our standard for the glory of heroes, and that of Cornelia[†] for the honour of matrons.

37   It appears, that there never was any quality recommended by any one, as a virtue or moral excellence, but on account of its being *useful*, or *agreeable* to a man *himself*, or to *others*. For what other reason can ever be assigned for praise or approbation? Or where would be the sense of extolling a *good* character or action, which, at the same time, is allowed to be *good for nothing*? All the differences, therefore, in morals, may be reduced to this one general foundation, and may be accounted for by the different views, which people take of these circumstances.

38   Sometimes men differ in their judgment about the usefulness of any habit or action: Sometimes also the peculiar circumstances of things render one moral quality more useful than others, and give it a peculiar preference.

39   It is not surprizing, that, during a period of war and disorder, the military virtues should be more celebrated than the pacific, and attract more the admiration and attention of mankind. "How usual is it," says Tully,[88] "to find Cimbrians, Celtiberians,[†] and other Barbarians, who bear, with inflexible constancy, all the fatigues and dangers of the field; but are immediately dispirited under the pain and hazard of a languishing distemper: While, on the other hand, the Greeks patiently endure the slow approaches of death, when armed with sickness and disease; but timorously fly his presence,[†] when he attacks them violently with swords and falchions!" So different is even the same virtue of courage among warlike or peaceful nations! And indeed, we may observe, that, as the difference between war and peace is the greatest that arises among nations and public societies, it produces also the greatest variations in moral sentiment, and diversifies the most our ideas of virtue and personal merit.

40   Sometimes too, magnanimity, greatness of mind, disdain of slavery, inflexible rigour and integrity, may better suit the circumstances of one age than those of another, and have a more kindly influence, both on

SBN 33

---

[86] Epist. lib. 1. epist. 7. Also lib. 1. ode 33. [Horace, *Epistles*, bk. 1, ep. 7, lines 26–8; also *Odes*, bk. 1, ode 33, lines 5–6.]

[87] Ode 28. Petronius[†] (cap. 126.) joins both these circumstances as beauties. [Anacreon, *Anacreontea*, ode 16 (current numbering), lines 9–11. Petronius, *Satyricon*, ch. 126.]

[88] Tusc. quæst. lib. 2. [Cicero, *Tusculan Disputations*, bk. 2, ch. 27, §65.]

SBN 33

SBN 33

public affairs, and on a man's own safety and advancement. Our idea of merit, therefore, will also vary a little with these variations; and LABEO, perhaps, be censured for the same qualities, which procured CATO[†] the highest approbation.

41 A degree of luxury[†] may be ruinous and pernicious in a native of SWITZERLAND, which only fosters the arts, and encourages industry in a FRENCHMAN or ENGLISHMAN. We are not, therefore, to expect, either the same sentiments, or the same laws in BERNE, which prevail in LONDON or PARIS.

42 Different customs have also some influence as well as different utilities; and by giving an early biass to the mind, may produce a superior propensity, either to the useful or the agreeable qualities; to those which regard self, or those which extend to society. These four sources of moral sentiment[†] still subsist; but particular accidents may, at one time, make any one of them flow with greater abundance than at another.

SBN 338

43 The customs of some nations shut up the women[†] from all social commerce: Those of others make them so essential a part of society and conversation, that, except where business is transacted, the male sex alone are supposed almost wholly incapable of mutual discourse and entertainment. As this difference is the most material that can happen in private life, it must also produce the greatest variation in our moral sentiments.

44 Of all nations in the world, where polygamy was not allowed, the GREEKS seem to have been the most reserved in their commerce with the fair sex, and to have imposed on them the strictest laws of modesty and decency. We have a strong instance of this in an oration of LYSIAS.[89][†] A widow injured, ruined, undone, calls a meeting of a few of her nearest friends and relations; and though never before accustomed, says the orator, to speak in the presence of men, the distress of her circumstances constrained her to lay the case before them. The very opening of her mouth in such company required, it seems, an apology.

45 When DEMOSTHENES prosecuted his tutors,[†] to make them refund his patrimony, it became necessary for him, in the course of the law-suit, to prove that the marriage of APHOBUS's sister with ONETER was entirely fraudulent, and that, notwithstanding her sham marriage, she had lived with her brother at ATHENS for two years past, ever since her divorce from her former husband. And it is remarkable, that though these were people of the first fortune and distinction in the city, the orator could prove this

---

[89] Orat. 33. [Lysias, *Orations*, Oration 32 (33 in older editions), 'Against Diogeiton', §§ 11–12.]

fact no way, but by calling for her female slaves to be put to the question, and by the evidence of one physician, who had seen her in her brother's house during her illness.[90] So reserved were GREEK manners.

46   We may be assured, that an extreme purity of manners was the consequence of this reserve. Accordingly we find, that, except the fabulous stories of an HELEN and a CLYTEMNESTRA, there scarcely is an instance of any event in the GREEK history, which proceeded from the intrigues of women.[†] On the other hand, in modern times, particularly in a neighbouring nation,[†] the females enter into all transactions and all management of church and state: And no man can expect success, who takes not care to obtain their good graces. HARRY the third,[†] by incurring the displeasure of the fair, endangered his crown, and lost his life, as much as by his indulgence to heresy.

47   It is needless to dissemble: The consequence of a very free commerce between the sexes, and of their living much together, will often terminate in intrigues and gallantry. We must sacrifice somewhat of the *useful*, if we be very anxious to obtain all the *agreeable* qualities; and cannot pretend to reach alike every kind of advantage. Instances of licence, daily multiplying, will weaken the scandal with the one sex, and teach the other, by degrees, to adopt the famous maxim of LA FONTAINE,[†] with regard to female infidelity, "that if one knows it, it is but a small matter; if one knows it not, it is nothing."[91]

48   Some people are inclined to think, that the best way of adjusting all differences, and of keeping the proper medium between the *agreeable* and the *useful* qualities of the sex, is to live with them after the manner of the ROMANS and the ENGLISH (for the customs of these two nations seem similar in this respect[92]); that is, without gallantry,[93] and without jealousy. By a parity of reason, the customs of the SPANIARDS and of the ITALIANS of an age ago (for the present are very different) must be the worst of any; because they favour both gallantry and jealousy.

---

[90] In ONETEREM. [Demosthenes, *Against Oneter* 1, §§ 33–6.]

[91] 'Quand on le sçait c'est peu de chose:
Quand on l'ignore, ce n'est rien.'
[Jean de La Fontaine, *Contes et nouvelles en vers*, 'La coupe enchantée'.]

[92] During the time of the emperors, the ROMANS seem to have been more given to intrigues and gallantry than the ENGLISH are at present: And the women of condition, in order to retain their lovers, endeavoured to fix a name of reproach on those who were addicted to wenching and low amours. They were called *Ancillarioli*.[†] See SENECA, de beneficiis, lib. 1. cap. 9. See also MARTIAL, lib. 12. epig. 58. [Seneca, *Moral Essays*, bk. 1, 'De beneficiis', ch. 9, §4. Martial, *Epigrams*, bk. 12, epigram 58.]

[93] The gallantry here meant is that of amours and attachments, not that of complaisance, which is as much paid to the fair sex in ENGLAND as in any other country.

A Dialogue

49   Nor will these different customs of nations affect the one sex only: Their idea of personal merit in the males must also be somewhat different with regard, at least, to conversation, address, and humour. The one nation, where the men live much apart, will naturally more approve of prudence; the other of gaiety. With the one simplicity of manners will be in the highest esteem; with the other, politeness. The one will distinguish themselves by good sense and judgment; the other, by taste and delicacy. The eloquence of the former will shine most in the senate; that of the other, on the theatre.

50   These, I say, are the *natural* effects of such customs. For it must be confessed, that chance has a great influence on national manners; and many events happen in society, which are not to be accounted for by general rules. Who could imagine, for instance, that the ROMANS, who lived freely with their women, should be very indifferent about music, and esteem dancing infamous:[†] While the GREEKS, who never almost saw a woman but in their own houses, were continually piping, singing, and dancing?

51   The differences of moral sentiment, which naturally arise from a republican or monarchical government, are also very obvious; as well as those, which proceed from general riches or poverty, union or faction, ignorance or learning. I shall conclude this long discourse with observing, that different customs and situations vary not the original ideas of merit[†] (however they may, some consequences) in any very essential point, and prevail chiefly with regard to young men, who can aspire to the agreeable qualities, and may attempt to please. The MANNER, the ORNAMENTS, the GRACES, which succeed in this shape, are more arbitrary and casual: But the merit of riper years is almost every where the same; and consists chiefly in integrity, humanity, ability, knowledge, and the other more solid and useful qualities of the human mind.

SBN 341

52   What you insist on, replied PALAMEDES, may have some foundation, when you adhere to the maxims of common life and ordinary conduct. Experience and the practice of the world readily correct any great extravagance on either side. But what say you to *artificial* lives[†] and manners? How do you reconcile the maxims, on which, in different ages and nations, these are founded?

53   What do you understand by *artificial* lives and manners? said I. I explain myself, replied he. You know, that religion had, in ancient times, very little influence on common life, and that, after men had performed their duty in sacrifices and prayers at the temple, they thought, that the gods left the rest of their conduct to themselves, and were little pleased or offended with

relig⁶'s
unlike,
weak in
antiq'y
183

197

those virtues or vices, which only affected the peace and happiness of human society. In those ages, it was the business of philosophy alone to regulate men's ordinary behaviour and deportment; and accordingly, we may observe, that this being the sole principle, by which a man could elevate himself above his fellows, it acquired a mighty ascendant over many, and produced great singularities of maxims and of conduct. At present, when philosophy has lost the allurement of novelty, it has no such extensive influence; but seems to confine itself mostly to speculations in the closet; in the same manner, as the ancient religion was limited to sacrifices in the temple. Its place is now supplied by the modern religion, which inspects our whole conduct, and prescribes an universal rule to our actions, to our words, to our very thoughts and inclinations; a rule so much the more austere, as it is guarded by infinite, though distant, rewards and punishments;[†] and no infraction of it can ever be concealed or disguised.

SBN 34:

54   DIOGENES[†] is the most celebrated model of extravagant philosophy. Let us seek a parallel to him in modern times. We shall not disgrace any philosophic name by a comparison with the DOMINICS or LOYOLAS,[†] or any canonized monk or friar. Let us compare him to PASCAL,[†] a man of parts and genius as well as DIOGENES himself; and perhaps too, a man of virtue, had he allowed his virtuous inclinations to have exerted and displayed themselves.

55   The foundation of DIOGENES's conduct was an endeavour to render himself an independent being as much as possible, and to confine all his wants and desires and pleasures within himself and his own mind: The aim of PASCAL was to keep a perpetual sense of his dependence before his eyes, and never to forget his numberless wants and infirmities. The ancient supported himself by magnanimity, ostentation, pride, and the idea of his own superiority above his fellow-creatures. The modern made constant profession of humility and abasement, of the contempt and hatred of himself; and endeavoured to attain these supposed virtues, as far as they are attainable. The austerities of the GREEK were in order to inure himself to hardships, and prevent his ever suffering: Those of the FRENCHMAN were embraced merely for their own sake, and in order to suffer as much as possible. The philosopher indulged himself in the most beastly pleasures, even in public: The saint refused himself the most innocent, even in private. The former thought it his duty to love his friends, and to rail at them, and reprove them, and scold them: The latter endeavoured to be absolutely indifferent towards his nearest relations, and to love and speak well of his enemies. The great object of DIOGENES's wit was every kind of

SBN 34

superstition, that is every kind of religion known in his time. The mortality of the soul was his standard principle; and even his sentiments of a divine providence seem to have been licentious. The most ridiculous superstitions directed PASCAL's faith and practice; and an extreme contempt of this life, in comparison of the future, was the chief foundation of his conduct.

56   In such a remarkable contrast do these two men stand: Yet both of them have met with general admiration in their different ages, and have been proposed as models of imitation. Where then is the universal standard of morals, which you talk of? And what rule shall we establish for the many different, nay contrary sentiments of mankind?

57   An experiment, said I, which succeeds in the air, will not always succeed in a vacuum. When men depart from the maxims of common reason, and affect these *artificial* lives, as you call them, no one can answer for what will please or displease them. They are in a different element[†] from the rest of mankind; and the natural principles of their mind play not with the same regularity, as if left to themselves, free from the illusions of religious superstition or philosophical enthusiasm.[†]

13. 14. 09

PART 3

Supplementary Material

Annotations to the *Enquiry*

Scope of the Annotations

Each annotation is introduced by paragraph numbers in the text. Each serves one and often more than one of the following eight purposes.

1. *Definition.* Many terms are defined or explained in the Glossary. However, context-determined meanings, expressions, and sequences of words are treated in the annotations.

2. *Translation.* Translations are provided for all French, Latin, and Greek *quotations* supplied by Hume.

3. *Interpretation.* Interpretations are presented of difficult and misleading terms, phrases, sentences, and passages. If a relevant explanation has already been provided in the Introduction, reference is made to that source.

4. *Summarization.* A summary of the main arguments and conclusions in each section is provided at the beginning of the annotation for that section.

5. *Completion of a self-reference.* A few annotations identify a separate passage in *EPM* to which Hume is referring although he does not provide an explicit chapter or section reference.

6. *Information on passages in named authors.* A few annotations explain or paraphrase the context or content of a work that Hume identifies or to which he alludes. These reports are needed whenever Hume's surrounding sentences assume more than the reader could be expected to know. More complete information about Hume's references are sometimes provided.

7. *Identification of passages in unnamed authors.* Several annotations identify Hume's allusions to unnamed authors. Full names and titles are usually found only in the reference list.

8. *Identification of the intellectual background.* A few annotations discuss Hume's possible sources, especially where a passage suggests an author known to have been read by Hume. The mention of sources is selective and serves more as a pointer than a comprehensive discussion of the intellectual background.

Translations

All Greek and Latin words or passages presented by Hume are translated by M. A. Stewart. All French words or passages presented by Hume are translated by Tom L. Beauchamp.

SECTION 1

In this introductory section Hume distinguishes two rival schools of thought about the general foundation (source or origin) of morals: (1) morals are derived from *reason*; (2) morals are derived from *sentiment* or an internal *sense*. He says that good arguments exist to support each position and mentions a few of these arguments. He then begins to associate himself with the second school, maintaining that moral conduct does not spring from conclusions of reason or the understanding and that reason is incapable of drawing moral conclusions. Hume argues that morality cannot guide conduct without the presence of motivating feelings and that moral judgements require an internal sense.

Hume states that the objective of his inquiries is to reach 'the foundation of ethics, and ... those universal principles, from which all censure or approbation is ultimately derived' (1.10). He proposes to analyse qualities of persons that form their 'personal merit'. These qualities cause us to blame or praise persons who possess them.

This investigation of human nature is primarily a factual inquiry into the origin of morals, and Hume states his intention to follow the experimental method in the search for universal principles and the qualities that are universally blamed and praised.

1 **wit**] Hume categorizes wit as a *'companionable* virtue' at 9.18. See also 1.5 and 8.3.

2 **reality of moral distinctions**] A moral distinction is a moral standard or a moral difference. To make a moral distinction is either to use moral precepts properly or to distinguish between good and evil, obligatory and unlawful, just and unjust, and the like. 'Those who have denied the reality of moral distinctions' maintained that there is no genuine difference between virtue and vice, that no proper uses of moral terms occur, or that no conditions exist (in human nature, say) that support distinctions between the proper and the improper. In the late 17th and 18th c. Thomas Hobbes (English philosopher, 1588–1679) was often interpreted as one who denied the reality of moral distinctions.

converting an antagonist] In Hume's account of human nature, any person with capacities of moral responsiveness can set aside prejudice or scepticism and be 'converted' to the perspective of common sense shared by reasonable and impartial persons.

3 **a controversy . . . foundation of morals**] How best to explain moral judgement and moral motivation is the fundamental problem in this controversy. One side in the controversy appeals to moral sentiment and the other side to reason. Hume discusses this controversy and names the primary parties during a discussion of 'the Foundations of Morality', in *A Letter from a Gentleman to his Friend in Edinburgh* (*Letter*, 30). He identifies Samuel Clarke (English philosopher and theologian, 1675–1729) and William Wollaston (English moral philosopher and theologian, 1659–1724) as primary figures on the side of reason, and Scottish philosopher Francis Hutcheson (1696–1746) and Lord Shaftesbury (Anthony Ashley Cooper, third earl of Shaftesbury, English philosopher and politician, 1671–1713) as influential figures on the side of sentiment. Clarke and his followers hold that moral distinctions and knowledge are conveyed by *reason*, yielding moral knowledge of unalterable moral truths. Hutcheson developed Shaftesbury's rudimentary ideas about a moral sense (discussed in the Intro., 21–2).

finer internal sense] an indirect reference to moral sense theory. See Intro., 17–22. See also 1.3–4; 1.10.

4 **taste**] 'Taste' in the sense here proposed is a properly cultivated capacity to reach good judgements and opinions regarding what is appropriate, excellent, beautiful, and the like. Hume uses 'taste' and 'sentiment' to refer to both judgement and opinion. See Hume's 'Of the Standard of Taste', where he opposes scepticism regarding appeals to taste; and see 1.9; 7.28; Appx. 3.10.

ancient philosophers . . . modern enquirers] Hume could be referring to any one of several ancient philosophers. He often approvingly cites Cicero (Roman orator, politician, and moralist, 1st c. BC), but Aristotle (Greek philosopher, 4th c. BC) and various Aristotelians, Sophists, Cynics, and Epicureans are also candidates for ancients who derive morals from taste and sentiment. The 'modern enquirers' are post-medieval rationalists (see Intro., 14–15) who defend reason in the controversy mentioned at 1.3. Hume is referring to the rationalists when he says that some philosophers deduce their conclusions 'from the most abstract principles of the understanding' (1.4).

opposition] a clash of theories of the sort mentioned in the controversy at 1.3.

Lord Shaftesbury] This author was among the first to use the term 'moral sense' and to account for our recognition of virtue in persons through this sense (see Intro., 20–1). Shaftesbury's writings are 'elegant' in the sense that they are eloquent and refined.

5 **specious arguments**] arguments that are attractive and plausible, but that none the less may be incomplete, or otherwise unsound.

not taste] Hume thinks that factual statements are true or false and can be disputed by appeal to evidence; matters of taste are neither true nor false and so not disputable on a factual basis. See ann. 1.4; 1.7; Appx. 1.6; Appx. 1.7.

systems in physics] systems of natural philosophy (see also 1.10; 5.17; 6.6), which study the nature, powers, motions, and operations of natural bodies. Hume is pointing out that these systems aim at factual truths and are often controversial.

fixing the other] Hume is asking whether the understanding establishes the second point, namely that the actions were innocent and lawful, or only proves facts.

6 **impossible for reason**] See Intro., 17, 19.

7 **beget correspondent habits**] lead to routine behaviours in persons so that they will fulfil their duties.

8 **practical study**] If reason or understanding alone were employed in moral thinking, independent of feeling, persons would not be motivated to act or to develop practices. Persons would aim at discovering truth, not at pursuing practical undertaking.

9 *reason* and *sentiment* **concur**] Reason and sentiment generally work together to reach moral conclusions, rather than being opposed. Sentiment sets practical goals, and reason determines how to reach those goals.

final sentence] concluding judgement. The internal (or moral) sense reaches these judgements.

false relish] a taste, preference, or liking developed from an inadequate understanding.

10 **complication of mental qualities**] combination or mixture of various features of the mind, especially character traits and motives (see Intro., 31–3). Hume conceives these traits (for example, cheerfulness and kindness) and motives as qualities of the mind and as the basis for ascriptions of personal merit, esteem, and affection.

personal merit . . . praise or blame] See Intro., 7, 29, 31.

panegyric or satire] commendation or scorn. The distinction is classical. Panegyric is usually understood as a form of public appraisal (encomium), not merely a private evaluation.

quick sensibility . . . so universal] the shared human capacity to make quick, non-inferential moral judgements (of praise, blame, and the like). On universality, see 1.9; 1.10; 9.8; Dial. 26–7; and Intro., 26–8.

10 **framing the catalogue**] listing the qualities that make up personal merit and demerit. The catalogue is primarily a list of moral virtues and vices. Hume later provides several lists of virtues that collectively seem to form his catalogue.

good sense, and . . . in the opposite] Hume is speaking of words offering praise and blame.

acquaintance with the idiom suffices] The point is that understanding the meanings of terms in moral language is sufficient to guide us to both the good and the blameable qualities of persons.

foundation of ethics . . . universal principles] See Intro., 12–13, 23–4. The foundation is a 'question of fact' because it is a part of human nature and is discovered by an experimental method.

abstract science] a science such as mathematics whose conclusions are derived from reason rather than experience.

experimental method] This method and Isaac Newton's role in Hume's conception of it are discussed in the Intro., 12–13. 'Experimental philosophy' relies on observation and experiment to find correct causal generalizations (the laws of science). Hume tends to use 'experimental' so that it includes both the observational and the experiential. Francis Bacon (philosopher, politician, and essayist, 1561–1626), Robert Boyle (experimental scientist, 1627–91), and Newton all influenced Hume's thinking about the experimental method. See ann. 5.17.

other scientifical method] This method has been associated, at least since Aristotle (*Posterior Analytics* 71^{b}18–23), with a theory claiming that science begins with rationally self-evident axioms. Though not themselves demonstrable, these axioms are the foundational principles necessary for all derivative scientific knowledge. Hume opposes this conception for his science of human nature, because it lacks a basis in experience.

11 **social virtues**] virtues that benefit other persons in society. Hume offers a list of social virtues in addition to benevolence and justice, at 5.44: 'fidelity, honour, allegiance, and chastity . . . humanity, generosity, charity, affability, lenity, mercy, and moderation'. See also Intro., 29–31.

SECTION 2

The first universal principle that Hume discusses is benevolence, one of his two major categories of the 'social virtues'. This principle, embedded in human nature, causes humans to act benevolently; the quality or trait of benevolence in a person is a virtue. Hume is concerned with both natural principles and traits of character. An 'internal sense' in our nature makes approval of actions performed by others possible. Hume maintains that we approve of benevolent actions primarily because of their utility—that is, because they benefit persons by promoting basic human goods. He also thinks that we approve benevolent actions because we find them immediately agreeable—that is, pleasing or enjoyable. Similarly, we disapprove of actions that are of no benefit or that cause harm. Thus, the utility and agreeableness of benevolence in persons explain our approbation of it.

Annotations: Section 2

Hume argues that benevolence is both universal in persons (as a principle of human nature) and universally approved by impartial inquirers.

1 **softer affections**] Various of these humane, responsive qualities are listed in italics in Hume's text three lines below (*sociable, good-natured*, etc.). See also 7.18 and the use of 'tender sympathy' at 2.5.

prosperous success] prosperity achieved through a person's efforts.

2 and n. 2 **Pericles**] Hume is observing that Pericles (Athenian politician and leader, 5th c. BC) displayed exalted capacities as a statesman that, combined with his humane concern for citizens, elevated him above other leaders. His qualities promoted approbation rather than the envy that many public figures encounter. According to Plutarch (Platonist philosopher, biographer, and historian, 1st–2nd c. AD), Pericles expressed amazement at the citizens' praise and commemoration of achievements that he thought were due as much to good fortune as to his character. He considered among his greatest achievements that he never caused an Athenian to 'go into mourning' because of his political and military decisions, and he thought his most admirable qualities were modesty and self-control (*Lives*, 'Pericles' 38.4). The word 'insensible' in this passage means 'incapable of sensing', which contrasts with insensibility at 1.2 and elsewhere.

2 **nine trophies**] According to Plutarch, Pericles had, as Athens' victorious general, set up nine trophies (structures erected as war memorials) to honour the city.

3 and n. 3 **Cicero**] Cicero maintains that 'courage' in flawed persons who act from treachery and cunning lacks justice, and thus is an effrontery rather than true courage. Cicero believes that a motive of justice is required to possess the virtue of courage (*De officiis* 1.19.62–3, 1.44.157).

4 and n. 4 **Juvenal**] Juvenal (Roman satirist, 1st–2nd c. AD) says that our ability to cry and feel pity is a capacity that exhibits *tenderness* and elevates humans above other animals (*Satires* 15.139–47). Hume attributes to Juvenal the view that the extensive benevolence in the human species creates more opportunities to influence other persons through kindness than occurs in the animal kingdom.

sole prerogative] The point is that eminent persons must act benevolently by protecting inferiors who might, lacking proper protection, expose the eminent person to risk and turmoil.

5 **sally of panegyric**] issuance of praise. On panegyric, see anns. 1.10.

more the speculative] The objective is a philosophical explanation of morals, not practical recommendations, character development, or moral praise and blame.

humanity] At 5.46 Hume speaks of 'any such *principle in our nature* as humanity or a concern for others' (italics added). Hume also refers to humanity as a *virtue* of concern and attention to others. 'Humanity' is closely associated with fellow-feeling and sympathy with the plight of others. See also 5.17–18 and Appx. 4.6.

transfuse] The point is that impartial beholders of these qualities of persons react in similarly favourable and affectionate ways.

6 **intercourse and good offices**] social interaction and proper performance of duties, functions, or services.

inferior minister] The sun provides many of nature's benefits, but the sun is none the less subordinate to divine providence.

7 **higher station**] higher office or place of duty; service in a public office.

8 **topics of praise**] themes or considerations of praise for the humane, beneficent person.

part **of their merit**] This thesis about utility (usefulness) is a central theme in *EPM*; see Intro., 31, 35–8 and Hume's summary of his views at 2.22 and 2.23.

11 **monk and inquisitor**] member of a religious order who is also part of a tribunal of the Roman Catholic Inquisition. Hume regards these activities as useless and pernicious, but he recognizes that persons in this role would not so evaluate their activities.

14 and n. 5 **gods, says Cicero**] Cicero notes (*De natura deorum* 1.36.100–1) that religions began when people worshipped objects, such as the sun, for their usefulness. Even the Egyptians deified animals for their utility; for example, they worshipped the ibis, which destroyed snakes. However, the Epicureans' gods performed no service, as if idleness were a virtue.

15 and n. 6 **sceptics assert**] Sextus Empiricus (physician and philosopher, 2nd–3rd c. AD), a basic authority on the sceptic school, quotes Prodicus of Ceos (a Sophist living in the 5th and early 4th c. BC) as asserting that 'The ancients accounted as gods the sun and moon and rivers and springs and in general all the things that are of benefit for our life, because of the benefit derived from them, even as the Egyptians deify the Nile' (*Against the Physicists* 1.18).

and n. 7 **deification**] Diodorus Siculus (historian, 1st c. BC) claims that heroes, demigods, and the like were honoured virtually as deities because of the widely shared benefits that they conferred on society (4.1.4–7; 4.2.1 ff.).

16 **religion of Zoroaster**] Hume's suggestion is again that the merit in these acts depends on their usefulness. In Zoroastrianism, agriculture is a special good: Whoever plants a tree will benefit from a yield of food, and a sown field of harvestable crops will make a person fortunate in life. There is also a Zoroastrian belief that procreation of children among the faithful is meritorious and rewarding in this life and in the 'other life'.

19 *Tyrannicide*] Hume's thesis is that the popularity or approval of the assassination of tyrants in some societies is to be explained by the utility of the acts for that society. In some cases assassination eliminated 'usurpers', that is, persons who wrongfully seize the property of or take away the rights of others (and who therefore are 'monsters'). For example, Timoleon (Corinthian military commander, 4th c. BC) assassinated his brother, the tyrant Timophanes, after attempting in vain to persuade him to change his ways. Influential Corinthians applauded Timoleon for setting country before family. Others saw his deed as abominable, and he was driven into isolation (*Lives*, 'Timoleon' 3.3).

Marcus Junius Brutus (Roman politician, 1st c. BC) was appointed to important posts by Caesar but joined a conspiracy to murder him. Plutarch reports that 'Antony . . . declared that in his opinion Brutus was the only conspirator against Caesar who was impelled by the splendour and by what seemed to him the nobility of the enterprise. . . . Brutus relied not so much on his armies as on his virtuous cause' (*Lives*, 'Brutus' 29.5–6).

20 **Liberality in princes**] These reflections on rulers' generosity in giving to their subjects may be inspired by either Cicero, *De officiis* 1–2, or Machiavelli, *The Prince* 16. Both conclude that a prince should exhibit miserliness more than liberality in order to govern efficiently and retain respect. Hume's treatment seems closer to Cicero's.

21 **Luxury**] This reference to luxury is one of three direct references in *EPM* to a thriving 18th-c. dispute over the positive and the negative effects on society of human desires for luxury goods. Hume believes that an important dimension of this debate is whether luxury is useful rather than harmful. Prior to the 18th c. the pursuit of luxury had been condemned as sinful, harmful to society, and a form of self-gratification. As prosperity and commerce expanded, many found it in the national interest to abandon the notion that luxury fosters moral degeneracy. Bernard Mandeville celebrated the social utility of luxury in his *Fable of the Bees*. The theory of 'those, who prove' summarized in Hume's paragraph is similar to Mandeville's.

regulate anew] The point is that changing the status of luxury from harmful and blameworthy to permitted and laudable involves a moral as well as a political shift of perspective.

22 **benign an influence . . . desirable an end**] The reference is to social virtues of persons that have a positive influence on society similar to that of benevolence. They advance worthy goals.

dominion over the breasts] the social virtues' moderate control over the feelings of persons.

23 **disquisitions**] discussions, in particular those in Sections 3–4 immediately below.

SECTION 3

Hume provides an account of the origin and nature of justice. His basic proposition is that public utility is 'the sole origin of justice'. Whereas we approve benevolent actions *primarily* because of their social utility, we approve systems of justice *exclusively* because of their social utility. To prove this claim, he uses a series of arguments that appeal to human circumstances under which the rules of justice would be useless and therefore inapplicable (see Intro., 36–7). Conventions of justice require both personal conflict and social co-operation; in the absence of either conflict or co-operation, rules of justice are useless and would never be formulated. Although rules of justice are universally needed in complex societies, Hume maintains that particular rules of justice depend on particular conditions of need and utility, and therefore differ from society to society. Near the end of Section 3, he argues that utility partially explains the merit found in virtues such as friendship and public-spiritedness and fully explains the merit found in the virtues of fidelity, integrity, and veracity.

1 *sole* **origin of justice**] Hume will consider whether usefulness to society is the sole source of the rules of justice. See Intro., 34–7.

5 **and n. 10 property in water . . . land**] The passages in Genesis cited in n. 10 refer to wells near Beersheba in Israel. Access to these wells was essential for nomadic life; land was not regarded as private property.

6 **use of justice . . . suspended**] Rules of justice would have no function under these conditions. See Intro., 35–6.

force and vivacity] strength and intensity. In *THN* Hume frequently uses 'force and vivacity' along with terms such as liveliness, violence, vigour, firmness, and intensity to explain the vivid nature of perceptual impressions (see Intro., 11–12).

second self] Hume may be assuming Aristotle's theory that friendship among virtuous persons entails a mutual concern for the other's good; a friend acts so that the other becomes like a 'second self'. See Aristotle's language of 'second self' and 'another self' in *Magna moralia* 2.12, 15 (esp. 1213ª10–26); *Eudemian Ethics* 7.12 (esp. 1245ª29–39); *Nicomachean Ethics* 9.4 (esp. 1166ª30–ᵇ1).

6 **lie in common**] Everything would be shared in common, without regard to distinctions of property.

7 **human heart**] Human nature being what it is, we cannot reasonably expect to find persons so free of self-interest and jealousy that they exhibit perfect or extremely high levels of trustworthiness and helpfulness in their dealings with others.

enthusiasms ... fanatics] zealous inspirations, beliefs, or plans ... inspired and extravagant visionaries or pretenders to inspiration. The 'community of goods' here refers to a social situation in which private property is abolished and all goods are held in common. Hume often links enthusiasm in religion to such fanaticism: See 3.23–7; 5.25; Appx. 2.2; Dial. 57; and his 'Of Superstition and Enthusiasm'.

8 **foregoing suppositions**] namely, the hypothetical situation (posited near the beginning of Section 3) in which a superabundance of goods or of human benevolence eliminates the need for rules of justice. Hume is moving now to a discussion premissed on an extreme lack of goods and human benevolence. In both extremes, the rules of justice 'are suspended' and no longer oblige us. See Intro., 35–7.

necessaries] common necessities of life.

opens granaries] Hume envisages the public opening food warehouses and distributing grain without the consent of owners.

authority of magistracy] civil authority; powers of public officials.

10 **rules of justice ... suspended**] It may seem odd to say that the rules of justice are suspended in punishing a criminal, but Hume is not thinking of justice in terms of criminal justice. He is discussing political rights and rules of property. When a criminal's property is confiscated or rights restricted, rules of justice are suspended because of the criminal activity.

11 **laws of war**] rules or international agreements regarding what is permissible and wrong in war. See ann. 3.15 and n. 11; 3.29; 4.2.

12 **owe their origin**] Hume is arguing that justice is a created set of rules that are needed because of human nature and the social circumstances in which persons interact. If social conditions are altered, the rules of justice may need to be modified. See Intro., 36–7.

14–15 **golden age ... reign of Saturn**] The reference is to the ancient legend that an ideal period existed on earth during the reign of Saturn (Greek Cronus). Rules of justice and property did not then exist, and, according to the early poet Hesiod of Boeotia (8th–7th c. BC), men lived like gods in perfect felicity, without women and without fear of suffering, hardship, or death (*Works and Days*, lines 109–20).

15 **of a piece**] in agreement or in keeping with.

and n. 11 *state of nature*] This state is a condition of human existence lacking all government and rules of law, though not necessarily all moral standards. It is 'fictional', Hume thinks, because such a state never existed in a pure form. Hume is considering Thomas Hobbes's philosophy that a fierce war of all against all prevails in a true state of nature (as explicitly mentioned by Hume at 4.3). Hume also links the state of nature to the earlier writings of Plato (Greek philosopher, 4th c. BC) and Cicero. Hobbes argues that in the state of nature there is no recognized authority or law among the parties (*Leviathan* 13.8–9), but Hume is more concerned about the lack of conventions of trust in Hobbes's theory than about the absence of authority, law, or contract. Plato reflects on the theses that no strong individual would enter into a social contract, and that only the weak seek a social arrangement in order to protect themselves from the strong (*Republic* 358 E ff.). Cicero considers how human society emerged from a state of savagery through principles of justice and humanity (*Pro Sestio* 42.91–2). The passage from Cicero quoted by Hume in n. 11 may be translated as follows:

> Which judge among you is not aware of the natural course of events? There was once a time when neither natural nor civil law had yet been defined. Mankind led a wandering existence, scattered and dispersed across the land, and possessed no more than they could seize or retain by their own hand and strength, inflicting wounds and slaughter. Those therefore who first distinguished themselves by their merit and wisdom, having observed the distinctive learning skill and natural talent of human beings, brought together the scattered population into a single place, and transformed their savagery into justice and gentleness. They established what we call the public domain, serving the common good, and created communities of people which were afterwards called states. They then linked dwellings together and surrounded them with defensive walls, having introduced both divine and human law: These are what we call cities. Between this civilized life and the previous savagery there is no clearer demarcation than that between law and violence. Whichever of these we reject, we must employ the other. Do we wish to eliminate violence? Then law must prevail, that is, the legal institutions within which all law is sustained. Are legal institutions not to our taste, or do they not exist? Then violence will inevitably reign. Everyone knows these things.

savage nature] This passage extends Hume's theses about the golden age and the social contract (see 3.14 and 3.15 and n. 11). 'Savage nature' refers to human beings in an undomesticated or untamed state prior to the formation of civilized society.

17 **satisfactory**] As we collect information about human behaviour, the experimental *method* (see 1.10) will allow us to form correct accounts of the origins of justice. The final part of this sentence is a recapitulation of the *substantive* thesis that justice originates in social circumstances in which rules of justice are useful and necessary.

18 **species of creatures**] Hume thinks that principles of human nature such as benevolence, compassion, and kindness would bind us to the performance of certain moral acts toward this hypothetical inferior species. These principles provide a curb to immoral conduct ('our lawless will'). Rules of justice presuppose an equality of persons that is not present in this relationship with inferior creatures; the rules of justice would therefore be useless.

19 **possess reason**] Hume believes that animals have some reasoning capacities, especially powers of causal inference. None the less, their capacities are insufficient to create rules of justice in Hume's sense. Hume discusses the nature and extent of reason in animals in *EHU* 9, and in *THN* 1.3.16.

barbarous Indians] Hume is pointing out that, unlike animals, humans in uncivilized regions have the capacities requisite for justice and cannot be treated as inferior creatures merely because of cultural disadvantages. Hume is probably referring to the natives of the Americas, especially as encountered by the Spaniards. Many writers prior to Hume had debated appropriate treatment of American Indians. In a famous public dispute between Juan Ginés Sepúlveda and Bartolomé de Las Casas in 1550–1, the question of the lawfulness of Spanish conquest and war against the American Indians was debated. Hume might have viewed this debate as about whether Europeans could 'throw off all restraints of justice, and even of humanity, in our treatment of them'. Sepúlveda argued that the Indians were idolatrous, sinful, rude in nature, and lacking in appropriate religious faith; Las Casas saw the conquests as violations of natural justice. (Hanke, *Aristotle and the American Indians*, 30–43; Wagner, *The Life and Writings of Bartolomé de Las Casas*, 170–82.)

19 **reduced to like slavery**] Hume gives an example below of this enslavement of women in one of these 'many nations'. See his discussion of women in ancient Athens at Dial. 43–4 and n. 89.

21 **boundaries of justice still grow larger**] a reference to the creation of treaties, international law, and the like. The boundaries of justice naturally expand or contract as social arrangements increase ('the rules . . . enlarge themselves . . .') or decrease, in accordance with the utility of the arrangements. See the discussion of *laws of nations* at 4.2.

23 **theocracy**] a form of government with God as the immediate ruler and judge. God would know each person's true personal merit and could distribute possessions according to a rule of merit.

dominion is founded on grace] the right to govern rests on the free and undeserved favour of God. See Rom. 5: 17; 6: 14. Possible fanatics are discussed in ann. 3.23 below.

saints alone inherit the earth] the blessed alone shall be given dominion over the land. See Matt. 5: 5; Ps. 37: 9–11, 29; Isa. 57: 13; 1 Cor. 6: 2; Dan. 7: 27.

sublime theorists] fanatics who propose great, lofty, elevated, or refined theories. 'Sublime' is perhaps used ironically, or even sarcastically.

24 *religious* **fanatics**] The reference is to diverse religious groups whose influence peaked during the administration of Oliver Cromwell (English political and military leader, 1599–1658). Hume's comments are linked to the comments about enthusiasm and fanaticism at 3.7. Religious fanaticism often supported political fanaticism, and the converse.

levellers] The only fanatics Hume specifically mentions here are the Levellers, whose name was applied to them (*c.*1647) because of their commitments to (1) social equality to be achieved through a levelling of social ranks and (2) a government equally shared between the nobility and the commonality. Hume thinks that thoughtful and experienced persons have the foresight to see that equality of property is impractical, even if in some respects pleasing.

avowed their pretensions] stated their aspirations, intentions, or claims.

25 **nature is so liberal**] nature provides so many resources and opportunities.

rob the poor] Hume is not supporting a claim that such a system of equality deserves our support. He questions the practicability of 'perfect equality' in the following paragraph.

frivolous vanity] For the background context of this mention of lavish or extravagant use of resources by the rich, see the discussion of luxury in ann. 2.21.

particularly that of Sparta] 'The rule of equality' was, as Hume puts it, achieved 'in an imperfect degree'. In Sparta (after 600 BC) the ruling class, or Spartiates, were alone entitled to citizenship and equal distributions; they shared in the allotment of serfs (helots), who were bound to the land.

Agrarian laws] The Agrarian laws of Rome dealt with the allotment of land using holdings from conquered territories that were suitable for settlement. Thousands of small parcels were distributed to impoverished peasants, mitigating their deprivation.

26 **break that equality**] A distrust of schemes of perfect equality (especially those rendering property equal) was common in the Enlightenment, when justice and liberty were typically more important principles than equality.

check these virtues] If restrictions are placed on art and industry in order to maintain social equality, poverty will be increased in the larger community. See the discussion of luxury at 2.21.

27 **false, though specious**] What appears to be true, because plausible and attractive, may be false. Hume recommends a search for rules that are truly useful and beneficial; neither custom nor appearance is satisfactory.

extensive enthusiasm] The point is that it is possible to find appropriate rules through common sense and ordinary experience, unless persons are too strongly influenced by selfish goals or some form of enthusiasm that overpowers good judgement. The term *vulgar sense* here has the meaning of common sense.

28 **alienated by consent**] the transfer of property by consent of the owner; voluntarily conveyed.

29 **writers on the laws of nature**] writers in the natural law tradition in ethics, political theory, and legal theory. See Intro., 18–19. Hume thinks that the rules they recommend are ultimately grounded in the benefits the rules confer.

prosecution of them] Hume seems to be calling on classical rhetoric to mean the following in this difficult sentence: An acknowledgement of the validity of this point by use of arguments from utility, which stand in contrast to the principles of natural law in certain philosophical theories, gains more intellectual influence than would be gained by using the arguments to indict theories of natural law.

30 **uninstructed nature**] Nature itself does not allocate property to individuals; before property rules come into existence, items are not naturally 'mine' or 'yours'. Rules of justice are required to turn items into *property*.

31 **slightest *analogies***] When two or more possible rules governing property have equally beneficial social outcomes, analogies from prior precedents (as in legal reasoning) are used to choose one rule rather than another rule.

32 **supreme law**] This maxim appears to be an English rendering of a Roman legal saying found in Cicero's *De legibus* 3.3.8: 'ollis salus populi suprema lex esto'—'the safety of the people shall be their supreme law'. The maxim is here invoked to justify violations of the rules of justice in extraordinary emergencies in which the public safety must be protected.

33 **natural *code***] the code of natural law, which includes authoritative and universal rules of justice. The expression *supply the place of* here has the meaning of supplant or replace. 'Natural justice' often referred to fundamental rules of justice antecedent to particular rules (such as civil laws) established by governments. See 3.34, 4.1, and Appx. 3.9 for Hume's use of 'natural justice' and 'nature'.

different *utilities*] the various consequences (of different laws). See Glossary for the meaning of 'prescription'.

34 ***convenience* of each community**] utility for each community. The rules of natural justice do not vary, but they are shaped and used differently in different communities.

and n. 12 late author] The 'late author' is Baron de Montesquieu (French author,

1689–1755). His *Spirit of the Laws* treats the subjects mentioned in this paragraph. The general background of Hume's remarks in n. 12 are discussed in ann. 1.3 and 1.4. Each thinker named in Hume's note (Montesquieu, Malebranche, Cudworth, Clarke) represents some aspect of rationalism. Each theory is sufficiently different that generalization across the theories is perilous, but paradigmatic of Hume's concerns articulated in the note is Clarke's statement that 'Thus have I endeavoured to deduce the original *Obligations of Morality* from the *necessary and eternal Reason* and *Proportions of Things*' (*Discourse*, in *Works*, 2: 630).

34 n. 12 *in foro humano . . . conscientiæ*] The Latin may be translated as follows: 'In a human court . . . before the bar (court) of conscience'.

36 **vulgar superstitions . . . particular regards**] Vulgar superstitions are religious beliefs, especially unreflective traditional beliefs, that are widespread in a population—for example, popular beliefs about observances, sacrifices, and asceticism. (See 2.2 and 3.27.) 'Folly' refers to difficulties in justifying the required rules, practices, or sentiments. (See 3.37.) 'Particular regards' refers to specific laws, rules, and rituals governing food, holidays, holy places, dress, manners, movement of the body, and the like.

Syrian . . . Egyptian] According to Lucian (Hellenic poet and satirist, 2nd c. AD), the Syrians 'consider fish something sacred and they never touch one. They eat all other birds, apart from the [pigeon] dove. For them this is sacred' (*De dea Syria* 14). According to Herodotus (Greek historian, 5th c. BC), 'Swine are held by the Egyptians to be unclean beasts. Firstly, if an Egyptian touch a hog in passing by, he goes to the river and dips himself in it, clothed as he is . . . Nor do the Egyptians think [it] right to sacrifice swine to any god save the Moon and Dionysius . . . then they eat of the flesh. . . . But they will not taste it on any other day' (Herodotus 2.47).

precise circumstance be pitched on] specific feature or property be successfully located (or picked out).

38 and n. 13 **articulating certain sounds**] Hume is pointing out that rules of justice, such as property rights, make no sense and seem without foundation unless one understands the underlying social practices, such as reaching agreements and consenting. The distinctions and theses here (and in n. 13) about speech, intention, and action are mentioned in some of the writings of the writers on laws of nature mentioned at 3.29 and n. 63, especially Hugo Grotius (Dutch jurist and statesman, 1583–1645); see *On the Law of War and Peace* 2.11.1–4.

n. 13 **Jesuits . . . Loyola**] In his *Dictionary*, entry on Loyola, Pierre Bayle (French philosopher and encyclopaedist, 1647–1706) criticized the Jesuits' methods of reasoning for promoting endless dogmatic wrangling; their methods were to blame more than any 'corruption of the heart'. 'Casuistry' was understood in the 18th c. as the application of general rules of religion and philosophy to particular moral cases and problems. A 'relaxed casuist' is one who is lax in the use of rules. By 'a metaphysical schoolman', Hume means a theologian or philosopher associated with the Aristotelianism of the late Middle Ages and Renaissance.

n. 13 **invalidate any sacrament**] An intentional action is here understood as a purposeful act or forbearance under appropriate knowledge. The Council of Florence (1439–45) and the Council of Trent (1545–63) declared that the minister of a sacrament must intend what the Church intends. The priest therefore must intend what the rite means when administering a sacrament, and the priest invalidates a sacrament if the intention deviates in an inconsistent manner.

n. 13 **put . . . on a balance**] put on the same level; make consistent with.

40 **original instinct**] An original instinct is an innate capacity or predisposition. Hume is denying that justice is, like benevolence, an original instinct, even though both are social virtues. See Intro., 36–8.

43 **innate ideas**] inborn concepts that are not the product of experience. Proponents believe that these ideas provide information about the world other than by experience. Hume denies this thesis, but does not deny that there are inborn features of human nature such as 'instincts', as he puts it in the next paragraph. A chancellor is a high and honourable officer, usually of government (in Scotland also a jury foreman); a *praetor* is an ancient Roman magistrate.

48 **excellence**] virtue.

force . . . energy] Hume suggests that force and energy in the mental world are analogous to force and energy in the physical world (as presented in a theory such as Newton's).

and n. 14 rules of philosophy] Hume is suggesting that when a 'principle' or condition—of utility or usefulness, in this case—has an influence in one type of circumstance, it can be expected to have a like influence in relevantly similar circumstances. Isaac Newton formulated four such 'rules of reasoning in philosophy'; see his *Mathematical Principles* 3 (398). In early editions of *EPM* Hume referred explicitly to Newton's second rule.

SECTION 4

Building on his arguments that (1) rules of justice exist only because of conflict and co-operation and that (2) we approve of systems of justice because of their utility, Hume now argues that government and political society exist because of the need to enforce the rules of justice. Just as rules of justice originate under social circumstances of competition for scarce resources and limited benevolence in persons, so political society originates under circumstances in which persons have put their own pleasure and advantage ahead of the rules of justice. If we lived in a society in which 'natural justice' were steadfastly maintained, without need for social mechanisms of enforcement, there would be no reason for political controls and law. Neither local government nor the laws of nations (international law) would exist. The sole foundation of allegiance to government is advantage (usefulness) to society, and laws of nations function successfully only when they are useful for international political situations. *Obligations* to obey political authorities and social rules hold in proportion to usefulness. Even in corrupt societies, such as communities of robbers and pirates, political stability depends on enforced rules of distributive justice that have utility for the members of those societies. Without this utility, both justice and political society would be without purpose.

Section 4] The discussion in this section is a reduced and recast version of the more ample discussion in *THN* 3.2.

1 **positive law . . . natural justice**] 'Natural justice' is discussed at 3.33, 3.34, and n. 12.

Here the contrast is between laws enacted by governments (positive law) and natural laws (of justice). Natural justice is not reducible to positive (or enacted) law. Social norms that are consistent with natural justice are often sufficient constraints in society.

2 **laws of nations**] These rules are international laws that apply to nations in both peace and war. Hugo Grotius (see 3.29; 4.1; n. 63) was an influential early modern writer on the subject.

ambassadors . . . quarter in war] Samuel Pufendorf (German jurist and historian, 1632–94) discussed 'the law of nations', the special privileges of ambassadors, universal condemnations of the use of poison, and the treatment of captives in war (*De jure naturae* 2.3; *Duty of Man* 2.16). He says that ambassadors are 'inviolable' and 'free from jurisdiction and control' so long as they are not spies. By 'quarter in war' Hume means exemption from immediate death and other fair treatments offered to a vanquished opponent in war (typically in return for surrender). The expression 'We gave no quarter' derives from this circumstance.

3 **the war of all against all**] See 3.15 and n. 11 for passages indicating that Hume has Hobbes in mind in choosing this language.

proportion with the *usefulness*] The strength of the moral obligation is proportional to the social usefulness of the rule of justice that states the obligation.

reasons of state] reasons for government action.

4 **Achæan republic . . . Swiss Cantons and United Provinces**] In all three of these federations, states joined into a league for common defence, retaining sovereignty in other matters. The Achaean League was an ancient confederation of cities on the Gulf of Corinth (the north-west coast of Peloponnesus) concerned with mutual protection against pirates. Switzerland is divided into cantons (regions or provinces) and is also called the Swiss Confederation. A defensive league emerged in this territory between 1273 and 1291. 'United Provinces' is a name for the Netherlands that was widely used after independence gained during the Thirty Years War (1618–48).

5 **virtue of chastity**] personal qualities of fidelity or abstinence in sexual intercourse. Hume argues that utility in raising children accounts for the great value placed on chastity and for its position in the catalogue of virtues. A noteworthy discussion occurs in THN 3.2.12.

n. 15 **Plato**] The passage from Plato may be translated, 'For it is an admirable saying, and will remain so, that what is beneficial is beautiful and what is harmful is ugly.'

n. 15 **Phædrus**] The passage from Phaedrus (Roman fabulist, 1st c. AD) may be translated, 'Unless what we do is useful, the glory is vain.' Phaedrus' fable 'Trees under the Patronage of the Gods' has Minerva express a preference for the olive tree because it bears fruit. The father of the gods congratulates her for selecting what is useful.

n. 15 **Plutarch**] The passage from Plutarch may be translated, 'Nothing that is harmful is beautiful.' Plutarch is discussing harmful 'disorders', such as a tendency to have undue respect for others.

n. 15 **Sext. Emp.**] The passage from Sextus Empiricus may be translated, 'The Stoics, therefore, identify good with utility, or not other than utility, meaning by "utility" virtue and right action.'

7 **Mississippi . . . stock-jobbers**] This rage (wild financial speculation) resulted from the Mississippi Scheme of the Mississippi Company, founded in France by financier, gambler, and speculator John Law of Edinburgh (1671–1729). His stated intention was

to meet the financial needs of the Prince Regent of France by commercially exploiting French colonial areas. Banknotes backed by the king were issued in anticipation of revenue from the Mississippi territory in America. Haste and the lack of real assets caused an abrupt failure. The 'Mississippi Bubble' burst on 20 Oct. 1720 when the public rushed to redeem the company's shares, whose value rested only on the unrealized Mississippi projects. The Rue de Quincempoix, today the Rue Quincampoix, is a street in Paris where Law set up his operation. 'Stock-jobbers' are buyers and sellers of stocks; they used the hump of the fellow mentioned by Hume as a writing-desk.

beauty arises . . . from ideas of utility] On this thesis, see 5.1 and 5.38.

women . . . liberty of indulgence] Hume is observing that general rules of chastity are extended beyond the point of their original usefulness, which Hume identified at 4.5 as the rearing of children in marriage. Hume maintains that if the rule did not apply to all women, young women would take the duty less seriously, thereby reducing the rule's usefulness.

9 **criminal correspondence . . . intercourse**] See ann. Dial. 44 and n. 89. 'Criminal correspondence' refers to wrongful or illicit interaction. Athenian laws and customs ('manners') discouraged or restricted various forms of homosexuality, adultery, and incest. Female adultery and male homosexual prostitution were viewed as morally disgraceful and as grounds for social isolation and exclusion, but were not punished directly by law. Adultery by males was viewed as a deep threat to family and honour and was punished as a criminal activity. Hume is attempting to explain the existence of these customs and variations in the customs in Athens and Rome in terms of social utility.

10 **any thing that escaped**] Hume's point is that repeating private information to a person's detriment is morally blameworthy; constraints must be placed on such uses of information if rules of fidelity and privacy are not already strictly observed.

11 **giving of one's author**] disclosure of one's source.

13 **lesser morality**] Hume depicts good manners, genteelness, and the like as '*companionable* virtues' at 9.18. Hobbes referred to politeness as 'small morals' (*Leviathan* 1.11), and Addison said, 'By Manners I do not mean Morals, but Behaviour and Good Breeding' (*Spectator* 119). On 'breeding', see 8.2.

14 **promiscuously together**] The reference is to casual meeting-places where many strangers or unattached people mix without a preconceived plan or arrangement.

acquaintance] It is not a breach of either morals or manners if a close rapport is not maintained with casual acquaintances.

15 **Robbers and pirates**] 'False honour' refers to deceitful or pretended honour among robbers and pirates. Hume is interested in how common interest and utility generate standards of right and wrong even in immoral contexts. Issues about thieves and distributive justice have had a long history in philosophical, political, and theological writings. For example, Julius Caesar described how robbery that takes place beyond state borders is often considered favourably (*Gallic War* 6.23), and Cicero discussed justice in the impartial administration of a 'code of laws' among robbers (Cicero, *De officiis* 2.11.40).

16 **I hate . . . forgets**] The saying 'I hate a drinking companion with a memory' derives from Martial (Roman poet, 1st c. AD), *Epigrams* 1.27. Hume is pointing to a subtle rule or expectation of social drinking.

17 **parliament of love in Provence**] During the Middle Ages, 'amour courtois' or 'courtly love' referred to the codes of proper behaviour for the conduct of upper-class love affairs, often involving adultery. There is little scholarly agreement on the nature of this 'immoral gallantry' or courtly love, and its origins are mired in obscurity. 'Courts of love' in France and Flanders supposedly cultivated the code of chivalrous conduct in general and courtly love in particular; problems in interpreting and applying the code of love were reported to have been argued before noble women who presided and delivered 'judgements of love'.

18 **societies for play**] societies organized to play games.
   public conveniency] the public agreements or arrangements that (for reasons of utility) establish standards of right and wrong conduct.

19 **Waggoners . . . postilions . . . give the way**] Wagon drivers . . . coach or carriage drivers . . . give way (yield).

SECTION 5

Having established the function and importance of social utility, Hume asks why utility pleases us and causes us to shower moral praise on persons possessed of the social virtues. Why do we praise qualities in persons that are socially beneficial? He argues, opposing egoism, that the public utility of these virtues 'must please, either from considerations of self-interest, or from more generous motives. . . . As much as we value our own happiness and welfare, as much must we applaud the practice of justice and humanity, by which alone the social confederacy can be maintained'. He notes that even when we see an enemy acting against our interest, the virtue and utility found in that person's actions occasionally please us. His explanation is that human nature is constituted to take pleasure in many events that are beneficial to other persons even though not beneficial to ourselves.

In Part 2 of this section Hume criticizes the egoists' beliefs that self-love alone can account for our concern for the public and that politicians manipulate persons into moral conduct. He argues that the fact that we approve some remote actions and even some actions taken against our own interests shows that our actions cannot always be explained by self-love. Mechanisms such as sympathy with others play an important role in his arguments. Hume concludes that it is not reasonable to doubt either that there is such a 'principle in our nature as humanity or a concern for others' ('the benevolent principle') or that actions from this principle are approved only because of enculturation or political indoctrination and manipulation. Section 5 is the middle section of the nine sections of *EPM*, and it occupies a pivotal role in connecting the first four sections to the final four.

1 **service the fabric was intended**] use for which the building was intended (see also 1.3).

2 **effects of usefulness**] Hume is referring to his opening comment in this section, at 5.1, that we 'would expect to meet with this principle [of ascribing praise to utility] every where in moral writers'. He now suggests that we need to explain this principle through a theory of human nature.

3 **education**] Sceptics deny both the reality of moral distinctions and that there is an appropriate manner of morally discriminating or perceiving. They maintain that such

human acts arise exclusively from 'education', here meaning enculturation or training. (See also ann. 1.2 and 1.3.)

natural principle] The point is that education, training, and enculturation can be so powerful that they increase or even bypass normal human responses (natural principles) and create powerful feelings of approval and disapproval, as is especially evident among the superstitious, fanatics, and the like.

original constitution] native capacity; human nature considered apart from the effects of education. See 3.43.

place in any language] The claim is that egoism cannot account adequately for the presence of moral language.

paradox of the sceptics] This comment seems directed largely at Mandeville's scepticism about the reality and praiseworthiness of virtue, as expressed in the *Fable of the Bees*. See Intro., 19–22, and 2.21 and 5.3. See also Appx. 2.6.

5 **social confederacy**] social union; persons joined together for a common cause.

6 **self-love . . . sceptics**] 'Self-love' is a principle in human nature leading one to act in one's own interest or promoting one's own happiness. Hobbes was the first philosopher in modern philosophy to attempt to ground morality in self-love. He and other egoists were regarded in Hume's period as sceptics about morals. See Intro., 19–21 and references at Appx. 2.3.

and n. 18 **Polybius**] The passage in n. 18 on undutifulness to parents may be translated, 'Seeing what is to come, and reckoning that something similar will befall each of them.' The passage on ingratitude may be translated, 'Joining in their neighbour's resentment and attributing a similar feeling to themselves, from which each individual derives a sense of the function and principles of fit conduct.' These passages are embedded in a discussion of natural human duty and justice. Polybius (historian of Rome, 2nd c. BC) is sketching a speculative natural history of the development of moral notions in the human species.

selfish theory] See Intro., 19–20.

7 **appearance of self-interest**] See Intro., 27–9.

9 **are very wide of**] reach well beyond.

11 **Æschines and Demosthenes**] Demosthenes (Athenian orator and statesman, 4th c. BC) attacked King Philip II (Macedonian political and military leader, 4th c. BC) in a famous series of orations (*Philippics*), and also led a patriotic party in opposition to Philip. See ann. 7.12 and n. 43; Appx. 4.5. Later, Demosthenes was made an ambassador, joining Aeschines (Athenian orator, 4th c. BC) in an attempt to establish a treaty with Philip. Aeschines was eventually bribed by Philip and formally accused by Demosthenes of accepting the bribe. There ensued a bitter series of disputes and orations over this accusation and over a gold crown proposed as an award to Demosthenes. Aeschines lost, but subsequently the Macedonian party accused Demosthenes of taking bribes from a departed finance minister. After imprisonment, Demosthenes escaped and fled.

13 **distant ages**] The point is that it is a weak and unconvincing defence of egoism to say that we can judge people in distant times favourably because we use our imagination to make a connection between our self-interest and their acts. The argument Hume here criticizes had been used by Archibald Campbell, in *Enquiry into the Original*, Treatise 2, Section 7 (365), but arguments and examples similar to Hume's reply had been used earlier in several works by Hutcheson (see 1.3).

13 *real* **interest is still kept in view**] actual benefit or advantage is continually kept before the mind.

14 **brink of a precipice**] Pascal (*Pensées*, 'Imagination', Sellier no. 78; Lafuma no. 44), presents this example and links the person's feelings directly to the functions of the imagination (Levi, 17). An earlier version of the example is found in Montaigne's essay on Raimond Sebond (*Essays*, 671).

associations of ideas] See Intro., 13, on laws of association.

that principle] the principle that experience shapes our associations of ideas.

16 **philosophers . . . found it simpler**] The reference is to the egoists; see Intro., 19–20. Hume has already named Hobbes and Locke.

unity of principle] A pretext or rationale (see Appx. 2.1) exists for explanation using a single principle. This explanation is tempting because actions that promote the interest of others are typically also actions that promote self-interest, but Hume thinks the egoists' explanation confuses two different interests.

17 *experimentum crucis*] This phrase may be translated 'crucial experiment', or, more literally, an 'experiment of the crux'. At a crucial point in the course of research, an experiment may indicate that one theory is better supported. It thus 'points out the right way'. The meaning of the term is broad enough to refer either to a crucial experiment or to a crucial point in an experiment. Hume is claiming to use an *experimentum crucis* against egoism by showing that when our 'private interest' is contrary to public interest, we yet may choose to promote the public interest. The concept of a crucial experiment seems to have its origins in Francis Bacon's *Novum organum* 2.36, where he referred not to an *experimentum crucis*, but to a 'decisive instance'.

disjunction of interests] clash of one's private interest with the public and moral interest.

contradiction in terms] Hume thinks it is incoherent (not merely erratic or paradoxical) to assert that we can be pleased about a means to an end when we are indifferent to the end itself. See the restatement of this point at 5.46 in terms of impossibility and again at 9.12 in terms of absurdity.

18 and n. 19 **humanity and benevolence**] On Hume's use of 'humanity', which is here closely associated with fellow-feeling, see 2.5. See also ann. 5.39; 5.42; 5.46. These descriptions of humane feelings of goodwill and dispositions of sympathy are part of the science of human nature. These passages deserve close study by comparison to *THN* 3.3.1–5, which emphasizes sympathy no less than benevolence as the given principle in human nature.

and n. 20 **Horace**] The passage cited from Horace (Latin poet and satirist, 1st c. BC) may be translated, 'As human faces laugh with those who laugh, so do they weep with those who weep.' Hume's point is that our humanity and benevolence often lead us to react directly and sympathetically (see 5.20) to the pleasures and pains of others.

20 **a pleasing sympathy**] 'Sympathy' is a pivotal moral category throughout *EPM* 2.5. Sympathy had been central to Hume's moral theory in *THN* (esp. 3.3.1–2). Through it one experiences a receptive and responsive sharing of another's opinion, distress, pleasure, or emotion. In *EPM* 'sympathy' has a similar use and shows a resemblance to Hume's use of the terms 'fellow-feeling' (see n. 19 and 7.29), 'pity' (see n. 34), and 'compassion' (especially with human happiness or misery). Often when Hume uses the word 'sympathy' he is designating not a particular sentiment, but a psychological capacity to feel or arrive at sentiments.

24 **aspect, a superior sensibility**] appearance, an enhanced capacity to discern or be moved.

27 **crosses our wishes**] goes counter to our desires for an appropriate outcome.

29 **Sannazarius**] Pastoral poetry portrays the life of shepherds. Sannazarius is Jacopo Sannazaro (Italian poet, 1458–1530), author of *Arcadia* and *Piscatorial Eclogues*. The pastoral work *Arcadia* moves from opening scenes of shepherds pasturing sheep to descriptions of moonlit paths, pleasing landscapes, decorated houses, and the like (see 7.20). The *Piscatorial Eclogues* transfers the scene to the sea-shore. There Sannazaro describes 'a weary fisherman' with a 'sorrowful heart' and 'sick mind'. He is 'wretched for loneliness' and believes he is despised (Eclogue 2, 'Galatea'). Bernard le Bovier de Fontenelle was critical of Sannazaro for his use, as Hume puts it, 'of toil, labour, and danger, suffered by the fishermen'. Fontenelle thought it essential that pastoral poetry depict tranquil scenes and portray a 'quiet life' ('Discours sur la nature de l'églogue'). Samuel Johnson also found Sannazaro's sea eclogues unsatisfactory because the sea presents terrors and offers far less descriptive variety than the land (*Rambler*, no. 36, 21 July 1750). Richard Steele (*Guardian*, no. 28, 13 Apr. 1713) also criticized Sannazaro for his arbitrary change from the pleasing aspects of the pastoral countryside to the 'uncomfortable and dreadful' seashore.

30 **French poet**] The French poet is Jean-Antoine du Cerceau, SJ (1670–1730). The lines appear in his *Recueil de poésies diverses*, first published in 1715. The Latin poet Ovid was influenced by Horace, but the two near-contemporaries are often contrasted. Ovid dwelled on themes of the arts of love and beauty (including erotic poems, some about his mistress, Corinna) and also wrote mythological poems that were particularly appealing to people of a younger age. He included instructions on how to attract and retain a lover. Even in ancient Rome, Ovid made a strong appeal to youthful audiences. By contrast, Horace wrote satires, lampoons, interpretations of Roman culture, and literary criticism that appealed to a more mature audience. He was a stern moralist who encouraged patriotic devotion, and he actively opposed rather than supported material about the passions of the young in the style of Ovid.

33 **Thucydides and Guicciardin**] Thucydides of Athens (5th c. BC), a military commander and historian of the early wars between Athens and Sparta, discusses the Athenian disaster in *History of the Peloponnesian War* 7.51–87. Italian historian Francesco Guicciardini (1483–1540) wrote *Della historia d'Italia*, an influential historical work of the 16th c. The 'wars of Pisa' are those between Florence and Pisa, dating from the 13th c.; Guicciardini's history covers wars during the period 1492 to 1534. Hume apparently believes that some parts of these histories are unexciting, others very exciting, depending on the events described.

34 **Suetonius . . . Tacitus**] Suetonius (Roman historian and biographer, 1st–2nd c. AD) provides detailed portraits in *Lives of the Caesars* 3, 'Tiberius', and 6, 'Nero'. Cornelius Tacitus (Roman politician and historian, 1st–2nd c. AD) wrote his *Histories* as an account of the reigns of emperors. In *The Annals*, to which Hume refers here, he reports that 'Nero in the end conceived the ambition to extirpate virtue herself by killing Thrasea Paetus [a Stoic] and Barea Soranus [a consul and governor]' (16.21–35). Both men were condemned to death in the Senate on the basis of fabricated accusations. Tacitus describes both Nero and Tiberius in highly unfavourable terms.

36 **frivolousness**] insignificance; triviality. Hume is observing that sympathy operates powerfully even in relatively insignificant human circumstances.

37 **criticism**] evaluation of literary works or discourse; art of appraising writing or oration, including moral evaluation of the works discussed.

38 n. 21 **Quintilian**] The passage quoted may be translated, 'The horse whose flanks are spare is more becoming but also faster. The athlete whose arm muscles have been developed by exercise may please the eye but is also more equipped for contest. For outward appearance is never separate from usefulness. Any person of ordinary judgement can recognize this at least.' Roman rhetorician and teacher Quintilian (1st c. AD, born in Spain) is examining the relationship between beauty and utility, especially in oratory. Quintilian maintains that beauty and utility can be simultaneously present and complementary in oratory (*Institutes* 8.3.10–11).

39 **subjected to his censure**] submitted for his critical appraisal.

principles of humanity] The humane principles that motivate good actions (see Intro., 23–4; 2.5; 5.17–18; 5.43; 5.46).

40 and n. 23 **Timon . . . Alcibiades**] Timon (philosopher, 5th c. BC) was a notorious misanthrope who lived in Athens during the period of Pericles. Alcibiades, renowned for beauty and conceit, several times lost the confidence of the Athenians and Spartans, both of whom he served as a military leader. Plutarch's 'Alcibiades' 13.6 (4: 42–3), as cited in n. 23, contains the following passage:

> Timon the misanthrope once saw Alcibiades, after a successful day, being publicly escorted home from the assembly. He did not pass him by nor avoid him, as his custom was with others, but met him and greeted him, saying: 'It's well you're growing so, my child; you'll grow big enough to ruin all this rabble.' At this some laughed, and some railed, and some gave much heed to the saying. So undecided was public opinion about Alcibiades, by reason of the unevenness of his nature.

two principles of the Manicheans] Once an influential religion, Manicheism was founded by the prophet Mani (3rd c. AD), born of Persian descent in Babylonia. Influenced by Zoroastrian belief in a fundamental antagonism between good and evil deities, Mani's primary doctrine was a dualism that strictly separates good and evil and rejects the possibility that both come from the same source. In the Manichean system, the conflict between light and darkness corresponds, to the opposition of God and Satan, truth and error, and good and evil.

natural philanthropy] natural love of humankind in general, but not necessarily involving altruistic giving.

Nero . . . Tigellinus . . . Seneca or Burrhus] Nero is depicted by Tacitus and Suetonius as blinded by a desire for popularity, driven by fears and insecurities, and often controlled by his intimates (*Annals* 16.20–4 [366–75]; *Lives* 6, 'Nero', 2: 86–187).

Seneca the Younger (Roman Stoic philosopher, 1st c. AD), tutor and political advisor to Nero, urged that Nero adopt a policy of clemency toward his subjects in order to win their love and support and to secure the emperor's safety. Nero turned on Seneca, accusing him of complicity in a conspiracy. By order of Nero, Seneca took his life by cutting his veins.

Burrhus (1st c. AD) was associated with Seneca as adviser and tutor to Nero, and helped secure Nero's succession to the throne. Burrhus and Seneca both supported a policy of fostering favourable public opinion. The two advisers became accessories in the murder of the ambitious and ruthless Agrippina in 59 AD, but Burrhus refused to approve some assassinations that had been ordered by the emperor and died suddenly, possibly from poison.

After the death of Burrhus, Ofonius Tigellinus (Roman politician, 1st c. AD) became Nero's favourite counsellor. He was a Sicilian of low birth who had been exiled for adultery with Agrippina. He rose to wealth, power, and favour through his friendship with Nero, to whom he recommended many executions that were approved. Plutarch describes Tigellinus as the most publicly hated of Nero's counsellors (*Lives*, 'Galba' 17.2–5, 'Otho' 2).

41 **corrects the inequalities**] Hume is providing a rudimentary account of objectivity, impartiality, and adjustment of belief. Just as we correct the appearances of 'our external senses' by information, so we correct the biases or partialities of 'our internal emotions and perceptions' by our awareness of the nature and merit of persons and actions, however remote.

n. 24 **real accidental consequences**] Hume is pointing to what the person's intentional action or character tends to bring about, not the consequences that merely happen to occur. The contrast is between 'nature and accident', as Hume puts it at the end of this note. We evaluate action and character, not accidental outcomes, even if the accidental outcomes are useful to society.

42 **intercourse of sentiments**] social interaction of thoughts, inclinations, and passions. and n. 25 **takes not part entirely with**] does not entirely embrace or share in. Hume is noting in this passage that our partiality toward those to whom we are close often takes precedence over the impartial point of view. In n. 25 he suggests that this partiality is good and to be expected in many cases.

43 **proportionable vigour**] Hume is maintaining that the intensity of the censure or approval is proportional to the humanity of the person, as measured by the positive and negative factors mentioned.

remote gazette] news-sheet or periodical from a distant place or time.

fixed star] A star so distant from earth that its position appears to the naked eye not to change. The term 'fixed star' derives from the astronomers of antiquity, who could detect no motions in these stars. Motions were first detected by English astronomer Edmund Halley (1656–1742) in 1718.

in his meridian] at its highest altitude in the sky; at midday.

44 **inseparable from**] Hume thinks that utility is the source of the high regard paid to all the social virtues; these virtues cannot be separated from the circumstance of utility.

46 **end is totally indifferent**] See the formulation of this idea at 5.17 in terms of 'contradiction' and at 9.12 in terms of 'absurdity'.

same conclusion] namely, that principles of humanity and benevolence are embedded in human nature.

SECTION 6

Sections 6 to 8 explore the qualities of persons—their natural talents and acquired abilities—that lead us to classify them as having moral virtue and other forms of personal merit. At this point the reader might consult Hume's fourfold typology of personal qualities, as outlined in the Intro., 30–1.

Hume starts with 'qualities useful to ourselves', that is, qualities useful to the people who possess the qualities. These qualities confer advantages on us without conferring any social benefits on those people who judge us favourably for having these qualities. Why, then, are these qualities approved by others? Hume answers that observers of these qualities do not approve of them because it is in their self-interest to do so, but from a principle of human nature that 'interests us in the felicity [happiness] of the person whom we contemplate' (6.3). This principle also gives us pain and feelings of disapprobation when we see people who are incapacitated by their faults and imperfections.

Hume considers several examples of these qualities of people, including *discretion, industry, frugality,* and *strength of mind.* He argues that our capacity for fellow-feeling with others causes us to respond favourably to people with these qualities. He thinks we have the same sentiments of favourable response when we encounter people who are far removed from our personal lives and can be of no use to us.

2 **Peripatetics**] Peripatetics are 'those from the Peripatos', supposedly the covered walk in the garden of the Lyceum where Aristotle lectured. 'Peripatetic philosophy' was used in the 18th c. chiefly to refer to the philosophy of Aristotle, and derivatively to refer to his successors and interpreters. Aristotle maintained that moral virtue is possessed to the extent that the proper medium is achieved between excess and defect. Virtue is analysed as a disposition to choose in accordance with the mean, which is determined by a rule that a practically wise person would recognize (*Nicomachean Ethics* 1106^{a}14–1107^{a}2; see also 1104^{a}1 ff., 1107^{a}1 ff., 1138^{b}16–34). For example, the virtue of courage is a mean between foolhardiness and cowardice. In saying that 'a due medium . . . is the characteristic of virtue', Hume seems to be referring to Aristotle's theory, rather than a later Peripatetic doctrine. It is Hume, however, who asserts that the due medium is determined by *utility,* not the Aristotelians.

celerity . . . and dispatch] swiftness (or efficiency) . . . and nimbleness (at business).
4 **originally framed**] constituted by nature.

schoolman's ass] The schoolman's ass is a jackass that dies of starvation when placed equidistant between two equally inviting stacks of hay, because it lacks sufficient motive, reason, and will to choose one rather than the other. 'Schoolman' refers to a scholastic theologian or philosopher in the medieval period, during which the parable likely originated.

5 **rules of philosophy**] The 'rules of philosophy' may be the rules of experimental method used in the attempt to find laws. See Intro., 12–13, and ann. 1.10 and 3.48 and n. 14.

6 **in moral as in natural disquisitions**] in moral philosophy as in natural philosophy. *Moral* philosophy studies *human* nature (including the inner life of the mind and human behaviour), whereas *natural* philosophy studies *physical* nature. In *EHU* (3.12), Hume presents moral philosophy as *the science of man,* i.e. the systematic study of human nature.

8 **Cromwell**] Oliver Cromwell (see ann. 3.24) combined strict discipline with religious enthusiasm, was a consummate opportunist, engaged in regicide, often changed his mind about his goals, and waged a vicious campaign in Ireland. Although clever and capable, he was not notable for discretion (prudence; judgement).

de Retz] Cardinal de Retz (Archbishop of Paris and political figure, 1614–79) was given to intrigues in love and politics and was indiscreet in disclosing his love affairs with certain women. He was also known for quickly shifting his political and religious affiliations and allegiances.

Dr. Swift] Jonathan Swift (English satirist, pamphleteer, and Anglican priest, 1667–1745) used the expression 'aldermanly discretion' (circumspection characteristic of a municipal councillor) in a general discussion of discretion as form of prudence (*The Intelligencer*, in *Irish Tracts: 1728–1733*, 38–9).

greatest parts . . . elegant writer . . . Polyphemus] 'Greatest parts' refers to the highest human abilities, qualities, capacities, functions, and talents. Hume is maintaining that a person of many fine qualities who lacks discretion is seriously defective, like a giant with no eyes. The 'elegant writer' is evidently Joseph Addison, who makes a similar statement and uses the example of Polyphemus in *Spectator* 225, which is an 'essay on discretion' (see Box, 'An Allusion', *Notes & Queries*, 60–1). 'Elegant' here means eloquent and refined (see 1.4). Polyphemus is the principal figure among the race of gigantic, lawless giants who loses the one eye in his forehead when Odysseus blinds him with a burning wood stake (*Odyssey* 1.69 ff. and 9.380).

9 **St. Evremond . . . Turenne**] Turenne (Henri de la Tour d'Auvergne, Marshal of France, 1611–75) was a leading French general in the wars of Louis XIV and a renowned and extraordinary figure. Saint-Évremond (Charles de Saint-Denis, literary figure, 1613–1703) depicts Turenne as loyal to the prince, morally virtuous and practically wise, filled with almost superhuman valour and courage, and a genius exhibiting great presence of mind as well as a vast understanding of military history and strategy. This praise is found in two contiguous essays: 'Éloge de Monsieur de Turenne' and 'Parallèle de Monsieur le Prince et de Monsieur de Turenne' (*Works*, 2: 320–34).

Fabius . . . Machiavel . . . Scipio] Fabius Maximus (Roman military leader, 3rd c. BC) withstood the might of Hannibal (Carthaginian military commander) by conducting small harassing operations and avoiding major battles. Scipio Africanus (Roman military leader, 3rd–2nd c. BC) crushed Hannibal in the battle of Zama (19 Oct. 202). In 206 BC Scipio planned an African campaign to bring the long war between Rome and Carthage to an end. He was opposed by powerful members of the Senate, Fabius Maximus among them. The Senate refused to supply him with an army; none the less, he collected a volunteer force that defeated Hannibal. (See also ann. Appx. 4.17 and n. 75.)

Hume's reference is to the *Discourses* 3.9.2–3 of Niccolò Machiavelli (political historian, 1469–1527). Machiavelli says that 'Fabius Maximus, when in command of the army, proceeded circumspectly and with a caution far removed from the impetuosity and boldness characteristic of the Roman.' In his plans to go to Africa and end the war, Scipio, by contrast, was bold, daring, and innovative beyond Fabius' recommendation. See, further, Machiavelli, *Prince* 17; *Discourses* 3.21.

10 **gained the race**] from 'The Tortoise and the Hare' (Phaedrus, appx. 226 [465]). 'Gained the race' means 'won the race'.

11 and n. 27 **Plato**] Plato explores the possibility that those who enjoy a life-style of bodily pleasures will not be freed from the desires of the body after death, when their souls will long for the physical delights they refused to renounce. Plato surmises (*Phaedo* 80 C–81 E) that these souls will assume the forms of animals sharing their indulgences. For example, those who have pursued the pleasures of drunkenness and gluttony will become asses, while those who lead lives of injustice, tyranny, and robbery

will become wolves and hawks. Plato's person of bodily pleasures lacks frugality in Hume's sense of moderate use.

11 **organs of sensation**] sensory capacities in the body.

worthless prodigals] wastefully lavish squanderers who lack all frugality.

12 **extreme of frugality is** *avarice*] Hume thinks miserliness or stinginess sometimes involves an insatiable greed and hoarding of wealth. See Hume's essay 'Of Avarice'.

14 *chastity*] See 4.5–6 and also *THN* 3.2.12.

15 **distant profit**] long-range rather than short-range benefit (see 'distant views' at 6.15 and 'distant pursuits' at 6.15).

calm passions] The distinction between calm and violent passions played a role in Hume's *THN* 2.1.1.3 and 2.3.4, and *DIS* 6.1. Hume often proposes that social situations are most secure and individuals happiest when the calm passions predominate. Happiness, stability, virtue, and the common good are associated with calm passions; the reverse with violent passions. This distinction had a history before Hume in the work of writers such as Hutcheson (see ann. 1.3). Sometimes 'calm passion' referred to a type of passion that is always calm (such as fondness or the desire for another's happiness), but in some cases to a particular quality of a passion (e.g. fear might be calm at one time, violent at another).

pure *reason*] a reference to elements of the rationalist theories that Hume opposes. See Intro., 19–20, 45–9.

objects approach nearer] objects of our affections exert more influence because of their proximity.

entailed] brought down or settled.

16 and n. 28 **Dicæarchus . . . Polybius**] Polybius writes that wherever Dicaearchus (Aetolian commander of the fleet of Philip V, 3rd–2nd c. BC) 'anchored his ships he constructed two altars, one of Impiety and the other of Lawlessness, and on these he sacrificed and worshipped these powers as if they were divine' (*Histories* 18.54). Hume apparently regards this practice as foolish, but does not necessarily regard Dicaearchus (a resourceful pirate) as a fool.

well assured . . . started] confident . . . jumped.

17 *can perform nothing upon study*] cannot perform when deeper study (i.e. thought, deliberate mental effort, or application) is required.

contrary character . . . dint of application] the reverse phenomenon, where a person laboriously studies something and reaches no conclusions by quick insight.

18 **refined sense and exalted sense**] discriminating or subtle sense and elevated or artistic sense.

19 **make a figure**] establish a reputation.

and n. 29 **memory . . . Cæsar**] The ancient Greeks invented techniques to enhance memory which were passed on to the Romans and were of great consequence prior to the invention of printing (see Yates, *Art of Memory*). The translation of the passage from Cicero's *Philippics* 2.45.116 in n. 29 is, 'In him was talent, intelligence, memory, writing skill, attentiveness, reflective judgement, diligence'.

20 **private or selfish virtues**] The contrast is to the public virtues. A list of private virtues, those with a 'tendency to serve the person', is presented at 6.21.

21 *public spirit . . . benevolence*] In his essays, Hume discusses 'public spirit', but he names only figures in the ancient world. Many speculative thinkers (philosophers, essayists, and the like) relied heavily on benevolence in their writings. Hume is point-

ing out that too much bragging in society about one's virtues renders ordinary people sceptical about the existence of such virtues. The theme of false pretensions and denying the reality of benevolence and public spirit is expanded at 2.1.

a sullen incredulity on the head of] a brooding disbelief concerning.

perpetual cant] The Stoics and the Cynics both exalted the cultivation of virtue. Hume is referring to the asceticism promoted by both groups: the Cynics allowed only the subsistence level of amenities and dismissed the importance of social conventions; the Stoics were less severe. The reference to 'their magnificent professions and slender performances' indicates Hume's belief that these philosophers were either hypocritical or weak-willed, or otherwise failed to live up to their own ideals. See Hume's disparagements of Stoicism in his essay 'The Stoic'.

and n. 30 Lucian] The passages from Lucian, who wrote about the magnificent professions and slender performances here mentioned by Hume, may be translated as follows. *Timon*: people 'declaiming loudly on "virtue", "incorporeals", and [other] trumpery'. *Icaromenippus*: 'and collecting round them youths, they (the philosophers) perform their "vaunted virtue"', *Parliament*: 'where then are their vaunted "virtue", "nature", "fate", and "fortune"—names without substance, empty of reality'. Lucian used humorous dialogue and satire to criticize many types of human vice and moral failings, including the ineptitude of philosophers.

22 **resolve into self-love . . . selfish virtues**] The mentioned selfish virtues are listed and explained at 6.21; see also 6.20. Hume thinks we cannot explain our approval of these virtues in terms of self-love, as egoists attempt to do, because impartial observers who gain nothing themselves still approve of and see the merit of these virtues in terms of what they contribute to those who possess them.

a natural, unforced interpretation of the phænomena of human life] a doctrine-free representation of human experience.

23 **bodily endowments . . . goods of fortune**] Hume is now going to test his theory of personal merit by examining advantageous properties of the body, such as beauty and functional structure, and goods of prosperity and wealth, in the form of riches, power, and the like, to see if they are the basis of some type of personal merit.

24 **proportions of a horse**] Hume is referring to Xenophon (Athenian politician and historian, 5th–4th c. BC), *On the Art of Horsemanship* (esp. 296–307, 310–11), and to Virgil (Roman poet, 1st c. BC), *Georgics* 3, lines 72–102. Xenophon discusses criteria for selecting a horse. He writes about how to assess the feet, the knees, bone structure, chest, neck, and the like, primarily with regard to the utility of these body parts for war. Virgil describes the type of horse that should be bred for racing and discusses the value of temperament and form.

received at this day by . . . jockeys] accepted today by . . . horse-dealers.

26 **and nn. 31–2 Homer . . . Epaminondas . . . Pompey**] Homer and other ancient poets often discussed the importance of bodily strength in war; Hume assumes that his readers are aware of this fact and so does not 'insist' (dwell) on it. 'Scruple not to mention' (i.e. dispute not the need to mention) refers to assumptions made by historians without hesitation or doubt. Epaminondas (of Thebes, 5th–4th c. BC) was among the commanders who defeated the Spartan army at Leuctra, for which he was uncommonly celebrated. He is portrayed by Diodorus Siculus (15.88.3–4) as having a noble character, including the ideal qualities of supreme virtue that Hume refers to in n. 31 as 'perfect merit'. Pompeius, or Pompey the Great (Roman military commander,

1st c. BC), crushed insurrections, cleared the seas of pirates, and organized (with Julius Caesar and Crassus) the First Triumvirate. According to Plutarch, he was kingly in appearance, possessed a trustworthy character and dignity, and enjoyed above all Romans the respect and goodwill of the citizens (*Lives*, 'Pompey' 1–2, 21–4, 79–80).

26 n. 32 **Sallust. apud Veget.**] The passage from Vegetius (writer on military subjects, 4th–5th c. AD), may be translated as follows: 'He [Pompey the Great] would contend appropriately with the fit, with the agile at jumping, with the swift at running.'

28 n. 33 **king's evil**] scrofula, a variety of tuberculosis associated with the cervical lymph nodes. Many thought it curable by the touch of a king.

32 **not accept of**] not accept.

33 n. 34 **envy and of pity**] Hume thinks of pity as a natural human response induced by the imagination rather than by reason or reflection. He discusses envy and pity in similar passages in *THN* 2.2.8 and 3.3.2.

34 **favours of fortune**] Hume's point is that riches and power often come through rights of inheritance and good fortune, which are arbitrary and not to a person's credit. People are less esteemed by others when advantages are due to accident or chance.

35 **monarchies . . . republican government**] A birth-based system of political governance leads to a hierarchical structure of family rule, in the form of emperors, kings, queens, czars, and the like. The lure of riches promotes a system in which supreme authority and power is distributed to the people and their elected representatives.

SECTION 7

Qualities or traits that are immediately agreeable to observers, such as a person's cheerful disposition, form another group of mental qualities that produce satisfaction and approval in beholders. These immediately agreeable traits (virtues) form a 'species of Merit' that gives 'immediate pleasure' to observers of the trait. These qualities do not confer any form of benefit to the community or to the possessor other than their agreeableness. As examples, Hume cites magnanimity or greatness of mind, courage, restrained pride, and tranquillity. He uses historical examples to show that these qualities can give us great satisfaction and excite our applause and admiration even for people we observe under adverse or unpopular circumstances. Social utility cannot account for such approbation, because often no social utility derives from these qualities. Rather, sentiments of approval spring from a form of disinterested sympathy or fellow-feeling. Spectators approve these traits because they sympathize with the pleasures that people will experience in interacting with the person who possesses the trait.

1 **Horace**] The reference is to Horace, *Epistles* 1.18, lines 89–90: 'The grave dislike the gay, the merry the grave, the quick the staid, the lazy the stirring man of action.'
jollity is moderate and decent] Merry-making exhibits a suitable moderation.

3 **character . . . Cæsar gives of Cassius**] The quotation is from William Shakespeare (1564–1616), *Julius Caesar*, I. ii. 204–8, where Caesar had just confessed to Antony his fear of Cassius (lines 195–6):

> Yon Cassius has a lean and hungry look.
> He thinks too much. Such men are dangerous.

polite nations and ages] civilized nations and cultures such as the Athenians and late 17th-century French. See *Dial.* 25 (on polite Greeks).

and n. 36 French writer] This verse occurs at the end of a letter that Seigneur de Saint-Évremond sent to 'Count Magalotti, Counsellor of State to his Royal Highness the Great Duke of Tuscany'. A translation of the passage in n. 36 is as follows:

> Virtue, if not sour, I choose;
> Pleasure, if not wild and loose;
> Life I love, but do not fly
> At Death's approach, nor fear to die.

(Des Maizeaux translation, 2: 451, with English modernized.)

4 **greatness of mind**] This virtue of dignity and distinction in life is among Hume's favourite examples of the virtues. It is more a division of the heroic virtues than a single character trait (*THN* 3.3.2.13). It is in Hume's model of perfect virtue (see 9.2), and his most admired figures typically exhibit greatness of mind. The term *signal* here carries the meaning of extraordinary or remarkable.

and n. 37 Longinus] The anonymously written work on the sublime (long erroneously attributed to Longinus) cited in n. 37 was the leading source for reflection on the *sublime*—one of the more important topics in aesthetics in Hume's lifetime. 'Longinus' held that the sublime is the feature in a work of fine or literary art that gives it a distinctive power; sublimity is the 'echo of magnanimity' in the metaphorical sense of the resonance of a noble mind (*On the Sublime* 9.2–4).

silence of Ajax] *On the Sublime* discusses the relevant passage in Homer, *Odyssey* 11 (lines 543–67). Ajax—represented in the *Iliad* as second in bravery only to Achilles—is full of wrath for a defeat and refuses to respond to words of consolation and reassurance. This silence, which so aptly expresses his anger and indignation, is grander than any use of language.

5 **Darius . . . Parmenio**] Parmenio (Macedonian military leader, 4th c. BC) served under Philip and Alexander the Great (Macedonian king as well as Philip's son and successor, 4th c. BC). Darius III (king of Persia) offered terms of peace, whereupon Alexander solicited the advice of Parmenio and responded as Hume reports.

a like principle] Alexander's saying is from a 'like principle' about the sublime because it excites our admiration and applause and for similar reasons of noble disdain and the like found in the principle(s) noted immediately above regarding (1) the echo of magnanimity and (2) Ajax's silence.

6 **refused to follow**] 'The same hero' is Alexander, who did not invade further into the East Indies (India), because his soldiers were exhausted and refused to continue.

Condé] Condé is the name of a family of French nobility, the chief of whom bears the title 'Prince de Condé'. The particular Condé is Louis II (1621–86), known as 'the Great Condé'.

7 **and n. 39 confident of Medea . . . true sublime**] 'Confident' is Hume's spelling of confidant. 'Of true sublime' refers to true greatness or grandeur in literature (and art), placing a work in the most exalted regions of thought and passion.

Pierre Corneille (French dramatist, 1606–84) wrote a tragedy, *Médée*, which is

229

discussed in the source cited in n. 39 by Nicolas Boileau-Despréaux (French poet and critic, 1636–1711). The confidant suggests caution and possibly submission in the face of grave problems and threats, asking what other recourse is left. Medea responds, as quoted by Hume, 'Moy, Moy, dis-je, & c'est assez' ('Me, me, say I, and that is enough') (*Medée*, in *Le Théâtre*, 2: 297).

8 and n. 40 **Phocion**] This story presumably illustrates Hume's observations about greatness of mind, dignity, and noble pride and spirit. Phocion (Athenian politician and military leader, 4th c. BC) was renowned for virtuous conduct and desire for peace. When democracy was restored to Athens (318 BC), Phocion was falsely accused of treason and executed at age 85. Plutarch, the source in n. 40, recounts several stories about Phocion's calmness, dignity, nobility, and bravery in the final moments of his life. In context, Phocion is chastising those sent to die with him for their complaints (*Lives*, 'Phocion' 36.2–3). Hume contrasts Phocion's behaviour with that of Vitellius.

9 and n. 41 **Tacitus . . . Vitellius**] Aulus Vitellius (Roman emperor, 1st c. AD) was proclaimed Roman emperor by his army. Vespasian opposed him. The Eastern legions at first swore allegiance to Vitellius, but later switched loyalty to Vespasian, who was victorious. Vitellius was then led through the forum and murdered. The passage cited in n. 41 from Tacitus may be translated as follows: 'He was led away, clothing in shreds, a pitiful sight. Many shouted at him; none wept. The ugliness of his exit had driven out compassion.'

10 **generous pride**] noble sense of inner worth and dignity. Pride is self-value and sense of dignity in the form of 'a certain satisfaction in ourselves, on account of some accomplishment or possession', as Hume puts it in *DIS* 2.1, 10. See also *THN* 2.1.7. Hume thinks that pride is often created or stimulated by a recognition that other people approve of one's accomplishments or possessions. However, he also recognized that some pride can constitute a vice when people lack the qualities they attribute to themselves (*THN* 3.3.2.6–10).

11 **a like sublimity of sentiment**] a similarly lofty or refined feeling (see 7.27).

12 and n. 43 **Demosthenes represent Philip**] In *On the Crown*, cited in n. 43, Demosthenes discusses his advice to the Athenians that they oppose Philip, whose purpose was to establish a despotic empire. He praises Philip ('under . . . shining colours') only for his sacrifices and lofty ambitions. Demosthenes '*apologizes* for his own administration' in the sense of *justifying the advice* he gave Athenians in the face of charges brought against him by his enemy Aeschines (see 5.11). Demosthenes does not apologize in the sense of *asking pardon*.
Pella] Philip of Macedon made Pella the capital of Macedonia and it became the birthplace of Alexander the Great. Ruins are some twenty-five miles west-north-west of Salonika, Greece. The place is *mean* in the sense of undistinguished or of small value.

13 and n. 44 **Suevi**] The reference is to several ancient, warlike tribes of Germanic nomads. Hume is still discussing 'the utility of courage'. He is illustrating his observations by showing how courage was needed for the continual wars the Suevi faced, and therefore was elevated in social importance.

14 and n. 45 **Scythians . . . Herodotus**] Scythians are the inhabitants of ancient Scythia (present-day southern Russia). Herodotus 4.46 describes them as savage and nomadic.

15 **courage**] This passage returns to the themes of the social utility of courage and its

'peculiar lustre', deriving from its elevation in a culture. Ancient and primitive ethics exalt virtues such as courage and the martial temper because of their utility and the sublimity of sentiment that these virtues occasion. Hume suggests that in cultivated nations the social virtues, though starkly different in orientation, are also exalted because of their utility and agreeableness. The comments immediately below about Homer, Fénelon, and Thucydides continue these themes; soon thereafter, at 7.18, Hume compares the ancient and modern ages in terms of virtues exalted in each.

ethics of Homer] The reference is to the code of honour and sense of heroic excellence in pre-Socratic, Hellenic culture. The code emphasized courage and personal glory. Some scholars have argued that the code articulated none of the virtues later recognized as central to ethics, but others have argued that at least a modern sense of *justice* was recognized in the Homeric period.

Fenelon] François Fénelon (French writer and religious figure, 1651–1715) wrote *Aventures de Télémaque, fils de Ulysse* as a satire on the king of France. The work has often been said to imitate the style and use of characters in the *Odyssey* (attributed to Homer, 9th c. BC). Fénelon's book seems designed as a treatise on ethics, politics, and peace for a prince, but interpretation is difficult. Whether there is any deep-seated imitation of Homer is controversial. However, a sharp contrast between Homer's heroic ideals and Fénelon's peaceful ideals is apparent.

Thucydides] In a discussion of piracy among the Hellenes and the Barbarians, Thucydides remarks that, in the period prior to the Peloponnesian War, piracy 'did not as yet involve disgrace, but rather conferred something even of glory' (1.5).

and n. 47 Spencer] Edmund Spenser (English poet, *c.*1552–99), once lord deputy of Ireland, advocated the use of stern measures, consistently administered, in order to suppress resistance to English landowners and officials in Ireland (*A View of the State of Ireland*, 145). In speaking of the 'barbarous' parts of Ireland, Hume may be expressing the then common British view that many people are barbarous because they do not accept the same conventions of property as the British. In n. 47, 'kern' means Irish foot-soldier(s); 'straight' means directly.

16 **sage elevates himself**] In some ancient philosophical writings, the sage, or 'wise man', was a model of virtue, self-sufficiency, autonomy, and happiness. Such views were found among the Stoics and Epicureans. For example, the Stoic Seneca analysed how to better the human condition by introducing forms of tranquillity that 'elevate' one, in Hume's sense ('On Tranquillity of Mind', *Moral Essays* 9.2.4), and Epicurus of Athens (founder of the Epicurean school, 4th–3rd c. BC) recommended an untroubled, quiet life free from disturbance in which inner tranquillity became the highest good.

too magnificent] These ideals are too high to be realized.

magnanimity] 'Magnanimity' here seems to refer broadly to greatness of spirit and nobleness. See also 7.4; Appx. 4.11–12; Dial. 40.

17 **Epictetus**] Epictetus (Stoic teacher, 1st–2nd c. AD), born a slave in Rome, was later banished to north-western Greece. There he lived in a small house outfitted with simple items such as a mat, a pallet, and an earthenware lamp that replaced a stolen iron lamp. This theft led Epictetus to reflect on the relative unimportance of possessions and the greater importance of moral purpose (*Discourses* 1.18.15–20).

18 **narrow souls**] limited minds. Hume often uses 'soul' to mean 'mind'.

19 **delightful in themselves**] agreeable independently of their utility. See 7.29: 'valued for the immediate pleasure' and not for 'utility or future beneficial consequences'.

20 **Elysian fields**] In Homeric mythology, heroes exempted from death and mortal relatives of the king of the gods are taken to these fields to savour eternal ecstasy.

pastoral Arcadia] Arcadia was an ancient pastoral and isolated mountainous region in the central Pelopponesus. The region came to symbolize simplicity, tranquillity, and rustic enchantment. See ann. 5.29 on Sannazarius' *Arcadia*.

22 **imply more esteem than many panegyrics**] show more regard for the person than occurs in many forms of commendatory speech, such as speeches at tributes and celebrations. See ann. 1.10 on panegyrics.

applying the epithet of blame] adding a judgement of fault. The point is that persons who are too good, too intrepid, and the like hurt themselves through conduct that is excessive and sometimes even amounts to a weakness of character—as in the excessive love of Harry IV and the excessive bravery of Charles XII, discussed immediately below.

23 **Harry the IVth . . . the league**] Henry IV (1553–1610) was first Henry of Navarre. The Catholic League, founded in 1576 to defend Catholicism against Protestantism, refused to recognize a Protestant as king of France and persuaded King Henry III (1551–89; see ann. Dial. 46), who had instigated the massacre of the Huguenots, to bar Henry of Navarre from succession and to revoke the concessions that Henry III had previously made to the Protestants. In a resulting war, Henry of Navarre defeated Henry III and succeeded to the throne of France in 1589. As Henry IV, he renounced Protestantism, leading to the end of the Catholic League in 1593.

Henry's marriage to Margaret of Valois was annulled in 1599. Shortly thereafter, he married Marie de' Medici, but retained numerous mistresses. In part because of his amorous passions, Henry IV was popular and gained a reputation as gallant, affable, witty, and concerned about the common people of France.

24 **Charles the XIIth**] Dubbed 'the Invincible', Charles XII (King of Sweden, 1682–1718) was involved in a series of successful invasions and attacks on Denmark and Russia. He returned to Sweden to find the nation in a deplorable state. Voltaire wrote an influential biography, *History of Charles XII* (1731), which depicted the king as heroic but as bringing disaster to his country. He notes that Charles underwent astounding changes of character at about age 18, and depicts him as an aggressive and brave warrior. (*Lion of the North*, 42–3.)

25 **Darius and Xerxes**] The Persian Wars, 500–449 BC, were waged between the Persian Empire and Hellenic city-states. The empire of King Darius I (6th–5th c. BC) stretched from west Asia to Egypt. Darius' son, King Xerxes I (5th c. BC), succeeded him and continued to lay plans for conquest. Although Athens was taken in 480, the Persian fleet was crushed shortly thereafter and the army defeated at Plataea in 479. The Athenians thought their victories demonstrated the superiority of their culture over what they took to be barbarian (uncivilized or unrefined) cultures.

Lysias, Thucydides, Plato, and Isocrates] 'The same partiality' here refers to a bias toward warlike achievements. Lysias fled from Athens after it came under control of the Thirty Tyrants. After their expulsion, he returned to impeach the tyrant Eratosthenes in a classic oration (*Against Eratosthenes, Orations* 12). His oration in honour of those Athenians who perished in battle under Iphicrates is considered his masterpiece on the topics mentioned by Hume (*Funeral Oration, Orations* 2). Isocrates,

Lysias' near-contemporary, depicts Athens as mindful of agriculture and the educator of Greece, whereas Sparta is intent on military conquest (*Panathenaicus* 90, 94; *Panegyricus* 51–140). Thucydides, himself a military commander, wrote about war and exhibited pride in Athenian military achievements. Plato's writings show a reasonably balanced approach to Athenian achievements, but the vital role of soldiers in the state is apparent.

26 **convey a satisfaction**] Hume is arguing that a great poet generates feelings of satisfaction in readers even while arousing disagreeable passions, such as anger.

27 **pathetic and sublime**] stirring and exaltation of feeling (often achieved by poets), amounting to an extraordinary, elevated form of passion or sentimental experience (see 3.23; 7.4 and n. 37; 7.7 and n. 39; 7.11). The pathetic is identified with the gentle, though moving emotions; the sublime is grander, richer, and more admired in aesthetic writings during Hume's period. The talent of stirring such feeling constitutes a form of personal merit (see Virgil as an example, immediately below).

Augustus . . . Virgil] Augustus, or Octavian (1st c. BC–1st c. AD), descended from a wealthy family to become the first Roman emperor. Although celebrated for valour, steadiness, and justice, his fame and stature as a cultural symbol never approached that of his contemporary Virgil (Roman poet, 1st c. BC), whose *Aeneid* is a national epic emphasizing the divine origins of the Romans. During Hume's period, Virgil's *Georgics* and *Aeneid* were widely praised for what Hume here calls 'the divine beauties of his poetical genius', giving Virgil significant personal merit. See Addison, *Spectator* 417.

28 **delicacy of taste**] The capacity to *appreciate* beauty in poetry and the like is a form of personal merit no less than the capacity to *create* the beauty. See ann. 1.4.

29 **fellow-feeling**] In this conclusion to Section 7, Hume is maintaining that sympathy, or fellow-feeling, is the source of both types of 'sentiment of approbation'— namely, the sentiments that arise from the *agreeableness* and the *utility* of qualities of persons.

SECTION 8

This section treats personal qualities that others find immediately agreeable. Disinterested observers approve of these qualities even though they do not confer utilitarian benefits on either the community or the possessor. As examples, Hume cites good manners, wit, ingenuity, modesty, decency, and cleanliness. Observers approve of these qualities not because of any immediate pleasure they give the person who possesses them. Rather, they approve of these qualities only because others find them immediately agreeable. Because of this agreeableness, these qualities sometimes become the source of others' love and affection. Hume maintains that it is often mysterious (inexplicable) *why* these properties inspire a sense of satisfaction in others.

1 **eternal contrarieties**] ceaseless oppositions or disagreements.

good manners or politeness] See 4.13 on 'laws of good manners'. These terms had a history of discussion, often in a context of attempting to account for the human advance from primitive behaviour to cultivated morals and civility. Hobbes devoted a chapter to 'manners' in which he began by describing 'decency of behaviour' as 'the small morals' (*Leviathan* 1.11). In Hume's time, the simple term 'politeness' was used broadly and was applied to literary and political contexts, among others.

3 **wit ... not be easy to define**] Wit was the subject of a series of articles by Addison in the *Spectator* 58–63 (7–12 May 1711). He was concerned primarily to distinguish true wit from false wit. He opened by saying, 'Nothing is so much admired and so little understood as Wit.'

4 **solid qualities**] steady, sturdy, sober, and practical qualities of persons.

5 **evil eye**] major disapproval; disaffected view.

7 **dignity and nice discernment**] worth and subtle discrimination (including insight).

8 **Modesty ... chastity**] Modesty was chiefly but not exclusively applied to relations with the opposite sex. See Hume's discussion in *THN* 3.2.12 and also Hume's essays 'Of Impudence and Modesty' and 'Of Love and Marriage'. On chastity, see 4.5; 4.7; 6.14.

pudor] This complicated Latin term means sense of shame for having done something improper or bad, sense of propriety, modesty, or decency, and even sense of honour. The word is also used to refer to scruples relating to matters that affect one's honour, reputation, or character.

9 and n. 51 **Aristotle**] Aristotle observes in *Nicomachean Ethics* 1123ᵃ33–1125ᵃ34 that magnanimous persons of moderate pride and self-esteem can escape both vanity (an excessive evaluation) and humility (an undervaluation). The defect in both cases is inadequate knowledge rather than evil or malicious motives. Humble persons do not see themselves as worthy of goods when they are worthy, whereas vain persons overestimate their worthiness. Aristotle maintains that the unduly humble person is found more frequently than the vain person.

Montaigne's maxim] In 'Of Practice', Michel de Montaigne (French essayist, 1533–92) says: 'I hold that we must show wisdom in judging ourselves ... If I seemed to myself to be good or wise—or nearly so—I would sing it out at the top of my voice. To say you are worse than you are is not modest but foolish. According to Aristotle, to prize yourself at less than you are worth is weak and faint-hearted' (*Essays* 2.6 [426]). In 'Of Presumption', Montaigne discusses how we flatter ourselves and represent ourselves as something other than what we are, thereby failing to exercise wisdom in judging ourselves. He notes that we tend to set too great a value on ourselves, while placing too little value on others (*Essays* 2.17 [720]).

common societies] public groups, by contrast to private groups.

Maurice ... marquis of Spinola] Maurice (Prince of Orange, 1567–1625) led the Netherlands in the fight for independence against the Spaniards, who were led by Ambrosio di Spinola (the Marquis de Spinola, 1569–1630). Spinola was a formidable adversary of Maurice from 1602 until 1607.

10 **internal sentiment**] inner feeling and motivation (by contrast to the 'outward behaviour' exhibited to others).

excludes not a noble pride] See 7.10 and 8.9 and n. 51.

contumacy of Socrates] The reference is to Cicero, *Tusculan Disputations* 1.29.71. Cicero praises Socrates' integrity and noble resistance, especially during his trial and death.

and n. 52 **Iphicrates**] Iphicrates (Athenian military leader, 4th c. BC) defeated the Spartans in important battles and later commanded a fleet off the Macedonian coast. Quintilian says that Iphicrates 'asked Aristophon, who was accusing him on a ...

charge of treason, whether he would consent to betray his country for a bribe. When Aristophon replied in the negative, he continued, "Have I then done what you would have refused to do?"' (*Institutes* 5.12.10).

11 **things of course**] events that happen in due course; normal events.

12 *indecorum* **... Cicero**] The reference is to Cicero's *De officiis* 1.27–8.93–100, which treats decorum (propriety, seemliness) and its absence (indecorum).

13 **cleanliness**] English poet Thomas Tickell described cleanliness as 'one of the *Half-Virtues*' and provided a lengthy analysis of its status (*Spectator* 631).

   smaller vices] See the quotation from Hobbes in ann. 8.1, on 'small morals'.

14 **blind, but sure testimony**] uninformed, but reliable declaration.

SECTION 9

In Part 1 of this Conclusion, Hume begins by summarizing his views in *EPM*. He says he has defended the proposition that a person's merit (moral and otherwise) consists entirely in the possession of mental qualities that are either useful or agreeable to the person or to other persons. He maintains that this proposition has been disputed in philosophy, but is presupposed in the beliefs and practices found in common life. He discusses how we 'survey ourselves' by critically evaluating our own moral adequacy and maintaining self-respect as well as respect in the eyes of others. One of Hume's clearest statements about the *universality* of morals appears in this part.

Part 2 of this section is not about 'the moral *approbation* attending merit or virtue' treated in Part 1, but about 'our interested *obligation*' to act virtuously—in effect, an entirely new topic. The question is why a person should be moral (faithful, just, honest, etc.) if moral behaviour would disadvantage the person in life. Suppose a person could act like a 'sensible knave' against moral rules, thereby improving the person's circumstances in life. Hume suggests that we may not be able to respond to this knave (the egoist) in an entirely 'satisfactory and convincing' manner: 'If [a person's] heart rebel not against such pernicious maxims, if he feel no reluctance to the thoughts of villany or baseness, he has indeed lost a considerable motive to virtue.' Hume maintains that the obligation to act morally is found in human nature, not in the desire for divine rewards and sanctions for moral behaviour that some philosophers and theologians have identified as the origin of moral requirements. He argues that we understand enough about human nature and the human condition to believe that consistent moral conduct and satisfaction with one's moral character are, at least for most persons, 'very requisite to happiness', whereas knaves are usually 'betrayed by their own actions'. He offers the related suggestion that we are motivated to act morally and to keep our obligations because, if we did not, we could not confine moral violations to a few instances, and we would soon lose our reputation as trustworthy.

1 *useful* or *agreeable* **...** *utile* or the *dulce*] *Utile* is Latin for useful, *dulce* for agreeable.

   systems and hypotheses have perverted] Hume thinks his account of personal merit seems obvious unless some theories and speculative theses have distorted our perspective.

2 **Cleanthes**] Cleanthes is a name from the history of Stoicism that Hume used for a leading figure in his *Dialogues concerning Natural Religion*. Hume makes no connection

between the figure in that work and the present fictional 'model of perfect virtue'. Hume's model is noticeably different from a saintly ideal, which he criticizes at 9.2 and elsewhere.

2 **pencil**] artist's fine brush.

Gratian or Castiglione] Hume might be referring to any one of three Gratians. The most likely candidate is Baltasar Gracián y Morales (Spanish Jesuit and college rector, 1601–58), who wrote five widely disseminated works, one of which is *El heroe*. He was widely read in 18th-c. Britain and was cited by Addison as 'the famous Gratian' (*Spectator* 293). Gracián describes the qualities that are essential to a hero and leader: virtue, self-perfection, self-knowledge, resolve, discretion, wit, courtesy, charm, and persistence against fools. Fidelity to near-perfect virtue is considered essential to greatness. A second candidate is Lucas Gracián Dantisco (Spanish writer, 16th c.), who wrote the work *El galateo español*, which drew in part on Castiglione's work and contained proverbs and concrete rules of etiquette and good manners. The least likely candidate is Franciscus Gratianus (Italian jurist and monk, 12th c.), who compiled the *Decretum Gratiani* (*c.*1140), a collection of decrees and principles that supplies the initial formulation of Roman Catholic canon law on matters of proper faith and conduct.

Conte Baldassare Castiglione (Italian diplomat and writer, 1478–1529) was well known for his *Il cortegiano*. The book presents a picture of 15th- and 16th-c. court life and delineates the characteristics of the ideal courtier or excellent man, a noble, witty, graceful, pleasant warrior and horseman, skilled in several languages and informed about literature and the arts.

3 **monkish virtues**] These 'virtues' (Hume perhaps views them as vices) had been defended by Blaise Pascal and perhaps to some extent by Diogenes the Cynic; Hume comments on both at Dial. 54 in a similar context, mentioning also Saint Dominic and Saint Ignatius of Loyola. *Mortification* here has the meaning of subduing or conquering of lusts and passions by abstinence and prayer.

obscure the fancy] dim the imagination. Hume is maintaining that the cultivation of monkish virtues discourages constructive imagination (as well as the other valuable qualities mentioned in this sentence).

hair-brained enthusiast] hare-brained (having the sense of a hare) and zealous believer; giddy-headed zealot.

calendar] calendar (or registry) of the saints.

4 **vulgar dispute**] The dispute is vulgar in the sense of *commonly discussed*. The dispute is between egoists and their opponents, as well as between those who disagree about the degree of authentic benevolence in human nature. See Intro., 24–6.

dove . . . wolf and serpent] See Intro., 25–6.

one tenet . . . indissoluble connexion] Those who maintain the tenet that human nature is predominantly selfish likewise maintain the tenet that only weak sentiments of virtue are in human nature; the two theses are very closely connected.

5 **vulgarly, though improperly, comprized**] commonly, but improperly placed. Many philosophers (including Hutcheson) had categorized both avarice and ambition as founded on self-love, as lacking in a proper direction, and (depending on the definition, in the case of ambition) as vices.

proper direction] These forms of merit lack the universality of morals, as the following lines explain.

general approbation] See Intro., 27–9 for an explanation of this passage. This central theme in Hume's philosophy had predecessors in Hutcheson, and also in John Locke, who wrote that 'the measure of what is every where called and esteemed *Vertue* and *Vice* is this approbation or dislike, praise or blame, which by a secret and tacit consent establishes it self in the several Societies, Tribes, and Clubs of Men in the World' (*Essay* 2.28.10).

6 **human heart**] As long as human nature remains as it now is, it will respond in predictable ways to the good of the public and to the character and actions of individuals.

8 **Virtue and vice become then known**] This idea was introduced at approximately 8.8. Character traits regarded as moral virtues are so regarded because of universal sentiments of approbation, whereas the judgement that certain character traits are vices rests on universal sentiments of censure. See Intro., 28–31.

n. 57 **Horace ... tree**] Horace depicts a malevolent person who once 'when the omens were dark' planted a tree on land now owned by Horace. The malevolent person had intended to harm or even kill his own descendants and neighbours, but the tree subsequently fell on the undeserving Horace's head. He finds an outlet for his feelings of outrage by damning the planter, even finding him (on this slender basis) capable of violently killing his own father. (*Odes* 2.13.1–12.) Hume uses this example to illustrate his thesis in n. 57 that when we 'give vent to passions' such as rage, we commonly 'impute malice or injustice' and distort the behaviour and motives of others.

9 **Solon ... neuters**] According to Plutarch (*Lives*, 'Solon' 20.1), Solon (Athenian statesman and legislator, 7th–6th c. BC) supported a law that disfranchised all who remained neutral in a faction-generated sedition. Solon held that private good should not be advanced while disregarding the public good.

kindles not in the common blaze] does not become excited or motivated because of public feeling. In this difficult paragraph, Hume argues that we have moral capacities to resist powerful social influences that affect the emotions and encourage immoral actions.

principles ... *party* of human kind] Principles in our nature that counteract tendencies to vice and disorder, though lethargic, are found in all morally sensitive members of society.

in solitary and uncultivated nature] in the absence of a supportive social context.

dominion of our breast] authority in the seat of our affections.

10 **generous minds**] high-spirited or magnanimous persons (those lofty of purpose).

accomplished in every perfection] skilled in every form of excellence.

11 **force of many sympathies**] strength of the totality of sentiments arising from impartial observation of the *agreeable* and *useful* qualities of persons.

12 **accommodate matters**] reconcile the various parts of the argument and render them consistent.

resolve ... into] interpret ... in terms of.

end itself is totally indifferent] See the related formulations of this 'absurdity' at 5.17, using 'contradiction', and at 5.46, using 'impossible'. Hume thinks that virtues elicit approval (and vices disapproval) from observers because the virtues tend towards ends to which the observer is not indifferent. Some mental qualities cause pleasure only in an observer; others also cause pleasure in the possessor.

13 *excessive* scepticism] For Hume's views on excessive scepticism, see Intro., 15–17, and also *EHU* 12.

grossest absurdities] Hume often promotes this view about enthusiasm, superstition, and fanaticism. See 3.7 and 3.23–4.

order and œconomy of the heavenly bodies] organization, including the structure and causes, of the bodies seen in the sky.

infinite itself] infinite quantity or distance, as employed in mathematical calculations.

14 interested *obligation*] An interested obligation to virtue is a reason from self-interest to act virtuously. See 9.16: 'duties [in] the true interest of each individual'. Hume is changing the subject from reasons for the approbation of virtuous conduct to reasons for being virtuous and acting morally. Hume holds that, even if egoistic theories are false, acting according to the duties and virtues of morality may still be in a person's interest.

find his account] discover his interest or advantage.

foregoing theory] namely, the account of the approbation attending merit or virtue.

amendment of men's lives] the reform, alteration, or repair of human lives. Hume is discussing the practical effects of philosophical theories on human conduct.

dangerous and pernicious] Hume is not suggesting that pernicious theories or truths exist or do not exist, but only that if they did exist, society would recognize their perniciousness and repudiate them.

15 dismal dress . . . many divines] Hume is pointing to the positive outcome of his theory, by contrast to other theories. Virtue is here personified to contrast Hume's useful-or-agreeable account to other accounts. The 'dismal dress' covering virtue in other accounts is a philosophical or religious doctrine that distorts true virtue, such as occurs in a system championing 'the monkish virtues' (see at 9.3). 'Many divines' refers to theologians and ministers who recommend austerity, and perhaps also those who interpret virtuous behaviour as appropriately motivated by a desire for a divine reward (see Appx. 4.21).

just calculation] The appeal is to a fair balancing of different interests so as to produce good outcomes for all affected parties. This passage, taken alone, seems to support the interpretation of Hume as a classical utilitarian, but other passages do not. See Intro. on 'utilitarianism', 40.

austere pretenders] persons devoted to ascetic practices who mistake austerity for virtue.

16 foregoing system] namely, the account of virtue and personal merit found in *EPM*.

20 *selfish* and *social* sentiments] Hume is denying that self-regarding sentiments (those that promote our own interest) necessarily conflict with other-regarding sentiments.

21 modelling his own disposition] designing his own character and set of dispositions.

not feel themselves such] The grammar is deceptive here. Read: persons are not deficient in doing their duty because they do not wish to be generous, friendly, and humane, but rather because they do not feel generous, friendly, or humane.

22 sensible knave] a deceitful, dishonest person; a base and crafty rogue. The 'sensible knave' is among the best-known examples found in *EPM*. See Intro., 38–9. Using the theses about *interested obligation* introduced at 9.14 and now about the sensible knave, Hume is progressively arguing that there are good reasons to act virtuously.

23 **practice will be answerable to his speculation**] the way he acts will be responsive to the demands of his knavish thinking.

25 **luxury and expence**] what is costly, lavish, and extravagant. The connotation of 'luxury' differs from its previous uses; see ann. 2.21.

APPENDIX 1

In Appendix 1 Hume returns to some themes he initiated in Section 1. He associates his views with the sentimentalists in opposition to the rationalists. He argues that reason (or the understanding) collects facts about a situation, investigates matters of truth, and points to the utilities that might be achieved, whereas sentiment sets our goals, moves us to action, and confers value. Moral approbation and blame are functions of sentiment. Hume offers five arguments ('considerations') against the rationalist view that reason is the source or foundation of morals. He is particularly concerned to criticize the thesis that the moral and immoral are to be found in *moral relations* that reason discovers.

During this analysis, Hume offers a formal definition of virtue: *whatever mental action or quality gives to a spectator the pleasing sentiment of approbation*. He also proposes an aesthetic analogy: Moral beauty is discovered much in the way natural beauty is, namely, through a sentiment created in us by objects. It is true that beauty depends on proportions and relations in objects, but mere apprehension of proportions and relations by reason does not account for the perception of beauty.

The final paragraph contains a summary of the theses in this appendix: *Reason* conveys knowledge of truth and falsehood; *taste* imparts the sentiments associated with beauty, deformity, vice, and virtue. Taste is also a productive faculty; it gilds the objects we evaluate with 'colours' (properties such as virtue) that are taken from internal sentiment and projected onto the objects.

1 **foregoing hypothesis . . . question first started**] If the arguments throughout *EPM* are accepted, then the major problem stated in Section 1 can be addressed, namely, that of finding the general principles of morals and determining the proper roles of reason and sentiment in moral judgement. This task was postponed from Section 1 to this Appendix.

2 **nice views, and a small overbalance**] precise or finely discriminative viewpoints, and a slight preponderance or overriding balance. In saying that 'a preference must be given', Hume presumably means that, although there is a slight preponderance of support for one choice over another, a decision still must be made.

general rule] The general rule captures what, in the long run, serves the public interest. One's moral obligation is to follow the general rule, not to make judgements about the balance of utility in particular cases, because these judgements might violate the general rule. In saying that 'single instances' are 'pernicious', Hume seems to mean that balancing utilities in individual cases is against the public interest because it ignores the rules of justice that protect everyone's interest. See also Hume's discussion of public utility and individual cases at Appx. 3.6 and *THN* 3.2.2–3, 6.

3 **instruct us**] See Intro., 48–9.

4 **five following considerations**] Hume is here stating that five arguments—noted by numbers 1–5 in the next few paragraphs—will be directed against rationalists. These arguments defend the role of sentiment in morals.

5 **comparisons, instead of instances**] comparisons such as analogies instead of cases that confirm or refute the hypothesis (see 3.31 and Appx. 3.10).

crime ... which has place] moral violation or transgression . . . which occurs under the following conditions.

6 *matter of fact* **or of** *relations*] This distinction is between two capacities of human reason (or understanding) and also between two types of proposition. In other writings Hume develops the distinction as follows: (1) *Matters of fact* are propositions that reason grasps through observation, scientific experiments, and the like. (2) *Relations of ideas* are propositions that reason grasps in deductive and mathematical reasoning; here reason grasps what is 'intuitively certain' rather than facts about the world.

crime] Ingratitude, a 'crime' in the sense of an immoral action, resides in a certain mental quality in the person who is ungrateful. In particular, the mental quality is a motive of ill will or an attitude of indifference directed at one who has exhibited goodwill. We infer this mental quality from the ungrateful person's behaviour and, upon feeling a sentiment of blame, we consider the action or inaction a vice or crime. We 'gild the object' beyond the bare facts of the person's behaviour. See Appx. 1.21 and Intro., 33–4.

discovers itself] The crime of ingratitude makes itself manifest or known.

7 *moral relations*, **discovered by reason**] a reference to rationalist theories such as those of Samuel Clarke. Hume is arguing that the full set of relations in a circumstance is not sufficient to determine the morality of an action or inaction; a relation, such as *being contrary to*, never by itself determines moral wrongness. A judgement from sentiment is required to make the difference. See Intro., 17–22.

10 **defines virtue**] See Intro., 27–9 and n. 50. The 'spectator' mentioned here is an impartial spectator, not merely any spectator.

11 **disquisitions of the understanding**] These observations about the functions and limits of the understanding may be responses to rationalist dismissals of the importance of sentiment. Hume assigns only the tasks of finding facts and drawing conclusions to the understanding; determination of what is right is assigned to a sentiment.

12 **Œdipus killed Laius**] In Hellenic legend, an oracle forewarned Laius that his son Oedipus would kill him. The child was therefore abandoned, but was rescued by a stranger and raised in Corinth. An oracle told Oedipus that he would slay his father and marry his mother, which caused him to leave Corinth. While travelling he encountered and killed Laius. He proceeded to Thebes, was proclaimed king, and married Laius' widow, his mother. Hume's point is that Oedipus was not aware of the father–son relationship, formed incorrect views of his action, and therefore lacked a proper perspective from which to make a moral judgement.

Nero killed Agrippina] After a long feud, Agrippina threatened to depose her son Nero and worked to achieve a popular outcry against him. This threat prompted Nero to have her killed. (For a discussion of the surrounding events, see ann. 5.34 and 5.40.) By contrast to Oedipus, Nero knew all the relevant relationships and was positioned to make a proper moral judgement. But his 'savage heart' overwhelmed any generous moral sentiments he might have felt.

14 **Euclid**] Euclid of Alexandria (mathematician, 4th–3rd c. BC) wrote *Elements of Geometry*, which was a standard manual during Hume's lifetime. To say that 'beauty is

240

not a quality of the circle' is to say that the beauty is not a geometrical property or a part of the line, but an aesthetic property that depends on a sentiment we feel after observing the circle.

15 **Palladio and Perrault**] Andrea Palladio (Italian architect, 1518–80) refined and adapted ancient Roman architecture to his period and was responsible for the popularity of what came to be called Palladian motif. Claude Perrault (French architect and physician, 1613–88) was one of the designers of the east façade of the Louvre. Hume is apparently referring to *A Treatise of the Five Orders of Columns*, in which Perrault discusses the cornice, frieze, base, entablature, and shaft and architrave.

16 **Verres or a Catiline**] The crimes and immorality of these corrupt politicians reside not in the facts of their actions but in the universal disapprobation felt by those aware of their actions. Hume is referring to two works by Cicero: *In Verrem* (*Against Verres*) and *In Catilinam* (*Against Catiline*). Gaius Verres (Roman politician, 1st c. BC) was convicted of tax theft, extortion, embezzlement, pillage of art, and disregard of civil rights. L. Sergius Catiline (Roman politician and patrician, 1st c. BC) entered into a conspiracy to plunder Rome and assassinate the consuls.

17 **Nero . . . murdered Agrippina**] See ann. Appx. 1.12. Hume is arguing that if morality consisted in relations alone, the tree that kills its parent would be as guilty as Nero in killing his parent. Hume is interested in what it would take to demonstrate wrongfulness or viciousness merely from the idea of parricide. If parricide itself is wrongful, then the young tree did something wrongful. But for a person to judge that parricide is wrongful, more is needed than the concept of parricide and facts about the cause of death.

18 **accounted for by *reason***] The ultimate goals of human action cannot be explained by appeal to reason. These goals are desirable for their own sake, not for the sake of something else to which they are a means.

21 **gilding or staining**] adding something to objects as they stand in nature. See Intro., 33–4.

eternal and inflexible] Facts about the world, which are discovered by reason, do not vary in accordance with our feelings or with anything we will. A fact is eternally a fact.

Supreme Being] Standards of taste come from human nature, which derives from the Will of God. Hume is pointing to the apparent design in human nature and its functions. Whether his comment about God as the designer is to be taken literally is controversial. Hume may only be pointing to two types of theism that underlie rationalist–sentimentalist differences: (1) rationalist theories such as Clarke's that emphasize the 'eternal and inflexible' nature of truth and of God, and (2) sentimentalist theories such as Hutcheson's that emphasize divine freedom, providence, and design, including the design of human nature.

APPENDIX 2

Whereas Appendix 1 is anti-rationalist (see Intro., 14–15, 19), Appendix 2 is anti-egoist. Hume distinguishes different claims made in the 'selfish systems' of morals and discusses these systems. He maintains that their proponents can be defeated by locating evidence of altruism in human nature and by showing how difficult it is to demonstrate that all motives are self-interested. He maintains that our love for others and our desire for their good are different from and counterbalance our self-love. He maintains that we have unselfish affections and that the egoist idea that all these affections can be reduced to self-love is an overly simple hypothesis about human nature.

Appendix 2] This Appendix may have been influenced by the writings of Anglican Bishop Joseph Butler (1692–1752); see *Fifteen Sermons* (especially Preface and Sermons 1–3, 11–12). Butler argued that benevolence and self-love, though distinct, are both parts of human nature and that both can influence a person's actions.

1 **a principle**] The egoistic principle 'that all benevolence is mere hypocrisy' assumes that human nature has no real capacity for benevolence. It was often associated in Hume's time with Bernard Mandeville's *The Fable of the Bees*. See Intro., 19–20. 'Hypocrisy' here refers to counterfeit goodness or dissimulation.

wiles and machinations] artful, cunning tricks and subtle contrivances.

2 **another principle**] The first principle ('all benevolence is mere hypocrisy') is mentioned at Appx. 2.1. This second and 'resembling' principle ('no passion is, or can be disinterested') is attributed immediately below to Epicurus, Atticus, Horace, Hobbes, Locke, Epicureans, and Hobbists. Hume rejects both principles.

3 **much mistaken**] Hume's point is that even those who defend egoism often act benevolently in their relationships.

Epicurus . . . Atticus and Horace] Epicurus taught that living in accordance with the traditional virtues in Hellenic philosophy is essential to attaining the good life. Even enemies were said to have admired the Epicureans' practices of friendship. Atticus, a friend of Cicero's, was an Epicurean. He was esteemed by Athenian citizens for his amiability, good character, benevolence, and cultured refinement. Horace, to whom Epicurean beliefs have commonly been attributed, was prized by Augustus and the patricians of Rome, and was a friend of the poets Virgil, Tibullus, and Varius.

austerer schools] schools of classical philosophy with the most austere or ascetic demands of virtuous conduct, such as the Stoics and Cynics.

selfish system] 'The selfish system of morals' is egoism, which Hobbes and Locke are here said to espouse. In mentioning their 'irreproachable lives', Hume is referring to their solid reputations for character and integrity. Hobbes was considered prideful, but enjoyed a reputation for wit, good spirits, and a good moral disposition. Locke received esteem and affection from friends and was regarded as a modest, polite, and honest person of sound practical judgement.

4 **Hobbist**] 'Hobbist' was often used as a term of abuse. In *'Brief Lives' . . . by John Aubrey*, many major figures of the 17th c. were reported to have admired Hobbes for his work and character. However, persons who undoubtedly would have repudiated the label were also accused of 'Hobbism'. Samuel Johnson once referred to Hume as a Hobbist, and some scholars still today consider Hume a Hobbist. The particular position Hume here mentions was endorsed by the 'Hobbist' Bernard Mandeville.

meanly interested] basely self-promoting.

at bottom, the same] Hume is arguing against the common assumption that two persons acting from self-love deserve the same moral evaluation. The person with a genuine concern for others who acts to help them deserves moral praise in the way a purely selfish person does not, even though both may be motivated by self-interest.

philosophy] natural philosophy. See ann. 6.6.

5 **speculative science**] The contrast is between the practical and the theoretical, in par-

ticular, moral practice in everyday life and the articulation of a theory of human nature that is Hume's goal.

6 **love of** *simplicity*] the desire to admit as few principles or causes as are needed for purposes of explanation. See Intro., 12–13. See also 5.16, and Appx. 2.12. 'Many able philosophers' here refers to the opponents of egoism, such as Shaftesbury, Hutcheson, and Joseph Butler.

7 and n. 61 **witty philosopher**] Bernard le Bovier de Fontenelle (French literary figure, 1657–1757) wrote prose works (see References) that contain witty paradoxes and themes expressing various postulates similar to the principle mentioned by Hume. Fontenelle argued that humans often welcome obscure, speculative causes as explanations of phenomena and that philosophers are vulnerable to prejudice and false reasoning, because they often ask more of reason than it can deliver in the attempt to discover nature's secrets.

so fallacious an hypothesis] so deceptive or misleading a speculative explanation.

other motives] In inquiries into the human mind, the predominant motive underlying an action is often concealed from the actor because it is obscured by other motives. None the less, Hume thinks the elaborate reflections of egoists about mingled and hidden self-interested motives are not confirmed in ordinary experience.

9 **fond mother**] See Intro., 25.

12 **pleasure from that acquisition**] If we are not constructed so that something gives us pleasure, then no amount of teaching, design, reason, etc. would lead us to seek that something. In this passage, the item is fame.

13 n. 62 **Virg. . . . Seneca**] The passage from Virgil may be translated, 'And they leave their lives in the wound'. Virgil is speaking of a 'rage beyond measure' of the sort possessed by bees who deposit their stingers and die as a result. The passage from Seneca may be translated as follows: 'Having no thought for itself provided that it may injure another'. Seneca is considering how anger might be allayed. He maintains that anger, unlike many other emotions, is violent, involving a rage that absorbs the person in the desire to harm another.

APPENDIX 3

In Appendix 3 Hume builds on the arguments introduced in Section 3. In particular, he sets out to provide a supplement to the analysis of the *origin and nature* of justice that he began earlier. He argues that justice rests on human conventions in the sense that it relies on a concurrence with others to accept a general plan or system of rules and laws that promote the public interest. Whereas humanity and benevolence exert their influence on a single person, the whole scheme or system of social rules and conventions that constitutes social justice benefits society in general. Justice's inflexible rules are necessary for peace and order. A *sense of common interest* felt by each person gives rise to conventions that are mutually advantageous. In this respect, justice is natural, but in other senses of the term 'natural', justice is an artificial creation arising from social co-operation.

2 **scheme or system . . . single individual object**] Hume is establishing a fundamental distinction between the virtues that rest on principles of human nature (benevolence and humanity, chiefly) and virtues that are not principles (justice and fidelity, chiefly).

The former are found in human responses directed toward individual objects (friends, say), without consideration of broad social consequences. Justice, by contrast, is determined by 'the whole scheme or system' as it affects the larger society, although we say of individual acts that they are just or unjust when they conform to or violate the system's rules. See ann. Appx. 1.2. For Hume's account of these distinctions and a clarification of his point in Appendix 3, see Intro., 35–7.

3 **right of succession**] right of inheritance through a blood line. Although this right will hurt society in some cases, it may be more beneficial overall than an alternative rule. For example, rules of succession in government may produce the occasional bad ruler, but following the rule may be better than the alternative of successional anarchy.

4 **Cyrus**] In considering 'only the individual case before him', Cyrus lost sight of the inflexible rules of justice set up to handle such cases. Hume's story is about Cyrus I (founder of the Persian Empire of the Achaemenids, 6th c. BC). It is found in Xenophon, *Cyropaedia* 1.3.17:

> A big boy with a little tunic, finding a little boy with a big tunic on, took it off him and put his own tunic on him, while he himself put on the other's. So, when I tried their case, I decided that it was better for them both that each should keep the tunic that fitted him. And thereupon the master flogged me, saying that when I was a judge of a good fit, I should do as I had done; but when it was my duty to decide whose tunic it was, I had this question, he said, to consider—whose title was the rightful one; whether it was right that he who took it away by force should keep it, or that he who had had it made for himself or had bought it should own it. And since, he said, what is lawful is right and what is unlawful is wrong, he bade the judge always render his verdict on the side of the law. It is in this way, mother, you see, that I already have a thorough understanding of justice in all its bearings; and . . . if I do require anything more, my grandfather here will teach me that.

Hume's term 'governor' means tutor or teacher. The master mentioned also refers to a tutor.

5 **building of a vault**] Justice is like a vault—an arched roof, entry way, or ceiling of stones or bricks—in that it is an integrated system of mutually supporting rules, each of which could not stand independently of the others.

6 **laws of nature**] See ann. 3.29 and Intro., 18–19, 43.

case which offers] case that presents itself.

7 **human conventions**] A convention is a tradition or fixed pattern of doing things in a certain way. (See Intro., 36–7.) Hume refers to a convention as 'a general sense of common interest; which sense all the members of the society express to one another, and which induces them to regulate their conduct by certain rules' (*THN* 3.2.2.10). However, a convention need not rest on consent, on a promise, or on an explicit agreement.

promise] Because Hume views obligations to keep promises as resting on conventions, it would be 'absurd' to maintain that conventions rest on mutual promises. We are not bound or obligated to do what we say we will do unless there already exists a convention that we are to keep our promises. The agreements on which obligations of justice rest are not promises, but conventions like the use of a certain language or form of money.

8 **pull the oars**] For a discussion of this example, see Intro., 41.

n. 63 **Grotius**] The passage from Grotius may be translated,

> From them [several sources, some biblical] we learn why it was that the initial sharing, first of movable and later of immovable possessions, was abandoned: It was undoubtedly because people, not content to live on what grew naturally to hand, to live in caves, to go naked or clothed in the bark of trees or the hides of wild animals, opted for a choicer mode of life. That called for a life of application, each to his individual tasks. But too little produce was collected this way into the common store. The remoteness of the places people went to was the first obstacle, and then their deficiencies in justice and affection, which had the result that neither in the labour exerted nor in the produce consumed was fairness preserved. At the same time we learn how private property arose. It was not just by a mental act; because one party could not know what things another wished to have in order to abstain from them, and there could be more who wanted the same thing. It was rather by a kind of agreement, either explicit, as when one divides between the parties, or tacit, as when one takes possession of something.

Grotius argues that the concept of property implies a form of social convention, a view with which Hume concurs.

9 and n. 64 **word, *natural***] See anns. 3.33; 3.34 and n. 12; 4.1. In *THN* Hume wrote as follows: '[W]hen I deny justice to be a natural virtue, I make use of the word, *natural*, only as oppos'd to *artificial*. . . . Tho' the rules of justice be *artificial*, they are not *arbitrary*. Nor is the expression improper to call them *Laws of Nature*; if by *natural* we understand what is common to any species, or even if we confine it to mean what is inseparable from the species' (3.2.1.19).

n. 64 **merely verbal**] For further characterizations of disputes as merely verbal, see Appx. 4.1 and Appx. 4.2. Hume is perhaps influenced by Locke's view that 'the greatest part of the Disputes in the World' may be 'merely verbal' (*Essay* 3.11.7).

10 **to accustom the bench . . . to regard**] to allow it to become customary or usual in the courts . . . to take into account (in regulating actions or conduct). The point is that judges must be impartial and held to strict conflict-of-interest rules.

natural reason . . . positive laws] See 4.1 for some of the relevant distinctions. 'Natural reason' here refers to reason's discovery of the overriding public utility, or what is right in the nature of things, rather than what is determined to be right in positive law.

courts of judicature] See Appx. 3.10.

precedents] The reference is to the legal doctrine of precedent. When the decision of judges in a tradition of law becomes authoritative in a case, the decision is thereby positioned to become authoritative for other courts hearing cases with *similar* facts, allowing judges to reason analogically from the prior cases. Hume here cryptically formulates the idea that the first (precedent) case in a string of legal cases itself has no relevant precedent, and so is 'without any sufficient reason' in another case.

controverted case] case in controversy; disputed case. Presumably the case can be decided analogically in light of precedents.

truth or falsehood] The point is that legal debate, which is predicated on the skilful use of analogies, is not based on true or false statements, but rather on better or worse arguments.

jurisprudence . . . courts of judicature] The term 'jurisprudence', sometimes defined as the *science of law* and also *philosophy of law*, has several meanings. Hume seems to invoke the most general meaning: *knowledge of or competence in law*. Its 'nicer questions' are its intricate and subtle inquiries. 'Pleaders' are those who plead in a court of law (advocates). *Courts of judicature* are courts that interpret the law and oversee the administration of justice.

10 n. 65 *accession . . . civilians . . . alluvion*] 'Accessions' are increases through some form of addition, including increases in the value of property by natural growth. 'Alluvions', or alluvial deposits, are almost imperceptible increases of land on a shore or bank of a stream or sea, as a result of the flow or channelling of water; the increases are sufficiently gradual that it cannot be estimated how much is added at any one time. Civilians are those acquainted with the relevant civil law. A jurisprudential account of these matters is found in Grotius, the source on property cited by Hume in n. 63 (*On the Law of War and Peace* 2.8.8–17).

11 **public wrong . . . private harm**] The private harm of an injury to an individual is a public wrong if a rule of justice has been violated. The private harm 'could have no place' (i.e. could not be correctly described as an injury) unless the public system of rules declared the act wrongful.

APPENDIX 4

Appendix 4 discusses the question of whether an exact distinction can be made between species of personal merit such as moral virtues and personal talents, and also between vices and personal defects. Hume has previously argued that we approve personal traits such as wit, eloquence, and self-control for reasons different than we approve moral virtues such as benevolence, justice, and moderation. Now he argues that the boundaries are not precisely fixed and so do not allow us to distinguish sharply between moral virtues and personal talents, natural abilities, and the like. Entitled 'Of Some Verbal Disputes', Hume devotes much of this appendix to the ways in which philosophers dispute about the meanings of words such as 'virtue' and 'talent' when they think they are treating substantive controversies beyond the meanings of words. He argues that moral virtue and personal talent as well as moral vice and various forms of personal defect are 'at the bottom, pretty nearly of the same kind or species'. The many forms of personal merit suggest that we not be extremely 'scrupulous about a *word*' such as 'virtue', even if different sentiments of approbation are involved. Hume therefore dismisses these *conceptual* issues about the difference between moral virtue and other forms of personal merit as largely *verbal* disputes over the meaning of words.

1 **grammarians**] Philosophers encroach on the province of grammarians (scholars of language) when they dispute the meanings of words.

talents, rather than of virtues] Hume's point is that many forms of personal merit are called talents rather than virtues. His project is to show the 'precise boundaries', if any, that distinguish them. Instead of proposing a sharp distinction, he offers four philosophical reflections.

only a grammatical enquiry] only an inquiry about the definition, meaning, or classification of words.

2 *intellectual* **and** *moral* **endowments**] Aristotle's *Nicomachean Ethics* (1138^b18–1139^b13,

1143^{b}17–1145^{a}12) supplies a classic distinction between intellectual virtues or excellences of intellectual activity and moral virtues or excellences of human conduct. Aristotle also says that 'intellect by itself moves nothing' (1139^{a}35).

3 n. 66 *amour propre*] Although 'amour propre' is conventionally translated as 'self-love', other apt translations for its uses in the maxims of François de La Rochefoucauld (French author, 1613–80) include 'pride', 'conceit', 'egotism', 'vanity', and 'boastfulness'. The expression generally was used with a connotation of selfishness, but it also meant simply 'self-regard'.

5 **Demosthenes and Philip**] Both men exhibited a range of intellectual and moral virtues. Perhaps Philip's chief virtues were decisiveness, organization, and diplomacy (see Cicero's *Philippics*, a source cited by Hume, at n. 29). Perhaps Demosthenes' chief virtues were eloquence and discernment. So successful were Demosthenes' orations against Philip that, according to Plutarch, 'Philip said to those who reported to him the public speeches of Demosthenes against him, "I myself, if I had heard Demosthenes speak, would have elected the man general to carry on the war against me"' (Plutarch, *Moralia*, 'Demosthenes' 845 D). For the historical and political background, see ann. 5.11; 7.12 and n. 43; Dial. 45; and Hume's 'Of Eloquence'.

pass with the world for] be viewed by others as.

6 **denomination of virtues**] Hume here returns to what he said at the outset of this section (Appx. 4.1) about the subject of this appendix: how to fix the differences and boundaries between virtues and talents. He now maintains that talents and moral virtues are not of distinct and different classes. For example, 'industry' and 'frugality' seem to be personal talents, but also often are considered virtues.

Cæsar . . . Cato . . . Sallust] The reference is to Sallust (Roman historian and politician, 1st c. BC), *War with Catiline* 53.6 and 54.1–6. Sallust declared that Caesar and Marcus Porcius Cato (1st c. BC) were both men of 'towering merit'. Sallust viewed Caesar as generous, gentle, forgiving, compassionate, good-natured, and attentive to the unfortunate, as well a person who attempted to prevent the passions from overwhelming good judgement. Sallust described Cato as austere, steadfast, a 'scourge for the wicked', and a person of integrity. On balance, Cato is given the more favourable judgement because he was less ambitious for fame and more consistently virtuous than Caesar.

7 **and n. 68 poet**] John Armstrong (poet and physician, 1709–79) appears to be delineating central features of virtue rather than defining the word 'virtue'. Virtue, he says, requires wisdom ('sense'), spirited feeling, humanity, and strength and beauty in one's inner life (*Art of Preserving Health*, 114).

8 **gaming**] Playing games of chance (gambling) for stakes was a subject of both intellectual and moral inquiry in the 18th c. Chance was investigated by mathematicians, who computed the variety of chance in different circumstances with the practical goal of determining where the advantage lies in gambling.

9 **and n. 69 Achæus**] Achaeus (military commander under Syrian king Antiochus III, 3rd c. BC) was executed for seeking military independence from Antiochus. Polybius, Hume's source in n. 69, wrote as follows: 'Thus did Achaeus perish, after taking every reasonable precaution and defeated only by the perfidy of those whom he had trusted' (3: 501).

10 **and n. 70 Pompey . . . Cicero . . . Atticus**] Cicero wrote to Atticus (Roman historian and bibliophile, 2nd-1st c. BC) that he missed Pompey's friendship, but 'the ugliness

of his flight and his carelessness have estranged my love' (*Letters to Atticus* 9.10 [2: 224–7]).

11 and nn. 71–2 **Cicero's *Offices***] Hume is appealing to Cicero as an authority on virtue. Cicero observes in *De officiis* 1.6.18–19 that everything virtuous relies at some point on one or more of the four cardinal virtues (see ann. Appx. 4.11, immediately below), which are interwoven, but distinguishable. The passage from Cicero in n. 72 may be translated as follows:

> Virtue merits praise in itself and is essential to anything else that can be praised; it has, however, several sides to it, some of which are more appropriately praised than others. For there are some virtues that are exhibited in people's conduct and with a certain courtesy and humanity, and others that appear in some faculty of mind, or in magnanimity and strength. Clemency, justice, friendliness, honesty, fortitude in common dangers—these are the virtues we enjoy hearing extolled in eulogies, because they are all considered advantageous not so much to those who possess them as to the whole human race; whereas wisdom, magnanimity (which regards all human affairs as slight and nugatory), strength and invention of intellect, and even eloquence, though they elicit no less admiration, give less pleasure, because they seem to adorn and protect those on whom we bestow the praise rather than those in whose presence it is bestowed. Nevertheless these kinds of virtues should be included in our praises, because mankind likes to hear praised both what gives joy and pleasure, and whatever there is in virtue that is cause for admiration.

The Whole Duty of Man cited in n. 72 was a widely circulated English Calvinist book of devotion on Christian ethical and religious duty. Although the lists of virtues in Cicero and *The Whole Duty* significantly differ, the lists overlap, and the list of vices is similar. Unlike Cicero and Hume, *Whole Duty* analyses the virtues from a distinctly Christian perspective and adds virtues such as meekness and humility that neither Cicero nor Hume (see *THN* 3.3.2.13) would accept and might regard as negative traits or vices.

cardinal virtues] Cicero (*De officiis* 1.5–27) lists the cardinal virtues as temperance, fortitude, justice, and wisdom (the latter including prudence). Hutcheson discusses the cardinal virtues in *Short Introduction* 1.3, arguing that 'the Ancients' conceived of the cardinal virtues as four classes (prudence, justice, temperance, and fortitude) from which all 'branches of virtue' are derivable.

12 **Aristotle's Ethics**] Aristotle discusses the virtues listed by Hume at the following points in his *Nicomachean Ethics*: *Courage* 1115^{a}7–1117^{b}23; *Temperance* 1117^{b}24–1119^{b}19; *Magnificence* 1122^{a}19–1123^{a}33; *Justice* 1129^{a}1–1138^{b}14; *Friendship* 1155^{a}1–1172^{a}15. The other virtues on Hume's list are often translated differently. Aristotle first discusses *Prudence* or 'practical wisdom' at 1140^{a}24–^{b}30. *Magnanimity* or 'pride', also translated 'greatness of soul (mind)', is discussed at 1123^{a}34–1125^{a}35. *Modesty* or 'shame' is discussed at 1128^{b}10–36. *Manly openness* ('manly freedom' in all but the last of Hume's editions of *EPM*) or 'liberality' is discussed at 1119^{b}21–1122^{a}17.

14 **Epictetus ... Stoics ... Solomon**] The Stoics, among them Epictetus, recommended that the good or wise person remain free of control by the passions. The 'parables of Solomon' in the Book of Proverbs (see 1: 1–9) lay emphasis on wisdom, instruction, understanding, judgement, justice, and equity. Hume is perhaps referring

to the legendary importance that Solomon placed on wisdom, understanding, and impartial reasoning. On Stoicism, see ann. 6.21 ('perpetual cant').

15 and n. 73 **David**] Psalm 49 is concerned with the role of riches in human life. Both riches and the praise of others are seen as screens behind which some persons hide. The author is, by tradition, King David of Israel.

and n. 74 **Greek poet**] The passage from Euripides (Greek poet and playwright, 5th c. BC) may be translated, 'I hate the practitioner of wisdom who is not wise in his own eyes.'

16 **Plutarch**] The reference is to Plutarch's *Lives* (his 'history') and *Moralia* (his 'philosophy'). 'Cramped by systems' means hindered or restricted by a particular philosophical theory so as to cause distorted claims. Hume notes that Plutarch discusses 'blemishes and accomplishments of whatever kind' without presupposing a significant distinction between talents and virtues.

17 and n. 75 **Hannibal . . . Livy**] Hannibal (Carthaginian military leader, 3rd–2nd c. BC) served in Spain under Hasdrubal (Carthaginian military commander and brother-in-law of Hannibal, 3rd c. BC). Hannibal's most serious defeat, at the hands of Scipio, is discussed at 6.9. Livy (Paduan historian of Rome, 1st c. BC–1st c. AD), regards Hannibal as having many virtues that fit him equally well for the contrary offices of commanding and obeying. Livy attributes to him virtually superhuman qualities of endurance and a long list of virtues, but also lists faults and vices (*History* 21.4).

general] public; multitude.

perfidy more than *punic*] breaching trust or promise even more than is entailed by the usual Carthaginian traits (according to the Romans) of faithlessness, treachery, and falsehood. 'Punic' also means *Carthaginian*.

18 and n. 76 **Alexander . . . Guicciardin**] Alexander VI, or Rodrigo Borgia (1432–1503), was a Roman Catholic Pope depicted by historians as quintessentially degenerate, though generous to his children and associates. Hume's description of Guicciardini's portrait of Alexander closely paraphrases the text.

19 and n. 77 **Polybius**] Timaeus (historian, 4th–3rd c. BC) was exiled by Agathocles (Sicilian tyrant, 4th–3rd c. BC) and later judged Agathocles harshly in his written history. Polybius then criticized Timaeus' ignorance and dishonesty. Polybius argued that Agathocles possessed impressive personal characteristics unmentioned in Timaeus' account. Polybius tendered the following judgement: 'It is just as mendacious for a writer to conceal what did occur as to report what did not occur' (12.15.9).

20 and n. 78 ***whether virtue could be taught***] In Plato's *Meno* 70 A, Meno asks Socrates at the outset, 'Can you tell me . . . whether virtue can be taught, or is acquired by practice, not teaching?' Reasons are then offered for why it cannot be taught. In 'On Leisure', Seneca maintains that virtue is learned not through formal instruction, but through 'leisure', which allows cultivation of the virtues and contemplation of philosophical questions about virtue (2: 186–9). Horace proposes that virtue may be a natural gift. The quotation in n. 78 may be translated, 'Whether virtue is procured by teaching, or is the gift of nature'. The reference to Aeschines Socraticus is to Dialogue 1, 'De virtute'. Aeschines suggests that divine chance may account for the ability of individuals to be virtuous.

independent of the will] Hume's point is that, as the ancients noted, a person can be judged vicious or defective even if the qualities of the person's mind on which the judgement is based are independent of the person's will, and therefore involuntary. See also Appx. 4.21.

21 **terms of composition**] compromises; concessions on previously accepted doctrines. Hume suggests in this passage that theology is often dogmatic and hostile to new information that presents a challenge to doctrines that have been predetermined to be correct.

reward and punishment] The point is that some moral theologians argued that God rewards those who follow divine commands and punishes those who fail to do so. Reward and punishment as well as praise and blame were attached to voluntary acts, not to involuntary acts. Voluntary choice thus became central in these moral theories.

22 **duty to ourselves**] Many writers in the history of philosophy have insisted that there are moral duties to oneself, such as duties of self-respect and the self-improvement of moral powers.

vulgar system] common system; system reflecting common beliefs.

A DIALOGUE

In this free-standing essay, Hume discusses issues of relativism and universalism. He mentions apparent moral discrepancies found in disparate ages and societies and considers whether these differences invalidate claims of a universality of moral sentiment. He uses the medium of a conversation to discuss the merits of a fictitious oriental society named Fourli 'whose inhabitants have ways of thinking . . . particularly in morals, diametrically opposite to ours'. He presents the beliefs in this fictitious society through the lens of actual beliefs in ancient societies, with an emphasis on Athenian beliefs. He notes that many actions approved in one society—for example, tyrannicide—are often disapproved in another.

Hume suggests that these cultural differences are consistent with his claims throughout *EPM* that universal principles in human nature account for similar moral responses in all moral agents in all societies. He intimates that different circumstances and different degrees of fellow-feeling produce different moral responses, customs, and traditions, but that these differences all spring from the same 'universal, established principles of morals'. He puts in the mouth of one character the following thesis: 'That [people who differ in their conclusions] all reason aright . . . it is not incumbent on any moralist to show. It is sufficient, that the original principles of censure or blame are uniform, and that erroneous conclusions can be corrected by sounder reasoning and larger experience.' The point about *correction* is important to his arguments. Our judgement can be corrected (though Hume does not say to the point of uniform or complete agreement among people) if we gain experience, look more closely at the likely utilities in the circumstance, acquire missing facts, and maintain a proper measure of impartiality.

Hume also suggests that in all societies the basis of merit is found in what is *useful* and *agreeable*. These foundational elements provide adequate guidance in the moral life unless the 'illusions' found in certain religious superstitions and philosophical enthusiasms interfere with a person's native capacities of moral responsiveness.

1 **A Dialogue**] This dialogue resembles the dialogues in Baron de Montesquieu's highly successful *Persian Letters*. The dialogue style, many of the questions addressed, and one

of the characters in the dialogue (Usbek) are similar. The fictitious characters and locations in Hume's dialogue are in some instances modelled on specific historical figures and locations.

2 **Fourli**] At Dial. 13 Hume reveals that he is referring to certain 'Greeks, especially the Athenians, whom I have couched, all along, under these bizarre names I employed'. His fictitious state of Fourli exhibits various forms of cultural approbation similar to those associated with ancient Athens. In these early passages Hume explores cultural differences in the evaluation of homosexuality, incest, parricide, and assassination—and, more generally, in personal traits that are admired in the culture.

obliging manner] complimentary and generous terms.

3–8 **personal merit**] Hume presents what to a modern European would have appeared to be the deviant and shocking values of Alcheic, including his bisexual preference and regard for incest in marriage, as well as his limited support of parricide and murder of the innocent. The fact that Alcheic's qualities and motives are 'extremely celebrated' suggests that in his society he is a person of merit, even virtue.

8 **assassination of Usbek**] Compare Hume's comments about a 'noble' action of assassination to his comments immediately below about Caesar, Brutus, Cassius, Harmodius, and Aristogiton at Dial. 15.

10 **Vitzli**] Perhaps modelled on Zeus or a composite of Zeus and Jupiter, the supreme deities in Greek and Roman religions.

12 **Mingrelians, and Topinamboues**] These peoples were considered primitive and corrupt, based on reports that had filtered back to Western Europe. The Mingrelians lived along the Black Sea coast. Pierre Bayle described them as the cruellest, most impudent people on earth and as regularly engaging in murder, assassination, lying, use of concubines, adultery, bigamy, incest, and infanticide (*Œuvres diverses*, 1: 648–9).

The Topinamboues or Tupinombas were a cannibalistic Indian tribe in Brazil known for ferocity in battle and for the vengeance with which they killed, ate, and displayed the bodies of enemies. They ate enemies not from hunger but from hate and jealousy. A detailed account of their customs and religion is found in the writings of Hans Staden, a Dutchman held captive by this tribe in 1557. Staden depicts them as cunning in all forms of wickedness (Staden, *True History*, 127–63).

13 **Athenians**] Palamedes now discloses that he has been talking not about either an imaginary culture or an actual culture he has visited, but about the ancient Greeks so much admired by the narrator of the dialogue.

and n. 79 **amours . . . exposing of their children**] 'The exposing of their children' refers to the practice of infanticide. Legislation against seduction, procuring, and sexual abuse was prevalent in ancient Hellenic culture and included controls discouraging pederasty and injustice to slaves. However, neither prostitution nor homosexual conduct was illegal in Athens.

15 and n. 80 **traitors and assassins**] These traitors and assassins, as some would label them today, were regarded as moral heroes in some cultures of antiquity. The authors in n. 80, Appian (historian, 1st–2nd c. AD) and Suetonius, explain the events leading to Caesar's assassination at the hands of Brutus, Cassius, and others. Suetonius discusses the oath taken by senators, before Caesar's death, to watch over their honoured Caesar.

Aristogiton and Harmodius (6th c. BC) were Athenian tyrannicides. They attempted to kill the tyrant Hippias and his brother Hipparchus. The scheme failed when only Hipparchus died. Harmodius was slain at the scene; Aristogiton was captured and executed. Later the tyranny was overthrown and the two tyrannicides were honoured as vanguards of liberation and democracy. The Athenians erected statues in their honour, and elevated them in poetry to the status of epic heroes.

16 **Themistocles, and . . . Eurybiades**] Hume's account of the exchange between Themistocles (Athenian naval commander, 6th–5th c. BC) and Eurybiades (Spartan fleet leader, 6th–5th c. BC) closely paraphrases Plutarch (*Lives*, 'Themistocles' 11.2–3). The two military leaders met to determine the best strategy to thwart the Persian threat. Eurybiades was commander-in-chief of the combined forces, Themistocles the pre-eminent strategist. Eurybiades argued for retreat, and Themistocles resisted. Sharp words were exchanged. Eurybiades was impressed by Themistocles' intensity and allowed him to restate his case. The virtues of allegiance, solidarity, and patriotism that they exhibit stand in marked contrast to the traits of Brutus and others Hume mentioned in the previous paragraph; yet all were regarded as heroes.

17 **and n. 81 Socrates . . . Xenophon**] By 'my last story' Hume is referring to his story of Alcheic at Dial. 11. Hume says that he 'exactly copied' Xenophon's account, which is as follows (*Memorabilia*, 258–9):

> Whenever some of the members of a dining-club brought more meat than others, Socrates would tell the waiter either to put the small contribution into the common stock or to portion it out equally among the diners. So the high batteners felt obliged not only to take their share of the pool, but to pool their own supplies in return; and so they put their own supplies also into the common stock. And since they thus got no more than those who brought little with them, they gave up spending much on meat.

self-murder] See Alcheic's suicide by hanging at Dial. 10 and Hume's comment on 'ancient maxims' in n. 41.

18 **impeach their morals**] indict their morality; accuse them of immoral beliefs and conduct.

19 **nation, in which adultery**] The nation is probably medieval France. See ann. 4.17 and also Dial. 47 and 48 on an immoral gallantry and the court or parliament of love. On 'mistress', see Appx. 4.10.

prostitute her charms] put her attractiveness and beauty to unworthy use. Hume uses the term with a sexual connotation.

20 **proud of their slavery**] Hume is imagining a culture that would shock the Athenians: if one can imagine husbands who happily offer their wives to other men, it is a short step to imagining a people happily held in slavery.

21 **their favourite morality**] The nation under discussion in this paragraph may again be France, and Hume may be building on Montesquieu's similar discussion of the 'laws of honour' in France, including duelling, through which the French regulated their affairs (*Persian Letters* 90–1). Hume may also be contrasting the themes of assassination mentioned at Dial. 8 and 15; assassination would not shock the Greeks, but the reason here given for it might.

22 **sword . . . own breast**] On suicide, see Dial. 10 and 17 and Hume's comment on 'ancient maxims' in n. 41. Hume is pointing to the stark contrast in cultural attitudes present in different societies about the moral acceptability of suicide.

generous contempt of death] courageous, noble disregard of the horrors of death. This attitude and those in the previous entry are discussed in Hume's 'Of Suicide'.

23 **barbarous partiality**] The 'barbarous partiality' is the extreme parental favouritism of the eldest son—an example of the rights of primogeniture or some similar system of parental favouritism. These feudal rules of inheritance were brought into England at the time of the Norman Conquest—another link to medieval France. See also ann. Appx. 3.3.

24 and n. 82 **Saturnalia**] In Lucian's *Saturnalia* 10–39, the character Cronosolon wrote laws granting equal treatment to slave and freeman and to poor and rich, but the laws were in effect only during the course of a merry-making festival honouring Saturn (the Saturnalia).

25 **national character**] Hume's 'Of National Characters' considers several of the themes about national characteristics found in this paragraph. Hume comments in this essay that 'the Athenians were as remarkable for ingenuity, politeness, and gaiety, as the Thebans for dulness, rusticity, and a phlegmatic [lethargic] temper.' He says the Athenians were the only Ionians with a reputation for valour and military achievements. (*Essays*, National Characters 12, 29.)

less liable to exception] less vulnerable to objection; more favourable. Hume is strongly praising their character.

little in common] These lines summarize the position defended by Palamedes, which appears to be a form of cultural relativism.

27 **universal, established principles**] This argument against Palamedes is consistent with Hume's theory of human nature and universal principle in *EPM*. See further Dial. 36–7.

28 **Greek loves**] chiefly, homosexual practices.

29 **canon law**] the authoritative body of rulings (law) for civil and ecclesiastical affairs in the Roman Catholic Church. It is based on definitions and rules formulated by councils, popes, and Church fathers. The canon law makes no distinction between the marriages of full-blood and half-blood relatives; all such marriages are proscribed. However, stepchildren are not blood relatives and may marry. The Athenians went far in the other direction because marriages within the wider family were common: Half-brothers married half-sisters, uncles married nieces, etc.

30 and n. 85 **bereaved . . . of that life**] a second reference in 'A Dialogue' to Athenian practices of infanticide. See also Dial. 13. In 'On Affection for Offspring' (*Moralia* 497 E), Plutarch writes:

> When poor men do not rear their children it is because they fear that if they are educated less well than is befitting they will become servile and boorish and destitute of all the virtues; since they consider poverty the worst of evils, they cannot endure to let their children share it with them, as though it were a kind of disease, serious and grievous.

35 **self-murder**] More than one famous Athenian held that suicide should be forborne (with allowable exceptions), whereas more than one celebrated French writer defended the permissibility of suicide. Hellenic city-states generally prohibited suicide by law and deprived persons who committed suicide of funeral rites. Plato and Aristotle accepted the prohibition, but both allowed valid exceptions. French author Michel de Montaigne wrote a classic essay on suicide, 'Custom of the Island of Cea

[Kea]' (*Essays* 2.3) in which free poison was distributed to all who wished to kill themselves. Montesquieu also discussed the morality of suicide in *Persian Letters* 76. He maintains, as Hume would later argue in his 'Of Suicide', that suicide does not disturb the order of divine providence more than do other human acts.

36 and nn. 86–7 **Horace . . . Anacreon**] Horace praises 'black locks on a narrow brow', a reference to the beauty of a low forehead (*Epistles* 1.7, lines 26–8 [297]). Anacreon (lyric poet and musician, 6th–5th c. BC) describes the woman his heart adores (*Anacreontea* 16, lines 9–11):

> Her eyebrows neither join nor sever,
> But make (as 'tis) that selvage never
> Clearly one nor surely two.

n. 87 **Petronius**] Petronius Arbiter (Roman satirist and consul, 1st c. AD) describes a woman 'more perfect than any artist's dream', with a 'small forehead' and with eyebrows that 'almost met again close beside her eyes' (*Satyricon* 126 [278–9]).

Apollo . . . Venus] In Hellenic religion, Apollo was an Olympian god generally associated with the higher aspects of civilization, including music, poetry, the healing arts, and prophecy. In Roman religion, the name Apollo was retained, and he was portrayed in art as the perfection of strength, beauty, and youth. Also in Roman religion, Venus was goddess of vegetation (and of birth and growth). Greek sculptors and painters presented her as the ideal of female beauty.

Scipio . . . Cornelia] Scipio and his heroic actions, especially in defeating Hannibal, are discussed in ann. 6.9. By decisively defeating the Carthaginian army, Scipio alleviated an inordinate Roman fear of Hannibal. Plutarch reports that Cornelia (Roman matron, 2nd c. BC) was renowned for purity and excellence of character, especially as a mother who cultivated her children's excellences of character (*Lives*, 'Tiberius and Caius Gracchus' 1.4–5).

39 and n. 88 **Tully . . . Cimbrians, Celtiberians**] Tully—another name for Cicero—is maintaining that barbarians—for example, the Cimbri in ancient Europe (Germany) who inhabited the Cimbrian Peninsula in Jutland (Denmark) and Celtiberians of mountainous regions of ancient Spain—are good at enduring suffering on the battlefield, but their tolerance of suffering is limited when they are sick. By contrast, Greeks endure sickness even if they are not courageous on the battlefield. (*Tusculan Disputations* 2.27.65.)

timorously fly his presence] fearfully flee the risk of death (on the battlefield).

40 **Labeo . . . Cato**] Labeo (Roman jurist and praetor, 1st c. BC–1st c. AD) was distinguished in law, philosophy, and literature. He was known as a formidable opponent and a person of high moral integrity. He was also known for an independence of mind, to the point of speaking freely against the emperor (Augustus). Labeo risked censure for this independence.

Cato and the qualities that earned him highest approbation—integrity, austerity, steadfastness, wisdom, elocution, and opposition to the wicked—are discussed in ann. Appx. 4.6.

41 **degree of luxury**] For the context and implications of this mention of luxury, see ann. 2.21 and 9.25. The pursuit of luxury encourages industry and stimulates the production and sale of luxury goods.

42 **four sources of moral sentiment**] the four types enumerated in the previous sen-

tence. These types, which provide much of the structure of *EPM*, are: (1) Qualities useful to others (Sections 2–5), (2) Qualities useful to ourselves (Section 6), (3) Qualities immediately agreeable to ourselves (Section 7), (4) Qualities immediately agreeable to others (Section 8). See Intro., 30–1.

43 **shut up the women**] Women ('the fair sex') were systematically excluded from social intercourse in Athens. Men regarded women as subordinate and properly in service to their husbands. Women remained at home as much as possible, and girls were generally confined to women's quarters.

44 and n. 89 **Lysias**] See ann. 7.25.

45 and n. 90 **Demosthenes prosecuted his tutors**] According to Plutarch, Demosthenes lost his father at age 7, and the guardians of his father's estate dissipated much of his patrimony (inheritance). As a result, Demosthenes' teachers were deprived of their pay, and his early education was impeded. At age 17 he successfully prosecuted both his guardians and a debtor to his father's estate, but recovered only a small fraction of the patrimony (*Lives*, 'Demosthenes' 4.1–2, 6.1).

In *Against Oneter*, 1: 148–51, Demosthenes discusses the conspiracy of Oneter and Aphobus, who sought to steal his patrimony. The woman pretending to be Oneter's wife, Aphobus' sister, was still married when she left her husband Timocrates; she thereafter lived exclusively with Aphobus, without marrying Oneter or anyone else. Demosthenes recounts how he solicited a deposition from a physician and testimony from slaves who had witnessed the woman living with Aphobus. The outcome of the trial is unknown. Regarding Hume's final observation—'So reserved were Greek manners'—see Dial. 43 and 44.

46 **intrigues of women**] In Hellenic fable, as Hume means by 'fabulous', Helen, celebrated as the fairest woman in the world, was the precipitating cause of the legendary war between Hellenes and Trojans. Clytemnestra was the wife of Agamemnon when he went to the Trojan War and entrusted his family to Aegisthus, who subsequently influenced Clytemnestra to infidelity. The two murdered Agamemnon. Each set of events 'proceeded from the intrigues of women', but both Helen and Clytemnestra were manipulated by powerful males.

neighbouring nation] France (as the following example of 'Harry the third' indicates).

Harry the third] Henry III (king of France, 1551–89) suffered a gradual loss of popularity due to a fatal power struggle with Henri de Lorraine, duc de Guise. When Henry III had the duc assassinated, Paris was swept by violence. Henry and his few faithful turned to Protestants for assistance, an alliance that, together with the murders, led to a papal bull that excommunicated the king. The duchesse de Montpensier, the duc's sister, then enlisted the aid of a Dominican monk, Jacques Clément, who gained a private audience with the king and fatally stabbed him. Upon hearing the news, the duchesse—who had publicly sworn revenge—rode through the streets of Paris in an open carriage crying, 'The tyrant is dead!' Henry III's relationship to the Catholic League and other related events are discussed in ann. 7.23.

47 and n. 91 **maxim of La Fontaine**] The point is that if instances of sexual scandal become frequent, sensitivity to scandalous behaviour will be weakened in the one sex, and the other sex will learn some version of 'La Fontaine's maxim'. The subject of 'La coupe enchantée' by Jean de La Fontaine (poet and fabulist, 1621–95) is female infidelity and male cuckoldry (the topic of several books in the 17th and 18th c.). La

Fontaine explores the possibility that cuckoldry might be good. A jealous husband resorts to sorcery and must drink from 'la coupe enchantée' (the enchanted goblet) in order to determine whether his sorcery has caused him to cuckold himself (while in the form of another). La Fontaine's disdain of such consuming covetousness is summarized in the comment quoted by Hume.

48 n. 92 **women of condition . . . wenching . . . *Ancillarioli*]** Women of condition are those of social position, rank, or good character. 'Wenching' means associating with wenches (working-class women, often female maidservants) or whoring. '*Ancillarioli*' is the plural form of '*ancillariolus*'—a low sort of person who pursues maidservants or slave-girls. Seneca and Martial (see the sources in n. 92) both use this rare term to report comments by married women who describe their husbands as addicted to base pleasures and affairs with maidservants.

50 **esteem dancing infamous]** regard dancing as disgraceful or shameful.

51 **vary not . . . merit]** The original ideas of merit, being universal and rooted in human nature, do not vary even though local customs consistent with the original ideas do. The virtues recognized by mature persons (those of 'riper years') are almost universally the same.

52 *artificial* **lives]** Diogenes and Pascal, discussed immediately below, lived singular and artfully fashioned ways of life. It is difficult to render their different rules of conduct coherent, yet both have been much admired in different ages. Hume is leading up to the point in the final two paragraphs in the dialogue that it is difficult to find universal moral standards in lives so disparate and so different from 'the rest of mankind'.

53 **guarded by infinite . . . rewards and punishments]** safeguarded by the threat of unlimited punishments through divine retribution and the offer of divine rewards.

54 **Diogenes]** Diogenes of Sinope (Cynic philosopher, 4th c. BC) denounced all personal ambition for wealth and honour, and especially any dependence upon luxuries. He was reported to live in public places, existing on meagre contributions from others while cultivating habits of personal restraint, abstinence, and independence. Hume's statement that Diogenes indulged himself in beastly (i.e. disgusting or offensive) pleasures is perhaps a reference to his attempt to find happiness strictly in terms of simple, natural needs and to satisfy them in the most direct manner possible—in public, without shame, and in disregard of social conventions.

disgrace any philosophic name . . . Dominics or Loyolas] The Dominican Order was founded by Saint Dominic (Spanish priest, 12th–13th c. AD). The Jesuit Order was founded by Saint Ignatius of Loyola (Spanish priest, 1491–1556). Hume's subtle sarcasm that he would not disgrace real philosophers by comparing these two saints to Diogenes insinuates that they are much inferior thinkers to Pascal (discussed immediately below), even if all three shared similar values and commitments. Hume's earlier comment about 'monkish virtues' may also be directed at these two saints as well as Pascal.

54–5 **Pascal]** Blaise Pascal (French philosopher and mathematician, 1623–62) suspended innovative work in mathematics following an intense religious conversion. Afterwards he devoted himself almost exclusively to the Christian ideals of asceticism and serving the poor. Hume is referring to Pascal's obdurate Christian commitments, including his self-effacement, his view of himself as helpless and sinful, and his indifference to friends and practical affairs. Hume agrees with Pascal that religion arises from our apprehensiveness about our future destiny, but disagrees that the appropriate response to this apprehensiveness is a religious one of the sort Pascal practised.

57 **in a different element**] removed from common sense. Those who depart from the maxims of common reason lack a normal environment for interaction with other people and are deeply affected either by religious superstition or by philosophical enthusiasm.

religious superstition or philosophical enthusiasm] religious superstition such as that found in Pascal and philosophical enthusiasm such as that found in Diogenes. Hume often discusses superstition and enthusiasm as forms of corrupt, implausible, ardent, or fervent religious belief. See ann. 3.7; 3.36; and Hume's essay 'Of Superstition and Enthusiasm'.

Glossary

This Glossary treats words in the text and notes of *EPM* that many students find unfamiliar or otherwise puzzling. Often, but not always, these words are archaic and now rarely used. Synonyms are used rather than formal definitions whenever they are simpler, less controversial, and adequate to the task of eliminating uncertainty about the text. Occasionally, however, a formal definition is needed. If Hume provides a definition in one of his works, that definition is preferred. Hume's metaphors are also explained if they have potentially puzzling meanings.

The Glossary and the annotations are mutually supplementary. Words that occur only once in *EPM* and that are defined in the annotations do not appear in the Glossary; however, a cross-reference is occasionally provided, using the form 'See ann.' ('See the annotation at'). Words in the Glossary are not indicated by markers in the text of *EPM*.

Each term in the Glossary is followed by section-and-paragraph locations for terms. The appendices and 'A Dialogue' are given appropriate abbreviations and are also cited by paragraph numbers. When a term is used in *EPM* more than ten times, with the listed meaning, then the designation *passim*—'here and there'—is used to indicate frequent usage; section-and-paragraph numbers are not provided for these entries.

More than one meaning is listed for many terms. When a term is equivocal, the distinct meanings are segregated by numbers [(1), (2), . . . (*n*)], and the passages in Hume's text where the proper meanings occur are listed separately under each number. (See, for example, the entries under 'gallantry' below.) More commonly, a term is not equivocal, but a family of related, English-language synonyms is helpful in the attempt to identify Hume's usage. More than one synonym or definition is often listed in explicating a single term. Several alternative synonyms or definitions often can be applied to a single passage, because it is not altogether clear which term most adequately captures Hume's meaning. Rather than dictate 'the meaning' by presenting only a single possibility, a range of the possible senses of the term is provided. Of course, some listed meanings will not fit every appearance of the word in Hume's text.

The Glossary does not attempt to capture all meanings of the terms listed. Only *relevant* meanings in light of the Glossary's purpose are presented. For example, two meanings of 'affection' are included, but 'affection' meaning 'loving regard' is not presented; and the meaning of the noun 'frame' is provided, but not the verb and adjective uses.

Verb (*vb.*), noun substantive (*n.*), adverb (*adv.*), and adjective forms (*adj.*) are distinguished if needed for clarity.

Sources and Acknowledgements

The glossing has relied heavily on the following sources: Nathan Bailey (ed.), *Dictionarium Britannicum* (1730; fac. Hildesheim: Georg Olms, 1969); Ephraim Chambers (ed.), *Cyclopaedia; or, An Universal Dictionary of Arts and Sciences* (London, 1728); Thomas Dyche and William Pardon, *A New General English Dictionary*, 3rd edn. (1740; fac. Hildesheim: Georg Olms, 1972); John Harris, *Lexicon technicum* (London: 1704–10; fac. New York:

Glossary

Johnson Reprint, 1966); Samuel Johnson, *A Dictionary of the English Language* (London, 1755); several editions; *Oxford English Dictionary*, primarily the 2nd electronic edition (Oxford: Oxford University Press, 1992). Although editors of glossaries often cite such authoritative sources in entries, these works have been used so extensively below that constant citation would be intrusive and constantly repeated. For example, the *OED* and Dyche and Pardon have been consulted for almost every entry.

Searches have been made of the texts of other philosophers in the history of modern philosophy to see how these philosophers use various terms. The database in the Intelex PastMasters series has been particularly helpful. Finally, I have profited from the previous work of many other editors and owe a particular debt to David and Mary Norton, Edwin Curley, and P. H. Nidditch.

abstruse: deep, demanding, and theoretical. 5.17; Appx. 1.10; Appx. 2.7.

acquaintance: acquaintances. 6.32; 8.4; 8.15; Appx. 4.5.

address: bearing of a person; manner. 3.19; 6.21; 7.27; 9.12; Appx. 4.4; Dial. 49.

admirable: wonderful. 7.5.

affect: given to; like. 6.30.

affection: (1) mental state. 1.6; 3.14; 3.36; n. 25; 6.22; 8.14. (2) feeling; emotion; passion. *passim*.

agreeable: conformable. 3.48; Appx. 3.7.

amiable: worthy; estimable. 1.6.

animal conveniencies: material comforts and advantages. 9.10.

application: careful attention to or examination of something. 6.17; 9.2.

artificial: singular or very different—in particular, as applied to human customs, practices, or conventions amounting to a unique style of life and set of governing norms. Dial. 52–3; Dial. 57. See Hume's comment in n. 64.

ascendant: powerful influence. Dial. 53.

aspect: sight; appearance; contemplation. 5.18; 5.24.

awful: awe-inspiring; worthy of commanding respect. Appx. 4.6.

bad grace: unseemly behaviour; ungracious behaviour. 9.14.

birth: rank, station, or position inherited from parent(s). 2.1; 6.31; 6.35; 7.27.

breast: mind; location of thought, passions, and affections. *passim*.

buckler: shield; defensive armour for the body. 3.9.

capricious: guided by imagination or fancy; fantastical. 4.18; 4.19.

cates: delicate or luxurious foods. 2.20.

cavil: frivolous or quibbling objection or argument. 5.3; 6.22.

character: (1) trait or quality of a person. *passim*. (2) distinguished status or position. *passim*.

chicanes: trickery; uses of subterfuge. n. 12.

chimerical: imaginary; visionary—and without ground of truth. Appx. 4.8.

civilians: authorities on the civil law. Appx. 1.2; n. 65.

claimed: required; needed. 3.24.

Glossary

clemency: mildness; gentleness. 3.2; 7.18.

cloaths: clothes; wearing apparel. 3.2; 3.14; 5.38; 6.33.

closet: a study or private room (**in the closet**: in a private place). Dial. 53.

come about: come back to; reach to. 4.11.

competent fortune: sufficient wealth. 6.32.

complacency: tranquillity; satisfaction. 2.22; 5.40; 6.3; n. 26; 7.2; Appx. 1.13; Appx. 2.4; Appx. 2.9.

complaisance: civility; politeness; courtesy. n. 93. See also **gallantry**.

complication: combination; joining or mixing; conjunction. 1.10; Appx. 1.6; Appx. 1.16.

composition: compounded item constituted by parts; mixing or joining of items together. n. 67.

condition: social standing; position. 6.31; 6.32.

constitution: the states, qualities, dispositions, and principles that make up human nature. 1.3; 3.25; n. 17; 5.3; n. 26; 9.10; Appx. 1.21; Appx. 2.12.

contagion: contagious or catching influence (not communication of contagious disease). 7.2; 7.21.

conveniency: convenience; comfort; ease. 2.10; 4.14; 4.17; 4.18.

convenient: suitable; appropriate. 5.19; 6.34. See also **inconvenient**.

converse: deal; have to do. 5.42.

correspondent: corresponding. 1.7; 5.18; 5.32; 9.11.

council: counsel. n. 22.

cudgelled: beaten, corrected, or chastised with a stick. Dial. 16.

cudgel-players: those in a contest who compete by using cudgels, which are short, thick sticks that can be easily handled. 4.20.

damp: pall; fog. 6.22; Appx. 4.3.

deceitful: misleading (deceptive), but without intent to deceive. 6.22.

delicacy: sense of what is becoming, virtuous, or proper. 6.21; 7.19; 7.28; Dial. 49.

delicate: perceptive; sensitive; keen. 5.14; 5.37; 5.39; 7.19; 9.12.

delusive: deceptive. 5.14; 9.3.

determined: ruled; governed; provided reasons for. 3.22; 3.47; 6.2; Appx. 1.9.

dispersed: diverse; disparate. 9.4.

distemper: sickness; disease. Dial. 39.

education: beliefs acquired by acculturation, exposure, or habituation; 'opinions and notions of things, to which we have been accustom'd from our infancy' (quoting *THN* 1.3.9.17). 3.36; 3.47; 5.4; 7.18; 9.18.

elevation: eminence; lifted up or raised in position or status. 6.3; 7.4; 7.11; 7.22; 8.10; 8.11.

eloquence: the art of oratory or the artful use of words. 5.11; 6.15; n. 31; 8.7; Appx. 4.4; Dial. 18; Dial. 19; Dial. 27; Dial. 49.

emergence: emergency; unexpected or sudden event or state of affairs. 3.8; Appx. 1.11.

empire: authority; supreme political control. 7.6; 7.9; 7.12.

Glossary

engage: (1) gain; secure. 2.1. (2) influence; persuade. 1.1; 2.5.

enthusiasm: zealous or frenzied inspiration or belief; groundless fancies believed to have divine support. 3.7; 3.27; 5.25; Appx. 2.2; Dial. 57.

enthusiast: See **enthusiasm** and ann. 1.6; 3.23–4; 9.3.

execration: cursing; utter detestation. Dial. 17; Dial. 25.

experience: (1) empirical testing; experimental trial. *passim.* (2) observation; accumulation of data as the basis of conclusions. *passim.*

experiment (and **experimental method**): See ann. 1.10 and 5.17.

exquisite: extreme. Dial. 22.

fabric: internal structure; frame. 1.3; 1.6; 5.1; Appx. 1.6; Appx. 1.14; Appx. 3.5.

faculty: capacity or power of mind; mental ability such as sensation, cognition, imagination, and memory. 1.5; 1.10; 3.20; 6.19; Appx. 1.2; Appx. 1.6; Appx. 1.21.

falchions: short, broad swords turning up like a hook. Dial. 39.

fallacious: deceitful; deceptive; misleading. Appx. 2.7; Dial. 18.

false: deceitful; pretended; feigned. 3.27; 4.15; 5.14; 6.21; Appx. 2.1.

fanatic: inspired and extravagant visionary; religious enthusiast. 3.7; 3.23; 3.24.

fancy: (1) *vb.* imagine; mentally invent. 6.3; Dial. 2. (2) *n.* the imagination. 5.16; 6.3; 6.5; 6.33; 7.20; 9.3; n. 65.

fetter: chain up; load with irons or other encumbrances. n. 72.

field: battlefield. 5.22.

fine: subtle; refined. 3.46; Appx. 1.9; n. 65.

fly: avoid; flee from. 2.9; Dial. 39.

fond (and **fondness**): kind; tender. 2.6; 5.40; 7.19; Appx. 2.9.

forwarded: prompted; promoted. 5.18.

frame: *n.* construction; nature; state. 3.25; 5.45; 7.19; 9.4; 9.6; Appx. 1.21; Appx. 2.12; Appx. 2.13.

full: fully. 6.33; 9.16.

gain: win; get advantage. 6.10; 7.10; 9.8; Dial. 9; Dial. 19.

gallantry: (1) amorous relationship or intrigue in love affairs, often involving adultery. 4.17; Dial. 32; Dial. 47; nn. 92–3. (2) genteelness, or polite attention to women; making oneself agreeable through politeness, courtesy, bravery, and the like. 9.2; Dial. 48; n. 93.

generation: procreation; generative reproduction. 3.44; 4.7.

generous: noble-minded and courageous; high-spirited; magnanimous. 2.5; 5.8; 5.41; 6.35; 8.10; 9.4; 9.10.

gewgaws: trifles or playthings for children and those who are childlike. 9.25.

gloss: interpretation; exposition. 9.3.

grace: genteel air (as in a graceful person). 8.14; 9.10; Dial. 51.

head: topic; subject; category. 1.10; 1.11; 6.21; Appx. 1.19.

humour: temper of mind; disposition or constitution. 7.2; Appx. 4.6; Dial. 49. Contrast **in**

Glossary

humour: pleased, satisfied, or agreeable. 9.21. Compare **good-humoured**. 5.19; 7.1; Dial. 9.

hurt: disadvantage. 3.6.

importunate: wearying or annoying, as a result of pressing the case. 8.11.

impression: original perception, not merely a copy; first appearance of sensations or passions. 1.2; Appx. 1.11; Appx. 2.7.

impudence: defect of civility; foolishness. 8.8; Appx. 4.3.

inconvenience: unsuitableness; incongruity; inconsistency with rule. 3.18; n. 13; Appx. 3.6.

inconvenient: lacking in utility; disadvantageous. 4.12; n. 16. See also **convenient**.

indifferent: of no special importance; of small value or little consequence. 4.14; 5.15; 5.17; 5.18; 5.30.

indulgence: admiration; appreciation. 2.19; Dial. 18.

infallible: unfailing. 3.16; 5.12; 5.40; 5.43.

in generals: to general terms. Appx. 1.5.

injury: violation of right. 3.3; 3.10; 4.4; 5.16; 5.21; 5.39.

insensibility: See **sensibility**.

insinuation: a covert, often cunning way of finding favour or affection. 3.19; 6.21.

interested: self-interested; self-promoting. 9.14; Appx. 2.4; Appx. 2.7; Appx. 2.12. See also ann. 9.14.

issue: end; discharge. 9.4; Appx. 1.5; Dial. 9.

jealous (of): vigilant in guarding; scrupulously careful to protect; suspiciously watchful. 6.16; 6.21; 8.5; 8.9.

landlord: owner and resident; host. 5.19; 8.2.

lawful: morally permissible. 1.5; 3.35; 3.36; 3.37.

law-topics: legal themes, rules, and considerations. 3.46.

lay hold of: grasp. 3.8; Appx. 4.2.

lenity: meekness; gentleness. 2.1; 5.44; 9.12.

licentious: going beyond customary or proper bounds as established by law or morals. 4.3; 6.21; Dial. 55.

luxury: See ann. 2.21.

magical syllables: (as used metaphorically) mysterious words; inexplicable expressions. 3.37.

manners: customs; practices and rules; ways of life. *passim.*

man of rank: person of standing in the community (though not necessarily a morally worthy or well-off person). Dial. 22.

man's time: person's lifetime. 6.10.

manufactory (also **manufacture**): manufacturing; industry. 2.11; 6.35.

meanness: lack of dignity, spirit, or greatness of mind; smallness of condition, character, or mind. n. 34; n. 42; Appx. 4.4; Appx. 4.20; Dial. 19.

Glossary

mechanics: the science of motion. 5.1.

mediocrity: mean or middle between two extremes; moderation of living. 6.2.

medium: (1) mid-point; middle state. 3.13; 6.2; Dial. 48. (2) principle; ground or device for reaching conclusions. 9.16.

merchandize: trading, buying, and selling (in business, particularly foreign trade). 2.11.

mess: food; meal. Dial. 11.

miscarriages: mistakes; failures. 6.8.

modification: mode. 5.16; Appx. 2.2; Appx. 2.6.

mortal: extremely great. Dial. 2.

municipal: state (not limited to local government of a town or city). 3.37; 3.45; Appx. 1.2; Dial. 29.

natural philosopher: person versed in or who examines natural science. 6.6; Appx. 2.7.

nay: term used to introduce a more precise, better-formulated, or correct statement than one previously made. n. 13; 5.37; 9.15; Dial. 56.

necessitous: marked by need; needing assistance. 3.4.

nice: subtle; precise; fine. 1.9; 8.7; 9.1; Appx. 1.2; n. 60.

nicety: sensitive feeling; scrupulousness of mind. 8.8.

œconomy: (1) organization or management of affairs. 6.21; Appx. 4.2. (2) organization, structure, or arrangement in the various parts of something. 9.13.

office: duty; service; assigned charge. 2.6; 3.6; 5.19; Appx. 1.5; Appx. 1.7; Appx. 1.21; Appx. 4.8; Appx. 4.17; Dial. 5.

order: type; species; class. 1.9; 2.11; Appx. 1.21.

organ: part of a person adapted to a particular function (including moral sensibility). 5.37; 6.11; Appx. 1.13; Appx. 1.16.

original: natural (prior to experience, as in original instinct). 1.6; 3.40; 3.41; 3.43; 3.46; n. 19; 9.20; Appx. 2.4; Appx. 2.12; Dial. 51.

ornaments: finery; attire. 3.2; Dial. 51.

paint: depict; portray; represent. 2.5; Appx. 1.16. See also **painted out** at 3.15.

paradox: statement contrary to received opinion; evident absurdity. 5.3; Appx. 2.6.

parts: talents; capacities; high intellectual ability or cleverness. 6.8; Appx. 4.5; Dial. 54.

passion: emotion; feeling; affection. *passim*.

peculiar: (1) singular; particular. 4.4; 5.42; 6.17; 9.6; 9.16; Appx. 1.21. (2) special; distinctive. 7.11; 7.26; 8.9; 9.8; Appx. 1.14; Dial. 38.

peevish: foolish; perverse. 6.21.

penetration: the intellectual faculty or virtue of discovering something by gaining access to its inner content. 9.2; Appx. 4.2.

perfection: accomplishment of a high order. 3.39; 6.21; 9.10.

phænomenon (pl. **phænomena**): any thing or event that is perceived or observed. 6.22; 6.23; 6.32; n. 34; 9.4; Appx. 2.7; Appx. 4.21.

poet: author of literature or fiction. *passim*.

Glossary

poinard (also *sp.* poniard): dagger. 2.19; 7.9.

polite: polished; refined; cultivated. 7.3; 8.4; Dial. 25.

politeness: See **polite** and ann. 4.13 and 8.1.

positive: (1) absolute; categorical. n. 13; 9.13; (2) (positive law) laid down; enacted. Positive law is law specifically enacted by proper government authority. 3.43; 4.1; Appx. 3.10; n. 65.

power: inherited authority or prerogative. 2.1.

preponderate: overbalance; outweigh. Appx. 3.6.

prescribe: expire or terminate owing to the culmination of an established period of time; lapse. 3.33; Appx. 3.7.

prescription: a mode of acquiring title to property, as a result of long and uninterrupted use or possession. 3.21; 3.33; 3.41.

pretence: (1) rationale. 5.16. (2) declaration. n. 57; Appx. 2.1.

pretend (also **pretension**): claim; maintain; assert. *passim*. See also **pretend to**.

pretend to: lay claim to; assert responsibility for. 7.25.

private connexions: close personal relationships, as with near friends. n. 25.

prosecution: the pursuit of. 3.29; n. 13.

prospect: outlook; extensive view; mental insight. 5.20; 5.22; 6.3; 6.11; 6.15.

purity (of manners): separation (lack of mixture) of the standards of manners for men and women. 4.8; Dial. 46.

purpose: *vb.* intend; propose; plan. 9.24.

quadrate with: square with; correspond to. Appx. 1.10.

rake into: investigate; gather a heap of information about. 9.14.

rally: play and jest; banter or play with words. Dial. 12.

refined: abstract and intricate; subtle. 6.18; Appx. 2.7; Appx. 2.8; Appx. 3.10.

rencounter: skirmish; hostile encounter. 3.11; 5.33.

rent-roll: list of lands or tenements belonging to a person; total of incomes or estates, as indicated by rolls of lands, renters, and resulting incomes. 6.34.

rude: unpolished; ignorant; unlearned. 9.1; n. 57.

run over: review; think about. 5.37; Dial. 1.

schools: scholastic philosophers or the subject-matter taught in medieval and early modern European universities. 9.2.

scope: purpose; aim. 4.16.

scruple: (1) *n.* dispute; doubt. Appx. 3.6; Dial. 15; Dial. 31. (2) *vb.* doubt; question the truth of. 3.32; 6.26; Appx. 4.8.

secrecy: keeping confidences; confidentiality. 6.21; 9.12; 9.24; Appx. 4.2.

secret: concealed; hidden. (Does not require an intentional action.) n. 13; 6.22; 8.11; Appx. 4.3; Dial. 4.

secretly: privately. 5.11; 6.14.

security: confidence; assurance. 3.8; 3.14; 3.15; 3.23; n. 13; 5.7; 6.9; 6.14; Dial. 31.

sensibility: (1) capacity to discern, be aware of, or make a judgement. 1.10; 7.28. (2) (also **sensible**) capable of sensing; ability to perceive. 5.24; 6.12.

sensible to: cognizant of; being properly endowed with understanding. 2.10.

sensibly: substantially; appreciably. 5.17.

sentiment: This term typically refers to an inner sensing, feeling, or emotion of which a person is aware—for example, anger, approval, disgust, sympathy, and compassion; but it is often used, like 'taste', to refer to judgement and opinion. Hume does not sharply distinguish sensing, judging, believing, responding, preferring, and the like. *passim*.

shock: conflict; clash. 5.11; 8.1.

solidity: soundness; good sense. 3.34.

specious: plausible and attractive; seemingly allowable and just. 1.5; 3.26; 3.27; Appx. 1.5.

spleen: depression; melancholy. 5.40; 6.21.

statuary: the art of sculpture or the art of making statues. 6.28.

still: *adv.* regularly; consistently. 3.39; 5.13; 5.23; 5.37; 6.15.

stupidity: incomprehension. 6.16; Appx. 4.3.

suffrage: approbation; support. 9.13.

superficies: outer surface of a body, as apparent to the eye; top, surface, or outside. Appx. 2.4.

symphony: harmony; agreeable concerted response. 9.6.

system: theory; organized body of principles; comprehensive philosophy. *passim*.

taste: See ann. 1.4; 1.5; 7.28.

tenderness: delicate, circumspect, sensitive feeling in regard to reputation, esteem, or respectability. 8.8.

tenure: condition on which a person holds property. 3.18.

theatre: platform (stage) erected for a ceremony or play. 5.42; Dial. 49.

topic: subject (in writing or discourse); matter; consideration. 2.8; 3.4; 5.9; n. 33; 9.2; Dial. 18.

train and equipage: retinue of personal attendants and equipment needed for a journey. 6.32.

violence: intensity of influence; passionate quality; commanding effect. 3.8; 3.14; 9.21.

vogue: common or general approbation of a person. Dial. 19; Dial. 25.

votary: devotee; follower. 9.15.

vulgar: common; ordinary. 2.2; 3.27; 3.36; 3.38; 4.7; 6.14; 9.4; Appx. 4.22. See also **vulgarly**.

vulgarly: commonly; in common speech. 6.34; 9.5; 9.20.

wanton: frisky; unrestrained. 5.6.

wrested: twisted; wrung. 7.21.

References

The authors and works in this reference list are of two types: (1) works cited by Hume either in the text or in the notes; (2) works cited by the editor in the annotation or introduction to this volume. Whenever specific references are made by the editor to the works in this reference list, the editions listed below were relied upon.

In the case of editions having more than one volume, the number of volumes is reported; if volumes were issued in a multi-volume edition in more than a single year, both volume numbers and individual dates of publication are reported. Only works actually cited by Hume or the editor are listed. Loeb Library editions are used for classical works wherever possible (abbreviated 'Loeb Library'); the dates listed are printing dates, not original dates of publication or dates of revised editions. The title as it appears on the title-page is listed. In a few cases involving non-standard titles, the original title and standard translation of the title are used.

English capitalization is normalized to modern practice; entries for Latin, French, Italian, and Spanish sources follow late twentieth-century forms. These titles are accompanied by a translation of the title into English. An attempt has been made to supply more accurate translations than those found on the title-pages of many standard, published sources in English. The reader therefore should not expect the translation to follow conventional English renderings.

ADDISON, JOSEPH. See *The Guardian* and *The Spectator*.

AESCHINES SOCRATICUS, *Dialogues*, in *Dialogi tres*, ed. and trans. Joannes Clericus (Amsterdam, 1711). Note 78.

ANACREON, *Anacreontea*, in *Elegy and Iambus with the Anacreontea*, trans. J. M. Edmonds, 2 vols., Loeb Library, 2 (1961). Note 87.

APPIAN, *Roman History*, trans. Horace White, 4 vols., Loeb Library, 3 (1913). Note 80.

ARISTOTLE, *Nicomachean Ethics*, trans. H. Rackham, Loeb Library (1947). Appx. 4.12.

——*Posterior Analytics*, in *Posterior Analytics*, *Topica*, trans. Hugh Tredennick, Loeb Library (1960).

ARMSTRONG, JOHN, *The Art of Preserving Health. In Four Books*, 2nd edn. (London, 1745). Note 68.

ARRIAN (FLAVIUS ARRIANUS), *Anabasis Alexandri* [*Anabasis of Alexander*], trans. P. A. Brunt, 2 vols., Loeb Library, 1 (1976), 2 (1983).

——*Epictetus: The Discourses*, in *The Discourses as Reported by Arrian*, *The Manual*, *Fragments*, trans. W. A. Oldfather, 2 vols., Loeb Library, 1 (1926).

References

AUBREY, JOHN, 'Brief Lives', chiefly of Contemporaries, set down by John Aubrey, between the Years 1669 & 1696, ed. Oliver Lawson Dick (London: Secker & Warburg, 1950).

BACON, FRANCIS, Novum organum [The New Instrument], in vols. 1 and 4 of The Works of Francis Bacon, ed. James Spedding, Robert Leslie Ellis, and Douglas Denon Heath, 14 vols. (London, 1857–74; repr. Stuttgart: Frommann, 1961–3). Section 5.17.

BAIER, KURT, The Moral Point of View (Ithaca, NY: Cornell University Press, 1958).

BARFOOT, MICHAEL, 'Hume and the Culture of Science in the Early Eighteenth Century', in Studies in the Philosophy of the Scottish Enlightenment, ed. M. A. Stewart (Oxford: Clarendon Press, 1990), 151–90.

BAYLE, PIERRE, The Dictionary Historical and Critical of M'. Peter Bayle, ed. Pierre Desmaizeaux, 2nd edn., 5 vols. (London 1734–8; fac. New York: Garland, 1984). Note 13.

——Œuvres diverses [Various Works] (The Hague, 1727; fac. Hildesheim: Olms, 1970).

BENTHAM, JEREMY, A Fragment on Government, ed. J. H. Burns and H. L. A. Hart (London: Athlone, 1977).

BIBLE, The Holy Bible . . . The Authorized Version Published in the Year 1611 (Oxford: Oxford University Press, 1985).

BOILEAU-DESPRÉAUX, NICOLAS, Réflexions critiques sur quelques passages du rhéteur Longin [Critical Reflections on Some Passages of the Rhetor Longinus], in Œuvres complètes, ed. Françoise Escal (Paris: Gallimard, 1966). Note 39.

BOX, MARK, 'An Allusion in Hume's An Enquiry Concerning the Principles of Morals Identified', Notes & Queries, 231/1 (Mar. 1986), 60–1.

BUTLER, JOSEPH, Fifteen Sermons Preached at the Rolls Chapel, in vol. 2 of The Works of Joseph Butler, ed. W. E. Gladstone, 2 vols. (Oxford: Clarendon Press, 1896).

BURTON, JOHN HILL (ed.), Letters of Eminent Persons Addressed to David Hume (Edinburgh, 1849; repr. Bristol: Thoemmes, 1989).

CAESAR, GAIUS JULIUS, The Gallic War, trans. H. J. Edwards, Loeb Library (1946).

CAMPBELL, ARCHIBALD, An Enquiry into the Original of Moral Virtue (Edinburgh, 1733).

CASTIGLIONE, BALDASSARE, Il cortegiano [The Courtier], ed. Antonio Ciccarelli (Venice, 1593). Section 9.2.

CHAMBERS, EPHRAIM, Cyclopaedia: or, An Universal Dictionary of Arts and Sciences, 2 vols. (London, 1728).

CICERO, MARCUS TULLIUS, De legibus [On Laws], trans. Clinton Walker Keyes, Loeb Library (1928).

——De natura deorum [On the Nature of the Gods], in De natura deorum, Academica, trans. H. Rackham, Loeb Library (1972). Note 5.

——De officiis [On Duties], trans. Walter Miller, Loeb Library (1921). Section 8.12; notes 3, 71.

References

Cicero, Marcus Tullius, *De oratore* [*On the Orator*], trans. E. W. Sutton; completed by H. Rackham, 2 vols., Loeb Library, 1 (1942). Note 72.

——*In Catilinam* [*Against Catiline*], in *The Speeches: In Catilinam I–IV, Pro Murena, Pro Sulla, and Pro Flacco*, trans. Louis E. Lord, Loeb Library (1959). Appx. 1.16.

——*Letters to Atticus*, trans. E. O. Winstedt, 3 vols., Loeb Library, 2 (1921). Note 70.

——*Philippics*, trans. Walter C. A. Ker, Loeb Library (1969). Note 29.

——*Pro Sestio* [*In Defence of Sestius*], in *The Speeches: Pro Sestio and In Vatinum*, trans. R. Gardner, Loeb Library (1966). Note 11.

——*Tusculan Disputations*, trans. J. E. King, Loeb Library (1966). Section 8.10; note 88.

——*The Verrine Orations*, trans. L. H. G. Greenwood, 2 vols., Loeb Library, 1 (1928), 2 (1935). Appx. 1.16.

Clarke, Samuel, *A Discourse concerning the Unchangeable Obligations of Natural Religion, and the Truth and Certainty of the Christian Revelation* (1705), in vol. 2 of *The Works of Samuel Clarke, D.D.*, 4 vols. (London, 1738; fac. New York: Garland, 1978).

Corneille, Pierre, *Medée* [*Medea*], in vol. 2 of *Le Théâtre de P. Corneille: Texte de 1682*, ed. Alphonse Pauly, 8 vols. (Paris, 1881–6). Section 7.7.

Cudworth, Ralph, *A Treatise concerning Eternal and Immutable Morality* (London, 1731; fac. New York: Garland, 1976).

——*The True Intellectual System of the Universe*, 2 vols. (London, 1678; fac. New York: Garland, 1978).

Demosthenes, *De corona* [*On the Crown*], in *De corona and De falsa legatione*, trans. C. A. Vince and J. H. Vince, Loeb Library (1926). Note 43.

——*In Oneterem* [*Against Onetor*], in *Private Orations*, trans. A. T. Murray, 3 vols., Loeb Library, 1 (1936). Note 90.

Diodorus Siculus, *The Library of History*, 12 vols., Loeb Library, 1 (1946), 2 (1953), 4 (1946), trans. C. H. Oldfather, 7 (1952), trans. Charles L. Sherman, 8 (1963), trans. C. Bradford Welles, 10 (1954), trans. Russel M. Geer. Notes 7, 31.

Du Cerceau, Jean Antoine, *Recueil de poësies diverses* [*Collection of Various Poems*], 4th edn. (Paris, 1733). Section 5.30.

Epictetus. See Arrian.

Euclid, *The Thirteen Books of Euclid's Elements*, ed. and trans. Thomas L. Heath, 3 vols. (New York: Dover, 1956).

Euripides, *Fragmenta* [*Fragments*], in *Tragicorum Graecorum fragmenta*, ed. Augustus Nauck (Leipzig, 1889). Note 74.

Fénelon, François de Salignac de La Mothe-, *Les Aventures de Télémaque, fils d'Ulysse* [*The Adventures of Telemachus, Son of Ulysses*], in *Telemachus*, ed. and trans. Patrick Riley (Cambridge: Cambridge University Press, 1994). Section 7.15.

Fontenelle, Bernard le Bovier de, *The Achievement of Bernard le Bovier de*

Fontenelle, ed. Leonard M. Marsak (London, 1688; fac. New York: Johnson, 1970).

——*Discours sur la nature de l'églogue* [*Discourse on the Nature of the Eclogue*], in *Poesies pastorales* (The Hague, 1688).

——*Entretiens sur la pluralité des mondes* [*A Plurality of Worlds*], in *The Achievement of Bernard le Bovier de Fontenelle*. Note 61.

——*The History of Oracles and the Cheats of the Pagan Priests*, in *The Achievement of Bernard le Bovier de Fontenelle*.

GRACIÁN DANTISCO, LUCAS, *Galateo espagnol; or, The Spanish Gallant* (London, 1640).

GRACIÁN Y MORALES, BALTASAR, *El discreto* [*The Discreet*], in *Obras escogidas de filósofos*.

——*The Hero* (London, 1726).

——*Obras escogidas de filósofos*, vol. 65 of *Biblioteca de Autores Españoles* (Madrid, 1873).

——*Oráculo manual y arte de prudencia* [*Oracle Compendium and the Art of Prudence*], in *Obras escogidas de filósofos*.

GRATIANUS, FRANCISCUS, *Decretum D. Gratiani* [*Gratian's Decretals*] (Venice, 1567).

GROTIUS, HUGO, *De jure belli ac pacis* [*On the Law of War and Peace*], ed. James Brown Scott, 2 vols., Classics of International Law (Oxford: Clarendon Press, 1925), vol. 1, fac. Amsterdam, 1646; vol. 2, Eng. trans. Francis W. Kelsey *et al.* Note 63.

The Guardian, by Joseph Addison *et al.*, ed. John Calhoun Stephens (Lexington, Ky.: University Press of Kentucky, 1982).

GUICCIARDINI, FRANCESCO, *History of Italy and History of Florence*, ed. John R. Hale, trans. Cecil Grayson (New York: Twayne, 1964). Section 5.33; note 76.

HANKE, LEWIS, *Aristotle and the American Indians* (London: Hollis & Carter, 1959).

HERODOTUS, *History*, trans. A. D. Godley, 4 vols., Loeb Library, 1 (1931), 2 (1938), 3 (1928), 4 (1930). Note 45.

HESIOD, *Works and Days*, in *The Homeric Hymns and Homerica*, trans. Hugh G. Evelyn-White, Loeb Library (1936).

HOBBES, THOMAS, *Leviathan*, ed. Edwin Curley (Indianapolis: Hackett, 1994). Appx. 2.2–4; note 11.

HOMER, *Iliad*, trans. A. T. Murray, 2 vols., Loeb Library, 1 (1978), 2 (1976). Section 7.15.

——*Odyssey*, trans. A. T. Murray, 2 vols., Loeb Library, 1 (1966). Sections 7.4, 7.15.

HORACE (QUINTUS HORATIUS FLACCUS), *The Art of Poetry*, in *Satires, Epistles and Ars poetica*. Note 20.

——*Epistles*, in *Satires, Epistles and Ars poetica*. Section 7.1; notes 78, 86.

——*Odes*, in *The Odes and Epodes*, trans. C. E. Bennett, Loeb Library (1978). Notes 57, 86.

References

HORACE (QUINTUS HORATIUS FLACCUS), *Satires, Epistles and Ars poetica*, trans. H. Rushton Fairclough, Loeb Library (1942).

HUME, DAVID, *A Letter from a Gentleman to his Friend in Edinburgh*, ed. Ernest C. Mossner and John V. Price (Edinburgh, 1745; fac. Edinburgh: Edinburgh University Press, 1967).

——*An Abstract of a Book lately Published; Entituled, A Treatise of Human Nature, &c.*, in *A Treatise of Human Nature*.

——*A Treatise of Human Nature*, ed. David Fate Norton and Mary Norton (Oxford: Clarendon Press, forthcoming).

——*Essays: Moral, Political, and Literary*, ed. Eugene F. Miller, 2nd edn. (Indianapolis: LibertyClassics, 1987).

——*The History of England from the Invasion of Julius Caesar to The Revolution in 1688*, 6 vols. (Indianapolis: LibertyClassics, 1983–5).

——*The Letters of David Hume*, ed. J. Y. T. Greig, 2 vols. (Oxford: Clarendon Press, 1932).

——*The Natural History of Religion and Dialogues concerning Natural Religion*, ed. A. Wayne Colver and John Valdimir Price (Oxford: Clarendon Press, 1976).

——*New Letters of David Hume*, ed. Raymond Klibansky and Ernest C. Mossner (Oxford: Clarendon Press, 1954).

HUTCHESON, FRANCIS, *An Essay on the Nature and Conduct of the Passions and Affections. With Illustrations on the Moral Sense* (fac. London, 1728), in vol. 2 of *Collected Works of Francis Hutcheson*.

——*An Inquiry into the Original of our Ideas of Beauty and Virtue; In Two Treatises* (fac. London, 1725), in vol. 1 of *Collected Works of Francis Hutcheson*.

——*A Short Introduction to Moral Philosophy* (fac. London, 1747), in vol. 4 of *Collected Works of Francis Hutcheson*.

——*A System of Moral Philosophy* (fac. London, 1755), in vols. 5–6 of *Collected Works of Francis Hutcheson*.

——*Collected Works of Francis Hutcheson*, 7 vols., fac. edn. by Bernhard Fabian (Hildesheim: Olms, 1969–71).

ISOCRATES, *Orations*, trans. George Norlin, 3 vols., Loeb Library, 1 (1928), 2 (1929).

——*Panathenaicus*, in *Orations*.

——*Panegyricus*, in *Orations*.

JOHNSON, SAMUEL, *The Rambler*, no. 36 (21 July 1750), ed. W. J. Bate and Albrecht B. Strauss, in vol. 3 of *The Yale Edition of the Works of Samuel Johnson* (New Haven: Yale University Press, 1969), 195–200.

JUVENAL (DECIMUS JUNIUS JUVENALIS), *Satires*, in *Juvenal and Persius*, trans. G. G. Ramsay, Loeb Library (1930). Note 4.

LA FONTAINE, JEAN DE, 'La coupe enchantée' ['The Enchanted Goblet'], in *Fables, contes et nouvelles* (Paris: Pléiade, 1948). Note 91.

LA ROCHEFOUCAULD, FRANÇOIS DE MARSILLAC, DUC DE, *Maxims*, trans. John Heard, Jr. (New York: Houghton Mifflin, 1917). Note 66.

References

LIVY (TITUS LIVIUS), *From the Founding of the City* [Livy's History], trans. B. O. Foster, 13 vols., Loeb Library, 3 (1924), 4 (1926), 5 (1929). Note 75.

LOCKE, JOHN, *An Essay concerning Human Understanding*, 4th edn., ed. Peter H. Nidditch (Oxford: Clarendon Press, 1975). Appx. 2.3.

LONGINUS. See *On the Sublime*.

LUCIAN, *De dea Syria* [*The Syrian Goddess*], ed. and trans. Harold W. Attridge and Robert A. Oden (Missoula, Mont.: Scholars Press, 1976).

—— *The Goddesse of Surrye*, trans. A. M. Harmon, Loeb Library (1925).

—— *Icaromenippus; or, The Sky Man*, trans. A. M. Harmon, Loeb Library (1929).

—— *The Parliament of the Gods*, trans. A. M. Harmon, Loeb Library (1936).

—— *Saturnalia*, trans. K. Kilburn, Loeb Library (1959). Note 82.

—— *Timon; or, The Misanthrope*, trans. A. M. Harmon, Loeb Library (1929). Note 30.

LYSIAS, *Against Diogeiton*, in *Orations*.

—— *Against Eratosthenes*, in *Orations*.

—— *Funeral Oration*, in *Orations*.

—— *Orations*, trans. W. R. M. Lamb, Loeb Library (1930). Note 89.

MACHIAVELLI, NICCOLÒ, *The Discourses*, ed. W. Stark, trans. Leslie J. Walker, 2 vols. (London: Routledge & Kegan Paul, 1950). Section 6.9.

—— *The Prince*, ed. Quentin Skinner and Russell Price (Cambridge: Cambridge University Press, 1988).

MALEBRANCHE, NICOLAS, *The Search after Truth*, ed. and trans. T. M. Lennon and Paul J. Olscamp (Columbus: Ohio State University Press, 1980).

MANDEVILLE, BERNARD DE, *The Fable of the Bees: or, Private Vices, Publick Benefits*, ed. F. B. Kaye, 2 vols. (Oxford: Clarendon Press, 1924; repr. Indianapolis: LibertyClassics, 1988).

MARTIAL (MARCUS VALERIUS MARTIALIS), *Epigrams*, trans. Walter C. A. Ker, 2 vols. Loeb Library, 1 (1947), 2 (1950). Note 92.

MILL, JOHN STUART, 'Bentham', in vol. 10 of *Collected Works of John Stuart Mill* (Toronto: University of Toronto Press, 1969).

MONTAIGNE, MICHEL EYQUEM DE, *Essays*, in *The Complete Essays*, ed. and trans. M. A. Screech (London: Penguin Books, 1993). Section 8.9.

MONTESQUIEU, CHARLES LOUIS DE SECONDAT, BARON DE, *Persian Letters*, 'Cashan edition, done into English' (London: Athenaeum, 1901).

—— *The Spirit of the Laws*, ed. and trans. Anne Cohler, Basia Miller, and Harold Stone (Cambridge: Cambridge University Press, 1989). Note 12.

NEWTON, ISAAC, *Philosophiae naturalis principia mathematica* [*Mathematical Principles of Natural Philosophy*], in *Sir Isaac Newton's Mathematical Principles of Natural Philosophy and His System of the World*, trans. Andrew Motte, rev. Florian Cajori (Berkeley: University of California Press, 1960). Note 14.

NORTON, DAVID FATE (ed.), *The Cambridge Companion to Hume* (Cambridge: Cambridge University Press, 1993).

References

On the Sublime (incorrectly attributed to Longinus), trans. W. Hamilton Fyfe, Loeb Library (1927). Bound with Aristotle and Demetrius. Notes 37, 38.

PALLADIO, ANDREA, *I quattro libri dell'architettura* [*The Four Books of Architecture*], in *The Architecture of A. Palladio; in Four Books*, 2 vols. (London, 1715). Appx. 1.15.

PASCAL, BLAISE, *Pensées and Other Writings*, trans. Honor Levi (Oxford: Oxford University Press, 1995).

PERRAULT, CLAUDE, *A Treatise of the Five Orders of Columns in Architecture*, 2nd edn., trans. John James (London, 1722). Appx. 1.15.

PETRONIUS ARBITER, GAIUS, *Satyricon*, trans. Michael Heseltine, Loeb Library (1951). Bound with Seneca, *Apocolocyntosis*. Note 87.

PHAEDRUS, *The Aesopic Fables of Phaedrus the Freedman of Augustus*, in *Babrius and Phaedrus*, ed. and trans. Ben Edwin Perry, Loeb Library (1965). Note 15.

PLATO, *Meno*, in *Laches, Protagoras, Meno, Euthydemus*, trans. W. R. M. Lamb, Loeb Library (1924). Note 78.

——*Phaedo*, in *Euthyphro, Apology, Crito, Phaedo, Phaedrus*, trans. Harold North Fowler, Loeb Library (1938). Note 27.

——*Republic*, trans. Paul Shorey, 2 vols., Loeb Library, 1 (1946). Notes 11, 15.

——*Symposium*, in *Lysis, Symposium, Gorgias*, trans. W. R. M. Lamb, Loeb Library (1939). Note 83.

PLUTARCH, *Lives*, trans. Bernadotte Perrin, 11 vols., Loeb Library, 1 (1914), 2 (1928), 3 (1915), 4 (1916), 5 (1917), 6 (1918), 7 (1919), 8 (1919), 9 (1920), 10 (1921), 11 (1926). Notes 2, 23, 40.

——*Moralia* [*Moral Essays*], 16 vols., Loeb Library, 1 (1927), 2 (1928), trans. Frank Cole Babbitt, 6 (1939), trans. W. C. Helmbold, 7 (1959), trans. Phillip H. De Lacy and Benedict Einarson, 10 (1936), trans. Harold North Fowler. Notes 15, 85.

POLYBIUS, *The Histories*, trans. W. R. Paton, 6 vols., Loeb Library, 3 (1960), 4 (1925), 5 (1926). Section 6.16; notes 18, 28, 69, 77.

PUFENDORF, SAMUEL, *De jure naturae et gentium* [*On the Law of Nature and Nations*], trans. C. H. Oldfather and W. A. Oldfather, 2 vols. (Oxford: Clarendon Press, 1934), vol. 1 fac. 1688; vol. 2 translation.

——*On the Duty of Man and Citizen According to Natural Law*, ed. James Tully, trans. Michael Silverthorne (Cambridge: Cambridge University Press, 1991).

QUINTILIAN (MARCUS FABIUS QUINTILIANUS), *Institutio oratoria* [*Institutes*], trans. H. E. Butler, 4 vols., Loeb Library, 2 (1953), 3 (1921). Notes 21, 52.

REID, THOMAS, 'Dedication', *An Inquiry into the Human Mind, on the Principles of Common Sense* (1764), in *Philosophical Works*, ed. Sir William Hamilton, 2 vols. in 1 (Edinburgh, 1895; fac. Hildesheim: Olms, 1983).

SAINT-ÉVREMOND, CHARLES MARGUETEL DE SAINT-DENIS, SEIGNEUR DE, 'A Parallel between the Prince of Condé and Monsieur de Turenne', in vol. 2 of *The Works of Monsieur de St. Evremond*. Section 6.9.

——'The Character of the Mareschal de Turenne', in vol. 2 of *The Works of Monsieur de St. Evremond*. Section 6.9.

References

—— 'Lettre à M. le Comte Magalotti' [Letter to the Count of Magalotti], in vol. 1 of *Lettres*, ed. René Ternois, 2 vols. (Paris: Didier, 1967–8). Note 36.

—— *The Works of Monsieur de St. Evremond*, trans. Pierre Des Maizeaux, 3 vols. (London, 1714).

SALLUST (GAIUS SALLUSTIUS CRISPUS), *The War with Catiline*, in *Sallust*, trans. J. C. Rolfe, Loeb Library (1960). Appx. 4.6.

SANNAZARO, JACOPO, *Arcadia*, in *Arcadia & Piscatorial Eclogues*. Section 5.29.

—— *Arcadia & Piscatorial Eclogues*, trans. Ralph Nash (Detroit: Wayne State University Press, 1966).

—— *Eclogues*, in *Arcadia & Piscatorial Eclogues*. Section 5.29.

SENECA, LUCIUS ANNAEUS, *Moral Essays*, trans. John W. Basore, 3 vols., Loeb Library, 1 (1928), 2 (1935), 3 (1935). Notes 62, 78, 92.

SEXTUS EMPIRICUS, *Against the Physicists*, trans. R. G. Bury, Loeb Library (1936). Note 6.

—— *Outlines of Pyrrhonism*, trans. R. G. Bury, Loeb Library (1933). Note 15.

SHAFTESBURY, ANTHONY ASHLEY COOPER, THIRD EARL OF, *Characteristics of Men, Manners, Opinions, Times*, ed. John M. Robertson, 2 vols. in 1 (London, 1900; repr. Indianapolis: Bobbs-Merrill, 1964). Section 1.3.

—— Letter to Michael Ainsworth, 3 June 1709, in *The Life, Unpublished Letters, and Philosophical Regimen of Anthony, Earl of Shaftesbury*, ed. Benjamin Rand (New York: Macmillan, 1900), 403–5.

SHAKESPEARE, WILLIAM, *Julius Caesar*, ed. John Jowett, in *The Complete Works*, ed. Stanley Wells and Gary Taylor (Oxford: Oxford University Press, 1986). Section 7.3.

SMITH, NORMAN KEMP, *The Philosophy of David Hume* (London: Macmillan, 1941).

The Spectator, by Richard Steele, Joseph Addison, *et al.*, ed. Donald F. Bond, 5 vols. (Oxford: Clarendon Press, 1965).

SPENSER, EDMUND, *A View of the State of Ireland*, ed. W. L. Renwick (Oxford: Clarendon Press, 1970). Note 47.

SPINOZA, BARUCH DE, *Ethics*, in vol. 1 of *The Collected Works of Spinoza*, ed. and trans. Edwin Curley (Princeton: Princeton University Press, 1985).

STADEN, HANS, *The True History of his Captivity*, ed. and trans. Malcolm Letts (London: Routledge, 1928).

STEELE, RICHARD. See *The Guardian*.

SUETONIUS TRANQUILLUS, GAIUS, *Lives of the Caesars*, trans. J. C. Rolfe, 2 vols., Loeb Library, 1 (1935), 2 (1930). Note 80.

SWIFT, JONATHAN, 'A Description of What the World Calls Discretion', in *The Intelligencer*, in *Irish Tracts: 1728–1733*, ed. Herbert Davis, in vol. 12 of *The Prose Works of Jonathan Swift* (Oxford: Basil Blackwell, 1971). Section 6.8.

TACITUS, CORNELIUS, *The Annals*, trans. John Jackson, in *The Annals Books I–III*, Loeb Library (1979). Bound with *The Histories Books IV–V*; and in *The Annals Books XIII–XVI*, Loeb Library (1981). Section 5.34.

References

TACITUS, CORNELIUS, *Germania*, trans. M. Hutton, rev. E. H. Warmington, in *Agricola, Germania, Dialogus*, Loeb Library (1980). Note 44.

—— *The Histories*, trans. Clifford H. Moore, 2 vols., in *The Histories Books I–III*, Loeb Library (1980) and *The Histories Books IV–V, The Annals Books I–III*, Loeb Library (1979). Note 41.

THUCYDIDES, *History of the Peloponnesian War*, trans. Charles Forster Smith, 4 vols., Loeb Library, 1 (1935), 3 (1931), 4 (1923). Section 5.33; note 46.

TICKELL, THOMAS. See *The Spectator*.

VEGETIUS (FLAVIUS VEGETIUS RENATUS), *Epitoma rei militaris* [*On Matters of the Military*], ed. Carolus Lang (Leipzig, 1885). Note 32.

VIRGIL (PUBLIUS VERGILIUS MARO), *The Aeneid*, trans. H. Rushton Fairclough, 2 vols., in *Eclogues, Georgics and Aeneid I–VI*, Loeb Library (1974) and *Aeneid VII–XII, The Minor Poems*, Loeb Library (1930).

—— *Georgics*, trans. H. Rushton Fairclough, in *Eclogues, Georgics and Aeneid I–VI*, Loeb Library (1974). Section 6.24; note 62.

VOLTAIRE, FRANÇOIS MARIE AROUET DE, *Lion of the North, Charles XII of Sweden* [Altered title of *Histoire de Charles XII Roi de Suède* (*History of Charles XII, King of Sweden*)], ed. and trans. M. F. O. Jenkins (Rutherford: Fairleigh Dickenson University Press, 1981).

WAGNER, HENRY R., *The Life and Writings of Bartolomé de Las Casas* (Albuquerque: University of New Mexico Press, 1967).

The Whole Duty of Man (London, 1706). (Authorship now generally attributed to Richard Allestree, 1658, under the title *The Practice of Christian Graces; or, The Whole Duty of Man . . .*). Note 72.

XENOPHON, *Cyropaedia*, trans. Walter Miller, 2 vols., Loeb Library, 1 (1925). Appx. 3.4.

—— *Memorabilia*, in *Memorabilia and Oeconomicus*, trans. E. C. Marchant, Loeb Library (1923). Note 81.

—— *On the Art of Horsemanship*, in *Scripta minora*, trans. E. C. Marchant, Loeb Library (1925). Section 6.24.

YATES, FRANCES A., *The Art of Memory* (Chicago: University of Chicago Press, 1966).

Index

This index encompasses the entire book, but it has been constructed to emphasize names, titles, and concepts in Hume's text (pp. 73–199). Entries for book titles are limited to titles (or authors of those titles) mentioned or intimated by Hume. Entries of authors are limited to persons mentioned either by Hume or by the editor in the section on suggested supplementary readings.

Index

Index

Index

Index

Iliad (Homer) 229
ill-offices 158–9
ill-will 78, 158–9, 173
images 73, 111–15, 120, 128–9, 136
imaginary interest 107–8, 168
imagination:
  as affected by news 111–12
  connections of the 92, 97, 101, 106–8, 115,
    131, 164, 174–5, 220
  its function of combining ideas 11
  use of, in reflecting on distant ages 106–7,
    129, 219
Immerwahr, John 61
impartial administration of law 92, 217, 245
impartial moral responses 7, 24, 27–8, 41, 44–5,
  204, 223
impartial observers 29, 34, 166, 207, 227, 237,
  240
impartiality 16, 19, 27–8, 34–5, 223, 250; *see also*
  partiality
impatience 142, 183; *see also* patience
impiety 124, 182, 226
impressions 11, 14, 73, 161, 167, 209
impudence 141, 178, 234, 251
In Defence of Sestius (Cicero) 88, 211
incest 101, 189, 217, 251
inconveniencies 85, 88, 95, 102–3, 171–2, 193
indecorum 143, 235
indifference 92, 108–20, 135, 137, 148–50,
  158–9, 168, 197–8
indignation 95, 110, 112, 132, 162, 229
indulgence 81, 101, 140–1, 154, 189, 190, 196
industry:
  Hume's youthful 8
  property acquired due to 96, 174, 254
  as a useful quality 30, 80–3, 87, 90–1, 122, 224
  as a virtue 120, 125–6, 151, 177–9, 247
inequalities 91, 115–16
infallibility 88, 107, 114, 117
infanticide 251, 253
infidelity 100, 124, 155, 186, 196, 255
ingenuity 28, 31, 73, 139, 153–4, 178, 233, 253
ingratitude 106, 124, 134, 158–9, 219, 240; *see
  also* gratitude
inheritance 43, 96, 110, 174, 228, 244, 253, 255
iniquity 99, 155, 162, 175
injury 83, 86, 100, 108, 110, 113–14, 117, 141,
  149, 175, 195
injustice 74, 84–7, 97, 100, 124, 150, 173, 179;
  see also justice
innate capacities 20, 84, 215
innate ideas 97, 215

insolence 134, 142, 149, 162
instincts 96–7, 170, 173, 215
Institutes (Quintilian) 113, 142, 222, 235
integrity 38–9, 98, 155, 194, 197, 209, 234, 242,
  247, 254
intellectual faculties 76, 160–1, 163, 173, 247–8
intellectual virtues 177, 246–7
intentions:
  role of, in moral judgement 32, 115, 223
  secret or concealed 95, 167, 214–15
intimacy 133, 141, 147, 185
intrigues 196, 224, 255
inutility 88, 100, 113, 128
involuntary actions 161, 182–3, 250; *see also*
  voluntary abilities and actions
Iphicrates 142, 232, 234
Isocrates 137, 232

Jenkins, John J. 62
Jessop, T. E. 66
Jesuits 18, 95, 214, 236, 256
Johnson, Samuel 221, 242, 259
judicature 173–4, 246
jurisprudence 174, 245
justice:
  abundance of resources and 83–7
  among robbers 102, 217
  boundaries of 87–9, 210–12
  conventional basis of 24, 35–7, 43–4, 49,
    170–4, 244
  natural 44, 93, 96–7, 171–3, 212–13, 215, 245
  and natural law 18, 92–3, 99, 171, 213,
    215–16
  particular laws of 90–7, 139, 157, 172–5
  property as the object of 83–8, 155, 170–5,
    213–14
  public utility as the origin of 35–6, 40–2,
    83–98, 117, 151, 157, 170–5, 209, 243
  rules of 43–4, 86ff, 99–102, 210–11, 214–15,
    244–6
  superstition distinguished from 94–5
  virtues of 24, 30, 38, 77, 83–90, 93, 126, 135,
    170, 179, 181, 192
  see also property; virtues; convention
Juvenal 79, 207

Kames, Lord 58
Kant, Immanuel 52, 59
kindness 7, 24, 88, 155, 167, 205, 207, 211
Klibansky, Raymond 57
knave, the sensible 38–9, 155–6, 178, 235,
  238–9

283

Index

Index

Index